Schizophrenia To

Schizophrenia Today

Edited by

D. KEMALI,
G. BARTHOLINI
AND
D. RICHTER

PERGAMON PRESS
OXFORD · NEW YORK · TORONTO · SYDNEY
PARIS · FRANKFURT

U.K.	Pergamon Press Ltd., Headington Hill Hall, Oxford OX3 0BW, England
U.S.A.	Pergamon Press Inc., Maxwell House, Fairview Park, Elmsford, New York 10523, U.S.A.
CANADA	Pergamon of Canada Ltd., P.O. Box 9600, Don Mills M3C 2T9, Ontario, Canada
AUSTRALIA	Pergamon Press (Aust.) Pty. Ltd., 19a Boundary Street, Rushcutters Bay, N.S.W. 2011, Australia
FRANCE	Pergamon Press SARL, 24 rue des Ecoles, 75240 Paris, Cedex 05, France
WEST GERMANY	Pergamon Press GmbH, 6242 Kronberg-Taunus, Pferdstrasse 1, Frankfurt-am-Main, West Germany

First edition 1976

Library of Congress Catalog Card No 76-19215

0 08 020928 9

Printed in Great Britain by A. Wheaton & Co., Exeter

Contents

List of Participants

ABBATE, G.	Via Pietravalle 85, Napoli, Italy
ALFANO, G.	Wyeth S.p.A., Via Generale Carascosa 39/41, Napoli, Italy
AMATI, A.	Cattedra di Psichiatria, I^ Facoltà di Medicina e Chirurgia, Piazza Miraglia 2, 80138, Napoli, Italy
ANCONA, L.	Istituto di Psicologia generale e clinica, Università Cattolica del Sacro Cuore, Via della Pineta Sacchetti 644, 00168 Roma, Italy
ANDÉN, N.-E.	Dept. of Pharmacology, University of Göteborg, Fack, S-400 33 Göteborg, Sweden
ANDREOLI, V.	Istituto di Farmacologia, Università di Milano, Italy
ARIETI, S.	125 East 84th Street, New York, N.Y. 10028, U.S.A.
BALESTRIERI, A.	Clinica Psichiatrica dell'Universita, Centro Ospedaliero Clinicizzato di Borgo Roma, 37100 Verona, Italy
BARTHOLINI, E.	10, Avenue Foch, Paris 16°, France
BARTHOLINI, G.	Synthélabo & Co Ltd., 58 Rue de la Glacière, 75621 Paris 13, France
BECKMANN, L.	Psychiatrische Klinik der Universität, 8 München 2, Nussbaumstr. 7, Germany
BENASSI, P.	Istituto Psichiatrico, Viale Amendola 2, Reggio Emilia, Italy
BERTOLINO, A.	Ospedale Psichiatrico "Casa della Divina Provvidenza", Bisceglie, Bari, Italy
BIEBER, I.	132 East 72nd Street, New York, N.Y. 10021, U.S.A.
BOGETTO, F.	Istituto di Psichiatria dell'Università, Via Cherasco 15, 10126 Torino, Italy
BOOK, J.A.	Institute for Medical Genetics, 24 V. Ågatan 752, 20 Uppsala, Sweden
BRIA, P.	Istituto di Clinica delle Malattie Nervose e Mentali, Università Cattolica del Sacro Cuore, Largo A. Gemelli 8, 00168 Roma, Italy
BRODY, E.B.	Institute of Psychiatry and Human Behavior, 645 West Redwood Street, Baltimore, Maryland 21201, U.S.A.

BUSCAINO, G.A.   Clinica Malattie Nervose e Mentali, II Facolta di Medicina e Chirurgia, Via S. Pansini 5, Napoli, Italy

CABOARA, F.   Ospedale Provinciale Psichiatrico, Quarto Via G. Maggio 6, Genova, Italy

CAIANIELLO, E.R.   Laboratorio di Cibernetica, C.N.R., Arco Felice, Napoli, Italy

CALLIERI, B.   Ospedale Psichiatrico "S. Maria Immacolata", Via Tiburtina Km. 20, 5 Guidonia, Roma, Italy

CAMPAILLA, G.   Istituto di Clinica Psichiatrica, Facoltà di Medicina e Chirurgia, Università di Trieste, Via S. Cilino 16, Trieste, Italy

CARLSSON, A.   Dept. of Pharmacology University of Göteborg, Fack, S-400 33 Göteborg 33, Sweden

CAZZULLO, C.L.   Istituto di Psichiatria dell'Universita, Via G. Besta 1, 20121 Milano, Italy

CEDROLA, G.   Ospedale Psichiatrico "Materdomini", Nocera Superiore, Salerno, Italy

CELANI, T.   Cattedra di Psichiatria, I^ Facoltà di Medicina e Chirurgia, Piazza Miraglia 2, 80138 Napoli, Italy

CERINO, S.   Via Posillipo 203, Napoli, Italy

CICCHETTI, V.   Direzione Medica D.L. Lepetit, Via Lepetit 8, 20124 Milano, Italy

COCORULLO, M.   Cattedra di Psichiatria, I^ Facoltà di Medicina e Chirurgia, Piazza Miraglia 2, 80138 Napoli, Italy

COENEGRACHTS, A.   Leopold Plaats 35, PB 12 Hasselt 3500, Belgium

COPPOLA, C.F.   Ospedale Provinciale Psichiatrico "L. Bianchi", Napoli, Italy

CORSINI, G.U.   Clinica Malattie Nervose e Mentali, Università, Via Ospedale 54, 09100 Cagliari, Italy

CURCI, G.   Cattedra di Psichiatria, II^ Facoltà di Medicina e Chirurgia, Via S. Pansini 5, Napoli, Italy

D'ALESSANDRO, C.   Cattedra di Psichiatria, I^ Facoltà di Medicina e Chirurgia, Piazza Miraglia 2, 80138 Napoli, Italy

D'ANDREA, F.   Clinica Neurochirurgica, II^ Facoltà di Medicina e Chirurgia, Via S. Pansini 5, Napoli, Italy

D'ANGELO, A.   Cattedra di Psichiatria, I^ Facoltà di Medicina e Chirurgia, Piazza Miraglia 2, 80138 Napoli, Italy

DA PRADA, M.   Hoffmann – La Roche & Company Limited, 4002 Basle, Switzerland

DAVISON, K.   Newcastle General Hospital Psychiatric Unit, Westgate Road, Newcastle-upon-Tyne, NE4 6BE, England

DE CAPRARIS, E.	Ospedale Psichiatrico "Casa della Divina Provvidenza", Foggia, Italy
DECLICH, M.	Ospedale Psichiatrico Provinciale, Sondrio, Italy
DEL VECCHIO, M.	Cattedra di Psichiatria, I^ Facoltà di Medicina e Chirurgia, Piazza Miraglia 2, 80138 Napoli, Italy
DE MARTIS, D.	Clinica Psichiatrica dell'Università di Pavia, Italy
DI DONNA, F.	Wyeth S.p.A., Via Generale Carascosa 39/41, Naples, Italy
DI FURIA, G.	Western State Hospital, Fort Steilacoom, Washington 98494, U.S.A.
DI PAOLO, P.	Ospedale Psichiatrico "S. Maria Immacolata", Via Tiburtina Km. 20,5 Guidonia, Roma, Italy
EBERHARD, G.	Dept. of Psychiatry, General Hospital, Helsingborg, Sweden
ERIKSSON, E.K.	Lillhagens Sjukhus, 422 03 Hisings, Backa 3, Sweden
FAGIANI, M.B.	Istituto di Psichiatria dell'Università di Torino, Via Cherasco 15, 10126 Torino, Italy
FALENI, R.	Av. Santa Fé 3694, Buenos Aires (25), Argentina
FATTORI, A.	Wyeth, Via delle Montagne Rocciose 60, 00144 Roma, Italy
FELICI, F.	Clinica delle Malattie Nervose e Mentali, I^ Facolta di Medicina e Chirurgia, Piazza Miraglia 2, 80138 Napoli, Italy
FERRARI, E.	Clinica delle Malattie Nervose e Mentali dell'Università di Bari, Ospedale Policlinico, Bari, Italy
FIEVE, R.R.	New York State Psychiatric Institute and Columbia University, 722 West 168th Street, New York City, N.Y. 10032, U.S.A.
FRIEDHOFF, A.J.	Millhauser Laboratories, New York University School of Medicine, 550 First Avenue, New York, N.Y. 10016, U.S.A.
FUSCO, F.	Wyeth, Via delle Montagne Rocciose 60, 00144 Roma, Italy
FUXE, K.	Karolinska Institutet, Dept. of Histology, S104, 01 Stockholm 60, Sweden
GADDINI, E.	Via Sebastiano Conca 13, Roma, Italy
GADDINI, R.	Via Sebastiano Conca 13, Roma, Italy
GAMBARDELLA, A.	Ospedale Psichiatrico "S. Maria Maddalena", Unità, Biagio Miraglia 8103, Aversa, Italy
GENTILI, C.	Clinica Psichiatrica dell'Università di Bologna, Via S. Lucia 9/2, 40135 Bologna, Italy
GIBERTI, F.	Clinica Psichiatrica dell'Università di Genova, Italy
GIORDANO, G.G.	Cattedra di Neuropsichiatria Infantile, I^ Facoltà di Medicina e Chirurgia, Piazza Miraglia 2, 80138 Napoli, Italy

GIRI, G.	Piazza Roma 6, 60019 Senigallia (Ancona), Italy
GIUDICELLI, R.	Synthélabo & Co Ltd. 58, Rue de la Glacière, Paris 13, France
GOLD, H.	Clinique Belle Allée, Fourneaux 45610 Chaingy, France
GRITTI, P.	Cattedra di Psichiatria, I^ Facoltà di Medicina e Chirurgia, Piazza Miraglia 2, 80138 Napoli, Italy
HARLE, C.	INPS, Clinica Psiquiatrica, Av. Rio Claro 75, 17500 Marilia, São Paulo, Brazil
INFANTE, S.	Cattedra di Psichiatria, I^ Facoltà di Medicina e Chirurgia, Piazza Miraglia 2, 80138 Napoli, Italy
IORIO, G.	Cattedra di Psichiatria, I^ Facoltà di Medicina e Chirurgia, Piazza Miraglia 2, 80138 Napoli, Italy
ITIL, T.M.	Division of Biological Psychiatry, 150 White Plains Road, Tarrytown, N.Y. 10591, U.S.A.
KEMALI, D.	Cattedra di Psichiatria, I^ Facoltà di Medicina e Chirurgia, Piazza Miraglia 2, 80138 Napoli, Italy
KEMALI, M.	Laboratorio di Cibernetica, C.N.R., Sezione di Neuroanatomia, Arco Felice, Napoli, Italy
KETY, S.S.	Psychiatric Research Lab., Massachusetts General Hospital, Boston, Mass. 02114, U.S.A.
LADEN, N.	6 Rue de Bosquet, 05000 Gap (Hautes Alpes), France
LA MURA, G.	Ospedale Psichiatrico "Casa della Divina Provvidenza" Bisceglie, Bari, Italy
LEONE, L.	Ospedale Psichiatrico "Casa della Divina Provvidenza" Bisceglie, Bari, Italy
LEVI, G.	Istituto di Neuropsichiatria Infantile, Via dei Sabelli 108, 00185 Roma, Italy
LIVREA, P.	Clinica delle Malattie Nervose e Mentali, Università di Bari, Italy
LONGO, V.	Via Posillipo 9, Palazzo Donn'anna, Napoli, Italy
LUZZATTO, L.	Istituto Internazionale di Genetica e Biofisica, Via G. Marconi 10, Napoli, Italy
MAFFEI, G.	Clinica Psichiatrica, Università di Pisa, Italy
MALM, U.	Dept. II, Lillhagen Mental Hospital, Box 3005, 422 03 Hisings, Backa 3, Sweden
MANARA, F.	Centro Studi Sclerosi Multipla, Via Pastori 3, 21013 Gallarate, Italy
MANGONI, A.	Istituto di Clinica delle Malattie Nervose e Mentali dell'Università, Ospedale Civile, Cagliari, Italy

MARGHERITA, G.	Via Tasso 480, Napoli, Italy
MARINO, A.	II Cattedra di Farmacologia, Facoltà di Medicina Università, Policlinico, Piazzale Giulio Cesare, Bari, Italy
MASTROSIMONE, F.	Clinica Malattie Nervose e Mentali, I^ Facoltà di Medicina e Chirurgia, Piazza Miraglia 2, 80138 Napoli, Italy
MATTE BLANCO, I.	Via Luigi Gherzi 8, 00136 Roma, Italy
MONTERA, C.	Cattedra di Psichiatria, I^ Facoltà di Medicina e Chirurgia, Piazza Miraglia 2, 80138 Napoli, Italy
MORCALDI, L.	Ospedale Psichiatrico Don Uva, Potenza, Italy
MOSCHETTI, P.	Reparto Neuropsichiatria, Ospedale Militare Principale di Napoli, Italy
MUNKVAD, I.	Sct. Hans Hospital, DK-4000 Roskilde, Denmark
NAPOLITANI, A.	Viale Maria Cristina di Savoia 44, Napoli, Italy
NAVARRO, F.	Via Posillipo 382, Napoli, Italy
PAOLOZZI, C.	Clinica Malattie Nervose e Mentali, I^ Facolta di Medicina e Chirurgia, Piazza Miraglia 2, 80138 Napoli, Italy
PERRIS, C.	Dept. of Psychiatry, University of Umeå, S-901 85 Umeå, Sweden
PINOTTI, F.	c/o Wyeth, Via delle Montagne Rocciose 60, 00144 Roma, Italy
PLETSCHER, A.	Research Dept., Hoffmann – La Roche, 4002 Basle, Switzerland
PLOOG, D.	Max-Planck Institut für Psychiatrie, 8 München 40, Kraepelinstrasse 2und 10, Germany
POLANI, E.N.	Little Meadow, West Clandon, Near Guildford, Surrey, England
POLANI, P.E.	Paediatric Research Unit, Guy's Hospital Medical School, Cameron House, London SE1 9RT, England
PONTALTI, C.	Istituto di Psicologia Clinica, Facoltà di Medicina, Università Cattolica del Sacro Cuore, Lg. Gemelli, Roma, Italy
PUCCIO, G.	Cattedra di Psichiatria, I^ Facoltà di Medicina e Chirurgia, Piazza Miraglia 2, 80138 Napoli, Italy
RAVIZZA, L.	Cattedra di Psicofarmacologia, Istituto di Psichiatria dell'Università, Via Cherasco 15, 10126 Torino, Italy
RESNIK, S.	20 Rue Bonaparte, Paris VIe, France
RICCIO, D.	Via Petrarca 20, Napoli, Italy
RICHTER, D.	I.B.R.O. Secretariat, 41 Queens Gate, London SW7 5HU, England
RINALDI, F.	Clinica Psichiatrica, II^ Facoltà di Medicina e Chirurgia, Via S. Pansini 5, Napoli, Italy
ROSENFELD, H.	9 Meadow Bank, Primrose Hill Road, London NW 3AY, England

SACCHETTI, E.	Clinica Psichiatrica dell'Universita, Via F. Sforza 35, 20122 Milano, Italy
SALMONI, G.	Via U. Ricci, 8 Napoli, Italy
SANTAGADA, V.	Wyeth, Via delle Montagne Rocciose 60, 00144 Roma, Italy
SARTESCHI, P.	Clinica Psichiatrica, Università di Pisa, Italy
SCHULSINGER, F.	Dept. of Psychiatry, Kommunehospitalet, 1399 Copenhagen K., Denmark
SHEPHERD, M.	Institute of Psychiatry, De Crespigny Park, Denmark Hill, London SE5 8AF, England
SHIELDS, J.	Institute of Psychiatry, Genetics Dept., De Crespigny Park, Denmark Hill, London SE5 8AF, England
SIMONE, F.	Clinica Malattie Nervose e Mentali, I Facolta di Medicina e Chirurgia, Piazza Miraglia 2, 80138 Napoli, Italy
SMERALDI, E.	Clinica Psichiatrica dell'Universita, Via F. Sforza 35, Milano, Italy
SPADETTA, V.	Ospedale Psichiatrico "Materdomini" Nocera Superiore, Salerno, Italy
TISSOT, R.	Clinique Psychiatrique de l'Universitè Bel Air, près Genève 1225, Chene-Bourg, Switzerland
TORRE, E.	Istituto di Farmacologia dell'Università Torino, Italy
TORRE, M.	Istituto di Psichiatria dell'Università, Via Cherasco 15, 10126 Torino, Italy
VACCA, L.	Cattedra di Psichiatria, I Facoltà di Medicina e Chirurgia, Piazza Miraglia 2, 80138 Napoli, Italy
VELLA, G.	Viale Liegi 32, 00198 Roma, Italy
VIVO, M.	Anacapri, Napoli, Italy
VIZIOLI, R.	Clinica Malattie Nervose e Mentali, I Facolta di Medicina e Chirurgia, Piazza Miraglia 2, 80138, Napoli, Italy
VOLTERRA, V.	Via Indipendenza 67/2°, Bologna 40121, Italy
WETTERBERG, L.	Dept. of Psychiatry, Karolinska Institute, St. Görans Hospital, Box 12500, 112 81 Stockholm, Sweden
WITTENBORN, J.R.	Interdisciplinary Research Center, Rutgers University, New Brunswick, N.J. 08903, U.S.A.
ZANCHI, B.	Viale dei Mille 14, Milano, Italy

Poster Exhibition

L. BELLODI, E. SACCHETTI and E. SMERALDI
Effect of haloperidol on intracellular cGMP/cAMP ratio

A. BERTOLINO, G. LA MURA and L. CORFIATI
The pictorial expression in psychotic patients

P. DI PAOLO
Immunoglobulins (IgA, IgM, IgG) and creatinphosphokinase in 511 hospitalized chronic schizophrenics, with respect to age and to the duration of the illness

G. EBERHARD, G. FRANZEN and B. LÖW
Schizophrenia susceptibility and HL-A antigen

G. LEVI
Learning strategies and identity sense in psychotic children

A. MANGONI, G.U. CORSINI, G. CIANCHETTI and M. DEL ZOMPO
Central effects of apomorphine in neurological and psychiatric patients pretreated with sulpiride and other drugs

G. MARGHERITA, V. CEI and L. RINALDI
Paranoid-schizoid relations with body drawing in regressed institutionalized patients

S. RESNIK
On narcissistic depression

M. TORRE, F. BOGETTO, M.B. FAGIANI and E. TORRE
LSD-25 serotonin and behaviour

G. VELLA and C. LORIEDO
Family psychotherapy of the schizophrenic: theoretical and practical aspects

V. VOLTERRA
Chronic irreversible extrapyramidal syndromes in long time treated schizophrenics, and usefulness of correcting drugs

Foreword

Schizophrenia continues to be a subject in which experts disagree. While some regard it as a functional disorder resulting mainly from faulty upbringing, social stresses and the like, others attach greater importance to genetic predisposition and to physical factors affecting the basic neurophysiological functions of the brain. Current disagreements over the nature and causes of schizophrenia extend to the practical problems of the treatment and handling of the large numbers in every country who are chronically disabled by schizophrenic psychoses. In this situation it appeared that it might be helpful to bring together a group of leading representatives of the different disciplines and different schools of thought to take part in a multidisciplinary confrontation in which the present position in the different fields of research could be reviewed. Such, in brief, was the "Schizophrenia Workshop" arranged at Capri in October 1975.

The original proposal, which was made at a meeting in London attended by Professor Kemali, Professor Bartholini and Professor Polani, was developed in cooperation with other neuroscientists and psychiatrists whom we thank for their good advice. The local arrangements for the meeting were entrusted to Dr. A. Amati, Dr. M. Del Vecchio and Dr. L. Vacca of the University of Naples, to whom we are indebted for their very great help in achieving the smooth running of this venture.

Despite gloomy forebodings, the exchanges at the scientific sessions were entirely amicable. Since the definition of schizophrenia is a frequent source of disagreement special attention was paid to this aspect of the problem. Valuable help was given by several participants who arranged a Poster Exhibition in which they presented the results of a series of current investigations. In the general discussion of recent advances in the field a genuine attempt was made by all to achieve better understanding of the various conflicting viewpoints, while at the same time emphasising differences and focusing on specific questions that could serve as indications for further research. It cannot be expected that the written version of the contributions to a Workshop of this kind will provide a comprehensive discussion of every relevant aspect of the subject. We hope nevertheless that in presenting a broad survey of recent developments and current hypotheses it will help to clarify the new evidence coming from different fields of research and will contribute to a better understanding of the central problem of schizophrenia.

DARGUT KEMALI
GIUSEPPE BARTHOLINI
DEREK RICHTER

Opening Address

Ladies and Gentlemen,

The main reason for the organisation of this meeting is the need to survey the problems and the methodologies that are being applied in different fields of research, so as to obtain an overall picture of the current hypotheses relating to schizophrenia.

While we may expect that the main problems of epidemiology and symptomatology can be overcome, they still appear insurmountable so far as the etiology and pathogenesis of schizophrenia are concerned. The basic mechanisms underlying perception, cognition and affect are not yet understood and we still have little understanding of the factors affecting interpersonal relations, the biological basis of abnormal behaviour, the mechanism of the relief of symptoms by psychotropic drugs or the corrective effects of psychotherapy. Again, the genetic determinants, the influence of socio-cultural factors on thought content and even the nosology of schizophrenia are still open problems.

Another reason for this meeting is that we aim by publishing the proceedings to produce an informative account of the way in which different areas of research have developed and new concepts have arisen in this field. Clearly we cannot expect that every aspect of the subject will be covered in the lectures that have been arranged, but we hope that in the discussion further worthwhile material may also be brought to light.

Finally we trust that this Workshop will be of value, not only with respect to the basic scientific and medical aspects, but also in contributing to a better understanding of the environmental factors that affect the schizophrenic patient. Thus it can be hoped that public policy towards these patients will be influenced so as to ensure that the treatment they receive is both effective and humane.

In the name of the Organising Committee I would like to thank the Mayor of Anacapri for his generous hospitality, the Rector of the University of Naples, the representatives of the regional Departments of Health and of Tourism who made this Workshop possible, the Chairmen and speakers in the sessions and all who contributed to the success of this meeting.

Again, I thank you one and all.

DARGUT KEMALI

Societal and Cultural Aspects

Definition, Classification and Nomenclature: A Clinical Overview

MICHAEL SHEPHERD

The importance of taxonomy in the context of scientific thinking is now widely recognised. The case was stated authoritatively 50 years ago by Alexander Wolf: "Scientific classification", he asserted, "seeks to formulate a scheme of mutually exclusive and collectively exhaustive categories based on the most important characteristics of the things concerned and on the actual relations between them ... The more nearly a classification approaches the aforementioned ideal the better is its claim to be called a *natural* one; a classification that deviates from this ideal, as usually happens when it is made for some practical human purpose, is called artificial ... In the history of every science classification is the very first method to be employed; but it is much older than science. Every name, indeed almost every word, of a language is the expression of some implicit classification; and language is older than science. The classifications expressed in ordinary language are, however, the result of practical needs rather than of scientific interests, so that science has to correct them even when it starts from them."[1]

Wolf, of course, was concerned principally with the function of classification in the basic natural and biological sciences. The relevance of his argument to most branches of medicine, and especially to those most firmly rooted in a biological understanding of disease, is apparent. In other fields of medicine, however, — and perhaps most notably in psychiatry — the role of classification is less apparent and it has been suggested that it does not apply to some forms of mental disorder, including the schizophrenias. To discard classification, however, is to discard scientific thinking for, as Gerhard Wasserman has pointed out, "scientific theories, apart from introducing hypotheses, deal with class characteristics of classes of phenomena and systems and with relations between classes of phenomena. A scientist's initial task is to classify publicly observable properties of systems".[2] It can, therefore, be maintained that the need for the logic of classification is still more important for psychiatry precisely because its scientific basis is still so poorly developed. At the same time the limits of any classificatory schema must be clearly recognised and the use to which it is put should be clearly understood.

The application of these general principles to the taxonomy of mental illness were fully appreciated by the most powerful thinker to have concerned himself with the problem. In his *General Psychopathology* Karl Jaspers[3] divided the map of mental disorders into three broad areas, namely: (i) Somatic illnesses with psychic disturbances; (ii) the three major psychoses; and (iii) the personality disorders. To Jaspers the major, or functional, psychoses, were essentially syndromes or complexes characterised by a marked endogenous or hereditary element and lacking an anatomical cerebral pathology. They included the schizophrenias, the manic-depressive illnesses and, interestingly enough, the epilepsies. He further emphasised the hierarchical structure of his schema, since disorders in group (ii) become subsumed under group (i) when a somatic substrate is detected. Thus, while one may speak of a pseudo-neurotic schizophrenia, one would not speak of an encephalitic schizophrenia but of a schizophreniform psychosis associated with encephalitis.

Jaspers' principal concern was with the place occupied by the schizophrenias within the broad spectrum of mental disorders, rather than with the diagnosis of the illnesses themselves. He affirmed that "diagnosis proper is only possible and necessary in Group (i). With Group (ii) the majority of cases will fall by consensus of psychiatric opinion into one of the three major psychoses but the diagnosis has got no specific alternative character . . . Hence in Group (i) our diagnosis is accordingly the *classes of diseases* to which a case either does or does not belong . . . In Group (ii) we have classes of disease in mind although their definitive causes and nature are not known, but in fact one is always confined to types." For many years this typological approach commanded a working agreement among German-speaking clinicians for whom the diagnostic importance of Eugen Bleuler's primary symptoms and Kurt Schneider's first-rank symptoms served to anchor the concept of schizophrenia as encountered in psychiatric institutions. In clinical practice, Jaspers was justified in assuming that the types which were good enough for Kraepelin, Bleuler and the Heidelberg school would be acceptable elsewhere.

However, as the concept of schizophrenia gradually broadened, its boundaries became increasingly fluid and the sad decline of clinical nosology set in. The consequent state of affairs was clearly revealed at the World Congress of Psychiatry held at Zurich in 1957 and devoted entirely to schizophrenia. On that occasion the disputation among the distinguished international group of clinicians on the subject of classification was conducted in a manner reminiscent more of mediaeval schools of theology than of scientific opinions. Indeed, one of the symposia was appropriately devoted to the concepts of Aristotle and St. Thomas Aquinas. The divine right of the Ordinarius was prominently displayed and one participant summed up the matter with the irreverent but pointed riposte: "You say this is a case of schizophrenia. Do you mean schizophrenia as Dr. X. my chief uses it, or are you referring to schizophrenia as construed by your chief, Dr. Y.?"

Retrospectively, indeed, the late 1950s can be seen as a period when the whole field of psychiatric taxonomy had fallen into a state of total disarray, and in some quarters the old idea of a single, unitary mental disorder was seriously revived. Since then, however, we have witnessed a quickening of interest and even a modicum of progress. This has been attributable principally to three factors. Two of these were clearly the new areas of investigation associated with the growing awareness of the potential of epidemiological enquiry and the therapeutic momentum provided by the arrival of a host of new psychotropic substances. Since both epidemiologists and psychopharmacologists must be numerate to express their data in quantifiable form, an agreement on some form of classification becomes essential. The third factor, in my opinion, has been the active intervention of the World Health Organisation. In 1958 the late Erwin Stengel was invited by WHO to review the state of the classification of mental disorders. His report illuminated a Tower of Babel.[5] He was able to collect and comment on no fewer than 38 national or individual schemata of classification in addition to the section on mental disorders in the International Classification of Disease (ICD). He also ascertained that the ICD was in regular use among only a handful of member states of the World Health Organisation. Any serious hope of international agreement at the time was therefore ruled out. However, as Stengel explained, while the lack of aetiological knowledge precludes the construction of a truly scientific classification, communication can be greatly improved by the widespread use of operational concepts and definitions. And since operational definitions need a common language they call for an acceptable nomenclature or terminology. Here it is worth recalling, in the words of the ICD, that "A nomenclature, being a list or catalogue of approved terms for describing and recording observations, has to be extensive and unlimited in scope and detail to allow for the recording of the manifold individual variations of ill-health. A classification, on the other hand, is concerned with groups of conditions whose peculiarities have to be fitted within a limited number of categories chosen for their usefulness to the numerical study of disease phenomena".[6]

For schizophrenic disorders the consequences of this outlook are clear. In Stengel's words: "Schizophrenia, then, as an operational concept, would not be an illness, or a specific reaction type, but an agreed operational definition for certain types of abnormal behaviour ... The question, therefore, which a person or group of persons trying to reach agreement on a national or international classification ought to answer is not what schizophrenia ... is, but what interpretation should be placed on these concepts for the purpose of diagnosis and classification, i.e. for the purpose of communication".[7] And, it may be added, if this seems a modest objective, it is worth recalling Kraepelin's own assessment of the classificatory system which remains his major legacy: "I should like to emphasise that some of the clinical pictures outlined are no more than attempts to present part of the material observed in a communicable form".[8]

It was against this background that the World Health Organisation initiated a large-scale programme on the standardisation of psychiatric diagnosis, classification and statistics in the early 1960s. One of the primary aims of this work, of course, has been the promotion of an improved and acceptable version of section V of the ICD which "is intended primarily for the classification of patients seen at mental hospitals, psychiatric clinics, mental deficiency institutions and similar facilities where the main interest is in the mental state of the patient". With the reliable collection of morbidity statistics as its principal objective the ICD is, inevitably, the most public, the least private, of all systems of classification, and Norman Cameron clearly identified the defects of such systems in the sphere of the functional psychoses 30 years ago.[9] They are, as he pointed out, "not based upon final and convincing scientific evidence. They are children of practical necessities; ... the decisions are usually reached by the majority vote of the practising members of large associations;" and "The most this can express is the majority opinion as to a useful expedient in administrative decisions. It does not necessarily represent even the most advanced opinion in scientific matters, particularly when the science is young and the evidence is very conflicting". These observations remain valid to-day since no international schema can be other than what Stengel called "rather conservative and theoretically unenterprising", if it is to command acceptance. In the process of developing the 8th and 9th revisions of the ICD, however, a great deal of time and thought were devoted to some of the basic taxonomic issues affecting schizophrenia so that, as Helmchen has said: "... the ICD-8 reflects essential elements of to-day's clinical practice and it also reflects the history of empirical scientific work in the field of schizophrenia".[10] I therefore propose to use the ICD as the skeleton on which to put the flesh of my remarks before going on to mention alternative, private systems of classification.

The focus of attention in the first part of the WHO programme was the study of observer variation. The direct study of clinical observation was initiated at the first of a series of international meetings in 1965, when schizophrenia was the principal topic under review.[11] By the use of video-tapes and the presentation of uniformly-prepared case-histories the complex process of the clinical diagnostic procedure was rendered susceptible to detailed scrutiny. It should perhaps first to be emphasised that in many cases a substantial measure of agreement on the diagnosis of schizophrenia was demonstrated. In other cases, however, there was marked disagreement and a close and detailed study of its causes was then undertaken. Here we were following Oldham's cautionary advice to the effect that "... when the disagreements (in judgements of skilled observers) are quantitative, nothing will be gained, and much may be lost, by bringing the observers together for joint discussion of their disagreements; when the disagreements are qualitative, discussion will be fruitful if and only if a hypothesis about the likely cause of their disagreements has emerged from analysis of their separate judgements".[12] In this instance it was possible to establish that the causes of disagreement operated at three levels, namely (1) the clinical observation and perceptions themselves; (2) the inferences which were drawn from these observations; and (3) the different diagnostic labels employed by individual clinicians.

The many discussions which have followed and accompanied these diagnostic exercises have made it clear that some, at least, of the differences recorded — particularly those related to inference and labelling — were intimately linked with variations in the use of language and of words. The spreading awareness of this issue has drawn attention to the need for a glossary of descriptions and definitions of mental disorders. In addition to several national glossaries which have been compiled, the World Health Organisation has recently produced an international glossary which fairly represents the views of experts all over the world.[13] Its section on schizophrenia reads as follows:

"Includes a group of psychoses in which there is a fundamental disturbance of personality, a characteristic distortion of thinking, often a sense of being controlled by alien forces, delusions that may be bizarre, disturbed perception, abnormal affect out of keeping with the real situation, and autism. Nevertheless, clear consciousness and intellectual capacity are usually maintained. The disturbance of personality involves its most basic functions, those that give the normal person his feeling of individuality, uniqueness, and self-direction. The schizophrenic person feels that his most intimate thoughts, feelings and acts are known to and shared by others, and explanatory delusions may develop to the effect that natural or supernatural forces are at work to influence his thoughts and actions, in ways that are often bizarre. He sees himself as the pivot of all that happens. Hallucinations, especially of hearing, are common; they may comment on the patient, or address him. Perception is disturbed in other ways; irrelevant features may become all-important and, together with passivity feelings, may lead the patient to believe that everyday objects and situations possess a special, usually sinister, meaning intended for him. In the characteristic schizophrenic disturbance of thinking, peripheral and irrelevant features of a total concept, which are inhibited in normal directed mental activity, are brought to the forefront and utilized in place of the elements relevant and appropriate to the situation. Thus, thinking becomes vague, elliptical and obscure, and its expression in speech sometimes incomprehensible. Breaks and interpolations in the flow of consecutive thought are frequent, and the patient may be convinced that his thoughts are being withdrawn by some outside agency. Mood may be shallow, capricious, or incongruous. There may be a degree of perplexity. Ambivalence and disturbance of volition may appear as inertia, negativism or stupor. Catatonia may be present. A diagnosis of schizophrenia should not be made unless there is, or has been evident during the same illness, some characteristic disturbance of thought, perception, mood, conduct, or personality — preferably in at least two of these areas. The diagnosis should not be restricted to conditions running a protracted deteriorating or chronic course. In addition to basing the diagnosis on the criteria just given, the clinician should make every effort to specify one of the following subdivisions of schizophrenia according to the predominant symptoms".

As it stands, it will be seen that this long statement constitutes primarily a set of phenomenological criteria containing nothing about aetiology and little more than a mention of outcome. The recommendation that the schizophrenias be sub-classified according to the dominant symptomatology is in keeping with clinical tradition, but each sub-category raises problems of its own and may be taken each briefly in turn.

(1) The first four sub-categories are the familiar Kraepelinian groups – *simple* (295.0), *hebephrenic* (295.1), *catatonic* (295.2) and *paranoid* (295.3) *schizophrenia*. However, it was Kraepelin himself who stated that ". . . there are so many transitions between them that in spite of every effort it seems impossible to delimit them exactly and to allocate each case confidently". In addition, it may be observed that although the paranoid form of schizophrenia (295.3) is distinguished in the ICD from both paranoid states (297) and paranoid personality (301.0) this distinction is disputed by many clinicians for whom the "Paranoiafrage" remains a live and unresolved issue.[14]

(2) The *acute schizophrenic episode* (295.4) includes states characterised by clouding of consciousness and good prognosis. However, the incorporation of such "schizophreniform" states within the congeries of the schizophrenias becomes unacceptable to those clinicians who still separate schizophrenia from "schizophreniform" psychoses on clinical and prognostic grounds.[15]

(3) *Latent schizophrenia* (295.5) contains such controversial inclusion-terms as "border-line", "pre-psychotic", "prodromal", and "pseudoneurotic" and also the following bleak admission:
"It has not been possible to provide a generally acceptable description of this condition. The category is not recommended for general use but a description is provided for those who believe it to be useful". Nonetheless, it does raise a major issue, since on the one hand it is said to include "a condition of eccentric or inconsequent behaviour and anomalies of affect that give the impression of schizophrenia though the patient has never manifested any definite and characteristic schizophrenia disturbance",
yet at the same time the schizoid personality disorder (301.2) is explicitly excluded. The concept of schizoid personality, however, cannot be dismissed so casually and I shall have to return to it later.

(4) The "*schizo-affective psychosis*" (295.7) brings up the relationship of the schizophrenias to the affective disorders, the other large group of functional psychoses. The definition specifically mentions the "intermingling" of manic or depressive and schizophrenic features, but does not indicate that the characteristic symptom-clusters cannot only co-exist but on occasion succeed each other. All experienced clinicians are familiar with patients whose illnesses commence as seemingly affective disorders and then develop clear-cut schizophrenic symptomatology. It is not always recognised however, that there are patients with indisputably schizophrenic illnesses by clinical criteria, who have subsequently developed indisputably affective psychoses on follow-up. Further, there is the case made by many clinical observers – including such authorities as Kleist,[16] Leonhard,[17] Mitsuda,[18] and Perris[19] – that the term "schizo-affective" may embrace atypical, marginal or cycloid illnesses which constitute in effect a third group of functional psychoses.

(5) The category of "*other specified types*" of schizophrenia refers specifically to illnesses with their onset in childhood. It might equally have picked out equally well-recognised forms of schizophrenia with clinical or chronological associations, e.g. senile paranoid states, Spätkatatonie, Propfhebephrenie or recurrent hallucinatory alcoholic states. Clearly, however, no consistent form of classification can be constructed on such foundations.

As it stands, therefore, the structure of the 8th revision of the ICD remains essentially similar to its predecessors and retains most of the unresolved issues. Much the same can be said of the proposed 9th revision which is currently awaiting approval. Nevertheless, the WHO has already endorsed some significant shifts of opinion embodied in the acceptance of several general principles, of which two are directly relevant to our theme. These are, first, the discarding of combination categories and, secondly, the discontinuation of aetiological assumptions. In practice, this will result in a form of double coding, the psychiatric syndrome remaining in Section V while any coincident physical condition is coded elsewhere: for example, schizophrenia associated with cerebral arteriosclerosis would be coded 295 (schizophrenia) plus 437 (cerebral arteriosclerosis). This trend represents a tacit recognition of an increasingly important tendency in nosological thinking, namely the need to do justice to the multifactorial nature of most mental illnesses, including the schizophrenias. In so doing it brings the process closer to the traditional clinical preference for the formulation rather than the diagnostic term. A formulation normally takes account of factors other than the presenting symptomatology, including the history of the illness, the pre-morbid personality, the course and the outcome of the illness and the causal factors when known. To compress this information into manageable proportions calls for some form of multi-axial system of classification, and individual workers have, in fact, employed local schemata for many years in Sweden,[20] Norway[21] and France.[5]

In the field of schizophrenia the results of the WHO diagnostic exercises have shown that no reshuffling of the ICD along the lines of its present axis of classification can do justice to the clinical formulation. Stimulated by these considerations the WHO has recently sponsored the use of a novel tri-axial system of classification for the psychiatric disorders of childhood.[22] The three digits are devoted respectively to the phenomena of the illness, the level of intelligence and the biological basis of the condition when identified; the fourth digit is given over to the relevant psycho-social factors. The principle of this schema has been shown to operate surprisingly well in practice and it patently lends itself to a possible extension to adult illnesses, including the schizophrenias. Here, however, a major problem lies in the need to include some assessment of personality as part of the system, for a "fundamental disturbance of personality" is, after all, the first-mentioned feature of the disorder in the definition. Unfortunately, the available categories in this rubric are clearly inadequate, and further work is needed to refine the concepts.

So much for the issues associated with public systems of classification of schizophrenia. Whatever their value for the public health worker, their principal value for more rigorous scientific enquiry is the clear demonstration which they can furnish of the manifold difficulties which are inherent in the present state of knowledge. In turning to private systems of classification we at once encounter a major problem, namely, the existence of radically different opinions about, not merely the content, but also the very structure of the system itself. While the ICD and most of its congeners are based on the assumption that the schizophrenias are disease-entities or symptom-clusters of some sort, this view has been challenged by proponents of alternative systems of nosology. These include, for example, those psychologists who have employed conditioning theory, the psychoanalysts of various persuasions who lay emphasis on intrapsychic or family processes; the social theorists with an eye on deviant conduct and labelling theory,[23] and those who have turned to mathematical constructs to tackle the relationship between the schizophrenias and the personality-disorders in dimensional terms. I would also recall the ecological approach of Norman Cameron, especially as the recent work on cultural influences on schizophrenia may well have revived this perspective;[24] Cameron ascribed, as an example, the genesis of paranoid phenomena to a defective development of role-playing and a consequent inadequacy in social perspective, and he developed a complex division of schizophrenia into aggressive, submissive or detached sub-types, each with its own varieties.[25]

In the face of so many alternatives, how, then, are we to proceed with any private system? First, I would suggest, by adhering to the principle enunciated so clearly by Sir Aubrey Lewis 25 years ago when he commented that "more than one criterion, and, therefore, more than one system of sub-division, is justifiable in classifying schizophrenia, according to the particular purpose we wish it to serve", but "no new, unfamiliar system can properly be given more than a private and limited use unless it clearly attains its stated purpose, is seldom ambiguous in its application to a particular goal given adequate means of scientific communication".[26]

In practice these standards would be met by relatively few forms of classification in current use. Nonetheless, they would clearly commend themselves to the scientific community at large. It is no longer enough for an investigator to define the schizophrenias by fiat, however experienced a clinician he may be. Rules of some sort must be observed; otherwise there is confusion at the outset, even among experienced workers who share the same general outlook. Take, for example, the proponents of genetics as a mode of enquiry. Among this group, which numbers no more than a handful of reputable investigators, it is rather disturbing to have two workers, Shields and Gottesman, comment of their colleagues "that the picture is far from clear as to what really belongs to what Heston calls 'schizoid' disease, or to what Rosenthal and his colleagues call 'schizophrenic spectrum disorder', or what are the characteristics of children at high risk for developing schizophrenia".[27]

Yet in principle, the rules of the game are quite simple and were lucidly outlined in the report of a WHO Scientific Group on Biological Research in Schizophrenia,[28] which proposed three types of solution. The first, which appeals to computerised neo-Kraepelinians, read as follows:

"If it is possible to obtain an accurate detailed description of the patient's behaviour and present state and of changes in these factors over a period of time, it would appear to be unnecessary to insist on obtaining rigid agreement among different investigators on a precise diagnostic classification. The main requirement is that collaborating investigators in different centres should establish empirically that, despite theoretical differences, they can use the same clinical measuring instruments and arrive at similar quantitative conclusions concerning aspects of a patient's present state, such as pressure of speech, agitation, presence of delusions and hallucinatory activity. Given a sufficient number of reliable indices of this kind, correlations can be sought between individual clinical symptoms and syndromes and biological data. Agreement on a system of clinical diagnosis can then become a goal rather than a pre-condition for collaborative . . . studies of schizophrenia".

This approach has been developed extensively in the WHO International Pilot Study of Schizophrenia. Here I would merely comment that the combination of clinical data, computer-derived syndromes, numerical taxonomy and factor analysis can certainly help increase the reliability of data-collection. It may even be able to generate more fruitful indices for correlations with biological or psycho-social phenomena, though this has still to be proven. Elegant quantitative techniques can also demonstrate impressively the wavy borders between the schizophrenic and affective psychoses. What it cannot do *sui generis*, however, is to define precisely where those borders should be since, while we may be able to improve our recognition of the cards and the various ways in which they may combine, no amount of re-shuffling of the pack will in itself yield the rules of the game for, as Spitzer and Endicott have pointed out: . . . "the major constraints on further developments in computerised diagnosis appear to lie in limitations in the standard nomenclature itself".[29]

The second approach rests on two assumptions, namely that expert psychiatrists can agree on the diagnosis of certain illnesses as schizophrenia and that the major problems in the diagnosis of schizophrenia concern the limits within which a patient can be regarded as schizophrenic and beyond which he is not. Here a panel of psychiatrists representing different points of view and backgrounds is required, and patients' care selected only when this panel is unanimously agreed on the diagnosis. A similar criterion — unanimity concerning the absence of the disorder — can provide an adequate control group. This method has been employed by Shields who has discussed in detail its merits and limitations though, as the WHO report points out, it has two major disadvantages, namely "that criteria for inclusion and exclusion may not be clear and that certain possibly important sub-groups are excluded".

Finally, there are the techniques which dispense altogether with the need for homogeneity in the patient-population. Here the aim is to use correlational analysis to reveal significant relationships even though the patients represent a diagnostic continuum rather than a homogeneous group. This technique has been most popular among psychologists with an interest more in clusters and dimensions than in disease.

In so unsatisfactory a state of affairs, then, any and every method of classification can be expected to find its defenders according to the particular taxonomic purpose in mind. What is clearly needed is more factual information bearing on the background and genesis of the schizophrenic disorders so that the available knowledge can be re-distributed in a more rational and heuristic way. Nearly 70 years ago Eugen Bleuler remarked that: "The task of dissecting schizophrenia into natural sub-divisions is not yet feasible ... It is ... not a question of defining diseases but of grouping symptoms". A major objective of this meeting is to decide whether his observation remains valid to-day.

References

1. WOLF, A. (1929) Classification. In *The Encyclopaedia Britannica*, 14th ed., Vol. 5, p. 777, The Encyclopaedia Britannica Co. Ltd. London.
2. WASSERMANN, G.D. (1974) *Brains and Reasoning*, Macmillan.
3. JASPERS, K. (1963) *General Psychopathology* (translated by Hoenig, J. and Hamilton, M.W.), Manchester.
4. SURYA, N.C. (1959) Some remarks Concerning an Anthology of Psychiatric Definitions. In *2nd International Congress for Psychiatry, Congress Report*, Vol. IV, Zurich, p. 275.
5. STENGEL, E. (1959) Classification of Mental Disorders, *Bull. Wld. Hlth. Org,* **21**, 601.
6. Manual of the International Statistical Classification of Diseases, Injuries and Causes of Death. Vol. 1. (1957) World Health Organisation, Geneva.
7. STENGEL, E. (1967) Recent Developments in Classification. In *Recent Developments in Schizophrenia*, ed. by Coppen, A. and Walk, A., *Brit. J. Psychiat.* Special Publication No. 1, Headly Bros. Ashford.
8. KRAEPELIN, E. (1920) Die Erscheinungsformen des Irreseins, *Z. ges. Neurol. Psychiat.* **62**, 1. (Translated as "Patterns of Mental Disorder" in *Themes and Variations in European Psychiatry*, eds. Hirsch, S.R. and Shepherd, M., Wright: Bristol, p. 7.)
9. CAMERON, N. (1944) The Functional Psychoses. In *Personality and the Behaviour Disorders*, Vol. II, ed. by Hunt, J. MCV., The Ronald Press Company: New York, p. 861.
10. HELMCHEN, H. (1975) Schizophrenia: Diagnostic Concepts in the ICD – 8. In *Studies of Schizophrenia*, ed. by Lader, M.H., *Brit. J. Psychiat.* Special Publication No. 10., Headley Bros: Ashford.
11. SHEPHERD, M., BROOKE, E.M., COOPER, J.E. and LIN, T.Y. (1968) An Experimental Approach to Psychiatric Diagnosis, *Acta Psychiat. Scand.* Suppl. 201., Munchgaard: Copenhagen.
12. OLDHAM, P.D. (1968) Observer Error in Medicine. *Proc. Roy. Soc. Med.,* **61**, 447.
13. World Health Organisation (1974) *Glossary of Mental Disorders and Guide to their Classification*, WHO: Geneva.
14. FAZIO, C. and CALLIERI, B. (1972) Critical Observations on the Nosological Position of Paraphrenia, according to the Psychiatric Glossary of the World Health Organisation (8th ed., 1970). In *Dimensiones de la Psiquiatria Contemporanea*, ed. by Perez de Francisco, Cesar, p. 147.
15. VAILLANT, G.E. (1964) An Historical Review of the Remitting Schizophrenias, *J. Nerv. Ment. Dis.* **135**, 534.
16. KLEIST, K. (1928) Über zykloide, paranoide und epileptoide, Psychosen und über de Frage der Degenerationspsychosen, *Schweiz. Arch. Neurol. Psychiat.* **23**, 1. (Translated as "Cycloid, Paranoid and Epileptoid Psychoses and the Problems of Degenerative Psychoses", in *Themes and Variations in European Psychiatry*, ed. by Hirsch, S.R. and Shepherd, M., Wright: Bristol, p. 295.)
17. LEONHARD, K. (1957-69) *Aufteilung der endogenen Psychosen*, 1st-4th ed., Akademie Verlag, Jena.
18. MITSUDA, H. (1962) The Concept of Atypical Psychoses – from the Aspect of Clinical Genetics. *Folia Psychiat. et Neurol. Jap.* **16**, 214.
19. PERRIS, C. (1974) A Study of Cycloid Psychoses. *Acta Psychiat Scand.* Suppl. 253, Munksgaard: Copenhagen.
20. ESSEN-MÖLLER, E. and WOHLFAHRT, S. (1947) *Acta Psychiat. (Kbh.)*, Suppl. **47**, p. 551.
21. LANGFELDT, G. (1956) The Prognosis in Schizophrenia, *Acta Psychiat. Scand.* Suppl. 110.
22. RUTTER, M., SHAFFER, D. and SHEPHERD, M. (1973) An Evaluation of the Proposal for a Multi-axial Classification of Child Psychiatric Disorders. *Psychol. Med.* **3**, 244.
23. McGUIRE, R.J. (1973) Classification and the Problems of Diagnosis. In *Handbook of Abnormal Psychology*, 2nd ed., ed. by Eysenck, H.J., p. 3.
24. JABLENSKY, A. and SARTORIUS, N. (1975) Editorial: Culture and Schizophrenia. *Psychol. Med.* **5**, 113.
25. CAMERON, N. (1943) The Paranoid Pseudo-Community. *Am. J. Sociol.* **49**, 32.
26. LEWIS, A. (1952) The Classification of Schizophrenia. In *Premier Congres Mondial de Psychiatrie*, Vol. 2, ed. by Ey, H., Marty, P. and Abely, X., Hermann et Cie: Paris, p. 247.
27. SHIELDS, J. and GOTTESMAN, I.I. (1973) Genetic Studies of Schizophrenia as Signposts to Biochemistry, *Biochem. Soc.* Spec. Publ. 1, 165.

28. Report of a WHO Scientific Group (1970) Biological Research in Schizophrenia, *Wld. Hlth. Org. techn. Rep. Ser*, No. 450.
29. SPITZER, R.L. and ENDICOTT, J. (1975) Attempts to Improve Psychiatric Diagnosis. In *Annual Review of Psychology*, ed. by Rosenzweig, M.R., and Porter, L.N., Vol. 26, p. 643.

International Collaboration in Schizophrenia Research

N. SARTORIUS and T.A. LAMBO

In a recent paper Kramer[1] calculated the future projections of the incidence of schizophrenia on the basis of patient care episodes in the USA and obtained the following figures:

| Year | Number of patients | | |
	Total	White	Non-white
1970	146.789	110.833	35.956
1985	183.808	135.265	48.543
% difference	25.2	22.2	35.0

He stressed that the overall per cent increase in numbers of new cases of schizophrenia exceeds the overall per cent increase in the general population, because the incidence rate for schizophrenia is highest in those age groups in which the relative increase of population is highest. He comments:

"Indeed, it cannot be emphasised too strongly that the number of new cases of schizophrenia will continue to increase until research produces the knowledge needed to prevent its occurrence. As of this moment in time, it is impossible to predict the date by which sufficient knowledge about the etiology of this disorder and, equally important, the methods needed to apply this knowledge, will have developed. It is equally impossible to predict when it will be possible to begin achieving significant reductions in the rate at which new cases of this disorder are being added to our population. Even though a major research breakthrough would occur, the likelihood of achieving significant reductions in new cases would seem to be quite small in view of the large increases expected in the size of the population groups in which the risk of acquiring this disorder is known to be high. Very effective and efficient methods of prevention would be required to counter-balance the increase in numbers of new cases that can be expected to occur as a result of population increases."

The same trend can be expected in developing countries where the decrease of child mortality and overall improvement in levels of health care are likely to make this increase even more dramatic. In spite of advances in methods of treatment, schizophrenia remains the condition which is the main reason for psychiatric hospitalisation and other types of care. In the USA (1971) schizophrenia accounted for 31.7 per cent of all patient care episodes in inpatient mental health services and for 14 per cent (males) and 17.3 per cent (females) of all patient care episodes in outpatient care. Knowledge about the etiology, course and outcome of schizophrenia is therefore urgently needed. Up to now research undertaken in different countries has not yielded sufficient information to permit the development of a radically new way of managing this condition, and in the past two decades it has become increasingly clear that collaboration in research in schizophrenia is a principal way of achieving progress.

Collaboration in Schizophrenia Research

This collaboration has two main aspects: firstly coordination between the different disciplines that could produce new knowledge, and secondly international collaboration. The need for and potential benefits of a multidisciplinary approach to the problem of schizophrenia have been discussed in other contributions to this seminar and this paper will concentrate on the justification for and methods of international collaboration in research in schizophrenia. The main reasons for collaboration between different countries in this difficult field can be summarised as follows:

(i) International collaboration is the only way to establish whether schizophrenia has the same manifestations, course and outcome in different cultures and in different socioeconomic settings. The answer to this question would contribute to the resolution of the nature/nurture controversy and, at a more practical level, enable health decision makers and the care providers to establish whether methods of treatment and care have an equal chance of success in different sociocultural settings.

(ii) In view of our limited knowledge of the forms that schizophrenia can take (and its course and outcome) it is essential to study these aspects of the question on sufficiently large groups of schizophrenics. This could of course be achieved at a national level, but the investment of time and effort required makes the accumulation of sufficiently large samples of schizophrenic patients exceedingly difficult even for the most prosperous country. Collaboration on the other hand can help to create large samples at a lesser expense for the individual investigator(s) and can shorten the time necessary for the accumulation of the study population. Large samples will also contain sufficient numbers of the rarer forms of schizophrenia and allow the study of the whole spectrum of schizophrenic disorders. Furthermore, at the present time when psychopharmacological treatment is ubiquitous, such large samples can produce a sufficient number of previously untreated patients in whom biological and other investigations may yield important new knowledge.

(iii) Collaborative research leads to a sharing of knowledge and an increase in the scientific capacity of researchers and research centres. The proliferation of the medical literature, and paradoxical increased delay in the publication of new results, are a serious obstacle in present-day research: collaboration can overcome this difficulty because results can be exchanged directly and without delay.

(iv) The sharing of expenses and pooling of knowledge that are characteristic of collaborative research can help to overcome the growing cost of the sophisticated technology needed for basic biological research. Similarly, modern methods of data analysis in a field such as epidemiological research require so much in terms of expertise and computer cost that it becomes imperative to seek new, more economical ways of dealing with this problem.

The Need for a Common Language

A basic requirement for collaboration in research is the use of a common language in the definition of the morbid condition, in the development of methods of biological and other types of investigation, and in the presentation of results. The need for a common language came to be recognised several decades ago and many valiant efforts were made by prominent people to satisfy it. The lack of common methods of assessment, of agreed diagnostic and classificatory schemes, of adequate information and statistical systems was an obstacle to progress and the subject of an ever-increasing number of complaints. The need for agreement grew in parallel with the increasing recognition of the fact that mental disorders are a public health problem of a high priority, both because of the suffering and social distress they cause and because of the loss of economic and human potential that result from them; this is in fact a public health problem of such proportions that planned action by the health decision-maker became an inevitable necessity. The decision-makers turned to the professions; and they in turn looked to their most prestigious members for a solution. A large number of proposals were made, but the very prominence of the many authors acted against the wide acceptance of any single scheme, or any single diagnostic and classificatory system. At the turn of the century Hans Tuke wrote that the wit of man has rarely been exercised more, and with poorer results than in the efforts to produce a satisfactory classification of mental disorders. The need for a common language was felt equally strongly by researchers, particularly after it was recognised that some of the contradictory results of biological research in psychiatry could not be explained nor studied further because of differences in the clinical definition of the "cases" and the variation between the different methods used in the study of psychobiological functioning.

The World Health Organisation recognised these problems and in the early Sixties started a programme on the standardisation of psychiatric diagnosis, classification and statistics. In the following 10 years a proposal for an international classification was produced in collaboration with experts from more than 40 countries.[2] The new proposal has, for the first time in the history of the International Classification of Diseases, an "in-built" glossary containing definitions and instructions concerning the inclusions and exclusions for each of the categories in the chapter on mental disorders. In addition, a glossary has been produced to facilitate the classification of mental disorders in the Eighth Revision of the ICD.[3] Psychiatrists, statisticians, mental health administrators and other mental health workers from more than 60 countries made comments, suggestions and contributions to these documents.

The proposals for the classification of mental disorders in the Ninth Revision of the ICD are neither revolutionary nor particularly original: their main advantage is that they seem to be an acceptable compromise which will make most people least unhappy. A first important step on this difficult path has thus been made; it is being followed by others, for example by work on the development of an "impairment and disability" code, and preparations for the development of an (international) classification which could be used by people with very modest training in psychiatry. An international study to test a multiaxial classification of mental disorders in childhood has started in several countries[4] and work on an international glossary of the most frequently used terms describing syndromes and symptom groups is about to begin. Another equally important effort now is aiming at the development of internationally acceptable definitions of terms used in mental health statistics, to overcome the present lack of agreement on terms such as "psychiatric bed", or "psychiatric nurse".[5] In a more tentative and experimental way a project has also been initiated to develop a classification of the severity of disease, and of disorders of social functioning.

The International Pilot Study of Schizophrenia (IPSS)

Linked to these efforts are projects which aim at the development of commonly agreed instruments and procedures for the assessment of the clinical state of patients suffering from different types of mental disorder. An important beginning in this area has been made by the International Pilot Study of Schizophrenia in the course of which 1200 patients were assessed and followed over 5 years in nine different countries. This resulted, among other things, in a set of instruments for the assessment of functional psychoses in nine languages.[6]

The IPSS was carried out in three phases: a preliminary phase, an initial evaluation phase, and a follow-up phase. During the preliminary phase, administrative, operational and organisational procedures were established and tested. Approximately 400 patients were examined in a pre-pilot run during which instruments were developed, translated and back-translated, the investigators trained, and the administrative setup in the centres adjusted so as to ensure smooth running of the project. In the next phase, lasting about a year (1968/69), a series of patients was selected from consecutive admissions to a set of psychiatric facilities, using psychopathological criteria such as the presence of hallucinations. The exclusion criteria included signs of organic brain damage, abuse of alcohol and drugs, mental retardation, inability to establish contact with the patient because of language, hearing or speech difficulties, and chronicity of the condition. The 1200 patients who were examined in this phase were then, in the third phase of the study, followed up over a period of 5 years.

One of the most remarkable results of this study is that 10 years after the study began, the field research centres still remain in close contact and work together analysing results and elucidating further the problems identified in the IPSS. The field research centres were selected on the basis of a number of criteria which included: (i) the existence of a network of services capable of detecting a sufficient number of likely cases of schizophrenia: (ii) the presence of several well-trained and motivated psychiatrists; (iii) the availability of census data on the whole population and of a reporting system; (iv) the absence of high death and immigration rates which would make the follow-up difficult; (v) the existence of a recognisable and distinct local culture or cultures. The nine centres were situated in Aarhus, Denmark; Agra, India; Cali, Colombia; Ibadan, Nigeria; London, UK; Moscow, USSR; Taipei, China; Washington, D.C., USA; and Prague, Czechoslovakia. The coordination of the research activities and the major part of the data analyses were carried out by WHO Headquarters in Geneva, although some of the centres contributed considerably to the data analyses.

Having selected patients on the basis of their symptoms a standardised examination was carried out. This lasted approximately 5 hours per patient and in the course of it more than 1600 items of information were collected about each patient. This was done using eight instruments, of which the three basic ones were the Present State Examination, the Psychiatric History Schedule and the Social Description Schedule. The first of these, the Present State Examination (PSE), was developed some 13 years ago by Dr. Wing and his colleagues,[7] and has been tested extensively and used in a number of studies, including the US/UK diagnostic project. It is a guide to structuring the clinical psychiatric interview, aimed at obtaining a systematic, reliable and valid description of the present mental state of patients suffering from one of the functional psychoses or neuroses. Its 360 items cover systematically all the areas of psychopathology usually explored in the course of a comprehensive clinical examination of the patient's current mental condition. A glossary describing how items should be coded was provided. An important feature of the method is that in all instances, the rating on the items is the result of a clinical assessment by a psychiatrist of the presence or absence of a symptom, rather than a mere recording of a patient's answer to questions. The clinical principle of cross-examination is followed throughout.[8] For the purposes of this study the PSE, as well as all other instruments, were translated from English into seven languages: Danish, Hindi, Spanish, Yoruba, Russian, Chinese and Czech. The back-translation method, in which the instrument is first translated from English into one of the target languages, and then the translation given to a second person who translates it back into English, in order to permit a comparison between the original and the back-translation, was selected as the method for achieving inter-language equivalence. That equivalence had been achieved was tested by: (i) the target check, which includes a search for errors of meaning and which was carried out frequently in all centres; and (ii) statistical analyses which showed similar patterns of correlations between items rated in various centres. Additional safeguards were the training which psychiatrists and other members of the research team received about the meaning of the items in the schedule and the manner of using them, as well as the fact that many of the psychiatrists (and other team members) spoke English.

To assess the reliability of the psychiatric assessments within the same centre, every sixth interview was rated simultaneously by two psychiatrists. The median value of the intraclass correlation coefficient was found to be 0.77 for individual items, and 0.81 for groups of items representing psychiatric symptoms. In addition to these examinations, a total of 51 patients from the different centres were interviewed consecutively within a week by two psychiatrists to assess the repeatability of ratings and lower, but still acceptable, values of the intraclass correlations were found. The intercentre reliability was tested by joint ratings of 21 interviews held in different centres. These were rated live or from videotape or films by an average of 10 psychiatrists from different centres. The median R for symptoms was lower than in exercises within centres (0.45), the reliability level being consistently higher for ratings based on patient-reported experiences than for items rated from observation of behaviour.

Hence, the reliability of the study's main instrument, the PSE, was found to be at an acceptable level, in spite of the obvious difficulties associated with the design of a multicentre, crosscultural study.

The other two instruments, Psychiatric History and Social Description Schedules, were much more difficult to construct because of crosscultural and socioeconomic differences between the countries involved and the lack of previous international experience. The Psychiatric History Schedule was designed to cover areas, such as previous illnesses and hospitalisations, history, symptomatology and course of the present episode, treatment, premorbid personality traits, psychosexual adjustment, occupational history, use of alcohol and drugs, and satisfaction with the premorbid life situation. The Social Description Schedule contained items related to areas such as parents' and spouse's education and occupation, type of household, patient's education, religion, marital status and work activities.

The primary task in the development of these two schedules was seen to be the identification of items that would be applicable and useful in a variety of different cultures; less emphasis was therefore placed on testing the reliability of these instruments. In a study of the intracentre reliability of these instruments using data from 36 paired interviews, 70 out of the 120 items had 90 per cent or more agreement, and on only two items the agreement was 50 per cent. Tests of intercentre reliability were not so encouraging, and here the exercise served more to improve the instructions on rating than to provide a final answer to the question of intercentre reliability.

The psychiatrists also achieved a high degree of diagnostic reliability. In 190 simultaneous paired interviews an agreement of 87.3 per cent was reached on three-digit categories of the ICD. On schizophrenia the agreement was 91.3 per cent and for the rest of the diagnostic categories the agreement was also acceptably high except for mania, for which there was an agreement in 6 out of 11 interviews. Intercentre reliability in making diagnoses was tested by multiple rating of videotaped interviews, where it was found that the agreement was satisfactorily high, ranging between 82 and 100 per cent for three-digit diagnostic categories.

These surprisingly good results of reliability assessments are understandable in the light of the very intensive training which the participating psychiatrists received. Two training seminars were held in London at the beginning of the study. Subsequently the 26 paired interviews carried out in each centre in the preliminary phase served both for the assessment of the schedule and for the further training of the investigators under field conditions. The degree of uniformity was maintained or improved by simultaneous interviews carried out at regular intervals throughout the period when patients were being taken into the study. New psychiatrists joining the project had to do at least five simultaneous interviews with each of the other psychiatrists in their centre. Joint rating exercises involving psychiatrists from the different centres also took place at regular intervals, during the exchange visits by the collaborating investigators, held in each of the centres in turn.

The main findings of this study were that it is possible to carry out effectively a large crosscultural investigation, that it is possible to develop standardised and reliable research instruments and procedures for practical use in psychiatric studies and to train teams of research workers to use instruments and procedures of this kind in both developed and developing countries. It establishes further that there are patients in each of the nine countries who show symptoms that constitute a syndrome of schizophrenia.

Encouraged by these results the investigators proceeded with follow-up examinations in which every patient was reassessed twice: at the end of the second, and at the end of the fifth year after the initial evaluation. Over 2100 hours were spent assessing IPSS patients with the two-year follow-up schedules, and 4300 man-hours were spent carrying out home visits, 1200 of these by psychiatrists. The number of home visits required to gather follow-up information about patients differed markedly from centre to centre. For example, Aarhus and Cali were quite similar with regard to the number of patients about whom sufficient information was gathered for them to be included in the follow-up group. In Cali, however, 81 home visits were required compared to 29 in Aarhus. Ibadan was the centre which carried out the greatest number of home visits (104) to gather information.

The follow-up instruments and procedures were pretested on a 40 per cent sample of the patients one year after the initial evaluation. They included the Follow-up Psychiatric History Schedule, the Follow-up Social Description Schedule, and the Follow-up Diagnostic Assessment Schedule. The information gathered with these four instruments was supplemented in most centres by detailed narrative accounts of the clinical picture, course of illness, and social environment of the patient. As in the initial evaluation phase of the study, simultaneous interviews and multiple rating exercises were carried out to determine and maintain intra- and intercentre reliability of PSE assessment. In the 2-year follow-up, it was possible to trace and reinterview a very high proportion of the patients: an average of 82.1 per cent for all centres. In two of the centres the proportion of the reinterviewed patients was above 90 per cent.

Only 2.9 per cent of all patients could not be traced for reexamination. Before a second-year examination could be carried out, 2.4 per cent of all patients had died. In 6.9 per cent of the 1202 patients the follow-up interview was refused by either the patient or his family. In addition 12.1 per cent of the patients were not reinterviewed but could have been examined had more resources been available. Prominent among the difficulties encountered by the centres in attempting to trace and reexamine patients were the lack of population registers in some centres, the large size of the catchment area (e.g. 52 076 sq km in Agra), changes in street names or numeration, and seasonal weather variations.

In the 5-year follow-up 75 per cent of the total initial series of patients were reexamined. In one centre this percentage was over 90, in four centres it was between 83 and 90, and in only one centre was it below 60. A detailed analysis of the feasibility aspects of the 5-year follow-up will be available at a later stage, but the preliminary impression is that the reasons for the simple attrition during this phase were similar to those described for the 2-year follow-up.

The main findings from this study are published elsewhere.[6],[9] On the whole, it can be said that the study was a successful experiment in international collaboration, paving the way for further efforts in psychiatric research on a world-wide scale.

Directions of Future Work

(i) *Further investigations of the clinical and social characteristics of schizophrenia and of other functional disorders (e.g. depression) in different parts of the world.* The IPSS has established that there are patients with similar characteristics in the nine countries studied and perhaps these findings permit us to conclude that schizophrenia is a universally present disorder, common to all populations because it is probably linked to the very nature of human beings. However, further confirmation of this statement which could be of crucial importance for further research is needed, for two reasons: firstly, because the differences between the sociocultural settings that exist on earth are so enormous that a sample of nine countries can hardly be taken as representative of the population of the world: and secondly, because even if there were schizophrenic patients in all countries in the world, there seem to be considerable variations in the incidence of the disorder, as research in Yugoslavia[10] and Papua, New Guinea[11] has clearly demonstrated. Knowledge about the reasons for these differences may be exceedingly useful in elucidating the etiology of schizophrenia. Furthermore, while the IPSS produced evidence that there are schizophrenics with *similar* characteristics in all the centres, it has left open the question of whether and how many schizophrenics there are with characteristics that are very *different* from one centre to another. Collaboration between psychiatric epidemiologists, anthropologists, sociologists and others will be necessary to approach these difficult but highly interesting questions.

(ii) *Development of methodologies that permit collaborative, international, and multi-disciplinary research in the field of psychiatry.* Equally important to agreement on a common language is the agreement among researchers on the methods of biological investigation in psychiatry. Here the difficulties may be even greater than in the field of psychopathology because of the belief held by many that biological research methods are objective and that no work is needed to achieve standardisation of methods which are to be used by different researchers. Yet there is ample evidence of differences that exist in the reading and interpretation of findings of biological tests; and investigations have shown that there is relatively little agreement on the details of the methods used. The procedures used when taking cerebrospinal fluid or when plasma is stored have significant effects on the results of investigation.

WHO has recently initiated collaborative research in biological psychiatry. An exchange of visits of collaborating investigators working in the WHO centres for research and training in biological psychiatry took place in Moscow in May 1975.[12] The investigators agreed to carry out jointly several studies, but the first phase of all of these studies is collaborative work on the standardisation of biological research methods. Attention is given not only to the laboratory side of the techniques but also to the administrative and technical arrangements necessary for an exchange of samples of body fluids, description of the way in which these are obtained and so on. It is expected that this work will result, *inter alia* in manuals and guidelines for collaborative research in that area.

(iii) *Studies of the reaction to treatment and characteristics of the course and outcome of schizophrenia in different sociocultural settings.* Anecdotal evidence, clinical reports and isolated studies indicate that the course and outcome of mental disorders and the reaction to the same medicament differ from culture to culture. If confirmed, these findings would be of tremendous importance, not only for further research, but also for daily practice and the treatment of the mentally ill. The preliminary results of analyses of the IPSS seem to confirm the first of these two statements; and WHO has now started preparations for a study that will assess the reaction to treatment of patients living in different sociocultural and biophysical environments.

The increasing recognition of the multivariate nature of mental disorders makes the need for the multidisciplinary approach and international collaboration more evident now than ever before. In most countries there now seems to exist reluctant admission that collaboration may be the only answer to the need for new knowledge which will help to provide better treatment and a more satisfactory life for the schizophrenic and for other mental patients. Yet, many obstacles still bar the way. They include the traditional separation between biological and environment-oriented approaches; the reluctance of scientists to share resources and pool knowledge; the fierce striving of academic researchers to gather new knowledge in individual disciplines or highly specialised fields as opposed to a common planning and utilisation of research facilities; the split between the public health planner and the researcher, the lack of agreement on methods of investigation and many others. Technical difficulties merge with administrative barriers and create formidable obstacles to joint progress.

In overcoming these difficulties WHO can only rely on the hope that experts in different fields and of different backgrounds will realise that they must work together and that working together must become a way of life rather than an exception.

References

1. KRAMER, M. *Psychiatric services and the changing institutional scene* (in press).
2. SARTORIUS, N. The programme of the World Health Organisation on the epidemiology of mental disorders. In *Excerpta Medica International Congress Series No. 274, Psychiatry (Part 1)*, p. 13, Excerpta Medica, Amsterdam, 1973.
3. WORLD HEALTH ORGANISATION. *Glossary of mental disorders and guide to their classification.* WHO, Geneva, 1974.
4. RUTTER, M., SHAFFER, D. and SHEPHERD, M. *A multiaxial classification of child psychiatric disorders.* WHO, Geneva, 1975.
5. WORLD HEALTH ORGANISATION. *Classification and evaluation of mental health service activities. Report.* WHO Regional Office for Europe, Copenhagen, 1973.
6. WORLD HEALTH ORGANISATION. *International Pilot Study of Schizophrenia Vol. 1.* WHO, Geneva, 1973.
7. WING, J.K., BIRLEY, J.L.T., COOPER, J.C., GRAHAM, P. and ISAACS, A.D. Reliability of a procedure for measuring and classifying "present psychiatric state". *Brit. J. Psychiat.* **113**, 499, 1967.
8. WING, J.K., COOPER, J.E. and SARTORIUS, N. *The measurement and classification of psychiatric symptoms.* Cambridge University Press, London, 1974.
9. WORLD HEALTH ORGANISATION. *International Pilot Study of Schizophrenia Vol. 2.* WHO, Geneva (in press).
10. LEMKAU, P.V. and KULCAR, Z. *Epidemiology of psychoses in Croatia* (in press).
11. TORREY, R.F., TORREY, B.B. and BURTON-BRADLEY, B.C. The epidemiology of schizophrenia in Papua New Guinea. *Amer. J. Psychiat.* **131**, 567, 1974.
12. WORLD HEALTH ORGANISATION. *Report on an Exchange of Visits of Investigators.* WHO, Geneva (offset: OMH/75.5), 1975.

Societal Determinants of Schizophrenic Behaviour

EUGENE B. BRODY

Schizophrenic Behavior

This chapter is concerned with the ways of thinking, feeling and acting which, occurring together as a behavioral constellation, are usually labelled "schizophrenic", or as symptoms and signs of a disease called "schizophrenia".

Elements of "schizophrenic behavior", e.g. paranoid delusions or hallucinatory experiences, do not usually occur apart from some other elements of the behavioral patterns delineated by Kraepelin. These include (i) the gradually withdrawing and disintegrating constellations (simple, hebephrenic) usually beginning in adolescence and sometimes hidden behind a mask of vagrancy, alcoholism, inadequacy or mental retardation; (ii) the paranoid constellations, beginning in later life; and (iii) the episodic forms, often aggressive or catatonic in nature. Less well defined are (iv) the pan-neurotic or global psychopathic constellations, often marked by significantly narcissistic, masochistic or sadistic sexual behavior as well as somatic pre-occupations and sometimes punctuated by more obviously psychotic periods of short duration. These patterns of schizophrenic behavior all share a private frame of reference, a tendency to primary process thinking, and obvious problems in relating closely to others. They can be studied in relating to the sociocultural context in which they occur. They may reflect, while not necessarily being caused by, modal developmental experience, the adaptive requirements of particular environments, or socially sanctioned or reinforced ways of handling one's own feelings or dealing with other people. The term "schizophrenic behavior" deliberately avoids the implication of an underlying pathophysiology, a disease process which may be shaped by societal events but is fundamentally independent of them running its own predetermined course.

"Schizophrenic behavior" is also studied through social or psychotherapeutic attempts to modify it as well as through the impact of public policy upon the behavior of the mentally ill. Again, the success or failure of such attempts or the influence of such policy need say little about the origins of the behavior in question — although they can provide valuable clues. They are often, however, important in determining the life histories of patients or potential patients, especially as they interact with and influence their families. There seems little doubt, moreover, that social context, especially the presence of supporting or stressful persons and groups, can be a significant determinant of patient response to pharmacotherapy, just as it is a major influence on post-treatment or post-hospital behavior.

If "schizophrenia", i.e. a disease process with causal genetic and/or other determinants is assumed, an additional set of societal factors becomes important. These influence biological processes which may have a more immediate causal relationship with the behavior in question. They include, for example, patterns of mating, nutrition, and endemic disease. These can

23

influence the nature of the gene pool; the internal environment of the pregnant mother, developing infant or adult; and the fetal environment as by trauma, disease, or other factors impairing neural development. Included here, too, is the expanding list of iatrogenic factors with not yet identified long-term consequences. These range from diagnostic radiation exposure during pregnancy to the social impact of antipsychotic drugs, as they permit early release from hospitals and promote more frequent coitus and an increased birthrate from schizophrenic parents.

The ensuing discussion, while noting commonalities in schizophrenic behavior, assumes that people so labelled are, nonetheless, more similar to other human beings than they are different. While their ways of behaving, adapting and coping have their own idiosyncratic qualities they are not immune from the impact of events ordinarily regarded as stressful; their moods and ideas, reflections of the ongoing social process of which they are part, cannot always be regarded as symptomatic; and, descriptively at least, they cannot be regarded as schizophrenic 60 seconds a minute, 60 minutes an hour, and 24 hours a day. A discussion of the societal determinants of schizophrenic behavior, then, in a fundamental sense is a discussion of the influence of social context on how all human beings think, feel and act.

Societal Variables Influencing Behavior

Other chapters are concerned with cultural and epidemiological aspects of schizophrenia. This discussion of societal aspects deals with variables which have a separate, though related and often overlapping focus. The following section identifies some of the relevant societal variables.

Social organization, status and role. A society is a human group organized so as to ensure its survival. This is done through allocating goods, services and responsibilities as well as the loci and personnel for necessary decision-making. Every social organization has a structure. The people who constitute it are categorized according to a variety of ascribed and achieved statuses. These include age, sex, marital state, occupation, religion; parenthood and other kinship indicators; skin color and other socially visible ethnic markers; and their place in a power and prestige hierarchy which may be operationally defined according to a variety of criteria such as education, occupation, wealth or family membership. Many of these statuses are tied to a person's place in the social allocation system noted above.

Every social status has an attached social role. The concept of role articulates the study of society with that of culture as it refers to the expectations by members of a society regarding the behavior of its members in particular social statuses. If a middle-aged American male physician, for example, behaves in the manner expected of an adolescent Brazilian high school girl, the observer is apt to conclude (because of status-role incongruence) that he is ill, intoxicated or emotionally upset. Characteristic emotional difficulties arise when the same person does in fact occupy statuses associated with conflicting social roles (as in the case of some upwardly mobile minority group members).

The likelihood of role conflict is increased by the number of subgroups contained in the broader society; and its rate of social change. The United States is a pluralistic, transitional society. The inhabitants of its various social worlds (based on national origin, race, and religion), especially growing children, are faced with the problem of reconciling the behavioral standards and goals acquired at home with those encountered in schools and elsewhere. As Shibutani (1961) noted: ". . . when participating in societies in which the component group norms are not mutually consistent it becomes progressively more difficult for any man to integrate his various self-images into a single unit." This problem is most obviously present in marginal persons, in transition between social statuses and roles, e.g. upwardly mobile members of lower class and socially visible ethnic origin. These matters as they relate to emotional disturbance and mental illness have been discussed elsewhere by the author at greater length (Brody, 1961, 1963, 1964a, 1967, 1968, 1970).

Social labelling and institutional context. Status and role are important variables, then, for determining both the private and public perceptions of one's self and others. In the public sense they influence the process of appraisal, evaluation or labelling called "diagnosis". The initial act of labelling is partly a function of the institution (e.g. medical, judicial-penal, religious, educational, social welfare) to which the person goes voluntarily or is sent because of subjectively experienced discomfort or socially observed deviance. All such institutions, including private psychiatrists' offices, are in some measure behavior change stations. If the individual passes the test or change criterion employed at the institution he may be released to the larger society. If not he may be moved to a socially designated setting where his freedom is further constrained in the name of personal therapy or societal protection.

Society's techniques for dealing with deviance, involving variable degrees of collaboration by the labelled deviant, may utilize special settings or occur wherever behavior takes place. These range from shunning, ridicule and nurturing to institutional behavior change in place (as via outpatient treatment), extrusion from the system for punishment and deterrence (jail), or extrusion for behavior change (mental hospital). These ways of behaving are institutionalized in that they represent unthinking conformity to cultural norms defining proper, legitimate or expected modes of action or social relationship. Institutionalized behavior provides "a mode of integration" of the actions of the component individuals of society (Parsons & Shils, 1961). Institutional settings (e.g. mental hospitals, jails, military units, boarding schools) while differing in specific purpose and detail tend to share the features described by Goffman (1957) as characteristic of "total institutions": the normally separated life activities of working, playing and eating and sleeping are carried on in the same place with the same people in accordance with a master plan managed by a group of supervisors. Such settings exert powerful influences on the behavior of inmates. Thus the nature of the setting is an important societal determinant of the nature of behavior called schizophrenic. There is also some reason to believe that persons most likely to be institutionalized are those most vulnerable to change in response to the controlled setting. As Hollingshead and Redlich (1958) noted, these include the lower-class schizophrenics for whom psychotherapy is unavailable. If treatment with anti-psychotic drugs is ineffective they are moved into hospitals where, more passive and dependent than those with more education and skills, they have a greater tendency to accumulate and become "chronic". This tendency is reinforced by the fact that, in total institutions, nonconforming behavior reflecting the struggle for individualization, or an attempt to cope rather than adjust, is regarded as deviant or uncooperative, and may be actively, even punitively, discouraged.

Gibbs (1941) regarded the likelihood of a person's being isolated (e.g. hospitalized or jailed) for committing a deviant act as directly proportional to the degree to which he is a "social and cultural alien", i.e. one who differs in status and cultural traits from other members of the society, and particularly from the agents of social control and the power-holding dominant culture-bearers. In the United States, such persons have included those who are non-white, non-native, and in agricultural labor and other lower-class occupations. Similarly, the pathway to the medical diagnostician and the label, itself, can influence subsequent behavior, in terms of the subjective response of the patient as well as of the ways in which others deal with him; the question still remains regarding a "natural history" of schizophrenia apart from the sociocultural context in which the individual lives. This question recognizes that behavior, including that described as psychotic, is not solely a function of genetic programming or past personal history, but reflects a mode of participation in an ongoing social process (Stanton, 1949; Stanton and Schwartz, 1949, 1954; Caudill *et al.*, 1952; Caudill, 1958). Behavior seemingly determined by a private or nonrational frame of reference and interpreted primarily as ego-defensive may upon examination prove to have adaptive, coping or communicative functions related to the context in which it occurs.

It has been hypothesized that low expectations regarding work and social participation affect the outcome of treatment. Lower-class patients and/or those returning to parental homes would thus be expected to have fewer rehospitalizations. Freeman and Simmons (1958 and 1959), however, found that social class was unrelated to either expectations or successful community tenure although it was related to performance. Later (1963) they reported that former patients were expected to perform as anyone else did. Angrist *et al.* (1968) also found that tolerance of deviance (symptom tolerance) and role expectations did not predict rehospitalization and that social class did not have a marked relationship to rehospitalization. It did, though, influence performance indirectly via class-related role expectations.

Self labelling and reference groups. The significance of the sociocultural context for adaptive as compared to ego-defensive aspects of behavior has been described at length by the author (Brody, 1974). A person constantly monitors his own behavior as does his audience. But the monitoring process is usually outside his focus of awareness. People categorize their experience on the basis of standards developing while they mature; sorting, matching, and classifying information and evaluating its congruence or fit with these standards occur rapidly and automatically. This silent process, shared by most members of a community (because of regularities in developmental and adult experience) is part of an institutionalized behavior pattern. A general unexplicated consensus about the social significance of behavior is also implied by Clyde Kluckhohn's definition of culture as a society's blueprint for living: the socially transmitted behavior patterns utilized by everyone in relation to all of the important aspects of life from birth to death (1944).

Generally accepted moral or obligatory standards, along with a society's common knowledge, common psychological states, and common attitudes, constitute what Ralph Linton called the "covert or implicit aspects of culture" (1945). Related is the definition of culture offered by Kroeber and Parsons: ". . . the transmitted and created content and patterns of values, ideas and other symbolic-meaningful systems as factors in the shaping of human behavior, and the artifacts produced through behavior" (1958). Jaeger and Selznick's (1965) definition of culture is more sharply focused as "everything that is produced by and capable of sustaining shared symbolic experience". Human behavior, according to this view occurs in a cultural symbolic-meaningful matrix, of which values are an essential part. Within this context, a person may categorize behavior as symptomatic if he experiences it as alien or a foreign body in himself, i.e. it is not congruent with his own internalized norms, values, and expectations of himself.

Among any group's important roles is that of the person defined as "sick". Parsons conceived of the sick-role as a socially acceptable though sometimes temporary solution to psychosocial impasses (1951). He regarded exemption from the performance of certain normal social obligations, as well as from a certain type of responsibility for one's own state, as one of the features making it evident that "illness is not merely a 'condition' but also a social role". Different cultures and different social strata reinforce or counteract the sick role in varying degrees. Self as well as other appraisal of behavior as symptomatic will depend to some degree upon the guilt and shame-free availability, usefulness or necessity of the sick role in a particular socioculture as a conflict-resolving or otherwise rewarding position (Brody, 1964b).

Self-referral to mental health units, folk-healers, or their equivalents, may not always be a consequence of ego-alien behavior. People also refer themselves for psychological help because of the secondary anxiety attendant upon stigmatized ego-syntonic behavior: acts defined socially but not experienced personally as deviant, i.e. evaluated as such by observers. The individual engaging in ego-syntonic, e.g. homosexual, behavior does not experience it as painful, alien, or symptomatic. He may, however, become anxious about its social consequences.

Both ego-alien and ego-syntonic behavior may be subjectively appraised as sick or symptomatic in terms of the others, the referents with whom the person compares himself (Merton, 1957). A person's major comparative reference group is usually the particular subcommunity in which he lives. Its institutional, organizational, and behavioral patterns are familiar. But his behavior may also be determined by a more distinct community which he values highly, but to which he does not belong. This wealthier, better-educated, or somehow more advantaged community functions for him as an emulative reference group. Behavior modeled on such an over-evaluated, but not well understood reference group may be perceived by others as caricatured or even bizarre, and may be met with rejecting or humiliating responses.

Minority status, socioeconomic disadvantage and powerlessness. Minority status may be most meaningfully defined on the basis of lack of access to or distance from sources of societal power. The majority does not necessarily include more people, but it is always in possession of more power. Thus, one *de facto* synonym for minority status is powerlessness. This broadens the concept to include not only those who can be defined on the basis of ethnic or racial characteristics, but also those who are powerless by virtue of poverty. The person who is helpless in the face of external economic, political, or social circumstances must devote his available energies to the here-and-now struggle for survival. The poor person also fits into the group who "capable of being distinguished on the basis of some physical or cultural characteristic, are treated collectively as inferior" (Mack, 1963). They may be socially visible on the basis of skin color, physiognomy, or ethnically or socioeconomically linked appearance and behavior. Social visibility permits them to be categorized at a distance and, once this categorization has been made, individual characteristics tend to be replaced by stereotypes in the eye of the beholder. To this degree the minority group man, the target of prejudice, is behaviorally vulnerable. No matter how well schooled the majority person is in dissimulation, he will transmit the message: you are inferior, dangerous, hated, or otherwise obnoxious. He will tend to behave toward the minority man in a way which elicits responsive aggressive or hostile behavior and, following the "self-fulfilling prophecy", the elicited behavior, confirmatory of the original belief, tends to reinforce it (Merton, 1948). The specific vulnerabilities of discriminated-against minority groups to behavioral disorganization, as well as the symptomatic nature of prejudiced behavior, have been reviewed elsewhere (Brody, 1961, 1966, 1968, 1970, 1973).

Minority status, on the other hand, may produce successful coping behavior in the presence of a strong, transplantable, complex culture capable of providing solutions to new problems and a sense of identity in a new milieu. Members of segregated groups with a strong cultural or religious heritage may reveal their insecurities and try to resolve their problems through overachievement. They are able to do this and have their achievement gain consistent recognition within their own groups of origin because it fits their cultural heritage. Since all complex cultures have much in common, such achievement also has significance for and is rewarded by the dominant system as well. As Erikson (1950) has pointed out, "ego identity gains real strength only from the wholehearted and consistent recognition of real accomplishment, i.e. of achievement that has meaning in the culture." Minorities with strong cultural heritages and values may even strengthen their group identities when surrounded by a dominant society possessing enough values congruent with their own to permit them to survive and to play a functional role within it. Minority group members with no intact history or culture of their own, however, who can acquire only distorted fragments of the values and achievement techniques of the majority, have little chance of reward for activities with real cultural meaning. Following Erikson again, they have diminished opportunity for developing the sense of reality which comes from a life way which is an individual variant of a stable group identity. On the other hand exclusion from full participation in the majority culture (Brody, 1966), lack of economic potency (Derbyshire, Brody and Schleifer, 1963) and awareness of blocked opportunities for upward mobility, all contribute to low self-esteem, retaliative anger against power holders, mistrust of those who do not belong to one's immediate social or family group, and a sense of alienation and powerlessness. These societal conditions influence the occurrence and nature of disturbed behavior, including some elements of the schizophrenic syndromes. Their behavioral correlates are mainly adaptive (including submission-withdrawal) and coping in the sense that they represent efforts to survive in harsh and threatening environments. To the degree, however, that circumstances determine the relative priority of particular defense mechanisms, (e.g. denial in the fact of psychologically insupportable circumstances) the correlated behavior reflecting their operation may be, in fact, maladaptive. Thus, inappropriate cheerfulness and submissiveness (e.g. due to denying the actual harshness of work conditions and repressing rage against the employer) may aid survival in a particular work relationship, but inhibit the creative effort necessary to change the relationship or escape from it. Projection, reflected in adherence to beliefs in malevolent forces outside the actual socio-economic-political systems or ultimate divine intervention, may similarly aid short-term adaptation to a particular context, but preclude the moves essential to long-range survival for an individual and his family.

An examining psychiatrist may conversely mistake behavioral reflections of the adaptive process as ego-defensive and pathological. For example, litigiousness, suspiciousness and readiness to attack before being attacked characterize many adolescent male slum dwellers. These behaviors, necessary for survival in the jungle of an urban ghetto, may appear to the examiner as reflections of projection. This may lead to an erroneous diagnosis of paranoid behavior which ignores the strengths facilitating reality-oriented coping under adverse conditions. As in the case of migration the degree to which this kind of environmentally relevant behavior shades into or increases vulnerability to the schizophrenic syndrome remains uncertain. The distinction between life in a chronically stressful context, shaping behavior from an early age, and exposure to acute stressful circumstances with a discrete beginning and end, is especially important. Under the former circumstances, when several generations are involved, it has been postulated (Lewis, 1959) that a culture of poverty develops, so the behavior in question can no longer be related solely to societal variables, but to socially transmitted values, beliefs, myths, symbols, rituals and other cultural forms and patterns.

Hypothetically, the alienated individual with few social alternatives might be prone to massive resignation, surrender or apathy, blind goal-less rage, or a state of panic resolvable only through suicide; all of these may be conceived as psychotic behavior. Our own observations, however, and those of others suggest a greater degree of behavioral organization in the poor and powerless than implied by the above alternatives. Thus a variety of self-narcotizing activities, an emphasis on immediate physical gratification rather than on achieving delayed long-range goals, and, in Rodman's terms (1966), a "value-stretch" to bring certain kinds of activities, such as companionate marriage, the production of illegitimate children and deception of dominant group members, into the range of subcultural approval, have been observed.

These behaviors can be understood up to a point as defensive as well as adaptive, in Hartmann's (1958) sense of promoting a stable reciprocal relationship with the environment.

The point at which they shade into or set the stage for defensive processes, which maintain an intrapsychic equilibrium by denying external reality, projecting unacceptable wishes, or substituting fantasies at the cost of adaptive stability, i.e. processes resulting in psychotic behavior, is unclear.

A sense of powerlessness in the face of catastrophic natural as well as brutal or unpredictable human forces has been reported by Klein among Andean Indian serfs in Peru (1963). The most deprived of a Rio de Janeiro psychiatric patient sample revealed themselves through Rorschach and TAT responses as feeling completely at the mercy of forces beyond their control (Brody, 1973). In both Peruvian nonpatients and Brazilian patients, symptomatic behavior patterns associated with lowest socioeconomic status and feelings of powerlessness were regressively defensive, withdrawn, self-insulating and inflexible. The behavioral reflections of these defensive-adaptive manoeuvers resemble those of the schizophrenic syndrome. However, there is no epidemiological evidence that the suspicious, vigilant, aggressive survivor of socialization under competitive slum conditions, or the rigidly defended South American worker on the land, is more likely to develop a paranoid psychosis than anyone else. His behavior can be understood in characterological terms as well, and what seems to be a fixed-character picture may well be modifiable on the basis of later experience. If his socially reinforced styles of feeling, thinking and acting have crystallized into a mould of character disorder, there is no firm evidence, either, to suggest that he is more likely than others to produce behavior of psychotic quality on more than transitory basis, e.g. as has been reported for so-called "borderline states" in a transference micropsychosis during the course of psychotherapy (Brody, 1960). Nonetheless, the question remains concerning a relationship for particular individuals between life style emerging from a setting of cultural exclusion, and vulnerability to periods of psychotic behavior.

In the U.S., under less extreme circumstances similar phenomena which keep the question about schizophrenic behavior open have been observed. An extensive literature agrees that a disproportionate number of urban schizophrenics in industrialized countries are concentrated in the socioeconomically most deprived areas of large cities, and in lowest class occupations (Kohn, 1974). The evidence, however, is not conclusive for a systematic inverse relationship between social class in general and the occurrence of diagnosed schizophrenia. Rather, lowest class membership in particular appears to be significant (Stern, Mednick and Schulsinger, 1974).

Some lower class schizophrenic persons probably have moved down the class structure as they became ill. The available evidence, however, does not support a "social drift" hypothesis as generally significant (Kohn, 1974), though it may, as noted later be more important for migrants than nonmigrants.

Some lower class schizophrenics have not achieved the education and occupation expected on the basis of their parents' status (Turner and Wagenfeld, 1967). This kind of evidence, especially from the United States, supports to some extent and for some persons a "social selection" hypothesis. Rates of first treatment, however, are also disproportionately high for patients with lowest occupational status fathers (Turner and Wagenfeld, 1967).

Kohn (1974) concluded on the basis of his critical review that, while downward social mobility contributes to the class schizophrenia relationship, it seems probable that "schizophrenia is actually produced at the lowest socioeconomic levels". He notes some inconclusive evidence that this may be mediated in part through a progressive multigenerational concentration of genetically loaded persons. His main emphasis, however, is on a constricted view of social reality impairing the lower class person's ability to deal resourcefully with problems and stress. This point of view also fits data presented by Brody (1973) from lowest class Brazilian populations. The Copenhagen group, working with genetically loaded "high risk" children, has specifically identified being reared in an institutional setting as a vulnerability-producing lowest class child-rearing experience (Stern, Mednick and Schulsinger, 1974).

Non-hospitalized midtown Manhattan respondents of the lowest socioeconomic status studied by Langner and Michael (1963) were described by them as "probable psychotics", rigid, suspicious, and passive-dependent, with some related depressive features. In contrast to "probable neurotics" of higher socioeconomic status, they had suffered more devastating early life stress, experiences favoring dependence upon externalized versus internal controls, self-esteem and ego-strength-weakening experiences, and failures in training for identity, communication, relating sexually, obtaining or postponing gratification, and planning for the future. At any given level of stress they were more likely to become disturbed than people of higher social class. These elements may have their counterparts in inhabitants of socioculturally disintegrated as compared with more integrated communities described by Leighton *et al.* (Leighton, 1963) in the Stirling County study.

The more capable and motivated literate Rio de Janeiro patients (Brody, 1973) showed a higher prevalence of psychophysiological symptoms, such as tachycardia or gastrointestinal dysfunction (in contrast to somatic pain, body or organ anxiety) diffuse anxiety, and fear of loss of control than the non-literates. While the resemblance was less clear than it is between members of the most deprived groups, in different countries they were more comparable in symptom formation to upper-class than lower-class New Haven patients (Hollingshead and Redlich, 1958) and midtown (Langner and Michael, 1963) Manhattan non-patient respondents. The Rio patients showing these symptoms were less socioeconomically privileged than the middle- and upper-class United States samples. However, in comparison to other groups in the Rio sample they were responsible informed participants in the socioculture, with actively self-critical standards, more capacity to inhibit direct expression of feelings through action, more fear of status loss, and higher value placed on rational, conscious control of behavior. Diffuse anxiety and fear of loss of control were most prevalent among the white, educated, literate, better housed, and non-manually employed Rio patients. In contrast, acute anxiety attacks, somatic complaints, and paranoid delusions and hallucinations, silly, fearful and suspicious ideas of reference behavior were most prevalent among the least privileged who were subject to the most pervasive social, economic, and physical survival threats. These were the patients most often described by projective testing as searching futilely for succor in an overwhelmingly stressful and coercive world. Those with acute anxiety attacks also more frequently exhibited situational, often realistic, fears about their jobs and families.

It is difficult to separate subculturally determined child-rearing experiences from the social advantages and symbolic capacities associated with education and literacy. Adams (1950) has written, for example, of the social emasculation suffered by the Black man at the hands of the white world, and he, as well as Kardiner and Ovesey, suggested the problems of sexual identity formation, especially in the Black boy, which might stem from this circumstance (Kardiner and Ovesey, 1951). These factors, plus the matricentric character of the lower-class Black family and a majority of the most poverty-stricken families elsewhere, with absent or intermittently present fathers, appear to be important to the low self-esteem of culturally deprived and excluded men.

These are two elements which seem to be of theoretical significance for gauging the relation between minority group status and vulnerability to disorganized behavior. First, the early failure of the father as an adequate gender and instrumental role model might of itself be regarded as predisposing to later problems in sexual identity. These might include a defensive turning to homosexuality in the face of the dominant and seductive power of the mother or, conceivably as the next step, the development of paranoid sensitivity to the possibly derogatory thoughts or dangerous attacks of others. These originate in the sexual identity problem but are reinforced by the social concomitants of minority status, which require suspicious vigilance in the presence of those who are different. There was some evidence in the past that young adult or late adolescent Black men, more than comparable whites, tended to be occupied with sexual identity problems when psychotic and to become ill after the severance of significant same sex peer group relationships (Brody, 1961).

Second, the situation is complicated by the developing minority group child's need to resolve anxiety-laden conflicting identifications with figures of opposing symbolic significance, such as the Black parent on one hand and the representatives of white value-enforcing institutions on the other. These last include the white God as well as the white Christ, and the white Santa Claus as well as the white president, judge, and policeman. It seems plausible that the problem of reconciling these identifications become particularly intense at the time when adult responsibility must be assumed (Brody, 1963).

Do the clinical pictures associated with minority status and socioeconomic deprivation represent a response to stress with adaptive value, e.g. increased readiness to deal with attackers? Do they represent a type of stress-induced perceptual distortion which, already impairing the capacity to evaluate and act upon reality factors, increases vulnerability to massive regression or behavioral disorganization? Or, do they represent a culturally-fostered tendency to deal with inner problems by externalizing or attributing causal significance to outside agents, which need not suggest psychosis vulnerability? This tendency has been reported for people in civilizations less dominated by Western rational thought. The question may be rephrased to ask: does an environmentally induced lack of trust in others, coupled with relative powerlessness, increase vulnerability to psychotic withdrawal, rage, or expressive or defensive delusions or hallucinations?

In summary, there are many varieties of minority status, and the behavioral consequences of such status are determined by a multitude of social, historical, political, and economic, as well as individual psychological factors. Among these factors are the concomitant occurrence of low self-esteem and/or being discriminated against with low socio-economic level and cultural exclusion; the presence of a complex transplantable minority culture with transfer value for the dominant society; opportunities for meaningful reciprocal contact with emulative reference groups; the presence or absence of effective social power and self-determination; and the opportunity to grow up as a member of an intact family with a father who fills the instrumental leadership role. An evolving culture may protect its members from acute disintegration but restrict their psychological lives as it institutionalizes passivity; or it may temporarily increase the likelihood of acute disturbance while moving toward individual enrichment, as it becomes more of an actively coping force in conflict with the dominant society. All of these factors contribute to the absence or presence of a stable sense of identity, the capacity to collaborate with others in the achievement of meaningful goals, and the vulnerability or resistance of the minority group man to behavioral disorganization (Brody, 1968).

Public policy and mental illness. Public policy is an expression of social organization. As it, in turn, influences a variety of societal issues it exerts an indirect effect on various expressions of mental illness. Policy about hospital admissions and discharges has a direct impact on the life experience of patients, particularly the schizophrenic patients who constitute the bulk of the chronically hospitalized, their families and communities. Arnhoff's recent review (1975) discussed this issue in terms of social costs, recognizing in particular Anthony's point regarding early hospital release of psychotic family members, especially parents, that: "As the traffic between home and hospital multiplies, a point may be reached when the mental health needs of the community as a whole conflict with the mental health needs of individual patients". The major study of Pasamanick *et al.* (1967) illustrates the problem. They demonstrated that schizophrenic patients could be cared for at home, as most improvement in comparable home-care for hospitalized groups occurred within the first six months. It was also noted that disruption to family and community of the home-care groups was highest at the beginning. Arnhoff reviews a number of other studies reporting roughly comparable results (Brown *et al.*, 1966; Hoenig and Hamilton, 1967; Rutter, 1966; Wing and Brown, 1970). Most, from an anti-hospital stance make the point that community treatment is at least as favorable in both its short and long-term outcome. From Arnhoff's view, the point is restated that neither community or home treatment are necessarily superior to hospital treatment. More important is the evidence of a severe burden imposed during the home treatment period on relatives and community. Beyond this is the only marginally noted phenomenon so far (Kahn, 1969; Shearer *et al.*, 1968; Stevens, 1970) that schizophrenic patients who could not reproduce while they were hospitalized are, with the aid of drugs, back in the community and still biologically capable of procreation. The move away from the hospital has already been marked by an increase in both legitimate and illegitimate births for the mentally ill.

Social Change: Migration

Social change, as it might influence the nature and occurrence of disordered behavior, is defined most easily by reference to specific types of situations. Migration provides the example most easy to define. This has been conceptualized in relation to behavior by the author in an earlier publication (1970).

Migration provides a set of concrete operations for the study of adaptation and defense in relation to social change. A shift in residence involves not only new places, but new faces and new norms. As the person moves from one socioculture to another, behavioral modes useful in the old setting may prove maladaptive in the new. Acute sensitivity which permits empathic understanding in one group may be perceived as discomfort-provoking vigilance or paranoia in another. The culturally supported tendency to deal with the unknown or with the consequences of one's own inadequacy by attributing malevolent control to external forces, reinforced by magical belief systems in rural areas, may interfere with the evaluation of one's actual capacities necessary for survival in the city. Under these circumstances, the person may so rationalize his adaptive failure in the new setting that he is not motivated to make the necessary coping effort. One index of such failure is incompatibility between the migrant's self-image on the one hand, and the status, of which he is unaware, given him by the new social system on the other.

Behavior in the new environment is a function of the push factors that contribute to the migrant's decision to leave the culture of origin, the pull factors that lure him to the new, the transitional experiences en route, the receptor networks or resistances encountered upon entry into the host system, the talents and personal and economic assets he brings with him, congruences between the old culture and the new, the internal motives for moving. Some of these last are the distillate of ungratified wishes and needs, undischarged tensions, and unresolved conflicts. Others are more easily related to a person's place in his individual social change career. Potential migrants are differentiated from their fellows with the first stirrings of dissatisfaction with the status quo. Once in the new environment, personal change may continue indefinitely, with the greatest acceleration not reached for several years. It is often difficult, given the resistance and discomfort of family and friends, to differentiate behavior accompanying rapid personal growth and the achievement of a new identity (usually accompanied by a change in social statuses) from symptomatic behavior. Similar growth phenomena may be encountered during the course of psychotherapy. The personal growth of later life accompanying the move to a new setting, with its new occupations and new friends, can be as turbulent as the growth occurring in adolescence, and can create as much discomfort in spouse and children as it once did in parents.

Some migrants are risk-takers, people willing to go a step beyond the ordinary or expected; the appraisal of risk-taking as self-defeating symptomatic behavior or as exploratory growing behavior may not be possible without detailed longitudinal data. Some are geographic escapers, people who deal with personal or environmental disaster by physical flight; these often carry their problems with them wherever they go. In this category are those for whom the move may be understood as symptomatic of pre-existing psychiatric illness. Detailed reviews of the particular factors influencing a migrant's capacity to interact with the opportunity structure of his environment, and of the particular stress points he will encounter are available elsewhere.

Sanua (1970) has reviewed most of the recent literature on the specific relationship between migration and schizophrenia. This literature suffers mainly from being confined to hospital admission data; it reflects, therefore, the acceptance and availability of conventional medical resources, cultural psychotherapeutic alternatives to these resources, familial and other support systems, and the degree to which the deviant behavior of particular groups is tolerated in particular settings. Within the constraints of the hospital admission approach it is clear that the migrations of all peoples from all contexts do not have identical psychosocial significance. Voluntary international movement away from certain difficult situations may represent an adaptive search for more advantageous circumstances. Migration away from a relatively stable context in search of some elusive reward, or as an attempt to escape an inner conflict through geographical movement may, conversely, represent impaired reality testing and the maladaptive activity of a schizoid or prepsychotic person. Involuntary migration, as in the case of political refugees, may represent a complex series of stresses of which crossing social system boundaries and the loss of familiar identity supports are not the most crucial.

Among the explanations for the apparent correlation in some instances of migration and schizophrenia in Sanua's extensive review are those of downward drift and adverse selection. These are factors also considered in attempts to explain the apparent relationship between lower social class membership and the prevalence of schizophrenia. It has been hypothesized, for example, that adult prepsychotic individuals tend to leave their own community perceived as threatening or insecure. This was one of the major issues raised in Faris and Dunham's study (1939) which revealed that the downtown rooming house districts of Chicago included a greater share of schizophrenics. Others refer to conflict with elements of the new environment and loss of identity support. The insecurity engendered by repeated moves has received some attention, especially during childhood and adolescence. Leighton *et al.* (1963) found a strong association between the prevalence of psychiatric disorders in a noninstitutionalized population sample and the number of moves (at least three) prior to the age of 20. However, no relationship was found when the moves took place at a later age.

Some examples of studies revealing conflicting interpretations in this area include the following. Tietze, Lemkau and Cooper (1942) who observed that intra-city migrants rather than in-migrants from other communities had an excess prevalence of personality disorders suggested alternative interpretations: families on the move have consequent adjustment difficulties; or families with a tendency toward mental deviation change residence in consequence oftener than more stable families. Gerard and Houston (1953), on the basis of Worcester (Massachusetts) State Hospital admissions concluded that certain central urban areas "attract" schizophrenics, rather than "breed" them. Cases living "in a family setting" were distributed in the city at random; those living in an "out of family setting" were located largely in the central city zones. They suggested that schizophrenics tend to drift into deteriorated zones where they lodge in cheap rooming houses, and thus seem to segregate themselves. However, Hollingshead and Redlich (1958) clearly showed that schizophrenic patients committed to mental hospitals from Connecticut slum areas had not "drifted" into them as a result of illness. Hare (1956a, 1956b) in Bristol, England, on the other hand, favored the "drift hypothesis". In almost 50 per cent of 64 schizophrenics separation from families was consequent to interpersonal difficulties; however, isolation was considered an important causal factor in another one-fourth of the cases. Similarly, Clausen and Kohn (1960) in Hagerstown, who found that schizophrenics changed residence and jobs more frequently than others, considered this to be a symptom rather than an antecedent of the illness.

The influence of foreign birth *per se* is difficult to separate from that of movement between social systems and cultures. In a series of studies in New York and Canada, Malzberg and associates (1968) demonstrated a higher rate of admission for foreign born than native persons, with the difference diminishing when socioeconomic factors, age and sex were controlled. Many other investigators reviewed by Sanua reported similar results. Malzberg saw his findings mainly in terms of selective migration (of psychosis-prone individuals) and the stress associated with cultural shock. Others such as Kleiner and Parker (1970) explain differences in morbidity rates between particular populations (i.e. second generation, Philadelphia Blacks with more problems than the first migratory from the South) on the basis of discrepancy between aspiration and achievement. Still others have identified the discontinuity or interruption of an identity, lack of recognition of one's personal or professional qualities, loss of familial and other personal or sociocultural support systems, and related factors as central to the crisis of relocation resulting in schizophrenic behavior and mental hospitalization.

Within the schizophrenic population the prominence of paranoid features has been underlined by many others attributing it variously to cultural isolation, loss of status incident to migration, the abrasive qualities of the new environment, and the real adaptive strain of being isolated and insecure among unknown and unpredictable strangers who elicit suspicion and distrust. In respect to this last the findings of Mintz and Schwartz (1964) are relevant. They note that members of each foreign-born group experience their ethnicity differently, depending upon their integration as a group, the transplantation of their own customs and language, and the number of their compatriots in their immediate neighborhood. Predominantly Italian communities, for example, tended to yield fewer Italian hospital admissions diagnosed schizophrenic than less ethnically dense communities. Data from other authors tend to confirm the tentative conclusion that overall community integration may protect a vulnerable individual from mental hospitalization, and possibly from decompensating to the point of schizophrenic behavior.

Brody (1973) studied the impact of having recently migrated from predominantly rural parts of Brazil upon the symptomatic behavior of mentally hospitalized patients in Rio de Janeiro. Migratory behavior in this group could not be regarded as purely symptomatic since it had occurred in a national context in which geographic relocation is an accepted form of problem solving. Almost all the migrant patients had overcome major obstacles in order to relocate , themselves or their families in pursuit of widely accepted socioeconomic or personal goals. Their move to Rio was voluntary, and there were many supportive circumstances: over one-half the Rio population is non-native; migrant associations and social agencies were increasingly available as helpers; and some communication with family members was usually maintained. Yet, for them the stresses of the new urban context and the loss of support following departure from the home community appeared more important determinants of mental hospitalization than earlier predispositions of the sort reflected (in the native and settled patients) in prior failures to marry or to achieve. The recent (within 5 years) migrants who had become patients felt themselves alone, and their opportunities for emotionally meaningful communication were clearly less than those of the Rio native or settled (after 5 years) migrant who was a patient. The friendship and institutional network, including the work structure of the new environment had remained relatively closed to them. They suffered from inadequate and poorly located housing; exclusion from the cultural mainstream owing to lack of education and literacy; rural origins influencing their attitudes toward others and habitual cognitive and affective styles not appropriate to the complex adaptive demands of the urban setting. Suspiciousness and distrust of the unknown were characteristics brought from the rural environment and intensified in the strange city context. The effects of inadequate or distorted information about the new setting, resulting in a state of relative perceptual deprivation, were intensified by their comparative isolation from friends and relatives and inability to gain needed support from social agencies. Although many changed jobs upon arrival, most did so without upward mobility, remaining in the unskilled manual category; and, more than the settled, suffered from temporary unemployment in the year preceding hospitalization. The hard manual labor, unsanitary living conditions, and associated illnesses of the poor and unskilled contributed to fatigue, body concern, and depression compounded by a sense of hopelessness, powerlessness and low self-esteem voiced by many during their interviews.

While the recently migrant were more depressed, anxious, paranoid, deluded, and hallucinated than the settled and native patients, their families did not more often list frankly disturbed behavior as a reason for admission. A factor contributing to differential tolerance is suggested by the family diagnosis of "reaction to persecution" offered by twice as many recently migrant as settled families. A rational explanation of this sort, based on shared perceptions of strangers and the new environment might reduce the likelihood of a sick member's extrusion by the family into a hospital until his disturbed behavior begins to interfere with its survival as a socioeconomic unit. If such differences in family tolerance do in fact exist, they would account for at least part of the greater frequency of anxiety-produced functional impairment of reality testing among the recently migrant who finally became patients.

Psychosocial Events Correlated with the Occurrence of Schizophrenic Behavior

The possibly causal significance of life situations for behavioral or physiological disorder was a preoccupation of folklore and ancient medicine. The modern scientific history of this concern covers the entire twentieth century. It has assumed new importance, though, in consequence of the development of multivariate statistical techniques, an interest in rapidly administered predictive and screening devices, and the recognition of epidemiological thinking as an essential component of public health psychiatry as well as medicine. While another chapter will deal specifically with psychiatric epidemiology, it is important, for the present discussion, to identify schizophrenic behaviors or elements of the schizophrenic syndrome in people who do not occupy the sick status or role. The available data are, otherwise, limited to those living in contexts which promote the labeling and social constraint (or modification) of these deviant behaviors through conventional Western medical means.

This section's concern with events correlated with or antecedent to schizophrenic behavior will be cast into the societal mode insofar as possible. This excludes single "traumatic" happenings which may occur unpredictably and independently of particular settings, contexts or processes. The significant events, rather, will be those which occur predictably and recurrently as aspects of particular societal categories, e.g. low socioeconomic status, ethnicity or migration. Cultural factors exert their influence as they are attached to such categories. Society and culture help create individually important events by influencing the interaction between individuals, or imposing specific "stresses" e.g. by interfering with the achievement of personal goals through lack of educational opportunities or job discrimination, increasing the likelihood that significant relationships will be predictably terminated by early death from respiratory illness or occupational hazard. The noun "event" is qualified by the adjective "psychosocial" to underscore the psychological side of the society-behavior equation.

Psychosocial circumstances also influence the modal behavior and vulnerabilities to stressful events of people in particular contexts by imposing various regularities upon their lives or creating a modal environment in which most people's subjective and interpersonal behavior occurs most of the time. Aspects of this environment may range from the availability of certain kinds of language and symbol systems to generally accepted and followed childrearing practices and to the experience of discovering one's self a member of a socially oppressed minority, or a host of other regularities associated with life in particular statuses, roles and contexts. Discussions of the impact of developing and adult life in particular environments (in contrast to the impact of discrete events) upon later psychopathology have often been couched in psychoanalytic characterological terms. In the preceding section, for example, brief reference was made to the influence upon character and gender-identity of a minority group boy's experience of an absent or ineffective father.

Finally, the prevalence and frequency of recurrent stressful events may be influenced by public policy. Policy related to mental illness influences access to and the nature of facilities for diagnosis and treatment, including their availability over time. Policy related to poverty, employment opportunities; school facilities, racial discrimination; the status of women, family planning services and a host of other social-education-welfare concerns exerts an indirect but significant impact on behavior, including that of the mentally ill.

Identifying previously unlabelled schizophrenic behavior. The history of attempts to identify "true prevalence" of mental illness, and the methodological problems involved therein have recently been reviewed by Dohrenwend and Dohrenwend (1974). Since epidemiology is the subject of another chapter, these issues will not be explored at length here. Some points are, however, relevant to the questions raised above.

In most investigations, cases are defined by applying clinical judgment to behavioral data collected on the basis of personal interviews by trained psychiatrists with subjects willing to talk about themselves. In others explicit data collection schedules and procedures are used by people who are not mental health professionals, but are accustomed to survey research. Here case identification depends on psychiatrists' evaluations of protocols compiled from the interview responses and, sometimes, from ancillary data. As the Dohrenwends have noted: "The question of what information is required to make an informed clinical judgment and the question of what information is likely to bias such judgment are two horns of a dilemma that has received considerably less attention in epidemiological studies and in the field of clinical assessment in general than it deserves." From our point of view the sociocultural gulf between interviewer and subject, and the automatic biases imposed by his own background upon the interviewer's information processing are also relevant factors. The largest source of variability in the rates reported by epidemiological studies reflects contrasting conceptions of what constitutes a "case". However, while epidemiological investigators differ in their concepts, most present their findings in terms of accepted broad nosological distinctions. Moreover, there appears to be considerable agreement among them on these vividly contrasting sets of symptom complexes despite differences in boundaries drawn between the types of "psychopathology" and "normality".

Given the probable validity of existing broad nosological categories Dohrenwend (1974) suggests four sets of problems as possibly responsible for the difficulties in identifying unlabelled as well as labelled cases of psychiatric disorder:

(1) Subcultural differences in modes of expressing distress.
(2) Relations between symptoms of disturbance of cognition, affect and volition on the one hand and ability and disability in role functioning on the other.
(3) The situational specificity of symptomatology as opposed to its relative independence of external circumstances.
(4) Relations between physical illness and some types of psychiatric symptoms — especially those thought of as psychophysiological.

Societal correlates of first mental hospital admissions labelled schizophrenic. It was not until the pioneering work of Faris and Dunham (1939) relating the occurrence and distribution of schizophrenia to individual position in the social structure and residence in neighborhoods with particular socioeconomic characteristics, that the need to identify unlabelled persons (called "untreated" cases by most investigators) in the general population was underscored. Their work, revealing high concentrations of persons with a range of schizophrenic (in contrast to manic-depressive) behaviors in socially deprived greater Chicago neighborhoods, particularly around the urban center, stimulated a great deal of valuable research on the complex interrelationships of society and mental illness. An outstanding example was the study by Hollingshead and Redlich (1958) based on a January 1950 survey of all people resident in New Haven, Connecticut who carried a psychiatric diagnostic label in a current treatment relationship with an institution or medical-psychiatric practitioner. They, and succeeding investigators explicated the tendency of lowest class schizophrenics, without access to expensive individual outpatient psychotherapy and without familial and other support systems in the community, to accumulate within the mental hospital to which they had most often come via the police and the courts. The impact of lower social class and discriminated-against ethnic status on the mode of admission to the mental hospital with its corollary impact on behavior was demonstrated in respect to black male psychiatric admissions to Maryland mental hospitals (Brody, Derbyshire & Schleifer, 1967). Long delays in labeling deviant behavior as a reflection of mental illness occurred for two major reasons. One was the attitudes of the police in producing a pattern of repeated arrest and jail incarceration, sometimes over several years, before mental illness was identified. Second was the families' attribution of the behavior in question to reality aspects of the environment; they regarded it as adaptive rather than sick. In most instances, therefore, hospitalization was not initiated by these families unless the patient became violent or his failure to work became an intolerable economic burden.

There are no data indicating the proportion of severely disturbed people in the general populations at large who have not been identified as ill or admitted to psychiatric institutions and labelled as "patients". It seems likely that this proportion decreases with industrialization, consequent demands upon individuals to function at a complex level, the reduced protective capabilities of families and other naturally occurring sources of support, and the increased availability of socially designated institutions into which nonfunctional persons can be extruded from society. The above does not imply increasing "stress", associated with industrialization, and therefore symptom incidence, but rather increasing social visibility of deviant persons in a regulated society requiring more complex integrated behavior. People who are highly visible within the social system are most apt upon exhibiting deviant behavior to be sent to hospitals by family members or the larger society's control agents. Available data suggest that in United States urban slums, poor and sometimes Black persons must be more floridly and acutely ill than others in order to be identified as sick, rather than criminal, and admitted to mental hospitals (Monroe, Klee and Brody, 1967). This appears to be true in Rio de Janeiro as well, and also for men not part of a conjugal family group, and for migrants. Related factors such as illiteracy and distance from sources of societal power reinforce the likelihood of dramatic, aggressive behavior by otherwise inarticulate but suffering people as an unconscious attempt to force communication and gain assistance. In particular, the single residentially mobile male, a heavy drinker unable to find work, and withdrawing passively rather than becoming actively excited, is more apt to remain one of the drifting homeless or, in a developing country such as Brazil, to be picked up by a social service center than to be hospitalized (Brody, 1973). Such men are therefore underrepresented in the mental hospital population; those becoming patients have been obviously and frighteningly deviant in order to achieve that status.

The saturation with mental hospital facilities and the intense social monitoring of more highly developed countries appear to produce a different picture with respect to unattached individuals. Kramer (1967), reviewing data from the United States, England and Wales, Norway, Australia, demonstrated excessively high rates, per 100,000 general population, of first mental hospital admission for the never married and the separated, divorced, and widowed. Male rates are considerably higher than those for females in the never-married category only. These are persons who, becoming ill in early life, have never achieved the degree of social competence necessary to establish a consistent relationship with a woman and to become an economically productive family head. For the widowed, separated, and divorced female, admission rates are higher than for men. This probably reflects the more dependent role for females in this society, the lack of satisfactory careers alternative to marriage, and the consequently combined emotional identity and socioeconomic loss following bereavement.

In many developing countries, in contrast to those described above, women, including the nonmarried, appear to be underrepresented in comparison with the population at large and to be sicker than the men in the hospital population. In this instance family tolerance and ability to sustain a quietly psychotic female who can still fulfill certain sexual and homemaking roles seem important. By the time the woman is sent to a hospital and assumes the patient role, she, like the migrant and the Black, is apt to have moved to a point of behavior grossly unacceptable to those around her. The economic burden of a sick relative, who is no longer capable of work is also significant. Among migrant families in Rio, this is often a major cause for his being taken to a hospital. Here, as among the poor Baltimore Blacks, paranoid symptoms may be regarded as adaptive and justifiable, thus delaying hospitalization.

Psychosocial events correlated with schizophrenic behavior. The discussion of life circumstances or stressful events antecedent to or reinforcing schizophrenic behavior will be limited in this chapter, as noted above, to those associated with major sociological variables, e.g. social class, migration, and social attitudes toward deviance resulting in labelling. A classic study of mental illness rates reflected in hospital admission is Goldhammer and Marshall's (1953) review of Massachusetts data over the last century. They could not find evidence that psychosis was increasing in modern society and their conclusion still stands.

Certain regularities become apparent when patient populations are scrutinized with respect to both sociocultural and behavioral variables. As noted previously life circumstances associated with a person's place in his socioculture (as indicated by his various statuses) do seem to increase the likelihood that particular symptomatic behavior patterns will appear. These circumstances include recurring events which maintain or reinforce ongoing behavior as well as chronic or usual developmental and adult life contexts. The interaction between individual behavior and the recurrent reinforcements which it elicits from others is basic to the social process. While life circumstances may have direct impact upon the adult, their influence is understood here as resulting from a combination of such impact with earlier experiences conditioned by sociocultural factors mediated through the family.

The social context of adulthood may exert its impact through events mediated by a range of statuses such as occupation or economic level. Intervening variables may include, for example, organic disease. The significance of seizures, head injuries, or other similar events indicating brain damage as contributory to a variety of psychiatric symptoms, though not established, is widely accepted as probable. The extent of organically based behavior disorder leading to mental hospitalization in the United States is indicated by Kramer's (1967) estimate, based upon 1963 data, that more than 26 percent of admissions to state and country mental hospitals are due to brain syndromes. This does not include the over 16 percent diagnosed as alcoholic, nor does it take into account the possible contribution of organic factors to disorders with other psychiatric labels.

Knobloch and Pasamanick (1966) have estimated that interruption of a "cycle of reproductive insult" characterized by damage to the intrauterine infant during delivery or in the first few months of extrauterine life by illness, malnutrition, injury, or other poverty-related factors would result in a significant reduction of the United States institutionalized population. Pollin and Stabenau (1968) suggested a variety of damaging factors, especially those leading to intrauterine hypoxia, with associated "soft" neurological signs, as important for the final emergence of schizophrenic symptomatology in genetically loaded individuals. While such factors are undoubtedly significant in mentally hospitalized populations of developing countries with inadequate public health services, their relationship to specific symptom patterns and their frequency in comparison to the United States is not known.

A recent review (Kaplan, 1975) emphasizes the difficulty in arriving at conclusions about causally significant social events antecedent to the appearance of psychopathology in general. It highlights methodological issues and formulations presented in reports of several conferences. Some of these support a correlation between the magnitude of life-change and the seriousness of health change for chronic physical illness (Holmes and Masuda, Chapter 2 in Dohrenwend and Dohrenwend, 1974). Others suggest that the balance between undesirable and desirable events rather than the life change itself is probably antecedent to behavioral impairment (Gersten *et al.*, Chapter 10, Dohrenwend and Dohrenwend, 1974). One model proposes that the nature of the relationships between life events and their consequent objective and then subjective stress, strain and illness leading to illness behavior is determined by a series of interacting factors. These are personal (defenses, coping, capacities, needs, genetic pre-disposition, past experience, attitudes toward illness and medical care) and social (current life situation, social support, attitudes of peers and gatekeepers). (Cobb, Chapter 9 in Dohrenwend and Dohrenwend, 1974). Hinkle (Chapter 2 in Dohrenwend and Dohrenwend, 1974) similarly emphasizes interaction, i.e. changes in culture, society and interpersonal relations may result in health changes in an already ill or susceptible person who (a) perceives the change as personally important, or (b) whose general activities, habits, immediate environment and exposure to noxious agents are changed in consequence.

These observations and multifactorial models are congruent with those encompassing events antecedent to schizophrenic behavior. Thus, Stabeneau and Pollin (in Roff and Ricks, 1970, pp. 94-126) trace phase-by-phase differences in personality development and life experience for pairs of monozygotic twins who become discordant for schizophrenia. Ricks noted that although some people have measurably greater potential for psychotic breakdown than do others, this potential need not be actualized (Roff and Ricks, 1970, pp. 288-307). He offers a model pathway to psychotic disorganization including (a) heightened sensitivity-irritability based on genetic or other, including intrauterine or birth process, pathology, (b) reduced general competence, (c) lack of access to satisfying and nondemanding activities, as well as stressful experience, e.g. rejection. Environmental pressures impinging recurrently upon an inadequate organism over 20 to 30 years lead to the eventual breakdown. Ricks also notes that intellectual deterioration does not occur in schizophrenic patients not subjected to social and stimulus deprivation.

Mednick and Schulsinger (Roff and Ricks, 1970, pp. 51-93) view stressful stimuli as activators of conditioned avoidance thinking responses learned in a harsh environment by schizophrenics in order to control their tendency to autonomic hyper-arousal. These avoidance responses constitute the thought disorder labelled schizophrenia.

Another recent symposium (Gunderson and Rahe, 1974), not included in Kaplan's review presents material specific to psychiatric illness. Paykel (in Gunderson and Rahe) reports the highest magnitude of self-reported antecedent life events in patients who had made suicidal attempts, followed by those diagnosed as depressive and then by persons who had experienced episodes labelled schizophrenic. The higher incidence of stressful life events antecedent to depressive than schizophrenic behavior was also reported by Brown (in Dohrenwend and Dohrenwend, 1974).

There are a number of other diathesis-stress models in the literature (Rosenthal, 1970; Rosenthal and Kety, 1968) regarding schizophrenic behavior (the phenotype) as a consequence of (so far undefined) environmental circumstances impinging upon a constitutionally predisposed, genetically-loaded individual (the genotype). The nature and duration of interaction with a schizophrenic parent has been the focus of many investigators (Mednick and Shulsinger, 1968; Anthony, 1972, and others) with reference to the possible later development of schizophrenic behavior in the child. As Arnoff (1975) has pointed out, it is still not possible to weigh the significance for a child's later development of psychotic behavior of his remaining with or being removed from the care of a psychotic parent. Eitinger's (1964) report of the possible relationship of concentration camp internment to the later development of schizophrenia is of interest here. The concentration camp experience combines elements associated with migration with the experience of total powerlessness and hopelessness, as well as a variety of somatic factors and acute stress situations. After excluding all those with positive heredity, premorbid factors commonly associated with later psychiatric illness and tuberculosis, he concluded that in 30 of 41 schizophrenic patients, former camp inmates, in Israeli hospitals the illness was immediately associated with the experience of captivity. All became overtly psychotic in the period between their arrest and before they could live a normal life again. None had been together with a relative or friend for any length of time during the camp experience.

Integration: Society, Events, Behavior

Five categories of societal variables have been identified as possibly related to the incidence, prevalence and nature of schizophrenic behavior: social organization, status and role; social labelling and institutional context; self-labelling and reference groups; minority status, economic disadvantage and powerlessness; and public policy. In addition the process of social change as a possible behavioral influence has been illustrated through the discussion of migration. In this section an effort will be made to indicate the ways in which these societal variables, including migration, might influence schizophrenic behavior, by (a) creating a developmental context promoting vulnerable characters or personalities and/or (b) increasing the incidence of psychosocial events antecedent to schizophrenic behavior. There is no unequivocal evidence that these societal conditions or psychosocial events, in the absence of genetic loading or other constitutional or organic predisposition, can result in such behavior on more than a transitory or fragmented basis. It seems likely, however, that given some such vulnerability or predisposition, the presence or absence of certain societal conditions will determine whether or not a particular individual will develop a more or less consistent constellation, stable over time, of schizophrenic behaviors. It appears, also, that societal conditions can increase the likelihood of organic conditions which together with genetic loading or particular developmental or adult experience maximize the probability of occurrence of schizophrenic behavior.

Developmental context factors associated with societal variables. As suggested above these may be divided roughly into three categories; organic, genetic, and psychosocial.

(1) *Organic.* Life at the lowest socioeconomic levels is characterized by greater risk for fetuses, infants, children and adults for injury, disease and malnutrition without adequate treatment. Under these circumstances the likelihood of the brain damage postulated in a significant number of institutionalized patients in consequence of the "cycle of reproductive insult" (Knobloch and Pasamanick), and increasing the likelihood of overt schizophrenic behavior in genetically predisposed children (Pollin and Stabenau, 1968) appears greatest in low socioeconomic level, deprived populations. In this sense central nervous system damage may be an intervening variable between society and schizophrenic behavior.

Another possible variable, not completely explored as yet, is the presence of chronic or endemic somatic disease. While the United States studies reviewed above point to a relationship between severe life stress and the onset of disease or physiological dysfunction, a relationship between this latter and schizophrenic behavior has not been established. Raman and Murphy (1972), however, found that on the island of Mauritius, with a mixed population of Indian and African origin, the presence of somatic disease and psychosomatic symptoms were strongly associated with the chronicity of what they defined as "primary process schizophrenia." Since this finding was made simultaneously with the failure of prognostic indicators useful in the West to be similarly significant on Mauritius they suggest that assumptions regarding the relation of certain features to schizophrenia may be a function of the social setting. Again, depending on context, somatic disease may be an intervening variable between societal factors and schizophrenic behavior.

(2) *Genetic.* Most of the interpersonal factors associated with patterns of mating and their impact on the gene pool are cultural. These are mainly constraints such as kinship taboos which probably diminish the likelihood of transmitting schizophrenic vulnerability. It is at least possible, though, that the proximity between psychiatrically ill or vulnerable male and female residents of deteriorated or lodging house areas may encourage sexual relations and reproduction. This possibility has not been established and, in fact, it has been assumed that the withdrawn character of such persons would militate against such relationships. With the advent of new anti-psychotic drugs and policies of rapid mental hospital discharge, however, reproduction rates of former patients diagnosed schizophrenic have increased, as reviewed by Arnhoff above (1975).

(3) *Psychosocial.* The existing literature indicates a variety of ways in which interpersonal relations and stresses consequent to societal context might influence development in a manner increasing the likelihood of occurrence of schizophrenic behavior. These relations and stresses

could result directly in learned behavior, e.g. avoidance responses, which cumulatively over time, reinforced by the responses elicited from others, might produce a series or constellation of schizophrenic behaviors; they could lead to anxiety, guilt or other tension so intense as to disrupt cognitive function or activate the regressive defense mechanisms (e.g. projection) producing behavior ordinarily called schizophrenic; they could result in a failure of the identifications and learning experiences necessary to maturation; or they could lead to physiological dysfunction of a sort requiring particular kinds of protective or self-isolating behavior. While there is some evidence for all of these possibilities, it is not possible to be conclusive about any of them.

(a) *Psychosocially determined physiological dysfunction.* An example of this is the Mednick and Schulsinger (1970) hypothesis that conditioned avoidance thinking activated by stressful situations functions to control a tendency to autonomic hyperarousal. Conceivably, such stressful situations may be associated with socioeconomic deprivation, failure to obtain a job, being one of a discriminated against minority or other societal conditions. It is also possible that the autonomic hyperreactivity itself could develop in consequence of an infancy and childhood marked by precarious or unpredictable care at the hands of overworked, anxious, or resentful parents or surrogates.

(b) *Identity conflict: gender and social role.* Examples here stem from studies of Black children and patients in the recent transition era in the United States. As noted above (Brody, 1963) anxiety-laden conflicting identification with figures of opposing symbolic significance (i.e. Black parents and white value-enforcing institutions) could be a vulnerability producing factor for psychotic behavior occurring at the time when adult responsibility must be assumed.

Aim-inhibited hostility directed against white and introjected white attitudes, consequent to identification with the powerful white group have also been implicated as the basis for self-hatred, and ultimately for a variety of efforts to deny low self-esteem (Kardiner and Ovesey, 1951; Dollard, 1949). It was, in fact, demonstrated by Goldenberg (1953), using a psychological test battery, that Black patients diagnosed schizophrenic were more overtly hostile against Blacks and showed a greater tendency to identify with whites than a group of nonschizophrenic controls. These latter tended more to accept membership in their own group, and exhibited more fantasied retaliation against whites.

Gender role conflict in Black men may stem from matriarchal and matrifocal family settings with socially emasculated, passive, absent or remote fathers (Frazier, 1940; Kardiner and Ovesey, 1951). This is a situation in which a secondary social structure, i.e. the culturally excluded lower-class Negro community, influences a primary social structure such as the family in the direction of producing boys vulnerable to schizophrenic behavior or homosexual tendencies (Brody, 1961).

(c) *Extreme social powerlessness.* Examples of studies in this area are those of Klein (1966) in Peru and Brody (1973) in Brazil noted above. It may be hypothesized that a subordinate, excluded population needs to deny the threatening or provocative aspects of the dominant world and to repress or displace hostile and other wishes that might bring them into destructive contact with it. One solution to this inner conflict between the impulse to express anger and the fear and guilt about so doing could be regression to a state of complete immobilized dependency or to one in which the warded off impulses are dealt with by mechanisms reflected in delusion or hallucinations.

(d) *Symbolic de-differentiation and defective concept learning.* Continued denial and repression could also contribute to a semantic impoverishment, a reduction in the connotative richness of the symbols used by subordinate individuals. This reduction, along with the cognitive disruption due to extreme and unmanageable anxiety may lead to a possible bridge between the societal condition and schizophrenic behavior, i.e. defective symbol and concept learning. This may be theoretically related to a particular aspect of such behavior, i.e. its disorganization viewed as de-differentiation: the abandonment of complex in favor of simple ways of perceiving, making discriminations, and processing information (Brody, 1967). The outcome may resemble behavior found in earlier developmental periods or that characteristic of primitive peoples, e.g. animism, a tendency to magical thinking, or a tendency to react to people not in terms of fine discriminations based on their individual characteristics, but rather in terms of gross categorizations, such as being a member of a class of strange or dangerous persons. Similar consequences may follow deficits in the training for identity or verbal communication of low SES persons (Langner and Michael, 1963).

De-differentiation also involves a diminution of the capacity to distinguish between self and non-self, the world of independent objects, and attitudes and expectations concerning such objects. Werner and Kaplan (1963) described the reflected loss of this capacity in language which reveals a breakdown in the distinction between the meanings which the patient feels and seeks to convey, and the semantic values of conventional words.

Symbolic vehicles which function in normal thought as the clear carriers of ideal meanings tend to lose this status in psychotic thought and to be perceived as material, actual, concrete-objective entities. Or, conversely, ordinary things, objects and events may become in Werner and Kaplan's words, "proto-symbols, that is they assume profound significance far transcending their pragmatic-functional meaning" (1963).

A limited repertory of cultural symbols, and a defective or distorted set of values to serve as internal and external reference points might occur as a concomitant of low SES or cultural exclusion; of rapid social change or migration which reduces the stability of established value systems, cultural symbols and role positions for all levels of society (Brody, 1967); or membership in a disintegrated society as described by Leighton and colleagues (1963) with poor communication, inadequate leadership and broken homes.

(e) *Behavioral consistency.* Environmental vulnerability coupled with a reduced repertory of cultural symbols and coping techniques may be translated into impaired capacity to maintain perceptual and cognitive consistency in the face of stress. Specific elements would include coarsening of the categories by which the perceptions of people as well as other types of experiences are ordered (which may be regarded as a defect in interpersonal concept formation and the ability to discriminate); reduction in comparative ego-independence from inner or outer pressure leading to impaired ability to make judgments and to engage in rational thinking and reality testing; impaired capacity to label specific elements of experience and to form the kinds of hypotheses or predictions which shape goal-directed behavior and permit delayed gratification; and impairment in the individual's sense of belongingness to his society, his capacity to communicate with others, and his sense of common sharing with them. Behavioral consistency in the face of fluctuating and stressful environmental conditions is, to some degree, a function of internalized evaluative standards, lacking or fragmented in persons socialized and/or living for prolonged periods in minority-powerless status, with low self-esteem, in such contexts. Behavioral dependence upon current environmental cues is probably greatest in powerless persons with low self-esteem, without well-established internalized values and standards (Brody, 1968).

(f) *Alienation and isolation.* These interrelated aspects of behavior, often noted as preceding more florid schizophrenic symptoms, were noted above as developmental corollaries of a variety of societal conditions. Thus, Leighton *et al.* (1963) implicated frequent residential mobility prior to age twenty. The South Italian villagers studied by Banfield (1958) seemed unable to form collaborative relationships outside of the nuclear family; and young Black men in Baltimore (Brody, 1961) were shaped by experience to mistrust strangers, especially those of differing appearances, i.e. whites.

These behaviors can be understood up to a point as adaptive in Hartmann's (1958) sense of promoting a stable reciprocal relationship with the environment. The point at which they shade into or set the stage for defensive processes, which maintain an intrapsychic equilibrium by denying external reality, projecting unacceptable wishes, or substituting fantasies at the cost of adaptive stability, i.e. processes resulting in psychotic behavior, is unclear. There is no epidemiological evidence as yet to support the positions that persisting regressive defenses or alienated withdrawal as a consequence of societal conditions lead to persisting schizophrenic behavior. Nonetheless, the question remains for particular individuals concerning a relationship between life styles emerging from a setting of deprivation, alienation and cultural exclusion, and vulnerability to periods of psychotic behavior.

Psychosocial events antecedent to schizophrenic behavior. While the foregoing was discussed in terms of the atmosphere of growing up, much is appropriate to the stressful events of adult life as well. In addition there is some evidence that discrete and repeated events, not part of the childhood experience and, therefore, not having influenced character formation or particular vulnerabilities, may have a disorganizing impact on behavior.

(a) *Labelling.* There is little published systematic work in this area. Personal observations in a clinical setting indicate, however, that application of the schizophrenic label as part of having been moved to a mental hospital ward, is often followed by more floridly "crazy" behavior than before. Some observers have regarded this as a consequence of the patient having been given "permission to be crazy". Others (cf Stanton and Schwartz, 1954) have conceptualized it more in communicative terms or of participation in the ongoing social process of the ward.

Having been labelled as schizophrenic or mentally ill may logically be assumed to have other consequences, e.g. reinforcing a person's mistrust of himself or reducing his self-esteem, which in turn might increase the likelihood of schizophrenic behavior. However, there is no systematic evidence regarding these or related issues.

(b) *Crossing social system boundaries.* This issue was examined at length in the discussion on migration. There is no unequivocal evidence that the migratory experience of itself, in a previously integrated person, will lead to schizophrenic behavior. It does appear probable, however, that the strangeness, isolation and loss of accustomed support systems incident to recent entrance into a new society do increase the likelihood that emerging schizophrenic symptoms will be paranoid in nature.

(c) *Specific stressful events.* As noted above the appearance of schizophrenic behavior is less frequently reported following such events than the appearance of physiological disorder or depressive reactions. The only stressful social experience which may have had a significant schizophrenogenic impact was the massive prolonged one of concentration camp incarceration which because of its overall biological impact is difficult to assess (Eitinger, 1964).

(d) *Hospital and post-treatment experiences.* All available evidence supports the idea that the behavior of patients diagnosed as schizophrenic is influenced by the social system of the hospital as well as that of their own community. The literature does not, however, support the idea that social class is unequivocally related to familial expectations or successful community tenure of discharged hospital patients.

Summary

Societal variables possibly related to the incidence, prevalence and nature of schizophrenic behavior include: social organization, status and role; social labelling and institutional context;

self-labelling and reference groups; minority status, economic disadvantage and powerlessness; public policy; and social change as exemplified by migration. These variables might influence schizophrenic behavior by (a) creating a developmental context promoting characters or personalities vulnerable to psychotic disorganization; and (b) increasing the incidence of psychosocial events antecedent to schizophrenic behavior. There is no unequivocal evidence, however, that in the absence of genetic loading or other organic or constitutional predisposition societal variables can determine such behavior on more than a transitory or fragmented basis.

Developmental context factors determined by the societal variables above include:

(1) Organic defects such as brain damage associated with a poverty linked cycle of reproductive insult, or chronic somatic disease.

(2) Genetic predispositions associated with socially determined patterns of mating, and the increased birth-rate of schizophrenics discharged from mental hospitals as a consequence of new public policies.

(3) Psychosocial factors.

These last include: (a) psychosocially determined physiological dysfunction, such as autonomic hyperreactivity associated with a stressful infancy and childhood as a member of a disadvantaged minority family; (b) gender-identity and social role conflict associated with growing up as a member of a discriminated-against minority group, particularly one in which stable consistent fathers are not present as gender-role models for their sons; (c) extreme social powerlessness as in the case of illiterate hacienda workers in a serf-like status, e.g. Andean Indians in Peru or rural farm laborers in Brazil, necessitating the continued employment of regressive defenses, (d) symbolic de-differentiation and defective concept learning following from continued denial and repression associated with semantic impoverishment, a consequence of low socioeconomic status, exclusion from the culture of the dominant society, rapid social change as by migration, or membership in a disintegrated society; (e) impaired capacity to maintain perceptual and cognitive consistency in the face of stress associated with a reduced repertory of cultural symbols and coping techniques, and a failure during socialization to develop firm internal evaluative standards; (f) alienation and isolation, as following migration or growing up in a minority status.

Psychosocial events in adult life antecedent to the occurrence of schizophrenic behavior or variations in its form may include:

(1) Labelling, reinforcing a person's mistrust of himself or permitting the release of otherwise restrained behavior.

(2) Crossing social system boundaries, as by migration, resulting in strangeness, isolation and the loss of accustomed support systems.

(3) Repeated stressful experiences, as bereavements, although these are more frequently antecedent to physiological disorder or depression.

(4) Events reflecting the nature of the hospital and post-treatment social context, which influence the course of schizophrenic behavior.

There is no evidence that any single category of societal variables, either during development or in adult life, is of itself a crucial determinant of schizophrenic behavior. It is suggested that the relationship of social context to such behavior be further illuminated by continuing comparative studies in carefully described societies and cultures.

References

ADAMS, W.A. The Negro Patient in Psychiatric Treatment. *American Journal of Orthopsychiatry*, **20**, 305-310, 1950.

ANGRIST, S., LEPTON, M., DINITZ, S. and PASAMANICK, B. *Women After Treatment: A Study of Former Mental Patients and Their Normal Neighbors.* New York: Appleton-Century-Crofts, 1968.

ANTHONY, E.J. *J. Psychiatr. Res.* **6** (Suppl.) 293, 1968.

ARNOFF, F.N. Social Consequences of Policy Toward Mental Illness. *Science* **188**, 1277-1281, June 1975.

BANFIELD, E.C. *The Moral Basis of a Backward Society.* New York: The Macmillan Co., 1958.

BRODY, E.B. Borderline State, Character Disorder, and Psychotic Manifestations. Some Conceptual Formulations. *Psychiatry, 23,* 75-80, 1960.

BRODY, E.B. Social Conflict and Schizophrenic Behavior in Young Adult Negro Males. *Psychiatry, 24,* 337-346, 1961.

BRODY, E.B. Color and Identity Conflict in Young Boys: Observations of Negro Mothers and Sons in Urban Baltimore. *Psychiatry, 26,* 188-201, 1963.

BRODY, E.B. Color and Identity Conflict in Young Boys II: Observations of White Mothers and Sons in Urban Baltimore. *Arch. Gen. Psychiat.* **10**, 354-360, 1964a.

BRODY, E.B. Conceptual and Methodological Problems in Research in Society, Culture and Mental Illness. *J. Nerv. and Ment. Dis.* **139**, 62-74, 1964b.

BRODY, E.B. Cultural Exclusion, Character and Illness. *American Journal of Psychiatry,* **122**, 852-858, 1966.

BRODY, E.B. Recording Cross-Culturally Useful Interview Data: Experience from Brazil. *Amer. J. Psychiat.,* **123**, 446-456, 1966.

BRODY, E.B., DERBYSHIRE, R.L. and SCHLEIFER, C. How the Young Adult Baltimore Negro Male Becomes a Maryland Mental Hospital Statistic. In *Psychiatric Epidemiology and Mental Health Planning.* Monroe, R.R., Klee, G.D., and Brody, E.B., Eds. American Psychiatric Association Research Report, No. 22, 1967.

BRODY, E.B. Culture, Symbol and Value in the Social Etiology of Behavioral Deviance. In *Social Psychiatry.* J. Zubin, Ed. New York: Grune & Stratton, Inc., pp. 8-33, 1968.

BRODY, E.B. Adolescents as a United States Minority Group in an Era of Social Change. In *Minority Group Adolescents in the United States.* Brody, E.B., Ed. pp. 1-16, Baltimore: Williams & Wilkins Co., 1968.

BRODY, E.B. Minority Group Status and Behavioral Disorganization. In *Minority Group Adolescents in the United States.* Brody, E.B., Ed. pp. 227-243, Baltimore: Williams & Wilkins Co., 1968.

BRODY, E.B. Migration and Adaptation: The Nature of the Problem. In *Behavior in New Environments: Adaptation of Migrant Populations.* Brody, E.B., Ed. Beverly Hills, Calif.: Sage Publications, Inc., 1970.

BRODY, E.B. *The Lost Ones: Social Forces and Mental Illness in Rio de Janeiro.* New York: International Univ. Press, 1973.

BRODY, E.B. Symptomatic Behavior: Ego-Defensive, Adaptive, and Sociocultural Aspects. In *American Handbook of Psychiatry*, Vol. III, Arieti, S., and Brody, E.B., Eds. New York: Basic Books, Inc. 1974.

BRODY, E.B. Psychosocial Aspects of Prejudice. In *American Handbook of Psychiatry*, Vol. II, Part III. Caplan, G. Ed. New York: Basic Books, Inc., 1974.

CAUDILL, W. *The Psychiatric Hospital as a Small Society.* Cambridge, Mass.: Harvard Univ. Press, 1958.

CAUDILL, W., REDLICH, F.C., GILMORE, H.R. and BRODY, E.B. Social Structure and Interaction Processes on a Psychiatric Ward. *Amer. J. of Orthopsychiat.* **22**, 314-334, 1952.

CLAUSEN, J.A. and KOHN, M.L. Social Relations and Schizophrenia. In *Etiology of Schizophrenia.* Jackson, D.D., Ed. New York: Basic Books, 1960.

DERBYSHIRE, R.L., BRODY, E.B. and SCHLEIFER, C. Family Structure of Young Adult Negro Male Mental Patients: Preliminary Observations from Urban Baltimore. *J. Nerv. and Ment. Dis.* **136**, 245-251, 1963.

DOHRENWEND, B.S. and DOHRENWEND, B.P. *Stressful Life Events: Their Nature and Effects.* New York: John Wiley, 340 pp., 1974.

DOLLARD, J. *Caste and Class in a Southern Town.* New York: Harper, 1949.

EITINGER, L. Schizophrenia and Persecution. *Acta. Psychiat. Scand.* **40**, Suppl. 180, 141, 1964.

ERIKSON, E.H. *Childhood and Society.* New York: W.W. Norton & Co., Inc., pp. 426-442, 1950.

FARIS, R.E.L. and DUNHAM, H.W. *Mental Disorders in Urban Areas.* Univ. of Chicago Press, 1939.

FRAZIER, E.F. *Negro Youth at the Crossways.* American Council on Education, Washington, D.C., 1940.

FREEMAN, H. and SIMMONS, O. *The Mental Patient Comes Home.* New York: John Wiley & Sons, Inc. 1963.

FREEMAN, H. and SIMMONS, O. Mental Patients in the Community: Family Settings and Performance Levels. *American Sociological Review,* **23**, 147-154, 1958.

FREEMAN, H. and SIMMONS, O. Social Class and Posthospital Performance Levels. *American Sociological Review,* **24**, 345-351, 1959.

GERARD, D.S. and HOUSTON, L.G. Family Setting and the Social Ecology of Schizophrenia. *Psychiatric Quarterly,* **27**, 90-101, 1953.

GIBBS, J.P. Rates of mental hospitalization: a study of societal reaction to deviant behavior. *Amer. Sociol. Rev.* **27**, 782-792, 1941.

GOFFMAN, E. The Characteristics of Total Institutions *Symposium on Preventive and Social Psychiatry.* Walter Reed Army Medical Center, U.S. Government Printing Office, Washington, D.C. 1957.

GOLDENBERG, H. *The Role of Group Identification in the Personality Organization of Schizophrenic and Normal Negros.* Unpublished Ph.D. Thesis, Univ. of California, Los Angeles, 1953, p. 76.

GOLDHAMMER, H. and MARSHALL, A.W. *Psychosis and Civilization.* Glencoe, Ill.: Free Press, 1953.

GUNDERSON, E.K.E. and RAHE, R.H. Eds. *Life Stress and Illness.* Papers from a symposium, Beito, Norway, June 1972. Springfield, Ill.: Thomas, 264 pp., 1974.

HARE, E.H. Mental Illness and Social Conditions In Bristol. *Journal of Mental Science,* **102**, 349-357, 1956a.

HARE, E.H. Family Setting and the Urban Distribution of Schizophrenia. *Journal of Mental Science,* **102**, 753-760, 1956b.

HARTMAN, H. *Ego Psychology and the Problems of Adaptation.* English translation by D. Rapaport. New York: Int. Univ. Press, 1958.

HOLLINGSHEAD, A. and REDLICH, F.C. *Social Class and Mental Illness.* New York: John Wiley and Sons, 1958.

JAEGER, C. and SELZNICK, P. A Normative Theory of Culture. *American Sociological Review,* **29**, 653-669, 1965.

KAHN, A.J. *Studies in Social Policy and Planning.* New York: Russell Sage Foundation, 1969.

KAPLAN, H.B. Understanding the Social and Social-Psychological Antecedents and Consequences of Psychopathology: A Review of Reports of Invitational Conferences. *Journal of Health and Social Behavior,* **16**, 135-151, June 1975.

KARDINER, A.S. and OVESEY, L. *The Mark of Oppression: A Psychological Study of the American Negro.* New York: W.W. Norton & Co., Inc. 1951.

KLEIN, R. The Self-Image of Adult Males in an Andean Culture: A Clinical Exploration of a Dynamic Personality Construct. *University Microfilm* Ann Arbor, Mich., 1963.

KLEINER, R.J. and PARKER, S. Social-Psychological Aspects of Migration and Disorder in a Negro Population. In *Behavior in New Environments.* Brody, E.B., Ed. Beverly Hills, Calif.: Sage Publications, pp. 353-374, 1970.

KLUCKHOHN, C. *Mirror for Man.* New York: McGraw-Hill, 1944.

KNOBLOCH, H. and PASAMANICK, B. Prospective Studies on the Epidemiology of Reproductive Casualty. *Merrill-Palmer Quarterly,* **12**, 127-143, 1966.

KOHN, M. Social Class and Schizophrenia: A Critical Review and a Reformulation. In *Explorations in Psychiatric Sociology.* Roman, P. and Trice, H., Eds., Philadelphia: F.A. Davis, pp. 113-138, 1974.

KRAMER, M. Epidemiology, Biostatistics and Mental Health Planning. In *Psychiatric Epidemiology and Mental Health Planning.* American Psychiatric Association Research Report, No. 22. Monroe, R.R., Klee, G.D. and Brody, E.B., Eds., 1967.

KROEBER, A.L. and PARSONS, T. The Concept of Culture and Social System. *American Sociological Review,* **23**, 582-583, 1958.

LANGNER, T. and MICHAEL, S. *Life Stress and Mental Health.* Glencoe, Ill.: Free Press, 1963.

LEIGHTON, D.C. *et al. The Character of Danger: Psychiatric Symptoms in Selected Communities, The Stirling County Study.* Vol. 3, New York: Basic Books, 1963.

LEWIS, O. Five families: Mexican case studies in the culture of poverty. Random House, N.Y., 1959.

LINTON, R. *The Cultural Background of Personality.* New York: Appleton-Century-Crofts, 1945.

MACK, R.W. *Race, Class and Power.* New York: American Book Co., 1963.

MALZBERG, B. Migration in relation to mental disease. Research Foundation for Mental Hygiene, Albany, N.Y., 1968.

MEDNICK, S.A. and SCHULSINGER, F. In *The Transmission of Schizophrenia.* Rosenthal, D. and Kety, S.S., Eds. New York: Pergamon, pp. 267-291, 1968.

MEDNICK, S.A. and SCHULSINGER, F. In *Life History Research in Psychopathology.* Vol. I. Roff, M. and Ricks, D.F., Eds. Minnesota: Univ. of Minnesota Press, 1970.

MERTON, R. *Social Theory and Social Structure.* Glencoe, Ill.: The Free Press, 1957.

MERTON, R.K. The Self-Fulfilling Prophecy. *The Antioch Review,* 8, 193-210, 1948.

MINTZ, N.L. and SCHWARTZ, D.T. Urban Ecology and Psychosis: Community Factors in the Incidence of Schizophrenia and Manic Depression Among Italians in Greater Boston. *International Journal of Social Psychiatry,* 10, 101-118, 1964.

MONROE, R.R., KLEE, G.D. and BRODY, E.B. Eds. *Psychiatric Epidemiology and Mental Health Planning.* Am. Psychiat. Association Research Reports, No. 22, 1967.

PARSONS, T. *The Social System.* Glencoe, Ill.: The Free Press, 1951.

PARSONS, T. and SHILS, E.A. *Toward a General Theory of Action.* Cambridge Mass.: Harvard Univ. Press, 1961.

PASAMANICK, B., SCARPETTI, F. and DINITZ, S. *Schizophrenics in the Community: An Experimental Study in the Prevention of Rehospitalization.* New York: Appleton-Century-Croft, 1967.

POLLIN, W. and STABENAU, J.R. Biological, Psychological and Historical Differences in a Series of Monozygotic Twins Discordant for Schizophrenia. In *The Transmission of Schizophrenia.* Rosenthal, D. and Kety, S.S., Eds. New York: Pergamon Press, pp. 317-332, 1968.

RAMAN, A.C. and MURPHY, H.B.M. Failure of Traditional Prognostic Indicators in Afro-Asian Psychotics: Results of a Long-Term Follow-Up Survey. *J. Nerv. & Ment. Dis.* 154, 238-247, 1972.

RODMAN, H. Illegitimacy in the Caribbean Social Structure: A Reconsideration. *American Sociological Review,* 31, 673, 1966.

ROFF, M. and RICKS, D.F. *Life History Research in Psychopathology.* Volume 1. Minneapolis: Univ. of Minnesota Press, 1970.

ROSENTHAL, D. *Genetic Theory and Abnormal Behavior.* New York: McGraw-Hill, 1970.

ROSENTHAL, D. and KETY, S.S., Eds. *The Transmission of Schizophrenia.* New York: Pergamon, 1968.

SANUA, V.D. Immigration, Migration, and Mental Illness: A Review of the Literature with Special Emphasis on Schizophrenia. In *Behavior in New Environments.* Brody, E.B., Ed. Beverly Hills, Calif.: Sage Publications, pp. 291-352, 1970.

SHEARER, M.L., CAIN, A.C., FINCH, S.M. and DAVIDSON, R.T. *Am. J. Orthopsychiat.* 38, 413, 1968.

SHIBUTANI, T. *Society and Personality.* Englewood Cliffs, N.J.: Prentice-Hall, Inc., 1961.

STANTON, A.F. Medical Opinion and the Social Context in the Mental Health Hospital. *Psychiatry,* 12, 243-249, 1949.

STANTON, A. and SCHWARTZ, M. *The Mental Hospital.* New York: Basic Books, Inc., 1954.

STANTON, A. and SCHWARTZ, M. Observations on Dissociation as Social Participation. *Psychiatry,* 12, 339-354, 1949.

STERN, S., MEDNICK, S. and SCHULSINGER, F. Social Class, Institutionalization and Schizophrenia. In *Genetics, Environment and Psychopathology.* Mednick, S., Schulsinger, F., Higgins, J. and Bell, B. Eds., North-Holland/American Elsevier, Amsterdam and New York, pp. 283-292, 1974.

STEVENS, B. *J. Biosoc. Sci.* 2, 17, 1970.

TIETZE, C., LEMKUA, P., and COOPER, M. Personality Disorder and Spatial Mobility. *American J. of Sociology,* 48, 29-39, 1942.

TURNER, R. and WAGENFELD, M. Occupational Mobility and Schizophrenia: An Assessment of the Social Causation and the Social Selection Hypotheses. *Amer. Sociol. Rev.,* 32, 104-110, 1967.

WERNER, H. and KAPLAN, B. *Symbol Formation.* New York: John Wiley and Sons, 1963.

Genetic and Biochemical Approaches

The Contribution of Genetics and Biochemistry: Chairman's Opening Remarks

P.E. POLANI

In trying to assess the genetic contribution to the origin of schizophrenia, uncertainties of diagnosis and vagaries of manifestation of the disease undoubtedly create problems. However the main problem arises from the existence of seemingly important environmental influences, the nature of which totally elude us at present. Nevertheless this is no new problem to geneticists and indeed there is no reality in trying to oppose instead of apposing, nature and nurture. The actions and reactions of genes and the actions and reactions of environments are both indissoluble parts of a formula: genes and environment are closely interwoven. The only question that arises is that of their relative contributions to the phenotype under standard conditions, namely, those conditions that prevail in the real life experience of an organism. So, too, in schizophrenia nobody questions the existence of relevant, but unidentified, environmental forces. Nevertheless, as you will hear from Dr. Shields, there is evidence too of an important genetic contribution to the origin of the disease. So the questions that are open are the general one of the relative strengths of the two contributions, the genetic and the environmental, and the detailed ones of the specificities and of the modalities of the two sets of influences that are at the origin of the morbid state.

Perhaps the most important aspect that one must consider in an attempt to understand any disease and especially schizophrenia is its heterogeneity. We can consider this under two broad headings. First, there is clinical heterogeneity. Part of this is technical, due to problems of recognition and diagnostic criteria, but there are also differences in the types of the disease and its severity. These latter differences may turn out to be correlated with the second class of heterogeneity, that is to say, the aetiological. Aetiological heterogeneity means, for example, the existence of different discrete environments and of different co-existing genetic modes; and, of course, it may result from a variable interaction between genes and environment.

Turning to consider the genetic side, and genetic heterogeneity, it is important to think and know about this heterogeneity if we are to consider the ways biochemical research on schizophrenia can proceed and help us. Any hypothesis about the genetic contributions to the origin of schizophrenia – and at present we can only have hypotheses about this complex disorder – must take into account not only the risk of affection in various classes of relatives, including twins of the two types, but also, at the population level, the relatively high frequency of the disorder. This frequency must be maintained in the face of a diminished fertility of schizophrenic subjects, which will tend to reduce the frequency in the population of the detrimental genes.

There are two sets of general genetic models possible, the monogenic and the multigenic. The first set of these considers that the genetic contribution stems, in essence, from a single gene locus acting through an allele of large effect. In the second type of model, one considers the effect of multiple gene loci, with multiple alleles, each allele with a relatively small effect, but supplementing the other alleles, and supporting them, so that between them they *add up* to the production of clinical illness. As just defined, this strict type of multigene hypothesis is generally called polygenic, or additive polygenic, and in it equal and small effects are attributed to each allele at each locus, and the loci are considered to be many.

Of the monogenic hypotheses, one, the dominant hypothesis, was proposed by Huxley, Mayr and others in 1964. It considers that the disease is due to the action of a single allele at a single locus and that the presence of this allele in single dose, namely in the heterozygous state, causes the disease in a certain proportion of carriers. However the allele in question is thought to have another side to its action, namely a general, beneficial effect on vitality and viability. This latter effect would account for the spread and hence for the balanced frequency of the allele in the population.

A second monogenic hypothesis is that which Böök proposed for his North Swedish genetic isolate and Slater (1958) extended (Slater and Cowie, 1971). The allele at the single locus in question is taken to act in an essentially recessive manner: all those with a double dose of the allele are schizophrenic, some 10 per cent of cases, as is a proportion, around 13 per cent, of those who have it in single dose. Presumably in this case the carriers have some selective advantage as long as they are free of the illness. The model was recently re-investigated and accepted by Kidd and Cavalli-Sforza (1973) as one of the genetic hypotheses that fitted well the data. These authors incorporated the concept of threshold for the origin of the disease state, and concluded that also a proportion of those not carrying the allele, namely a proportion of the homozygous normal would be affected. Their illness would be accounted for by the action of environmental factors.

There is yet another type of monogenic model (Schultz, 1950: quoted by Shields, 1968) which can cover any mode of monogenic inheritance. This may be called the plural monogenic model. According to this model and in conformity with what happens in respect to mental deficiency, there are different monogenic schizophrenias, each independently caused by an allele at one locus. There are many different loci in each individual but a specific mutant allele at any one of these loci suffices to produce the schizophrenic syndrome. Most people would believe that, not even if one added together all the different genetic entities and added to them the purely environmental schizophrenia, would all examples of schizophrenia be accounted for. The gap would have to be filled by the other set of genetic models, the polygenic. For some, these, of course, could in practice be *the* genetic mechanisms for schizophrenia. These models address themselves essentially at the liability to the disease. This liability is thought of as a metrical trait varying in intensity in different subjects. At present, however, there are no direct ways of measuring it. The liability would be determined by the action of a number of alleles at a number of loci and there would be a level, or threshold of liability beyond which the disease would become overt. The more of these alleles are present, the greater the background liability. The intensity of the liability is assumed to be normally distributed, statistically speaking, in the population. The threshold itself could be fixed or might be variable, depending on the interactions with the environmental influences. So the quantitative variation of liability steps over into the pathological when the distribution threshold, which may have its own variability, is reached.

The polygenic model can be extended to allow for two thresholds, one for frank pathology and another one for clear schizoid personality (Gottesman and Shields, 1971) always interacting with the environment. The model also contemplates (Gottesman and Shields, 1973) that one or a very few loci could be of greater significance than the rest to the origin of the illness. In fact these would be key loci at which alleles can be considered, at the limit, as influential as genes of large effect. Alternatively, given a series of alleles at each locus, one (or more) of the alleles at some of the loci could be almost the key gene factor in the determination of the illness. Either way the polygenic model would drift into a monogenic one.

A related problem with polygenic systems is that sometimes it can be difficult, particularly when detailed breeding experiments are impossible, to distinguish between two alternatives: on the one hand multiple gene loci and their alleles acting *in the individual* and combining with the environmental influences to determine the morbid phenotype; on the other hand, many different genes and their alleles *in the population*, each capable of producing the phenotype with its overall variation. In addition, in this latter situation, variable environmental influences would be responsible, both for adding to the genetic influences and for contributing a whole series of what are in essence environmentally determined cases. They are often classed as phenocopies. For these reasons, if we accept that polygenic inheritance, smoothed by environmental influences, underlies the disease and the liability to it, we accept this only as a provisional first step towards a genetic understanding of the condition. The aim is to unmask the effects of single genes. Once this is done our next aim is to try to characterize the various alleles at each gene locus. It could turn out that we can identify a locus. If, now, we identify the various alleles at this locus, and if each allele turns out to have a certain measurable effect on liability, and especially if most of these alleles at this given locus are relatively common in the population, we will not be surprised if an apparently polygenically controlled liability, and thus origin of the disease, turns out to be largely, or even entirely, under the genetic control of a single locus, aided, naturally, by environmental forces. Anyway, as far as genetic heterogeneity goes, the net result of what I have said about genetic models is that only the two monogenic models, and only a fraction of the polygenic ideas are compatible with genetic homogeneity. Furthermore, as I have said, from the genetic view point in a proportion of instances schizophrenia may be determined monogenically by a plurality of different single major genes, and in the rest of the cases, polygenically. All of which would add to the aetiological heterogeneity of the disease.

As we contemplate these formal alternative genetic models, the differences between them become blurred the moment we are able to characterize the effects of each gene, or rather of each allele, in precise molecular terms. At this, the chemical level, penetrance, dominance or recessiveness, which are properties of characters — or, some might say, of the techniques whereby the characters are studied — disappear. By the same process phenotypic effects which do result from the action of multiple genes, are resolved into some, most or, hopefully, all their component monogenic effects.

However there are other ways, albeit very infrequent, which seem to underlie the genetic origin of schizophrenia. Although rare these ways are interesting and pose problems of a general nature in respect to the illness, while they bear witness to its aetiological heterogeneity. Thus, the schizophrenias which are seen in certain well-defined inborn errors of metabolism, those observed in numerical sex-chromosome anomalies and those rare special biochemical defects which lead to schizophrenia, like the folate deficiency variety, can provide us with important lessons, granted that we accept that the mental illnesses in these cases are schizophrenia. In this event there are two possibilities. Either the illness is a direct but not an obligatory consequence of the abnormal or unusual trigger, in which case we have valuable lessons to learn. For example we may ponder about the quantitative cellular effects of sex-chromosome imbalance, or about how many different metabolic pathways produce a quite specific abnormal behaviour. Or else the chromosomal or metabolic error is no more than a trigger that reveals an independently present liability to the disease and may simply lower the threshold of clinical manifestations.

Be all this as it may, we need to turn to biochemistry to resolve the phenotypes, and, one suspects, for help with the influence of the environment, at least, to some extent. Indeed this was the whole object of my stressing genetic heterogeneity. Boulton (1971) has recently critically reviewed some of the biochemical leads in schizophrenia. For example, it has been suggested that there may be disturbances in which phenyl-ethyl-amines are involved. Abnormalities of methylation of dopamine and/or noradrenaline could transform these substances into psychotogenic compounds, chemically similar to mescaline. On the other hand indoles have been implicated in the mental disturbances often present in Hartnup disease, pellagra and phenylketonuria, and it happens that psychotomimetic compounds are often methylated indoles. So the metabolism of these substances is of interest. But biochemistry can also provide leads to the mechanism whereby environmental stresses may act as triggers. For example, using monozygotic twins and subjects with different degrees of severity of illness, Wyatt and colleagues (1973a, b and c; Murphy and Wyatt, 1972) considered that the level of di-methyl-tryptamine – an indolamine – varied in response to *environmental* factors which induced an enhanced activity of the enzyme concerned in di-methyl-tryptamine formation. Conversely the degradation of di-methyl-tryptamine, which is controlled by monoamine-oxidase seemed to be impaired in both affected subjects and at risk persons for *genetic* reasons. Perhaps this story will not turn out to be as clear cut as this. The fact remains that this is the type of solution that could come from biochemistry and help with the genetic and environmental components of schizophrenia, and we shall hear on these matters from Dr. Richter.

In summary, various analytical and statistical approaches allow us to formulate hypotheses of genetic causation of schizophrenia, while we remain constantly aware of the existence of important environmental influences. However the ultimate aim in our understanding of the genetic processes is the characterization of the activity of the various possible alleles, revealed and studied as distinct and discrete genetic entities identified by their mode of transmission, their chemical effects and their modes of action. Meanwhile, on the formal genetic side we could place our preference on monogenic models, like, say, the Böök-Slater-Kidd & Cavalli-Sforza model. However, especially in view of its population frequency and supported by evidence on the risk of schizophrenia in relatives with genes in common, we will do well if we think that the genetic side of the syndrome may be due, at least in a good proportion of cases, to the action of relatively common alleles at different gene loci. These alleles could be "non-pathological" and hence not disadvantageous. Indeed, they could be quite the reverse, and could confer on those who carry them various selective advantages. This is one reason why they could be common in the population. According to this view it is not the alleles themselves that are potentially harmful, quite the contrary: it would be their particular combination in one individual which is detrimental in a given environment.

References

BOULTON, A.A. (1971) *Nature, London,* **231**, 22.
GOTTESMAN, I.I. and SHIELDS, J. (1971) *Human Hered.* **21**, 517.
GOTTESMAN, I.I. and SHIELDS, J. (1973) *Brit. J. Psychiat.* **122**, 15.
HUXLEY, J., MAYR, E., OSMOND, H. and HOFFER, A. (1964) *Nature, London,* **204**, 220.
MURPHY, D. and WYATT, R. (1972) *Nature, London,* **238**, 225.
SHIELDS, J. (1968) in D. Rosenthal and S.S. Kety, eds. *The Transmission of Schizophrenia*, p. 95. Pergamon Press, London.
SLATER, E. (1958) *Acta Genet. statis. Med.* **8**, 50.
SLATER, E. and COWIE, V. (1971) *The genetics of Mental Disease.* Pergamon Press, London.
WYATT, R.J., SAAVEDRA, J.M. and AXELROD, J. (1973a) *Amer. J. Psychiat.*, **130**, 754.
WYATT, R.J., SAAVEDRA, J.M., BELMAKER, R., COHEN, S. and POLLIN, W. (1973b). *Amer. J. Psychiat.* **130**, 1359.
WYATT, R.J., MURPHY, D.L., BELMAKER, R., COHEN, S., DONNELLY, C.H. and POLLIN, W. (1973c). *Science*, **179**, 916.

Genetics in Schizophrenia

JAMES SHIELDS

Historical Review of the Genetic Hypothesis

The idea that heredity can be a cause of mental illness goes back to time immemorial. Supporting evidence that it is a cause of something called dementia praecox or schizophrenia goes back to Rüdin's monograph of 1916.

From the beginning it was clear that schizophrenia itself was not a clear-cut simply-inherited genetic disease like Huntington's chorea or cystic fibrosis. The risk for the sibs of schizophrenics, for instance, is much lower than the Mendelian ratios of 50 per cent and 25 per cent expected for dominant and recessively inherited traits and found in these diseases. It need hardly be said that no simply-inherited biochemical error has yet been established which will account for even a small but recognisable proportion of schizophrenics, analogous to phenylketonuria among cases of low-grade subnormality. The evidence for the existence of genetic factors in schizophrenia, then, rests on the low observed rates in the general population compared with the higher rates in the families of schizophrenics, including twins and adoptees. Just in case there is still any lurking misunderstanding, I should point out at the outset that no geneticist has denied the existence of environmental factors in schizophrenia — it is just that genetic predisposition needs to be taken into account too.

Family studies. The genetic hypothesis has survived several attempts at refutation. Support first came from several family studies; many of them such as those by Schulz (1932) and Kallmann (1938) were carried out in the 1930s. Zerbin-Rüdin's (1967) account of this and later work from many different countries has served later summarizers well (Slater, 1968; Rosenthal, 1970; Slater and Cowie, 1971; Gottesman and Shields, 1972; Zerbin-Rüdin, 1972). Applying the European standards of diagnosis of the time, the lifetime risk of developing schizophrenia was usually found in these studies to be somewhere around 10 per cent for the sibs and children of schizophrenics. It was lower in the parents, particularly fathers, probably because of the low marriage rate of schizophrenics. Second-degree relatives such as uncles and aunts sharing on average only 25 per cent of genes with a schizophrenic were less extensively studied, but their risk of developing schizophrenia was usually around 3 per cent. For various groups of the general population the morbid risk was 1 per cent or somewhat lower. Recent European work has confirmed risks of these kinds — for example those for first and second degree relatives of schizophrenics in Manfred Bleuler's (1972) longitudinal study from the Burghölzli Hospital in Zürich and, the 10 per cent risk for sibs, in studies by Larson and Nyman (1970) in Sweden and by Stephens *et al.* (1975) in the UK.

It has been argued that family environment rather than family genes might account for these findings. However, no environmental factors have been discovered which will predictably produce a rate of schizophrenia of 10 per cent in persons not already known to be blood relatives of a schizophrenic. Furthermore the nature of the environment shared by parent and child is different from that shared by brother and sister, yet the schizophrenia risks are similar,

57

TABLE 1

Lifetime expectancy of schizophrenia for relatives of schizophrenics

Relationship	Earlier studies (from data reported by Zerbin-Rüdin, 1967)			Data of M. Bleuler (1972)	
	Number of studies	Total relatives (age-corrected)	Percentage schizophrenia or probable schizophrenia	Total relatives (age-corrected)	Percentage schizophrenia or probable schizophrenia
Parents	14	7675	5.5	597	6.7
Full sibs	12	8504.5	10.2	634	9.9
Children	6	1226.5	13.9	106.5	9.4
Second degree relatives*	12	6715	3.3	775	3.4
Unrelated	20	330725	1.2	756	1.1

* Half-sibs, uncles and aunts, nephews and nieces, grandchildren

as is the degree of genetic resemblance.

Twin studies. A more direct test of the environmental counter-hypothesis comes from the comparison of genetically identical (monozygotic, MZ) twins with genetically dissimilar (dizygotic, DZ) twins of schizophrenics brought up in the same family. Systematic twin studies were pioneered by Luxenburger in 1928, and the largest of the earlier studies were published in the 1940s and early 1950s (Kallmann, 1946; Slater, 1953). Though they appeared amply to confirm the hypothesis that the genes play an important role, these twin studies were strongly criticised in the late 1950s and early 1960s, (a) because of the supposed peculiarity of twins and the more similar environments of MZ than DZ pairs (Jackson, 1960) and (b) because the MZ concordance rates of up to 86 per cent were thought to be misleadingly high for a number of methodological reasons (Rosenthal, 1959, 1961, 1962a, b); and as if to bear out the latter criticism, a new study from Finland (Tienari, 1963) at first found no schizophrenia among the MZ twin partners of 16 cases. It was, however, subsequently confirmed that MZ twins as such are at no greater risk of developing schizophrenia than singletons and that concordance does

TABLE 2

Concordance for schizophrenia in twins

	Number of pairs	Both twins schizophrenic or probably schizophrenic (per cent)
6 earlier studies		
MZ	337	65.3
DZ (same sex)	458	12.0
5 recent studies		
MZ	261	45.6
DZ (same sex)	329	13.7
Twins reared apart		
MZ	28	64.3

Rates not age-corrected. From data as reported by Gottesman and Shields (1972) and Shields and Gottesman (1972). Rates for the recent studies have been calculated in terms of co-twins of probands. Concordance in twins at least partially reared apart includes 3 pairs where the second twin had a "disorder resembling schizophrenia".

not require the sharing of the same microfamilial environment, of a kind more similar for MZ than DZ pairs, since concordance for schizophrenia occurs at about the same rate in MZ twins brought up apart as in those brought up together. Well designed twin studies in Norway (Kringlen, 1967), Denmark (Fischer, 1973) and Great Britain (Gottesman and Shields, 1972) took into account the criticisms made of the earlier studies and confirmed the significantly higher concordance in MZ than DZ pairs. The rates reported by the investigators themselves vary depending on which conditions they count as definite, probable or borderline schizophrenia. We have calculated the rates for the recent studies, including the revised findings in the study from Finland, counting as affected those co-twins with schizophrenic-like functional psychoses but not "borderline" personalities. This shows the pooled rate in five recent twin studies to be about 47 per cent for 261 MZ co-twins and 14 per cent for 329 DZ co-twins of schizophrenic probands (Shields and Gottesman, 1972). The fact that concordance for schizophrenia may be less than 50 per cent in the MZ twins of schizophrenics shows the critical importance of environmental factors, at least for those persons who are genetically predisposed to develop the disorder.

Adoption studies. Parents usually provide their children with their early environment as well as their genes. It might therefore be thought that schizophrenia would develop in those predisposed only when brought up in the chaotic kind of environment sometimes provided by parents who are themselves schizophrenic or have schizophrenic genes. Since the late 1960s there have been well controlled adoption and fostering studies in America by Heston (1966), and in Denmark by Rosenthal, Kety and their colleagues (Rosenthal *et al.*, 1968; Rosenthal, 1972, 1975; Kety *et al.*, 1968, 1975; Wender *et al.*, 1974). The latter used Danish national registers of adoptees and of psychiatric cases. It has been shown that the presence in the environment of persons with schizophrenia or related disorders is not a relevant stress in the development of schizophrenia. The children of schizophrenics placed early for non-familial adoption develop schizophrenia at about the same rate as the children of schizophrenics brought up in their own homes. They do so even when the adopted parents could not have known about the schizophrenia in the biological parents – for in the Rosenthal studies the schizophrenia in the parents usually developed only after the child had been adopted. Schizophrenic adoptees are found to have more biological relatives with schizophrenia and related disorders than control adoptees, and there is no increase in their adoptive relatives. Even children adopted by a schizophrenic have no excess of schizophrenic disorders. The hypothesis that it might be the prenatal maternal environment rather than the postnatal family environment that is critical was disproved by the finding that maternal half-sibs of schizophrenics are no more often affected than paternal half-sibs. (This later hypothesis had been given some credence by conclusions – perhaps unwarranted – from studies of discordant MZ twins (Pollin and Stabenau, 1968, cf. Gottesman and Shields, 1972) and "high-risk"

TABLE 3
Psychiatric disorders in foster-home reared children
(data of Heston, 1966)

	Mother chronic schizophrenic	Controls
Number studied	47	50
Mean age	35.8	36.3
Schizophrenia	5	–
Mental deficiency, IQ < 70	4	–
Sociopathic personality	9	2
Neurotic personality disorder	13	7

TABLE 4
Interim findings in the Rosenthal-Kety adoption study of schizophrenia in Denmark

	Number of relatives	Prevalence per cent of schizophrenia, including uncertain latent or borderline schizophrenia
Families of adoptees (Kety *et al.* strategy)		
Biological parents of schizophrenic adoptees	66	12.1
Biological parents of control adoptees	65	6.2
Adoptive parents of schizophrenic adoptees	63	1.6
Adoptive parents of control adoptees	68	4.4
Biological half-sibs of schizophrenic adoptees	104	19.2
All adoptive sibs; full and half-sibs of control adoptees	143	6.3
Adopted children (Rosenthal, Wender *et al.* strategy)		
Biological parent Adoptive parent		
Schizophrenic Normal (Index)	69	18.8
Normal Normal (Control)	79	10.1
Normal Schizophrenic (Cross-fostered)	21	4.8

Calculated from data of Kety *et al.* (1975) and Wender *et al.* (1974)

prospective studies of the children of schizophrenics (Mednick and Schulsinger, 1968; cf. McNeil and Kaij, 1973; Mirdal *et al.*, 1974).)

The wide use of the term schizophrenia to include "uncertain latent schizophrenia" in the Danish adoption studies of Rosenthal and Kety, though not in Heston's study, gives rise to some problems. In some control groups, such as adoptees whose biological parents were not on the Danish psychiatric register, the crude prevalence of schizophrenia including uncertain cases was as high as 10 per cent or some ten times the age-corrected lifetime risk in most other studies. However, this particular rate is so far based only on ratings of thumbnail diagnostic formulations by the psychiatrist who interviewed them and not on the detailed account of behaviour and symptomatology contained in the full transcript of the interview. The high rate found in the half-sibs of schizophrenic adoptees — second degree relatives — is difficult to account for. Based on lengthy accounts of interviews, it was as high as 19 per cent in all half-sibs. In previous studies the comparable figure was more like 4 per cent or 5 per cent. Part of the explanation could be related to differences between the parents of schizophrenics whose children are placed for adoption and those of schizophrenics in general, combined with the wide concept of borderline schizophrenia. Despite these difficulties the highest rates are those found in the biological relatives of schizophrenics. In the continuing Rosenthal and Kety work, as in our own twin study from the Maudsley Hospital, diagnosis of the subjects was made in ignorance of that of other members of their family and there was good agreement among the raters about which of them were schizophrenics or (in the Rosenthal and Kety studies) latent schizophrenics. To paraphrase Dr. Kety (1974), if borderline schizophrenia is a myth, it may be a myth with a strong genetic component.

Conclusion. From the combined results of family, twin and adoption studies, as they stand at present, we can therefore conclude that over the years the genetic hypothesis has been strengthened, not demolished. But while the evidence strongly favours the importance of genetic factors in the development of schizophrenia, variously defined, it is much more difficult to say anything conclusive about their nature or how they operate in interaction with the environment. We turn now to current concern with these unanswered questions.

Unity or Diversity of the Schizophrenic Syndromes

Besides having had a decisive influence on opinion about the existence of genetic factors in schizophrenia, the adoption studies have thrown up the old problem of what clinical disorders might have a genetic connection with schizophrenia (E. Bleuler, 1911; Shields, 1971; Shields *et al.*, 1975) and the equally old problem of the aetiological unity or diversity of various schizophrenic disorders.

The nature of the schizophrenic "spectrum". In what sense can a spectrum of schizophrenic disorders, ranging from the deteriorating chronic cases through the well-preserved paranoid and the good prognosis schizoaffective psychoses to latent or borderline cases and socially adequate schizoid personalities be regarded as a genetic unity? (The possibility has also been raised that still other disorders belong to the spectrum, including sociopathy such as criminality, or manic-depressive psychosis, or, according to Heston's (1970) schizoid disease theory, any disorder occurring in the close relative of a schizophrenic.) These might constitute a unity either because they all require the same necessary gene or because they all increase the likelihood that schizophrenia will occur in their families though not all to the same degree.

The evidence is conflicting. In Heston's (1966) fostering study, schizoid psychopathy clearly differentiated the children of schizophrenics and controls, but in Kety's adoption study (Kety *et al.*, 1975) schizoid personality was diagnosed no more frequently in the biological relatives of schizophrenics than in other groups and on this showing would be out of the spectrum. On a small number of cases Rosenthal (1975), however, found that chronic schizophrenics mated with spectrum (mostly schizoid) spouses had more spectrum offspring than those whose spouses were not in the spectrum. But the pedigree study of Reed *et al.* (1973) found that non-psychotic abnormalities of all kinds in the second parent increased the psychosis risk for the offspring of schizophrenics. To decide how closely schizoid personality or other such conditions might be genetically related to schizophrenia we need to study the offspring of two such parents and see whether they show an increased incidence of schizophrenia. So far there is no suggestion of such an increase in the families of neurotics or psychopaths not suspected of being psychotic themselves.

Perhaps a useful working hypothesis is that as one moves from one end of the spectrum to the other the disorders become increasingly heterogeneous or mixed in origin (Shields, 1971); thus, while some eccentric personalities might be as genetically predisposed to develop schizophrenia as most hebephrenics (or perhaps rather less so), the majority might be no more than averagely predisposed to schizophrenia but have become eccentric for other reasons. Reich *et al.* (1975) suggest a method for determining how far different disorders might be related to the same aetiological process, provided the frequency of the disorders is reliably known in the population and in the families of each kind of patient. This is not yet the case with the suspected schizophrenia spectrum disorders.

The extreme views of a unitary psychosis, or even of a global inherited neuropathic taint where the nature of its manifestation depends entirely upon environmental factors, can be ruled out. While there may be more clinical heterogeneity within psychotic families than was once held to be the case (Ødegaard, 1972), the degree of resemblance in type of psychosis, even between family members reared or living apart, is far greater than chance would allow.

The problem of heterogeneity. The opposite hypothesis is that different clinical classifications within the schizophrenic syndromes largely reflect different aetiologies. In particular the group of acute, good prognosis, schizoaffective or reactive schizophrenias has been separated from the so-called process group. Some claim the former may be largely non-genetic (Kety *et al.*, 1975), some that they belong to the affective disorders genetically (Clayton *et al.*, 1968), and still others that they are a separate genetic entity with a dominant mode of inheritance (Mitsuda, 1972; Perris, 1975) or are themselves a heterogeneous group aetiologically (Angst, 1966). There is, however, evidence from studies by Achté (1961) and Larson and Nyman (1974) that good prognosis and poor prognosis probands both have a rather similar mixture of poor and good prognosis schizophrenics among their relatives. Bleuler (1972) found that the 22 per cent of his schizophrenic cases who had an acute onset ending in recovery contained nearly as many with a family history of schizophrenia (32 per cent) as the other more typical cases (38 per cent with family history); there were many instances of good and poor outcome schizophrenias in the same family. This conflicts with the suggestion of McCabe *et al.* (1971) that the schizophrenics should be divided according to outcome.

Within the classical schizophrenias there is usually a tendency for hebephrenics to have more schizophrenic relatives than paranoids. Kallmann's (1938) findings on this point were recently confirmed by Larson and Nyman (1973) and Tsuang *et al.* (1974). There is a modest tendency towards subtype resemblance within families, at least in some studies (Kallmann, 1938; Slater, 1947, 1953), and rather less in the case of the paranoid than the hebephrenic or catatonic forms, suggesting that the main or modifying genes contributing to schizophrenia are not entirely uniform in their effects. Winokur *et al.* (1974) have gone so far as to suggest that there are two genetic types of poor prognosis schizophrenia: hebephrenia, which may occasionally manifest as paranoid; and true paranoid schizophrenia in which the risk for relatives is lower but which runs true to type. This view would seem to be premature to say the least (*Brit. med. J.*, 1974).

For some time to come we may not know how far we are confronted in schizophrenia with clinical diversity in genetic unity or with genetic diversity in clinical unity. It does seem, however, that some schizophrenic-like psychoses, often paranoid in form, can be evoked by organic disease such as temporal lobe epilepsy (Slater *et al.*, 1963) in persons with no more than average genetic liability. Such symptomatic psychoses have been reviewed by Davison and Bagley (1969).

Mode of inheritance

Leaving the symptomatic psychoses out of account, the mode of inheritance of schizophrenia as conventionally diagnosed has been widely studied. Some of the many theories are discussed in the volume edited by Kaplan (1972). There are three main kinds of theory, monogenic inheritance, polygenic inheritance and genetic heterogeneity.

Monogenic. According to monogenic theory there is one necessary gene common to all schizophrenics which they must inherit from one or both parents for them to be at risk of developing the disorder. Recessivity has sometimes been put forward as the general mode of inheritance, but the fact that sibs are not more often affected than children goes against it. Most single gene theories assume some form of dominance, that is, most schizophrenics will have the essential gene in single dose only. Slater first put forward his monogenic theory in 1958 and it has since been elaborated in his book with Valerie Cowie (1971). Taking the frequency of schizophrenia in the general population as given, the latest version of the theory calculates that the gene has a frequency of 3 per cent in the population gene pool. All who inherit the gene in double dose will develop schizophrenia. However, such homozygotes will account for only 10 per cent of all schizophrenics. The remaining 90 per cent will be heterozygous, but only 13 per cent of heterozygotes will develop schizophrenia. Whether they do so or not will depend on many other genes and on the environment.

Other similar theories have been put forward according to which the rate of manifestation in heterozygotes is as low as 6 or 7 per cent (Elston and Campbell, 1970). Another such monogenic theory by Kidd and Cavalli-Sforza (1973) calculated that heritability would be only 10-15 per cent. Their model, however, has been criticised as biologically unlikely (Gurnow and Smith, 1975), since it allows only environmental factors and no genetic factors to modify the expression of the major locus. Karlsson (1973) has abandoned his two-gene for a one-gene theory.

One problem with monogenic theories is how the gene is maintained in the population, given the low fertility of schizophrenics. The condition is too common to be maintained by fresh mutations. No selective advantage has so far been reliably established for heterozygotes, such as resistance to stress or infection. But the fact that monogenic theories can be made to fit the data suggests to some that it might still be worth searching for a simply inherited biochemical error in schizophrenia. For others it seems preferable not to posit a single essential gene with *ad hoc* low penetrance as the most likely explanation until such a gene can be reliably identified by its effects.

An alternative formulation of the dominant gene theory was put forward by Heston (1970). This attempted to avoid the difficulty of the low manifestation rate by broadening the phenotype from schizophrenia into one called "schizoid disease". Heston noted that nearly 50 per cent of first degree relatives have something wrong with them. If one counted schizophrenia plus these other disorders one might have a trait that was simply inherited. Heston has subsequently modified his theory (Shields *et al.*, 1975). The kinds of condition which it is necessary to include among relatives before a 50 per cent rate of affectation is achieved is too wide for the concept to be useful. There will be too many false positives in the general population. Kay *et al.* (1975) found that schizoid and other personality disorders were significantly more often diagnosed in schizophrenics' relatives, but the observed risks did not fit well with Heston's major gene model.

Polygenic. Polygenic models assume that the genetic contribution to schizophrenia is the result of the combined effect of many genes, no one of which is essential. The genetic predisposition in the population will be graded. Some schizophrenics will have more of the genes than others. The combination of genetic and environmental factors will vary from case to case. Once an accumulation of such factors results in the crossing of a threshold, schizophrenic psychosis ensues. The liability is partly genetically and partly environmentally determined, and methods are now available for estimating how much of this liability in the population depends on genetic variation. This is done by comparing the incidence in the general population with that in the relatives of schizophrenics. Using the methods of Falconer (1965) and Smith (1970, 1971) Gottesman and Shields (1972) showed that, given a population risk of 1 per cent, such "heritability" estimates derived independently from MZ and DZ twins, siblings and second degree relatives agreed quite well and were of the order of 80 per cent. It is important to stress that finding a high heritability does not imply that curative or preventive measures will be ineffective, but only that one will have to look outside the range of environments experienced by the untreated population.

Polygenic or multifactorial models are thought by some to be useful for summarising and analysing data where more than one gene together with several environmental factors are likely to be involved. They may provide a useful if temporary tool during a period of ignorance

(Curnow and Smith, 1975; Shields, 1975). The existence of various subthreshold manifestations in relatives and the association between concordance and severity in twins fit the polygenic hypothesis; and the problem of how the genes are maintained in the population is less acute on this theory than on monogenic theory, since it is only in the exceptional individuals who have inherited a large number of schizophrenic polygenes that the genes will be exposed to natural selection. The tendency for other cases in the family to pile up on one side of the family only is, however, more in favour of a dominant gene theory than simple polygenic inheritance (Slater and Tsuang, 1968); but it would be consistent with a form of the polygenic theory favoured by Gottesman and Shields which suggests that within the polygenic system there might be a few genes which accounted for most of the effect.

Unfortunately family data are consistent with more than one theory. The Slater and Cowie and Gottesman and Shields theories come out with such similar predictions as to be non-discriminative. For the present it may be largely a matter of taste which model one prefers to work with.

TABLE 5
Predictions of schizophrenia risks from polygenic and monogenic models
(after Gottesman and Shields, 1972)

| | Risk for schizophrenia (per cent) | | | |
| | For sibs of schizophrenic | | For children of schizophrenic | |
Number of parents affected	0	1	1	2
Observed (pooled risks from literature)	9.7	17.2	13.9	46.3
Predicted, polygenic model	6.5	18.5	8.3	40.9
Predicted, monogenic model	9.4	13.5	8.8	37.1

Genetic heterogeneity. These theories consider that schizophrenia consists of an unspecified number of genetically distinct groups, which need not be distinct clinically. It is usually implied that there are a number of different rare genes each of which can cause schizophrenia, rather as in deafness and blindness. Few people will have more than one such gene. According to the theory disorders due to such genes will account for a sizable proportion of all schizophrenias, leaving a not too large residue of sporadic cases of environmental origin or of more complex inheritance. (If such genes accounted for only a small proportion of cases, it could be argued that each type should be given its own name — x, y or z deficiency — leaving the term schizophrenia for the remainder.) The mutation rate would not be too high to maintain these rare genes in the population. However, no rare simply-inherited genetic diseases have been discovered within the schizophrenias. No clinical type breeds true enough, or has an incidence of schizophrenia in relatives close enough to the classical Mendelian ratios to provide the theory with much empirical support at the present time.

Conclusion. Most theorists qualify their monogenic, polygenic or heterogeneity theories, so that in practice they overlap. They represent hypotheses about what accounts for most schizophrenias: one particular gene, various rare genes, or a combination of causes. Whatever theory is preferred, the tasks ahead are much the same: to discover how genotype and environment interact; to search for heterogeneity of one kind or another; and to look for stable biological or other characteristics in relatives which might identify a high-risk genotype. We know very little about any of these.

Nature of the Principal Factors

Environmental. Studies which look at the kind of environmental input which may be critical for the development of schizophrenia in the genetically predisposed, or which may prevent its development, have focused on pairs of MZ twins that are discordant for schizophrenia and on longitudinal observations of the so-called high-risk children of schizophrenic parents. It has also been shown that "life-events" or environmental changes of various nonspecific kinds can precipitate relapse in schizophrenics (Birley and Brown, 1970; Brown *et al.*, 1973).

As previously noted (p. 59), perinatal factors seem unlikely to be crucial in most cases. The most consistent finding in the discordant twin studies is that the relatively more submissive member of such pairs is more likely to be the schizophrenic. Twins often adopt or get cast in the roles of leader and follower. The findings are not specific to schizophrenia, and it is not clear how far they apply to non-twins; but if the submissive twin tended to be more emotionally involved with his parents and also more criticized by them, the findings would be consistent with those of Brown *et al.* (1972) who showed that emotional overinvolvement with close relatives, especially if these relatives are critical, is a kind of stress which is liable to cause schizophrenics to relapse.

Genetic. Another of the many unanswered questions, but one to which attention has been paid in recent years, is what is inherited in schizophrenia. It has been hoped that psychological or biological investigation of patients' relatives might give some leads. Claims that it might be a detectable disorder of thinking have not been substantiated (Hirsch and Leff, 1971); such traits are common in some groups of the general population (McConaghy and Clancy, 1968), and their presence in schizophrenics fluctuates according to the clinical state (Gottesman and Shields, 1972). In the Danish high-risk studies of Mednick and Schulsinger (1968, 1970) it is as yet too early to say which of the offspring of schizophrenics will be similarly affected, or to say how much hope can be placed on psychophysiological studies of the kind they have carried out. Fast electrodermal reaction and recovery time discriminated most consistently between their high-risk and low-risk groups — the latter were matched children of non-psychotic parentage — and between the sick and well members of the high-risk group; but this is not the finding they originally predicted, and it is not confirmed in Rosenthal's Danish adoptee study using similar measuring techniques (van Dyke *et al.*, 1974).

The problem in studying relatives is where to look. From time to time the claim is made that schizophrenics and their relatives differ from other groups. For example, Holzman *et al.* (1974) recently reported them as showing a high rate of eye-tracking dysfunction in a test of smooth-pursuit eye movement. The more promising of any such leads should be followed up, as should the informed hunches of experienced experimental psychologists, physiologists or biochemists. However, there is no special reason to suppose that a style of thinking, a perceptual anomaly, a physiological response latency or the activity of an enzyme will be any more simply inherited or less mixed in its aetiology than schizophrenia itself. One might nevertheless succeed in identifying variables that were loosely correlated with the liability.

What is required, if we are to identify genetic factors which contribute to the predisposition to schizophrenia, is a constitutional trait which will show up in an individual whether he is sick or well and is not just a consequence of his being schizophrenic. Cazzullo *et al.* (1974) hope that the leucocyte antigenic system HL-A may provide a genetic marker for schizophrenia. Wyatt *et al.* (1973a) thought that low monoamine oxidase (MAO) activity in blood platelets might be such a trait because it was found to be low both in schizophrenics and in their unaffected MZ co-twins. In theory this would be a better trait to study in relatives than the activity of the enzyme forming dimethyltryptamine, since the latter was raised in the schizophrenics but not in their twins (Wyatt *et al.*, 1973b). MAO activity has been found to be under genetic control in a study of normal twins (Nies *et al.*, 1973). Currently many consider MAO activity to be among the more promising leads, though Brockington *et al.* (in press) failed to confirm the low levels in chronic schizophrenics in England.

Enzyme activity is not strictly speaking a genetic marker in the sense that the blood groups and other genetic polymorphisms are (Giblett, 1969), since a wide range of activity is possible for individuals of the same genotype under different conditions (Harris, 1970). Perhaps the best hopes for a real genetic advance would be the identification of genetic variants in an enzyme whose activity is related to the biochemistry of schizophrenia. This might provide a useful handle in advancing our understanding of how some of the genetic factors in schizophrenia operate (Shields and Gottesman, 1973). It might help to solve some of the problems of the mode of inheritance, heterogeneity and factors common to more than one psychiatric condition.

Summary

The results of many family, twin and, most recently, adoption studies, using increasingly elegant methods, continue to confirm the hypothesis that genetic factors play an important if still imperfectly understood part in the aetiology of schizophrenia.

There is scope for further studies of the relatives of schizophrenics, clinically, biologically and environmentally. On clinical lines, using well defined, reliable diagnostic criteria (cf. Cooper *et al.*, 1972; WHO, 1973), such studies would test current theories about which other conditions might be related genetically to classically diagnosed schizophrenia and about how far the schizophrenias should be split up into aetiologically distinct disorders. Given advances in biological research, the study of relatives on biological lines might throw light on unsolved problems such as the nature of the genetic factors and the mode of inheritance. It is hoped that from such studies, together with those of the environment and the development of schizophrenics and their relatives, we shall reach a better understanding of how genetic and other factors interact in the development of schizophrenia.

Acknowledgement. Much of this paper is a result of long collaboration with Irving I. Gottesman.

References

ACHTÉ, K.A. (1961) Der Verlauf der Schizophrenien und der schizophreniformen Psychosen. *Acta Psychiatrica et Neurologica Scandinavica*, Suppl. 155.

ANGST, J. (1966) Zur Ätiologie und Nosologie endogener depressiver Psychosen. *Monographien aus dem Gesamtgebiete der Neurologie und Psychiatrie*, 112. Berlin: Springer.

BIRLEY, J.L.T. and BROWN, G.W. (1970) Crises and life changes preceding the onset or relapse of acute schizophrenia: clinical aspects. *British Journal of Psychiatry*, 116, 327-333.

BLEULER, E. (1911) *Dementia Praecox oder Gruppe der Schizophrenien*. Leipzig: Deuticke.

BLEULER, M. (1972) *Die schizophrenen Geistesstörungen im Lichte langjähriger Kranken- und Familiengeschichten*. Stuttgart: Thieme.

BRITISH MEDICAL JOURNAL (1974) Unsigned editorial, Unity and diversity in schizophrenia. 4, 673-4.

BROCKINGTON, I., CROW, T.J., JOHNSTONE, E.C. and OWEN, F. (in press). An investigation of platelet monoamine oxidase activity in schizophrenia and schizo-affective psychosis. In CIBA Foundation Symposium volume, (ed. Knight, J., Tipton, K.F. and Youdim, M.B.H.).

BROWN, G.W., BIRLEY, J.L.T. and WING, J.K. (1972) Influence of family life on the course of schizophrenic disorders: a replication. *British Journal of Psychiatry*, 121, 241-258.

BROWN, G.W., HARRIS, T.O. and PETO, J. (1973) Life events and psychiatric disorders. Part 2: nature of causal link. *Psychological Medicine*, 3, 159-176.

CAZZULLO, C.L., SMERALDI, E. and PENATO, G. (1974) The leucocyte antigenic system HL-A as a possible genetic marker of schizophrenia. *British Journal of Psychiatry*, 125, 25-27.

CLAYTON, P.J., RODIN, L. and WINOKUR, G. (1968) Family history studies: III. Schizoaffective disorder, clinical and genetic factors including a one to two year follow-up. *Comprehensive Psychiatry*, 9, 31-49.

COOPER, J.E., KENDELL, R.E., GURLAND, B.J., SHARPE, L., COPELAND, J.R.M. and SIMON, R. (1972) *Psychiatric Diagnosis in New York and London*. Maudsley Monograph No. 20. London: Oxford University Press.

CURNOW, R.N. and SMITH, C. (1975) Multifactorial models for familial diseases in man. *Journal of the Royal Statistical Society, A,* 138, 000-000.

DAVISON, K. and BAGLEY, C.R. (1969) Schizophrenia-like psychoses associated with organic disorders of the central nervous system: A review of the literature. In *Current Problems in Neuropsychiatry* (ed. Herrington, R.N.). British Journal of Psychiatry Special Publication No. 4. Ashford, Kent: Headley, pp. 113-184.

ELSTON, R.C. and CAMPBELL, M.A. (1970) Schizophrenia: evidence for the major gene hypothesis. *Behavior Genetics*, 1, 3-10.

FALCONER, D.S. (1965) The inheritance of liability to certain diseases, estimated from the incidence among relatives. *Annals of Human Genetics*, 29, 51-76.

FISCHER, M. (1973) Genetic and environmental factors in schizophrenia. *Acta Psychiatrica Scandinavica*, Suppl. 238.

GIBLETT, E.R. (1969) *Genetic Markers in Human Blood*. Oxford and Edinburgh: Blackwell Scientific Publications.

GOTTESMAN, I.I. and SHIELDS, J. (1972) *Schizophrenia and Genetics: A Twin Study Vantage Point*. New York: Academic Press.

HARRIS, H. (1970) *The Principles of Human Biochemical Genetics*. Amsterdam: North-Holland Publications.

HESTON, L.L. (1966) Psychiatric disorders in foster home reared children of schizophrenic mothers. *British Journal of Psychiatry*, 112, 819-825.

HESTON, L.L. (1970) The genetics of schizophrenic and schizoid disease. *Science*, 167, 249-256.

HIRSCH, S.R. and LEFF, J.P. (1971) Parental abnormalities of verbal communication in the transmission of schizophrenia. *Psychological Medicine*, 1, 118-127.

HOLZMAN, P.S., PROCTOR, L.R., LEVY, D.L., YASILLO, N.J., MELTZER, H.Y. and HURT, S.W. (1974) Eye-tracking dysfunctions in schizophrenic patients and their relatives. *Archives of General Psychiatry*, 31, 143-151.

JACKSON, D.D. (1960) A critique of the literature on the genetics of schizophrenia. In *The Etiology of Schizophrenia* (ed. Jackson, D.D.). New York: Basic Books, pp. 37-87.

KALLMANN, F.J. (1938) *The Genetics of Schizophrenia*. New York: Augustin.

KALLMANN, F.J. (1946) The genetic theory of schizophrenia. An analysis of 691 schizophrenic twin index families. *American Journal of Psychiatry*, **103**, 309-322.

KAPLAN, A.R. (ed.) (1972) *Genetic Factors in "Schizophrenia"*. Springfield, Ill.: Thomas.

KARLSSON, J.L. (1973) An Icelandic family study of schizophrenia. *British Journal of Psychiatry*, **123**, 549-554.

KAY, D.W., ROTH, M., ATKINSON, M.W., STEPHENS, D.A. and GARSIDE, R.F. (1975) Genetic hypotheses and environmental factors in the light of psychiatric morbidity in the families of schizophrenics. *British Journal of Psychiatry*, **127**, 109-118.

KETY, S.S. (1974) From rationalisation to reason. *American Journal of Psychiatry*, **131**, 957-963.

KETY, S.S., ROSENTHAL, D., WENDER, P.H. and SCHULSINGER, F. (1968) The types and prevalence of mental illness in the biological and adoptive families of adopted schizophrenics. In *The Transmission of Schizophrenia* (eds. Rosenthal, D. and Kety, S.S.). Oxford: Pergamon Press, pp. 345-362.

KETY, S.S., ROSENTHAL, D. WENDER, P.H., SCHULSINGER, F. and JACOBSEN, B. (1975) Mental illness in the biological and adoptive families of adopted individuals who have become schizophrenic: a preliminary report based on psychiatric interviews. In *Genetic Research in Psychiatry* (ed. Fieve, R.R., Rosenthal, D. and Brill, H.). Baltimore and London: Johns Hopkins University Press, pp. 147-165.

KIDD, K.K. and CAVALLI-SFORZA, L.L. (1973) An analysis of the genetics of schizophrenia. *Social Biology*, **20**, 254-265.

KRINGLEN, E. (1967) *Heredity and Environment in the Functional Psychoses*. London: Heinemann Medical Books.

LARSON, C.A. and NYMAN, G.E. (1970) Age of onset in schizophrenia. *Human Heredity*, **20**, 241-247.

LARSON, C.A. and NYMAN, G.E. (1973) Differential fertility in schizophrenia. *Acta Psychiatrica Scandinavica*, **49**, 272-280.

LARSON, C.A. and NYMAN, G.E. (1974) Schizophrenia: outcome in a birth year cohort. *Psychiatrica Clinica*, **7**, 50-55.

LUXENBURGER, H. (1928) Vorläufiger Bericht über psychiatrische Serienuntersuchungen an Zwillingen. *Zeitschrift für die gesamte Neurologie und Psychiatrie*, **116**, 297-326.

McCABE, M.S., FOWLER, R.C., CADORET, R.J. and WINOKUR, G. (1971) Familial differences in schizophrenia with good and poor prognosis. *Psychological Medicine*, **1**, 326-332.

McCONAGHY, N. and CLANCY, M. (1968) Familial relationships of allusive thinking in university students and their parents. *British Journal of Psychiatry*, **114**, 1079-1087.

McNEIL, T.F. and KAIJ, L. (1973) Obstetric complications and physical size of offspring of schizophrenic, schizophrenic-like, and control mothers. *British Journal of Psychiatry*, **123**, 341-348.

MEDNICK, S.A. (1970) Breakdown in individuals at high risk for schizophrenia: possible predispositional perinatal factors. *Mental Hygiene*, **54**, 50-63.

MEDNICK, S.A. and SCHULSINGER, F. (1968) Some premorbid characteristics related to breakdown in children with schizophrenic mothers. In *The Transmission of Schizophrenia* (ed. Rosenthal, D. and Kety, S.S.). Oxford: Pergamon Press, pp. 267-291.

MIRDAL, G.K.M., MEDNICK, S.A., SCHULSINGER, F. and FUCHS, F. (1974) Perinatal complications in children of schizophrenic mothers. *Acta Psychiatrica Scandinavica*, **50**, 553-568.

MITSUDA, H. (1972) The clinico-genetic study of schizophrenia. *International Journal of Mental Health*, **1**, 1-2, 76-92.

NIES, A., ROBINSON, D.S., LAMBORN, K.R. and LAMPERT, R.P. (1973) Genetic control of platelet and plasma monoamine oxidase activity. *Archives of General Psychiatry*, **28**, 834-838.

ØDEGAARD, Ø. (1972) The multifactorial theory of inheritance in predisposition to schizophrenia. In *Genetic Factors in "Schizophrenia"* (ed. Kaplan, A.R.). Springfield, Ill.: Thomas, pp. 256-275.

PERRIS, C. (1974) A study of cycloid psychoses. *Acta Psychiatrica Scandinavica*, Suppl. 253.

POLLIN, W. and STABENAU, J.R. (1968) Biological, psychological and historical differences in a series of monozygotic twins discordant for schizophrenia. In *The Transmission of Schizophrenia* (eds. Rosenthal, D. and Kety, S.S.). Oxford: Pergamon Press, pp. 317-332.

REED, S.C., HARTLEY, C., ANDERSON, V.E., PHILLIPS, V.P. and JOHNSON, N.A. (1973) *The Psychoses: Family Studies*. Philadelphia: Saunders.

REICH, T., CLONINGER, C.R. and GUZE, S.B. (1975) The multifactorial model of disease transmission. Description of the model and its use in psychiatry. *Brit. J. Psychiat.*, **127**, 1-10.

ROSENTHAL, D. (1959) Some factors associated with concordance and discordance with respect to schizophrenia in monozygotic twins. *Journal of Nervous & Mental Disease*, **129**, 1-10.

ROSENTHAL, D. (1961) Sex distribution and the severity of illness among samples of schizophrenic twins. *Journal of Psychiatric Research*, **1**, 26-36.

ROSENTHAL, D. (1962a) Problems of sampling and diagnosis in the major twin studies of schizophrenia. *Journal of Psychiatric Research*, **1**, 116-134.

ROSENTHAL, D. (1962b) Familial concordance by sex with respect to schizophrenia. *Psychological Bulletin,* 59, 401-421.

ROSENTHAL, D. (1970) *Genetic Theory and Abnormal Behavior.* New York: McGraw-Hill.

ROSENTHAL, D. (1972) Three adoption studies of heredity in the schizophrenic disorders. *International Journal of Mental Health,* 1, 1-2, 63-75.

ROSENTHAL, D. (1975) Discussion: the concept of subschizophrenic disorders. In *Genetic Research in Psychiatry* (eds. Fieve, R.R., Rosenthal, D. & Brill, H.). Baltimore and London: Johns Hopkins University Press, pp. 199-208.

ROSENTHAL, D., WENDER, P.H., KETY, S.S., SCHULSINGER, F., WELNER, J. and ØSTERGAARD, L. (1968) Schizophrenics' offspring reared in adoptive homes. In *The Transmission of Schizophrenia* (eds. Rosenthal, D. and Kety, S.S.). Oxford: Pergamon Press, pp. 377-391.

RÜDIN, E. (1916) *Zur Vererbung und Neuentstehung der Dementia Praecox.* Berlin and New York: Springer-Verlag.

SCHULZ, B. (1932) Zur Erbpathologie der Schizophrenie. *Zeitschrift für die gesamte Neurologie und Psychiatrie,* 143, 175-293.

SHIELDS, J. (1971) Concepts of heredity for schizophrenia. In *The Origin of Schizophrenia* (ed. Bleuler, M. and Angst, J.). Bern: Huber, pp. 59-75.

SHIELDS, J. (1975) Polygenic influences on abnormal behaviour. *Eugenics Society Bulletin,* 7, 39-43.

SHIELDS, J. and GOTTESMAN, I.I. (1972) Cross-national diagnosis of schizophrenia in twins. *Archives of General Psychiatry,* 27, 725-730.

SHIELDS, J. and GOTTESMAN, I.I. (1973). Genetic studies of schizophrenia as signposts to biochemistry. In *Biochemistry and Mental Illness* (ed. Iversen, L.L. and Rose, S.P.R.). Special Publication No. 1. London: The Biochemical Society, pp. 165-174.

SHIELDS, J., HESTON, L.L. and GOTTESMAN, I.I. (1975) Schizophrenia and the schizoid: the problem for genetic analysis. In *Genetic Research in Psychiatry* (ed. Fieve, R.R., Rosenthal, D. and Brill, H.). Baltimore and London: Johns Hopkins University Press, 1975, pp. 167-197.

SLATER, E. (19   Genetical causes of schizophrenic symptoms. *Monatsschrift für Psychiatrie und Neurologie,* 113, 50-58.

SLATER, E. (1953) (with the assistance of J. Shields). Psychotic and Neurotic Illnesses in Twins. Medical Research Council Special Report Series No. 278. London: Her Majesty's Stationery Office.

SLATER, E. (1958) The monogenic theory of schizophrenia. *Acta Genetica et Statistica Medica,* 8, 50-56.

SLATER, E. (1968) A review of earlier evidence on genetic factors in schizophrenia. In *The Transmission of Schizophrenia* (ed. Rosenthal, D. and Kety, S.S.). Oxford: Pergamon Press, pp. 15-26.

SLATER, E., BEARD, A.W. and GLITHERO, E. (1963) The schizophrenia-like psychoses of epilepsy. *British Journal of Psychiatry,* 109, 95-150.

SLATER, E. and COWIE, V. (1971) *The Genetics of Mental Disorders.* London: Oxford University Press.

SLATER, E. and TSUANG, M-t. (1968) Abnormality on paternal and maternal sides: observations in schizophrenia and manic-depression. *Journal of Medical Genetics,* 5, 197-199.

SMITH, C. (1970) Heritability of liability and concordance in monozygous twins. *Annals of Human Genetics,* 34, 85-91.

SMITH, C. (1971) Recurrence risks for multifactorial inheritance. *American Journal of Human Genetics,* 23, 578-588.

STEPHENS, D.A., ATKINSON, M.W., KAY, D.W.K., ROTH, M. and GARSIDE, R.F. (1975) Psychiatric morbidity in parents and sibs of schizophrenics and non-schizophrenics. *British Journal of Psychiatry,* 127, 97-108.

TIENARI, P. (1963) Psychiatric illnesses in identical twins. *Acta Psychiatrica Scandinavica,* Suppl. 171.

TSUANG, M.T., FOWLER, R.C., CADORET, R.J. and MONNELLY, E. (1974) Schizophrenia among first-degree relatives of paranoid and non paranoid schizophrenics. *Comprehensive Psychiatry,* 15, 295-302.

VAN DYKE, J.L., ROSENTHAL, D. and RASMUSSEN, P.V. (1974) Electrodermal functioning in adopted-away offspring of schizophrenics. *Journal of Psychiatric Research,* 10, 199-215.

WENDER, P.H., ROSENTHAL, D., KETY, S.S., SCHULSINGER, F. and WELNER, J. (1974) Crossfostering: A research strategy for clarifying the role of genetic and experiential factors in the etiology of schizophrenia. *Archives of General Psychiatry,* 30, 121-128.

WINOKUR, G., MORRISON, J., CLANCY, J. and CROWE, R. (1974) Iowa 500: the clinical and genetic distinction of hebephrenic and paranoid schizophrenia. *Journal of Nervous and Mental Disease,* 159, 12-19.

WORLD HEALTH ORGANIZATION (1973) Report of *The International Pilot Study of Schizophrenia, Vol. 1.* Geneva: World Health Organization.

WYATT, R.J., MURPHY, D.L., BELMAKER, R., COHEN, S., DONNELLY, C.H. and POLLIN, W. (1973) Reduced monoamine oxidase activity in platelets: a possible genetic marker for vulnerability to schizophrenia. *Science,* 179, 916-918.

WYATT, R.J., SAAVEDRA, J.M., BELMAKER, R., COHEN, S. and POLLIN, W. (1973) The Dimethyltryptamine-forming enzyme in blood platelets: a study in monozygotic twins discordant for schizophrenia. *American Journal of Psychiatry,* 130, 1359-1361.

ZERBIN-RÜDIN, E. (1967) Endogene Psychosen. In *Humangenetik, ein kurzes Handbuch*, Vol. V/2 (ed. Becker, P.E.). Stuttgart: Thieme, pp. 446-577.
ZERBIN-RÜDIN, E. (1972) Genetic research and the theory of schizophrenia. *International Journal of Mental Health*, **1**, 1-2, 42-62.

The Impact of Biochemistry on the Problem of Schizophrenia

DEREK RICHTER

1. The Neurological Basis of the Symptoms

One approach to the study of schizophrenia is to look for biochemical correlates of the symptoms. Hallucinations and other symptoms found in schizophrenia can be produced by relatively simple chemical compounds such as mescaline or LSD and the idea that an abnormal metabolite of some kind might be concerned has been current for many years. The symptoms generally regarded as diagnostically important include certain forms of thought disorder, faulty perception, inappropriate affect, auditory hallucinations and delusions of control, with changes in personality and behaviour. There is no single set of symptoms that occur consistently in every case: the term "schizophrenia" is applied to patients with certain combinations of symptoms which, like the onset and course of the illness, vary considerably in different cases. Some take a wider view of the conditions that should be included in the schizophrenias while others keep to a narrower definition. For purposes of investigation criteria such as the presence of Schneider's[1] first-rank symptoms (thought insertion, delusions of control, etc.) can be helpful in defining more closely the clinical state of those selected for inclusion in any particular study, but clearly there is no evidence that a group selected in this way is strictly homogeneous or that the causal factors are the same in every case.

The view that biochemical factors could be involved is supported by the observation that schizophrenia-like psychoses occur in conditions such as myxoedema, pellagra, Kleinefelter's syndrome, and Wilson's disease, where biochemical factors are known to operate. When a symptomatic psychosis is the presenting symptom the correct diagnosis is not always easy to make and patients with these conditions have frequently been diagnosed as suffering from schizophrenia. It is evident today that the "group of schizophrenias" which Bleuler originally described included patients with other conditions such as temporal lobe epilepsy, homocystinuria, porphyria, and even with toxic-infective psychoses. With the steady accumulation of new knowledge there has been a successive removal of sub-groups with schizophrenia-like psychoses caused by biochemical or physical abnormalities which, as a result of more recent advances, we are now able to recognise. This points to the possibility that schizophrenia, as at present defined, is still not a single homogeneous condition, but a group of conditions in which different causal factors have led to a final common pathway. On this basis "schizophrenia" denotes a condition comparable to "fever" in which certain combinations of symptoms can arise in different ways, and further work may be expected to reveal further sub-groups which new diagnostic techniques will enable us to identify.

In seeking information as to the biochemical factors that may be concerned, we may ask how do the symptoms of schizophrenia arise? What are the underlying neurological systems and

71

what transmitter mechanisms are involved? Since schizophrenia occurs without clouding of consciousness or impairment of memory, it would appear that the disturbance does not extend to all areas of the brain but that specific mechanisms are specially involved. An early attempt to relate the symptoms to underlying neurological mechanisms was made by Pavlov who, impressed by the tendency of schizophrenics to withdrawal, suggested that schizophrenia represents a state of "partial inhibition" of the cerebral cortex. Pfister[2] examined the responses of groups of patients and controls to stimuli of various kinds and found that in the early acute stage of their illness schizophrenics reacted with an exaggerated autonomic response, whereas in longstanding chronic cases the responses were often diminished: in both types of patients the responses were generally abnormal. Since this applied to parameters such as blood pressure and water balance which are not under voluntary control, he concluded that schizophrenia is associated with a basic disorder of the controlling mechanisms of the hypothalamus. This could also explain the disturbance of affect, since affective responses are also mediated by hypothalamic mechanisms.

Shakow[3] confirmed the tendency of schizophrenics to respond abnormally to stressful stimuli and he reported their inability to adapt in the normal way to repeated stimuli by decreasing the response (defective habituation). Those observations suggested a disturbance of brain-stem structures concerned with arousal and especially of the sensory filtering functions of the ascending reticular formation. Gruzelin and Venables[4] who reported further evidence of defective habituation and abnormal response, suggested that there is a disturbance of catecholamine-mediated mechanisms of the limbic system involving apparently the amygdala and hippocampus, which are believed to mediate the control of sensory input and habituation. On this view the acute schizophrenic is unable to adapt normally to stressful stimuli since his consciousness is flooded with irrelevant stimuli which he cannot exclude from his attention. The difficulty experienced in adapting to stressful stimuli may account for some of the common secondary symptoms such as neophobia (fear of novelty), lack of initiative and withdrawal, which can serve as defence mechanisms. Rado[5] has postulated an additional disorder of the limbic reward system as the cause of the purposelessness, lack of initiative and anhedonia (inability to experience pleasure) of many schizophrenics. This would agree with evidence of abnormal EEG activity in the region of the medial nucleus accumbens (septal area) reported originally by Heath[5] and more recently confirmed by other investigators (Stevens[6]). It may be concluded that the symptoms are referable mainly to a dysfunction of one or more of the neurological mechanisms in a relatively small brain-stem area affecting the functions of the limbic system and temporal lobes. Besides cholinergic mechanisms, noradrenergic, serotoninergic and doapminergic modes of transmission are prominent in this region and could therefore be involved.

2. Toxic Metabolite Hypotheses

One possible line of investigation is to look for abnormal metabolites that could cause the symptoms of schizophrenia. It is known for example that cerebral functions are affected by toxic amines such as are formed by bacterial action, and an early hypothesis was the idea that schizophrenia is caused by amines formed by bacterial action in the gut. In support of this view it was noted that schizophrenics are often sedentary in their habits and constipated, so that the amine content of their urine tends to be high: but careful studies failed to reveal any abnormal bacteria or toxic amines that could account for the symptoms. Another early hypothesis was that schizophrenia is a form of "autointoxication" due to an abnormal hormonal secretion from the gonads. This view was based partly on the sexual deviations reported in schizophrenics but mainly on the observation of atrophic changes in the testicles and other endocrine glands. However further investigation showed that these findings applied only to a special sub-group, probably of patients with Kleinefelter's syndrome, who were formerly included in the schizophrenias[7] and they were not applicable to schizophrenics as a whole.

More recently the idea of a toxic metabolite was revived by Hoffer, Osmond and Smythies[8] who first put forward the idea that schizophrenia is caused by an excessive formation in the tissues of *adrenochrome*, an oxidation product of adrenaline, which is an indole derivative and therefore structurally related to LSD and other hallucinogens. Some naturally occurring hallucinogens such as mescaline are methylated derivatives of catecholamines; and another suggestion was therefore that schizophrenia might be caused by toxic methylated derivatives formed from normal metabolites by abnormal processes of transmethylation or by failure of the normal demethylating processes. Interest in this *"transmethylation hypothesis"* increased when Friedhoff and Van Winkle[9] reported the presence of dimethoxyphenylethylamine (DMPEA) in the urine exclusively of 60 per cent of schizophrenics and not in the urine of controls. The presence of DMPEA was indicated by a "pink spot" when the urines were tested by paper chromatography. An observation of Pollin, Cardon and Kety[10] that methionine, which is a methyl donor, caused an apparent exacerbation of the psychosis when administered to chronic schizophrenics appeared at first to give strong independent support for the transmethylation hypothesis, but later it appeared that the response to methionine could be no more than a toxic reaction, since other compounds such as cysteine have a similar exacerbating effect.[11] While some investigators obtained a "pink spot" only with the urine of schizophrenics, others failed to obtain it or obtained it also with the urine of non-schizophrenic controls. Some urines were found to contain unknown compounds other than DMPEA which also gave "pink spots", and "pink spots" from schizophrenics were shown to be of dietary origin since they disappeared when the diet was changed. The "pink spot hypothesis" became less probable when it was shown that large doses of up to 1000 mg of DMPEA were almost without effect on human volunteers.[12]

A chance observation that the urines of some schizophrenics give a mauve-coloured spot on chromatograms suggested that this might be due to another toxic compound causing a disorder which Hoffer and his collaborators called "malvaria".[13] Further investigation showed that the mauve spot is not limited to schizophrenics, but produced by urine from patients of several other types as well as from normal controls. Moreover, the compound responsible, identified later as *kryptopyrrole* is frequently absent from the urine of schizophrenics.[14] Of greater interest was another methylated compound *bufotenine* (N,N-dimethylserotonin) which is highly toxic and reported to produce EEG changes and hallucinations when administered to man. Small amounts of a bufotenine-like substance have been found in human urines, but it is not established that more is present in the urine of schizophrenics than in the urine of controls.[15]

A recent addition to the list of suggested toxic metabolites is *6-hydroxydopamine*, which can cause local damage to noradrenergic nerve terminals and which might be formed by the oxidation of dopamine, if dopamine accumulated in the tissues.[16] An early report that schizophrenics accumulate dopamine owing to a reduced activity of the enzyme dopamine-β-hydroxylase has not been supported by more recent work.[17] There have been several other suggested toxic metabolites and this subject has now been extensively reviewed elsewhere. (15) The various speculative hypotheses that have been proposed may have served a useful purpose in stimulating research, but they have not led hitherto to the discovery of any toxic compound that is accepted as specifically concerned in the causation of schizophrenia.

3. Blood Proteins

In looking for factors related to the psychosis several investigators have examined the blood plasma of schizophrenics, using various different techniques. Heath[18] reported the isolation of a protein fraction ("taraxein") which produced EEG spiking in the septal area and behavioural changes when injected into monkeys or into human volunteers; some other investigators have been unable to confirm this finding.[19] The presence of an abnormal protein causing the symptoms of schizophrenia appeared less likely when it was shown that exsanguination of schizophrenics and blood volume replacement with normal blood did not change their clinical condition. Similarly, it was reported that cross-transfusion with a schizophrenic patient did not adversely affect a non-psychotic volunteer.[19] Heath and Krupp[20] later suggested that "taraxein" interferes with certain functions of the brain by acting as a specific antibody to antigens occurring in the septal region of the limbic system. This *autoimmune hypothesis* of schizophrenia was based on evidence of the local binding of fluorescein-tagged antiglobulin to cell nuclei in slices of brain tissue of schizophrenics obtained at post mortem: but other investigators have been unable to find circulating antibodies in the sera of schizophrenics.[19]

Winter and Flataker[21] used the rope-climbing activity of rats and Frohman[22] and his collaborators used the anaerobic metabolism of chicken red blood cells in further tests for a specific serum globulin reported to be present in greater amounts in schizophrenics than in controls. This alpha-globulin from the serum of schizophrenics, which apparently takes the form of an α-helix, increases the rate of uptake of amino acids such as tryptophan when incubated with brain tissue slices. There have been many reports of abnormal concentrations of enzymes and other proteins claimed to be present in the blood of schizophrenics and also many reports of failure by other workers to confirm the original observations. The difficulty of assessing the significance of these findings is increased by the fact that the blood proteins are affected by factors such as exercise, drugs, diet and incidental infections in which hospitalized patients often differ from controls. There is therefore always the possibility that findings reported are related to physical factors rather than to the mental symptoms, and this may account for the difficulty in confirming some of the observations that have been made.

4. Genetic Predisposition

One finding that is well established is the observation that schizophrenia is a familial disorder in which the risk of illness increases with closeness of blood relationship to a schizophrenic. A long series of genetic studies culminating in the recent work on adoptive children of schizophrenic parents has shown the importance of genetic predisposing factors;[23] and since the concordance in identical (one egg) twins is well below 100 per cent, the same genetic studies have confirmed the importance of environmental factors as well. We therefore need to consider, not one, but *two* sets of causal factors, genetic and environmental, of different kinds. Since genetic information is transmitted only through biochemical mechanisms, by the synthesis of enzymes and other proteins specified by the inherited DNA, that means that one at least of the main causal factors must be biochemical in nature.

At what age and at what functional level are the genes expressed in producing the genetic predisposition for schizophrenia? Do they act at adolescence, in infancy or earlier during foetal life? Are the genetic factors operative at the molecular level of a metabolic error, in the structural organisation of the brain, or in the behavioural characteristics of the personality as a whole? Again, are there gene-linked characteristics that could serve as genetic markers in helping us to recognise those who carry the defective genes and who are therefore at risk? A number of speculative biochemical hypotheses have been proposed, but attempts to find an enzymic defect such as occurs in phenylketonuria, or any other consistent biochemical abnormality, have hitherto had little success. Reports of a low monoamine oxidase (MAO) activity in the blood platelets, and an increased urinary excretion of catecholamines[24] have suggested that schizophrenics might have a genetically determined deviation in the metabolism of transmitter compounds, but further work is needed to establish this. Initial reports of a low dopamine-β-hydroxylase activity in the brain have not been upheld. There is some evidence of a reduced incidence of allergies in schizophrenics and a reduced response to histamine[15] but it is hard to relate this to the development of a psychosis.

One characteristic of schizophrenics that could relate to a neurological disorder is the increased incidence of foetal and neonatal deaths in the offspring of schizophrenics. Sobel,[25] who studied the records of women who had delivered in state mental hospitals, first reported a high frequency of infant deaths and congenital malformations in the offspring of schizophrenic women. This has now been confirmed in a controlled prospective study.[26] An increased frequency of stillbirths and miscarriages has recently been reported also in an independent investigation of the mothers of schizophrenics.[27] These findings could be caused by the inheritance of genes for metabolic errors causing foetal damage directly. Another possibility is that they produce an inherited susceptibility to a neurotropic virus such as genital herpes, which kills some of the foetuses and leaves others with residual brain damage. The viral infection could be due to factors such as abnormal membrane permeability or the late maturation of the genes for immunoglobulins. In this connexion interest attaches to recent reports of characteristic differences in the distribution of HL-A antigenes in schizophrenia.[55]

The statement has sometimes been made that schizophrenia is a "functional" psychosis with no organic pathology. Since several earlier reports of pathological changes in the brain were disproved by later work, there has been an understandable awareness of the need for caution in accepting reports of pathological findings in schizophrenia: but most of the earlier work related to the cerebral cortex which, in the light of more recent work, is probably not the region mainly concerned. More recent studies of the brains of schizophrenics by Nieto and Escobar[28] using newer techniques have shown no abnormality in the cerebral cortex, but consistent evidence in every case of a patchy glial proliferation localised to the region of the hypothalamus, hippocampus and other mid-brain and diencephalic structures. The lesions observed would be consistent with a viral infection or anoxic damage at an earlier age. Fisman[56] has recently confirmed the presence of glial nodules "suggestive of an encephalitic process" in the brain stem region of 6 out of 7 schizophrenics, but not of other mental hospital patients or normal controls. Further confirmation in other laboratories is desirable, but in the light of this new evidence the possibility of specific organic changes in the brain in schizophrenia cannot be excluded.

The view that genes conferring the predisposition to schizophrenia operate at an early foetal or paranatal stage is supported by the observations of Mednick and his collaborators[29] who studied the development of high-risk children of schizophrenic mothers and found that early birth complications associated with low birth weight and retarded development were a good predictor of those who would have a psychiatric illness later in life. They conclude that the high-risk offspring of schizophrenic mothers are genetically vulnerable to maternal toxemia, hypoxia or other perinatal factors, but clearly other interpretations of their findings are possible. Nearly 50 per cent of the high-risk children of schizophrenic parents examined by Mednick and Schulsinger showed significant neurophysiological deviations which included poor habituation, verbal irrelevance and defective autonomic control. The characteristics found in the high-risk children are in fact similar to those found also in adult schizophrenics, which impair the normal adaptation to stressful stimuli, and which could therefore lead to breakdown under conditions of stress. Associated with the neurophysiological abnormalities are also deviations at a behavioural level. Heston[30] found a high incidence of neurotic or psychopathic personality disorders as well as mental subnormality in high-risk offspring separated from their schizophrenic mothers soon after birth. Kety and his collaborators[23] also found an increased incidence of character disorders (schizoid personality, anhedonia, etc.) besides schizophrenia in the biological families of adopted schizophrenics.

If it is taken that schizophrenics all have the same common genes for the predisposing factors, that does not preclude the existence of sub-groups in which other genetic factors of a different and less common type contribute to the stresses or other factors leading to mental breakdown. That might apply, for example, in individuals carrying the genes for Huntington's chorea or homocystinuria who develop a schizophrenic psychosis. There may well be other genetic factors of a less distinctive kind that contribute by causing unspecific cerebral dysfunction. This is suggested for example by the reported finding of a sub-group of schizophrenics characterised by androgynoid body-build and reduced excretion of androgens.[31]

The frequency of schizophrenia is estimated at about 1 per cent of the population in most countries. Since mental breakdown probably occurs in less than 50 per cent of those with the genetic predisposition, it is likely that not less than one in fifty of the normal population are at risk. In view of the relatively low fertility of schizophrenics, the high frequency of genes for predisposing factors could be maintained only if they have survival value in conferring favourable as well as unfavourable qualities. The nature of the favourable qualities carried by these genes is not yet clear. The same characteristics of low habituation and autonomic liability which predispose to breakdown under stress imply an increased sensitivity to environmental stimuli, which could be advantageous under appropriate conditions. In this connection interest also attaches to recent reports of an increased constitutional resistance in schizophrenics or their families to allergies, psychosomatic disorders, certain virus infections and to malignant disease.[32] The greater aptitude for creative activity reported by Heston[30] in the high-risk children of schizophrenic parents could also be relevant as a factor with survival value.

5. Environmental Factors

Environmental factors operate to induce a psychosis in a considerable proportion of the "high-risk" population who are genetically predisposed to schizophrenia. In Pollin and Stabenau's[33] studies of identical (one-egg) twins with the same genetic predisposition the nature of some relevant environmental factors is indicated by the observation that the twin who developed schizophrenia was generally lighter in weight at birth, had more birth complications (including anoxia), more CNS illness as a child, and was weaker, smaller and later in developing than the normal twin. It is evident that the pre-schizophrenic twin was more vulnerable to environmental stresses and that the greater vulnerability was present early in life. During childhood the pre-schizophrenic twin was characteristically more neurotic, more sensitive, submissive, obedient, dependent and well-behaved.

Of the factors leading finally to mental breakdown stressful family relations may be expected to play a part. One possible clue to the kind of stresses that may trigger the development of a schizophrenic psychosis is the observation that the curve relating breakdown to age shows a peak at about the age of 20. This is an age when sexual arousal tends to be maximal, and not infrequently a schizophrenic breakdown has been found to coincide with the pain and frustration of an unhappy love affair. The associated endocrine changes could well be relevant in view of the mechanisms for the specific binding of steroid hormones by cells of the hypothalamus, septum, amygdala and hippocampus. The binding of steroid hormones is followed by altered firing patterns and habituation properties.[6] There is evidence that steroid hormones influence the organisation of neuronal circuits by affecting the activity of rate-limiting enzymes required for the synthesis of monoamine transmitters.[34] It would therefore be helpful to have further information about the endocrine changes associated with the onset of a schizophrenic psychosis.

Besides psychological stresses, physical factors must also play a part. Thus there are cases in which a schizophrenic psychosis has followed an attack of encephalitis, and some schizophrenics have been found to have a raised CSF protein content attributable to a subacute virus infection.[35] One indication of the nature of the environmental factors is the observation, now confirmed in several investigations, that in European countries there is a significant excess of births of schizophrenics in the first three months of the year.[36] It has been suggested that a seasonal dietary deficiency leading to haemorrhagic disease of the newborn might be responsible for this finding, but it would appear that a perinatal virus infection could also be the factor concerned, since a number of virus infections such as genital herpes show a seasonal variation, with a higher morbidity rate in the first few months of the year. Several workers have reported the presence of virus antibodies in the blood and CSF of some schizophrenics, and neurological symptoms not attributable to drug therapy, such as abnormalities of eye movement, head position and rigidity are not uncommon in chronic schizophrenics.[36,37] In view of these findings the existence in some populations of a subgroup of encephalitis-induced schizophrenia is a possibility that must be seriously considered.

The belief that dietary factors can play a part in the causation of schizophrenia comes mainly from reports of schizophrenics with an allergic reaction to specific food proteins such as those in wheat flour, eggs or milk, who improve when these items are removed from their diet. Dohan *et al.*[38] reported that the substitution of a gluten-free diet for the normal hospital diet reduced the time that schizophrenics remained in hospital, but the difference disappeared when gluten was secretly added to the gluten-free diet. It would appear that a severe allergic reaction can add to the stresses affecting the mental state of schizophrenics who are sensitive to certain foods: but the incidence of allergies in schizophrenics has been found to be relatively low.[39] It is well established that a diet low in nicotinic acid can cause the schizophrenia-like psychoses of pellagra, and in patients with malabsorption the requirement of nicotinic acid is increased; but there is little evidence that the majority of schizophrenics derive any benefit from treatment with large "mega-vitamin" doses of nicotinic acid or nicotinamide, which a number of investigators have found to have no more than a placebo effect.[15]

While environmental factors must operate in every case, that does not mean that they are always of the same kind or that environmental and genetic factors are equally important in every case. It is reasonable to believe that in some cases the environment and in others the genetic factors are of primary importance.

6. The Focus of Disturbance in Schizophrenia

The symptomatic psychoses which develop as a result of brain injury or in organic disease take many different forms. In cerebrovascular disease, multiple sclerosis and in brain injuries as a whole, the proportion who develop a schizophrenia-like psychoses is no greater than chance: but in certain other conditions the incidence is relatively high. That is true for example in Huntington's chorea, narcolepsy, Wilson's disease (hepatolenticular degeneration), temporal lobe epilepsy, carbon monoxide poisoning and tumours of the temporal lobe, in which the frequency of schizophrenia-like psychoses is many times higher than the chance expectation.[40] These conditions have a wide range of different pathologies, with lesions extending into many different areas of the brain, but there is a common factor in the focal involvement of upper brain-stem and diencephalic structures, which are known to be involved in all of these conditions. The association of schizophrenia-like psychoses with temporal lobe epilepsy has led some investigators to conclude that the temporal lobes are specially involved, but Feindel and Penfield[41] found that the automatism characteristic of temporal lobe epilepsy occurs only when the discharge extends centrally into upper brain-stem structures. The lack of memory impairment in schizophrenia suggests again that the temporal lobes are not necessarily involved. A computer analysis by Davison and Bagley[40] of the symptoms in 80 cases with mainly localised cerebral lesions showed strong associations between (a) diencephalic lesions and auditory hallucinations, and between (b) brain-stem lesions and thought disorder, including Schneider's symptoms of the first rank. From this evidence it would appear that the symptoms of schizophrenia can be related mainly to a disturbance focused on brain-stem and diencephalic areas of the brain.

The well-known psychotomimetic effects of drugs such as mescaline and psilocybin have suggested that by studying their pharmacological actions it might be possible to reveal the mechanisms operative in schizophrenia. However, the hallucinations, usually visual, produced by mescaline for example are different from the self-referred auditory hallucinations ("audible thoughts") most characteristic of schizophrenia. Levodopa produces a psychotic reaction in some individuals, but no drug is known which will reproduce directly Schneider's first-rank symptoms. In a different category are the amphetamines, which produce central arousal and, if administration is continued over a period, may lead to the development of a schizophrenia-like psychosis. It is known from animal experiments that the central excitant action of amphetamine is exerted especially at the brain-stem level through activation of the ascending reticular formation. It is known also that amphetamine is a MAO inhibitor which potentiates the action of the catecholamines and releases noradrenaline from adrenergic nerve fibres. There are therefore grounds, as Kety and others have pointed out,[42] for relating the schizophrenia-like amphetamine psychosis to a disturbance affecting the noradrenaline and dopamine-containing brain-stem system of Dalström and Fuxe,[43] which is closely concerned in the mechanism of arousal, habituation and the control of affective reactions.

Independent evidence has come from studies of the pharmacological action of drugs such as the phenothiazines which alleviate the symptoms of schizophrenia. Bradley and his associates[44] showed that chlorpromazine depresses the activity of the brain-stem reticular system by blocking the sensory input. It acts specifically on the neurons that respond to catecholamines, and both chlorpromazine and the butyrophenones act preferentially in blocking the dopaminergic transmission.[45,6] Four independent lines of investigation therefore point to a focus of disturbance in schizophrenia in a relatively small subcortical region of the brain:

    (a) The leading symptoms in schizophrenia are referable to brain-stem and diencephalic mechanisms.

    (b) In the symptomatic schizophrenias first-rank symptoms are associated with brain-stem lesions.

    (c) Amphetamines, which can cause schizophrenia-like psychoses, act especially on dopaminergic brain-stem receptors.

(d) Drugs which alleviate the symptoms of schizophrenia are blockers of dopaminergic brain-stem mechanisms.

It would appear that the symptoms of schizophrenia, which vary considerably in different patients, are consistent with a focal disturbance in the brain-stem and diencephalic region, which affects to a variable extent the functions of the amygdala, hippocampus, nucleus accumbens, hypothalamus and limbic system, and therefore ultimately the functions of the brain as a whole.

7. Central Transmitter Mechanisms in Schizophrenia

Recent developments in neurochemistry have increased our understanding of the mechanisms concerned in the synthesis, storage, release, reuptake and inactivation of a number of known and putative transmitters which are present in the brain. New histochemical techniques have helped us to determine their localisation and so to elucidate the mode of action of a variety of stimulant and inhibitory drugs. There is general agreement that the phenothiazines and butyrophenones, which relieve the symptoms of schizophrenia, block dopaminergic transmission, and hence the *"dopamine hypothesis"* which postulates that schizophrenics have too much dopamine liberated at the central synapses. This could occur as a generalised "inborn error" of metabolism or it could be limited to certain pathways such as those of the mesolimbic system. Dopamine, which is formed in the tissues by the decarboxylation of dihydroxyphenulalanine (DOPA), is normally oxidised in the side-chain to form noradrenaline, a reaction catalysed by the enzyme dopamine-β-hydroxylase. An accumulation of dopamine could therefore be caused if schizophrenics had a deficiency of the enzyme dopamine-β-hydroxylase in the brain, as proposed by Stein and Wise.[16] Another possibility is that there might be a defect in the adaptive regulation of the dopamine system, and therefore a relative under-activity of inhibitory cholinergic or GABA-liberating neurons. (46) Clearly the activity of the dopaminergic system of the brain-stem is determined, not by the level of dopamine alone, but by a balance in which other transmitters and metabolites including cations, peptides, prostaglandins and steroid hormones are also involved.

The post-synaptic receptor for dopamine in neurons in the brain is believed to be a specific dopamine-sensitive adenylate cyclase[47] which synthesizes cyclic adenosine monophosphate (cAMP). Another specific adenylate cyclase sensitive to noradrenaline is apparently the receptor for β-adrenergic transmission. In both cases the actions of the transmitters in the brain are mediated by cyclic AMP. The antipsychotic drugs block dopaminergic transmission either by inhibiting the dopamine-sensitive adenylate cyclase or by blocking the presynaptic stimulation-evoked release of dopamine.[48] It is not unreasonable to regard the mesolimbic dopaminergic system as probably the main target for the antipsychotic drugs, but we cannot yet be sure which of their several different actions are relevant for their therapeutic effect. Thus the phenothiazines raise the level of prolactin in the plasma by inhibiting the release of hypothalamic prolactin-inhibitory factor (PIF), and this has been regarded by some investigators as possibly their main antipsychotic action in schizophrenia.[49]

That chlorpromazine and the butyrophenones, which relieve the symptoms of schizophrenia, act by blocking dopamine receptors, was suggested originally by their extra-pyramidal side-effects; but with thioridazine, which is equally effective in treating schizophrenia, the extra-pyramidal side-effects are relatively slight. This apparent discrepancy has now been resolved by the demonstration that, besides blocking dopaminergic transmission, thioridazine also blocks the muscarinic acetylcholine receptors of the corpus striatum, so that it reduces the extra-pyramidal side-effects as well.[47,48] While the "dopamine hypothesis" offers an explanation for a number of facts relating to the symptoms of schizophrenia, it does not easily explain why some schizophrenics do not respond to treatment with phenothiazines or other dopamine blocking agents. The evidence that such patients may respond satisfactorily to treatment with propranolol,[50] which is a β-noradrenaline blocking agent, suggests that in some cases factors other than a raised dopamine level must also be considered. Again, the "dopamine hypothesis" leaves unanswered the question of how an abnormally high dopaminergic activity can persist for months and years in an organ with the adaptability and plasticity of the mammalian brain. A more likely occurrence might be an imbalance due to a defect in an antagonistic inhibitory system, such as the GABA deficiency which Roberts proposed.[46] Another difficulty for the dopamine hypothesis is the observation that the blocking effect of the phenothiazines on dopaminergic transmission operates quickly, within a day or two after administration, whereas their anti-psychotic action continues to increase for 2 or 3 weeks. It would therefore appear that their anti-psychotic effect may depend on processes of adaptation or something more than the simple blocking of dopaminergic transmission.

8. Periodic Catatonia

Some 30 per cent of schizophrenics have recurrent exacerbations of their symptoms or show other evidence of periodicity, and this may be attributed to the involvement of neuronal mechanisms in subcortical centres concerned in the regulation of biological rhythms. In periodic catatonia, which accounts for about 2 per cent of cases of schizophrenia, the periodicity is particularly marked and there is a regular alternation of *lucid phases* in which the patient may appear normal, with *psychotic phases* characterised by catatonic excitement, stupor or other symptoms of schizophrenia.

In a series of investigations extending over many years Rolf Gjessing[51] established that the periodic swings in mental state are associated with regular concurrent changes in autonomic activity, metabolic rate and nitrogen balance. Different patients vary to some extent in the time relations of the changes, but during the lucid phase there is generally a retention of nitrogen, which reaches a maximum near the start of the psychotic phase. The excess of nitrogen is then excreted in the urine, mainly as urea. In some cases as much as 30 g of nitrogen are retained and, since there is no equivalent increase in the blood proteins or non-protein nitrogen, it appears that the nitrogen must be stored mainly as proteins in the tissues. Most patients respond to treatment with thyroxin, which relieves the nitrogen retention and induces at the same time a lucid phase that persists indefinitely if sufficient thyroid is given to keep the basal metabolic rate raised by about 10-15 per cent. The patients may then become completely normal in mentality and behaviour. Gjessing's work was important both in establishing for the first time a form of schizophrenia definitely associated with a metabolic disorder and in finding an effective treatment. It was of value also in showing the merit of the longitudinal type of clinical investigation in which individual patients are studied over a long period of time, so that observations made during a psychosis can be controlled by similar observations made during periods of remission.

The investigation of periodic catatonia has now been taken further by a number of workers including Leif Gjessing,[52] who has defined more closely the characteristics of the psychotic phase. During the period of mental disturbance an increase in pulse rate, blood pressure, basal metabolic rate and body temperature is associated with an increased alpha frequency in the EEG and a severe disturbance of sleep with a marked reduction in REM time. This is accompanied by a rise in the fasting blood levels of glucose and free fatty acids, while there is a shift in the distribution of electrolytes and a large increase in the excretion in the urine of catecholamines and their metabolites including noradrenaline and dopamine. From this evidence it appears that the change from the lucid to the psychotic phase is associated with a swing from parasympathetic to increased sympathetic tonus, or from cholinergic to adrenergic activity of the autonomic nervous system. The periodicity has been attributed to a hypothetical "noxious peptide" which accumulates during the lucid phase and finally stimulates central adrenergic receptors in the brain-stem, leading to the release of thyroid hormone.[52] Treatment with thyroxin would then prevent the accumulation of the peptide and so avert the onset of the psychotic phase.

Antipsychotic drugs such as chlorpromazine, haloperidol or reserpine are effective in suppressing or abolishing most of the psychotic symptoms, but they do not generally bring about a complete recovery, and the patient may remain in a chronic state of partial disability, lacking in initiative and drive. Attempts to treat by electroshock or by leucotomy, psychotherapy or psychoanalysis were found to be ineffective. The observation that in some cases the psychotic symptoms can be suppressed by α-methyl-dopa (which inhibits the dopa decarboxylase) or by disulfiram (which inhibits the dopamine-β-hydroxylase), as well as by drugs which block dopaminergic transmission, supports the view that the symptoms depend on the balance of centrally acting catecholamine transmitters. Rolf Gjessing believed the accumulation of proteins in the body to be due to a defect in the proteolytic enzyme system in the hypothalamus. In this connexion interest attaches to the recent demonstration in the brain of specific peptide hydrolases which effect the breakdown of polypeptide hormones formed in the hypothalamus, including TRH, which stimulates the release of thyrotropin and prolactin from the pituitary.[53] It has been shown that TRH potentiates the behavioural effects of L-DOPA in mice and it is reported to cause a deterioration of the mental state when administered to schizophrenic patients.[54]

The relevance of the work on periodic catatonia to other forms of schizophrenia is not yet clear. Periodic exacerbation of the symptoms is not uncommon in schizophrenia and several investigators have reported an association between schizophrenia and thyroid disease in the families of schizophrenics.[33] It is therefore possible that in some forms of schizophrenia other than periodic catatonia a similar disturbance of metabolism in the hypothalamus, associated with a disturbance of thyroid function, is concerned, but that can be no more than a speculation until further evidence has been obtained.

The evidence at present available is consistent with the view that the symptoms of schizophrenia are due to local disorganisation of the transmitter mechanisms at points extending to a variable extent through certain diencephalic and brain-stem areas concerned with arousal, habituation, biological rhythms, reward, affect and autonomic control. Generally there is evidence of a relative increase in the activity of the mesolimbic dopamine system, which can be relieved by treatment with drugs that block dopaminergic transmission. It is known that the central disturbance is caused by an interaction of genetic and environmental factors which may not be the same in every case, and it appears likely that there are sub-groups of schizophrenia in which different factors are mainly responsible. Research has yielded a number of clues and hypotheses that can be tested. Further work is needed to identify the genetic and environmental factors mainly concerned and to show how their interaction can be prevented.

References

1. SCHNEIDER, K. *Clinical Psychopathology.* Grune & Stratton, London, 1959.
2. PFISTER, H.O. The responses of schizophrenics to stimuli. *Amer. J. Psychiat.* Suppl. 109, **4**, 94-99, 1938.
3. SHAKOW, D. Some observations on the psychology (and some fewer on the biology) of schizophrenia. *J. Nerv. Ment. Dis.* **153**, 300-316, 1971.
4. GRUZELIER, J. and VENABLES, P. Bimodality and lateral asymmetry of skin conductance orienting activity in schizophrenics. *Biological Psychiatry,* **8**, 55-73, 1973.
5. RADO, S. Hedonic self-regulation of the organism. In *The Role of Pleasure in Behaviour.* Heath, R.D. (ed.), p. 257. Hoeber, New York, 1964.
6. STEVENS, J.R. An anatomy of schizophrenia? *Arch. gen Psychiat.* **29**, 177-194, 1973.
7. RICHTER, D. The biological investigation of schizophrenia. *Biological Psychiatry,* **2**, 153-164, 1970.
8. HOFFER, A., OSMOND, H. and SMYTHIES, J. Schizophrenia: new approach: result of year's research. *J. Ment. Sci.* **100**, 29-45, 1954.
9. FRIEDHOFF, A.J. and VAN WINKLE, E. Conversion of dopamine to 3,4-dimethoxyphenylacetic acid in schizophrenic patients. *Nature,* **199**, 1271-1272, 1963.
10. POLLIN, W., CARDON, P.V. and KETY, S.S. Effects of amino acid feedings in schizophrenic patients treated with iproniazid. *Science,* **133**, 104-105, 1961.
11. SPAIDE, J., TANIMUKAI, H., GINTHER, R., BUENO, J. and HIMWICH, H.E. Schizophrenic behaviour and urinary tryptophan metabolites associated with cysteine. *Life Sciences,* **6**, 551-560, 1967.
12. BROWN, W.T., McGEER, P.L. and MOSER, I. Lack of psychotomimetic effect of para-methoxyphenylethylamine and 3,4-dimethoxyphenylethylamine in man. *Canadian Psychiatric Association Journal,* **13**, 91-92, 1968.
13. HOFFER, A. and OSMOND, H. Malvaria: A new psychiatric disease. *Acta Psychiat. Scand.* **39**, 335-366, 1963.
14. JACOBSON, S.J., RAPOPORT, H. and ELLMAN, G.L. The nonoccurrence of hemo- and kryptopyrrole in urine of schizophrenics. *Biological Psychiatry,* **10**, 91-94, 1975.
15. WYATT, R.J., TERMINI, B.A. and DAVIS, J. Biochemical and sleep studies of schizophrenia. *Schizophrenia Bulletin,* **4**, 11-16, 1971.
16. STEIN, L. and WISE, C.D. Possible etiology of schizophrenia. *Science,* **171**, 1032, 1971.
17. WYATT, R.J., SCHWARTZ, M.A., ERDELYI, E. and BARCHAS, J.D. Dopamine-Hydroxylase Activity in Brains of Chronic Schizophrenic Patients. *Science,* **187**, 368-370, 1975.
18. HEATH, R.G. Schizophrenia: Biochemical and physiologic aberrations. *Internat. J. Neuropsychiatry,* **2**, 597-610, 1966.
19. BOCK, E. and RAFAELSON, O.J. Schizophrenia. Proteins in blood and cerebrospinal fluid. *Danish Medical Bulletin,* **21**, 93-105, 1974.
20. HEATH, R.G. and KRUPP. Schizophrenia as an immunologic disorder. *Arch. gen. Psychiat.* **16**, 1-19, 1967.
21. WINTER, C.A. and FLATAKER, L. *Arch. Neurol. Psychiat.* **80**, 441-449, 1958.
22. FROHMAN, C.E., LATHAM, L.K., BECKETT, P.G.S. and GOTTLIEB, J.S. Evidence of a plasma factor in schizophrenia. *Arch. gen. Psychiat.* **2**, 255-262, 1960.
23. KETY, S.S., ROSENTHAL, D., WENDER, P.H. and SCHULSINGER, F. The types and prevalence of mental illness in the biological and adoptive families of adopted schizophrenics. In *The Transmission of Schizophrenia.* Rosenthal, D. and Kety, S.S. (eds.), pp. 345-362. Pergamon Press, Oxford, 1968.
24. POLLIN, W. A possible genetic factor related to psychosis. *Amer. J. Psychiat.* **128**, 311-317, 1971.
25. SOBEL, D.E. Infant mortality and malformations in children of schizophrenic women. *Psychiatr. Q.* **35**, 60-64, 1961.
26. RIEDER, R.O., ROSENTHAL, D., WENDER, P. and BLUMENTAL, H. The offspring of schizophrenics. *Arch. gen. Psychiat.* **32**, 200-213, 1975.
27. MACSWEENEY, D.A., JOHNSON, A.L. and TIMMS, P.E.S. The families of schizophrenics. In the press.

28. NIETO, D. and ESCOBAR, A. Major psychoses. In *Pathology of the Nervous System, Vol. III*. Minckler, J. (ed.), pp. 2654-2670. McGraw-Hill, Inc., New York, 1972.
29. MEDNICK, S.A., MURA, E., SCHULSINGER, F. and MEDNICK, B. Perinatal conditions and infant development in children with schizophrenic parents. *Social Biology*, 18 supplement. S103-S113, 1971.
30. HESTON, L.L. Psychiatric disorders in foster home reared children of schizophrenic mothers. *Brit. J. Psychiat.* 112, 819-825, 1966.
31. BROOKSBANK, B.W.L., MACSWEENEY, D.A., JOHNSON, A.L., CUNNINGHAM, A.E., WILSON, D.A. and COPPEN, A. Androgen excretion and physique in schizophrenia. *Brit. J. Psychiat.* 117, 413-420, 1970.
32. CARTER, M. and WATTS, C.A.H. Possible biological advantages among schizophrenics' relatives. *Brit. J. Psychiat.* 118, 453-460, 1971.
33. POLLIN, W. and STABENAU, J.R. Biological psychological and historical differences in a series of monozygotic twins discordant for schizophrenia. In *The Transmission of Schizophrenia*. Rosenthal, D. and Kety, S.S. (eds.). pp. 317-332. Pergamon Press, Oxford, 1968.
34. BALÁZS, R. Hormonal influences in brain development. In *Biochemistry and Mental Illness*, Iversen, L.L. and Rose, S. (eds.). pp. 39-57. *Biochem. Soc. Spec. Publ.* 1, 1973.
35. HUNTER, R., JONES, M. and MALLESON, A. Abnormal CSF total protein and gamma-globulin levels in 256 patients admitted to a psychiatric unit. *J. Neurol. Sci.* 9, 11-38, 1969.
36. HARE, E.H. Manic Depressive Psychosis and Season of Birth. *Acta psychiat. Scand.* 52, 69-79, 1975.
37. HALONEN, P.E., RIMON, R., AROHONKA, K. and JÄNTTI, V. Antibody levels to herpes simplex Type 1, measles and rubella viruses in psychiatric patients. *Brit. J. Psychiat.* 125, 461-465, 1974.
38. DOHAN, F.C., GRASBERGER, J.C., LOWELL, F.M., JOHNSTONE, H.T. and ABERGAST, A.W. The effect of wheat gluten on the detention of psychiatric patients in hospital. *Brit. J. Psychiat.* 115, 595-596, 1969.
39. CASSELL, W.A. and FISHER, S. Body-image boundaries and histamine flare reaction. *Psychosomatic Medicine*, 25, 344-350, 1963.
40. DAVISON, K. and BAGLEY, C.R. Schizophrenia-like psychoses associated with organic disorders of the CNS. In *Current Problems in Neuropsychiatry*. Herrington, R.N. (ed.), pp. 113-184. *Brit. J. Psychiat. Special Publication No. 4*. Headley Bros., Ashford, 1969.
41. FEINDEL, W. and PENFIELD, W. Localisation of discharge in temporal lobe automatism. *A.M.A. Arch. Neurol. Psychiat.* 75, 400-409, 1954.
42. KETY, S.S. Commentary on observations of Shakow. *J. Nerv. Ment. Dis.* 153, 323-326, 1971.
43. DALSTRÖM, A. and FUXE, K. Evidence for the existence of monoamine containing neurons in the CNS. *Acta Physiol. Scand.* 62, (Suppl. 232), 1-31, 1964.
44. BRADLEY, P.B. The effect of drugs on the electrical activity of the brain. In *Recent Advances in Pharmacology*. Robson, J.M. and Stacey, R.S. (eds.), pp. 311-348. Churchill, London, 1968.
45. SNYDER, S.H. Catecholamines in the brain as mediators of amphetamine psychosis. *Arch. gen. Psychiat.* 27, 169-181. 1972.
46. ROBERTS, E. An hypothesis suggesting that there is a defect in the GABA system in schizophrenia. In *Prospects for Research in Schizophrenia*, Kety, S.S. and Matthysse, S. (eds.) Neurosciences Res. Prog. Bull. 10, No. 4, 468-482, 1972.
47. SNYDER, S.H., BANERJEE, S.P., YAMAMURA, H.I. and GREENBERG, D. Drugs, Neurotransmitters and Schizophrenia. *Science*, 184, 1243-1253, 1974.
48. SEEMAN, P. and LEE, T. Antipsychotic drugs: Direct correlation between Clinical Potency and Presynaptic Action on Dopamine Neurons. *Science*, 188, 1217-1219, 1975.
49. LOVETT DOUST, J.W. Psychotropic drugs and gender as modifiers of the role of plasma tryptophan and serotonin in schizophrenia. *Compr. Psychiatry*, 16, 349-355, 1975.
50. YORKSTON, N.J., ZAKI, S.A., MALIK, M.K.U., MORRISON, R.C. and HAVARD, C.W.H. Propranolol in the treatment of schizophrenic symptoms. *Brit. med. J.* 4, 633-635, 1974.
51. GJESSING, R. Disturbances of somatic functions in catatonia with a periodic course and their compensation. *J. mental Sci.* 84, 608-619, 1938.
52. GJESSING, L.R. A review of periodic catatonia. *Biological Psychiatry*, 8, 23-45, 1974.
53. MARKS, N. and STERN, F. Novel enzymes involved in the inactivation of hypothalamo-hypophyseal hormones. In *Psychoneuro-endocrinology*. Hatotani, N. (ed.), pp. 276-284, Karger, Basel, 1974.
54. DAVIS, K.L., HOLLISTER, L.E. and BERGER, A. Thyrotropin-releasing hormone in schizophrenia. *Am. J. Psychiat.* 132, 951-953, 1975.
55. CAZZULLO, C.L., SMERALDI, E. and PENATI, G. The leucocyte antigenic system HL-A as a possible genetic marker of schizophrenia. *Brit. J. Psychiat.* 125, 25-27, 1974.
56. FISMAN, M. The brain stem in psychosis. *Brit. J. Psychiat.* 126, 414-422, 1975.

Pharmacological Approaches

Introductory Remarks

G. BARTHOLINI

It is my task to focus on the main problems which will be dealt with in this section, for those of us who are less familiar with the topic. I have therefore chosen five basic questions. Let me follow a scheme which takes into consideration the chronological development of our knowledge concerning the involvement of dopamine in schizophrenia and the consequent therapeutic approach.

The story began in 1958 when Carlsson and Bertler discovered in the striatum a high content of dopamine which they postulated to be involved in the control of extrapyramidal motor activity and muscle tone. At about the same time, the antipsychotic properties of neuroleptic drugs were confirmed beyond doubt and the work of Carlsson and of Andén showed that these compounds impair dopaminergic transmission. Thus, the idea was put forward that schizophrenia may be connected with an exaggerated dopaminergic activity. Since then, several pieces of evidence have accumulated supporting this idea. Dr. Carlsson's main task will therefore be to discuss the two following questions:

Is dopamine involved in the pathogenesis of schizophrenia?

and

Does the blockade of dopaminergic transmission mediate the antipsychotic action of neuroleptic drugs, or is it just an epiphenomenon?

If enough evidence is provided for the involvement of dopamine in schizophrenia, the next problem to be discussed is which dopamine pathway in the central nervous system may be connected with the psychosis. Actually, during the early stages of the development of the dopamine theory, the idea was widely held that the blockade of dopaminergic transmission in the *extrapyramidal* system is essential for relieving schizophrenia. This was based on the fact that no neuroleptic agent was known which was devoid of dopamine receptor blocking properties in this system. However, it soon appeared clear that neuroleptic drugs also act on another dopamine pathway in the brain, namely the mesolimbic dopamine system described by Fuxe and his collaborators. Concomitantly, increasing evidence was provided for the involvement of the limbic system in altered behaviour. Thus, we may ask:

Are the changes of striatal activity connected with the therapeutic action of neuroleptic drugs and/or with their extrapyramidal effects?

and

Is the limbic system the anatomical substrate of the antipsychotic action of neuroleptic drugs?

I am sure that Dr. Pletscher will try to answer these questions which have become particularly pertinent since the birth of a new generation of neuroleptic drugs which are claimed to be at least partially devoid of extrapyramidal side effects and which may act preferentially on an extrastriatal dopamine system.

The last question,

Is the blockade of dopamine receptors the only mechanism which can be considered to-day for relieving schizophrenia?

refers to a very recent trend in our research concerning the possible amelioration of the psychotic symptoms by changes in GABA-ergic activity in the central nervous system. This also probably results in an impairment of dopaminergic transmission which, however, for several reasons, may open new perspectives in the therapy of schizophrenia.

Finally, problems such as diagnostic criteria, choices of treatment and nosological questions concerning acute schizophrenic episodes will be pointed out by Dr. Cazzullo. Dr. Munkvad will underline the many problems arising from long-term treatment with neuroleptic drugs. We should keep in mind that these compounds do not cure schizophrenia and they may cause several troubles during chronic administration, such as tardive dyskinesias and endocrinological side-effects.

The Impact of Pharmacology on
the Problem of Schizophrenia

A. CARLSSON

Introduction

Drug research can contribute to disclosing the nature of the schizophrenic disturbance by investigating the mode of action of drugs affecting schizophrenic symptomatology. A sound basis for this approach is afforded by the fact that drugs specifically influencing schizophrenic symptoms in either direction are available: while some drugs — the antipsychotic or neuroleptic agents — specifically alleviate, others — the amphetamines — produce or aggravate schizophrenic symptoms. Considerable knowledge of the mode of action of these drugs has accumulated during the last two decades. These agents have been shown to exert specific actions on neurohumoral transmission mechanisms in the brain. There is good evidence that the catecholamines are the transmitters primarily involved and among these dopamine has attracted particular interest.

This research goes back to 1955, when Drs. Brodie, Shore and their colleagues (Shore *et al.*, 1955) discovered the ability of reserpine to deplete body tissues, including brain, of their 5-hydroxytryptamine (5-HT) stores. This was shortly after the discovery of the remarkable therapeutic effect of chlorpromazine and reserpine in psychotic conditions such as schizophrenia. Drs. Brodie and Shore suggested that the antipsychotic action of reserpine was due to continuous release of 5-HT onto receptors.

I had the privilege to work with Drs. Brodie and Shore on these problems during a most profitable stay in their laboratory in 1955-1956. After returning to Sweden I observed together with the late Dr. N.-Å. Hillarp, that the catecholamines are also released by reserpine (Carlsson and Hillarp, 1956). The depletion of the adrenergic transmitter noradrenaline, resulted in failure of adrenergic transmission (Carlsson *et al.*, 1957a).

Discovery of Dopamine, an Endogenous Agonist in the Brain

The failure of adrenergic transmission suggested to us that deficiency of amines was the most likely explanation of the pharmacological actions of reserpine. To test this hypothesis we gave the catecholamine precursor dopa to reserpine-treated animals and discovered the central activity of this amino acid, presumably mediated via its decarboxylation products (Carlsson *et al.*, 1957b). The dramatic reversal of the reserpine syndrome by dopa supported our deficiency theory and the simultaneously observed inefficiency of 5-hydroxytryptophan directed our attention to the catecholamines.

At this time the primary decarboxylation product of dopa, i.e. dopamine, had not yet been detected with certainty in the brain, owing to lack of a specific and sensitive method for assaying this compound. We developed such a method and found that dopamine is stored by a reserpine-sensitive mechanism in the brain in even greater amounts than noradrenaline, suggesting that it is an agonist in its own right and not just an intermediate in the biosynthesis of noradrenaline and adrenaline (Carlsson *et al.*, 1958). In support of this, the distribution of dopamine was found to differ greatly from that of noradrenaline, the largest amounts being found in the basal ganglia rather than the brain stem, where noradrenaline occurs in the highest concentration (Bertler and Rosengren, 1959).

Brain Monoamines: Neurohumoral Transmitters

The actions of reserpine and dopa, as well as the regional distribution data, suggested to us that the catecholamines are important agonists in the brain and that they are involved in the control of extrapyramidal motor functions (especially dopamine) as well as in higher integrative functions such as wakefulness (Carlsson, 1959; Carlsson *et al.*, 1960). However, many investigators expressed doubts at this time (around 1960), especially in the case of dopamine which was known by pharmacologists only as a poor adrenergic agonist. The scepticism was partly dissipated by Hornykiewicz' discovery of reduced dopamine levels in the brains of Parkinsonian patients (Ehringer and Hornykiewicz, 1960), and by the subsequent demonstration of the therapeutic properties of L-dopa (Birkmayer and Hornykiewicz, 1961). Probably more instrumental in this respect was the accumulation of evidence demonstrating the role of the brain monoamines as neurohumoral transmitters. Particularly strong support came from the demonstration, by means of fluorescence histochemistry, of the neuronal localisation of the brain monoamines (Carlsson *et al.*, 1962) and the subsequent mapping out of the monoamine-carrying neuronal pathways (Andén *et al.*, 1964; Dahlström and Fuxe, 1964, 1965; Fuxe and Andén, 1966). But also electron-microscopical, biochemical and physiological techniques contributed to make a strong case for the brain monoamines as neurohumoral transmitters: it was established that the monoamines (dopamine, noradrenaline and 5-hydroxytryptamine) are formed in nerve terminals and stored in synaptic vesicles; they are released by nerve stimulation; after release they cause physiological effects; efficient inactivation mechanisms to terminate their action exist; transmitter turnover is markedly dependent on the nerve impulses (for review, see Andén *et al.*, 1969).

Receptor-Blocking Antipsychotic Agents

I should like to come back now to the mode of action of the antipsychotic drugs. In the case of reserpine we were rather satisfied with the evidence. Reserpine appears to act by causing transmission failure in monoaminergic nerves, and this is due to depletion of transmitter, which can no more be concentrated in the synaptic vesicles (or storage granules) because of blockade of a specific uptake mechanism in these organelles (Carlsson, 1965). In fact, more recent studies, utilizing the principle of selective protection of individual transmitter stores, have confirmed our original suggestions and clearly demonstrated the dominating role of the catecholamines, notably dopamine, for the characteristic syndrome induced by reserpine, even though 5-HT appears to contribute (Carlsson, 1974a).

But we were puzzled by the virtual absence of an effect on monoamine levels exerted by some clinically important groups of antipsychotic agents, i.e. the phenothiazines, the thiaxanthenes, the butyrophenones, etc. As is well known, these drugs are remarkably similar to reserpine with respect to the whole spectrum of psychiatric, extrapyramidal, and endocrinological actions, and yet they must have an entirely different mode of action at the molecular level.

In 1963 Margit Lindqvist and I found that small doses of chlorpromazine and haloperidol specifically stimulated the metabolism of dopamine and noradrenaline in brain, and since this took place without any decrease in catecholamine levels we inferred that also the synthesis of the catecholamines was stimulated by these agents (Carlsson and Lindqvist, 1963). It was known at this time that the central effects of catecholamines (from administered dopa) could be antagonized by these agents, and thus we proposed the following mechanism to account for the observations made. The antipsychotic phenothiazines and butyrophenones act by blocking central dopamine and noradrenaline receptors. This blockade activates a negative feedback mechanism which leads to an increased physiological activity of catecholamine neurons, with an increased release, metabolism, and synthesis of the transmitter.

This concept of receptor-mediated feedback control of neuronal activity, represented in

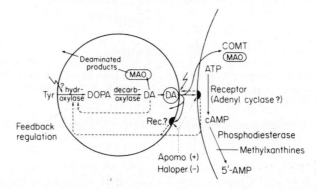

Fig. 1. Schematic illustration of some regulatory mechanisms controlling the activity of a dopaminergic neuron.

A dopaminergic nerve terminal is depicted to the left and the postsynaptic neuron to the right.

The nerve impulse causes release of dopamine (DA) from a synaptic vesicle in close contact with the nerve terminal membrane. After release into the synaptic cleft DA activates postsynaptic receptors resulting in activation of adenylcyclase and increased formation of cyclic AMP. Activation of dopaminergic receptors stimulates a feedback mechanism which results in inhibition of the dopaminergic neuron. The feedback mechanism appears to operate in part via a neuronal loop controlling impulse generation of dopaminergic cell bodies. However, in addition, a local feedback mechanism appears to exist, possibly operating via presynaptic, so-called autoreceptors. The local mechanism has a complex action on the dopaminergic nerve terminal: it controls the activity of tyrosine hydroxylase and the amount of transmitter released per nerve impulse.

Apomo = apomorphine, a dopaminergic receptor agonist capable of penetrating through the blood-brain barrier.

Haloper. = haloperidol, a dopaminergic receptor antagonist.

diagrammatic form in Fig. 1, has been amply confirmed and extended by numerous investigators, using biochemical as well as neurophysiological techniques (Andén *et al.*, 1969; Aghajanian and Bunney, 1974; see Fig. 2). Also in man, antipsychotic agents have been found to stimulate central catecholamine metabolism (Sedvall *et al.*, 1974). Moreover, the hypothesis that phenothiazines and butyrophenones act by blocking catecholamine receptors has received support through the work of Greengard and his colleagues (Greengard, 1974), who have demonstrated what appears to be dopaminergic receptor responsiveness of a cell-free adenylate cyclase system, obtained from striatal tissue. This system can be activated by dopamine, and the effect is blocked by phenothiazines, butyrophenones, etc.

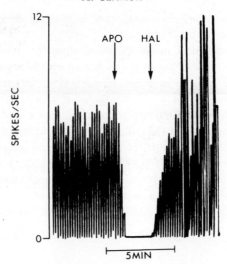

Fig. 2. Firing of dopaminergic cell bodies of the rat substantia nigra.

Apomorphine (APO, 0.1 mg/kg i.v.), a dopaminergic receptor agonist capable of penetrating through the blood-brain barrier, causes a complete inhibition of firing. A subsequent injection of haloperidol (HAL, 0.1 mg/kg i.v.) blocks the action of apomorphine and brings firing above the baseline level.

Courtesy of B.S. Bunney, 1975.

Central noradrenaline receptors, blocked by antipsychotic agents, appear to be similar to the peripheral α-adrenergic receptors. However, central dopamine receptors differ from these receptors, since either type of receptor can be selectively activated or blocked (Andén, 1973). A survey of the receptor-blocking properties of antipsychotic drugs indicates that all of them, except for those causing monoamine depletion, possess dopamine receptor-blocking activity. In addition, some of them are capable of blocking central α-adrenergic receptors, but certain agents appear to be devoid of such activity while maintaining antipsychotic properties (Andén *et al.*, 1970; Nybäck and Sedvall, 1970; see Table 1). Besides, no antipsychotic action of pure

TABLE 1

Classification of Neuroleptics with Respect to Dopamine (DA) and Noradrenaline (NA) Receptor Blockade and Turnover Increase in the CNS (Andén *et al.* 1963, 1970; Nybäck and Sedvall, 1970)

Group No.	Agents	Receptor blockade	Turnover increase
I	Pimozide Fluspirilene	DA receptors only	DA after low doses, NA after high doses only
II	Spiroperidol Haloperidol Perphenazine	DA receptors markedly, NA receptors slightly	See group no. 1
III	Chlorpromazine Thioridazine Chlorprothixene	Both DA and NA receptors	Both DA and NA
IV	Phenoxybenzamine	NA receptors only	NA only

α-adrenergic blocking agents has been reported so far. From these data, the conclusion seems justified that dopamine receptor-blocking activity is essential for the antipsychotic effect. This does not exclude the possibility that noradrenaline-receptor blockade may play a contributory role, however.

Role of Different Dopaminergic Pathways

It would thus appear that dopamine neurons are not only involved in the extrapyramidal but also in the antipsychotic actions of the neuroleptic agents. Are we dealing with one and the same dopaminergic pathway? This is unlikely. It is well known that the ratio of extrapyramidal to antipsychotic potency varies for different agents and that for a given agent this ratio can be

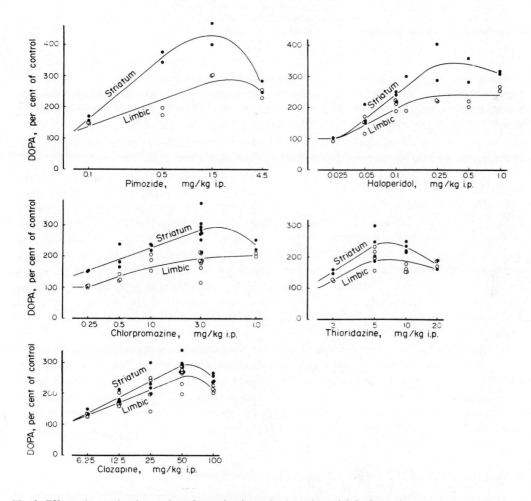

Fig. 3. Effect of neuroleptics on dopa formation in rat brain regions rich in dopamine.

The neuroleptics were given 60 min before NSD 1015 (100 mg/kg i.p.) and the animals were killed after another 30 min. (Unpublished data of this laboratory.)

NSD 1015 (3-hydroxybenzylhydrazine HCl) is an inhibitor of the aromatic L-aminoacid decarboxylase. After injection of this agent dopa starts to accumulate in brain. This accumulation is a measure of the catecholamine synthesis *in vivo.*

TABLE 2

Differential Action of Antipsychotic Drugs on DOPA Formation in Striatum vs. Limbic Regions

Drug	Dose, mg/kg	Diff. in % DOPA incr., striatum − limbic	Significance	Extrapyramidal side effects[a]
Pimozide	0.5 − 1.5	153 ± 18.3 (4)		?
Haloperidol	0.25 − 0.5	117 ± 26.1 (4)	p < 0.025	1
Chlorpromazine	3	104 ± 11.1 (8)		3
Chlorprom. + Atr.	3	73 ± 9.2 (5)	p < 0.005	−
Thioridazine	5 − 10	51 ± 9.3 (8)	p < 0.05	4
Clozapine	50 − 100	37 ± 8.8 (10)		5

The differences in % DOPA increase between the striatum and the limbic areas were obtained from the data represented in Fig. 3 and from similar data of an experiment with chlorpromazine and atropine (Atr. 40 mg/kg i.p. 10 min before NSD 1015). The data refer to the doses indicated in the Table. Statistics: t-test.
(a) from Snyder et al., 1974; rank by class; 1 indicates the most side effects.
Note. There seems to exist a correlation between a high striatal *vs.* limbic response and liability to extrapyramidal side effects, which may possibly also be related to anticholinergic activity (see Snyder et al., 1974).

modified by an anticholinergic drug. Moreover, choreatic side effects of dopa, which are probably due to excessive activation of dopamine receptors, are not strictly correlated to mental side effects. Therefore we are probably dealing with at least two different systems.

Dopamine occurs in many different parts of the central nervous system. The two quantitatively dominating locations are the striatum, where by far the largest amount occurs, and certain regions belonging to the so-called limbic (or mesolimbic) system, e.g. the olfactory tubercle, the nucleus accumbens, the central nucleus of the amygdala, and certain parts of the paleocortex. Recent observations suggest that the antipsychotic action of neuroleptic drugs is largely located in the limbic system, whereas the extrapyramidal actions reside in the striatum. Two observations point in this direction. First, anticholinergic agents are known to antagonise extrapyramidal side effects of neuroleptic drugs, while leaving the antipsychotic activity entirely or at least largely unaffected. It has been found, in different sets of experiments, that anticholinergics have a similar, differential activity in antagonising the effect of neuroleptic agents on dopamine metabolism in the two regions (Andén, 1972; Carlsson, 1975). Second, neuroleptics with a strong liability to extrapyramidal side effects in general cause a stronger effect on the dopamine metabolism in the striatum relative to the limbic system than neuroleptics with little or no extrapyramidal side effects (Andén and Stock, 1973a; Carlsson, 1974b; Fig. 3, Table 2).

If the antipsychotic action is located in limbic dopaminergic synapses, the question arises which of the various dopaminergic regions are involved. This question cannot be answered as yet. Local application of dopamine in the nucleus accumbens has been found to induce hyperkinesia and to stimulate food-reinforced lever pressing, and in the striatum, stereotyped behaviour (gnawing, licking, etc.) (Jackson et al., 1975). Further studies are necessary to clarify this point.

Antipsychotic Action of a Tyrosine Hydroxylase Inhibitor

As indicated by the evidence presented above, antipsychotic activity can be induced by interfering with central catecholamines, notably dopamine, in two different ways, (a) by blocking the function of the presynaptic storage organelles, leading to neurotransmission failure, and (b) by blocking postsynaptic catecholamine receptors. The question then arises whether inhibition of catecholamine synthesis will alleviate psychotic symptoms.

α-Methyltyrosine is a relatively specific inhibitor of tyrosine hydroxylase, the first enzyme involved in catecholamine biosynthesis. This agent has been administered in fairly large doses to psychotic patients, but no antipsychotic action could be detected (Gershon *et al.*, 1967). A possible explanation for this failure could be that the degree of enzyme inhibition was insufficient, clinical dosage being limited by renal toxicity. If insufficient dosage is the explanation, it might be possible to demonstrate an antipsychotic action of α-methyltyrosine by utilising the ability of receptor-blocking neuroleptics to potentiate the action of this enzyme inhibitor. Such potentiation, of a marked degree, has been demonstrated in animal experiments (Ahlenius and Engel, 1971, 1973; Fig. 4).

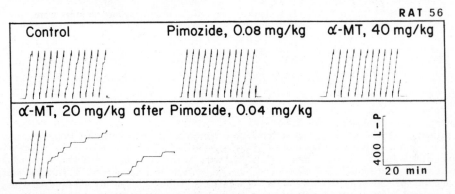

Fig. 4. Potentiation by α-methyltyrosine of the pimozide-induced inhibition of food-reinforced lever pressing. (Reproduced from Ahlenius and Engel, 1973.)
  The cumulative records show that pimozide, 0.08 mg/kg, and α-methyltyrosine methylester HCl (α-MT, H 44/68), 40 mg/kg, when given separately to a rat, have no significant influence on the lever pressing. However, a pronounced inhibition is seen if the two drugs are combined, the doses being only half of those given separately.

We have investigated the effect of combined treatment with a phenothiazine and α-methyltyrosine in altogether eight schizophrenic patients with a stationary symptomatology (Carlsson *et al.*, 1972, 1973; Wålinder *et al.*, 1975). In four of these patients two or three trials have been performed, in one trial for each patient using a double-blind crossover design (Wålinder *et al.*, 1975). Before each trial the patient had been treated with a single antipsychotic agent, usually thioridazine, in constant dosage for several months. The trial was started by rating the symptomatology by means of two different rating scales (Fig. 5). Then the dosage of the phenothiazine was reduced stepwise over several weeks, and the ratings were repeated at weekly intervals. After several weeks, when the phenothiazine dosage had been drastically reduced and the care of the patients started to be difficult because of a marked deterioration of the mental condition, α-methyltyrosine was given in a dose which was increased to 2 g daily. This was followed by a certain improvement in a few cases. The dose of phenothiazine was then slowly increased in order to titrate the dose necessary to attain the pre-trial level of ratings. This dose was found to be lower than the pre-trial dose in all cases, the average reduction being about 70 per cent (range 33 to 98.5 per cent). Plasma thioridazine levels were similarly reduced. This combined treatment regimen was maintained for periods varying between 4 weeks and 6 months without any signs of tolerance. During the treatment the concentration of homovanillic acid in the cerebrospinal fluid was reduced by about 80 per cent. The treatment period was ended by stopping α-methyltyrosine medication or replacing it by placebo, while keeping the phenothiazine dosage unchanged. In all cases a rapid

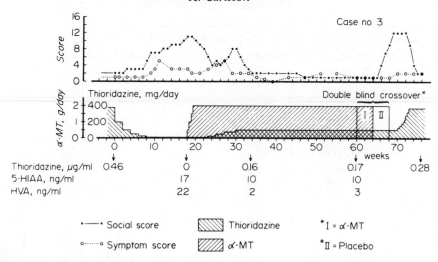

Fig. 5. Potentiation of the antipsychotic action of thioridazine by α-methyltyrosine (α-MT) in a schizophrenic patient (Wålinder *et al.*, 1975.)

The patient, a 44-year-old male, had suffered from schizophrenia with stationary symptomatology for more than 6 months. He had been hospitalised and treated with thioridazine as the only antipsychotic drug in constant dosage for more than 6 months. The trial was started by rating the symptoms verbally by a psychiatrist ("symptom score") and behaviourally by the head nurse ("social score"). Then the dosage of thioridazine was reduced stepwise until the care of the patient became difficult. At this time the scores were markedly elevated. α-Methyltyrosine therapy was now started, the dosage being gradually increased to 2 g/day, while keeping the thioridazine dosage at a constant level. This dose regimen was insufficient to control the condition, and thus the dose of thioridazine was gradually increased until the pretrial symptomatology level was attained. This occurred at a thioridazine dosage of 100 as compared to the pretrial dosage of 375 mg/day, the corresponding plasma levels of thioridazine being 0.16 and 0.46 μg/ml, respectively. The dose regimen was kept for 30 weeks. During this period the patient tended to be in an even better mental condition than before the trial. The α-methyltyrosine treatment caused a marked decrease in the level of homovanillic acid (HVA) in the cerebrospinal fluid.

At the termination of the trial α-methyltyrosine was replaced by placebo or α-methyltyrosine, using a double-blind crossover design. During the blind α-methyltyrosine period, which in this case came first, there was no change in the ratings, but during the placebo period a rapid deterioration occurred. The dosage of thioridazine was then gradually increased to the original level, and the pretrial symptomatology level was re-attained.

Similar results were obtained in 3 additional schizophrenic patients.

deterioration of the mental status occurred. The phenothiazine dosage was now increased to the same level as before the trial, and the pre-trial level of symptomatology was reattained.

The Nature of Antipsychotic Drug Effect

Thus, in the presence of a phenothiazine given in a dosage near the threshold for detectable antipsychotic activity, schizophrenic symptomatology appears to be profoundly influenced by alterations in tyrosine hydroxylase activity. Strong additional support is thus provided for the view that this symptomatology is closely related to central catecholamine neurotransmission. The question then arises what inference we can draw from this with respect to the pathogenesis of schizophrenia. The answer to this question is highly dependent on the specificity of the antipsychotic action. In other words, the crucial question is whether the so-called antipsychotic agents possess true antipsychotic activity. If the answer is "yes", we have strong reasons to believe that psychotic symptoms are due to a disturbance in catecholamine neurotransmission

TABLE 3
Effects of Apparent Deficiency or Excess of Dopamine at Central Receptor Sites
(Tentative scheme)

Neuronal pathway	Deficiency	Excess
Nigrostriatal	Hypokinesia* Rigidity (= α-motoneuron hyperactivity)* γ-Motoneuron hypoactivity* Tremor*	Hyperkinesia Hypotonia γ-Motoneuron hyperactivity Stereotyped behaviour
Limbic? Cortical? Other?	Inhibition of: (a)　　exploratory behaviour (b)　　conditioned responses (c)　　psychotic behaviour	Stimulation of: (a)　　exploratory behaviour (b)　　conditioned responses Psychotic behaviour
Median eminence	Galactorrhea (hyper- prolactinemia)	Hypoprolactinemia

* Antagonised by anticholinergic agents

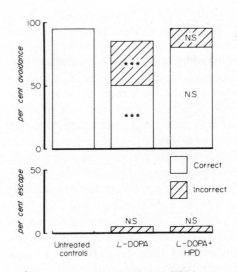

Fig. 6. Loss of discrimination ability after treatment with a large dose of L-dopa and restoration of correct performance by haloperidol. (Reproduced from Ahlenius and Engel, 1975.)

Rats were trained to pass through one of two passages in a shuttle box. If cue lights above the passages lit up when an auditory warning signal was given the animals were trained to pass through the right passage in order to avoid a grid shock. If the auditory warning stimulus was given without any light signal, avoidance was obtained by passing through the left passage.

Note. Untreated animals were trained to almost 100 per cent avoidance by using the correct passage exclusively. After treatment with L-dopa, 100 mg/kg i.p. 1 h before the test session (together with the inhibitor of the aromatic amino acid decarboxylase Ro 4-4602 = N^1-(DL-seryl)-N^2-(2,3,4-trihydroxybenzyl)-hydrazine HCl, 25 mg/kg i.p., to inhibit the enzyme in peripheral tissues), the animals still reacted to the warning stimulus by passing through one of the openings but no longer discriminated between the correct and the incorrect passage. The addition of haloperidol (HPD), 0.25 mg/kg i.p. 20 min before the test session, restored the performance almost completely to *** $P < 0.001$; N.S. $P > 0.05$ (comparisons with untreated controls, Wilcoxon T-test; the values shown are medians, N = 8).

or in a functionally closely related mechanism. If on the other hand the so-called antipsychotic action is only a manifestation of a general depression of mental activity, we are not justified in implicating the catecholamines in the pathogenesis of schizophrenia. Of course we have also to consider the possibility that a true specificity of the antipsychotic agents exists but is limited to certain components of the schizophrenic process or to a certain group of schizophrenic patients. The implication of the catecholamines in the pathogenesis of schizophrenia may then be at least partly justified.

Several clinical reports suggest that antipsychotic agents do not simply suppress abnormal behaviour but may, in addition, favour normal behavioural components (May, 1968; Snyder *et al.*, 1974). Also, in animals in which an inadequate behaviour has been induced by e.g. a large dose of L-dopa, antipsychotic agents have been shown to restore adequate responding (Ahlenius and Engel, 1975; Fig. 6).

Amphetamines and Schizophrenia

If drug-induced suppression of central catecholamine functions alleviates schizophrenic symptoms, a psychotomimetic effect would be expected from agents causing excessive stimulation of these functions.

The psychotomimetic agents form a heterogeneous group both from a chemical and pharmacological point of view. Many of them have attracted quite a lot of interest over the years, mainly in view of the possibility that they might provide useful schizophrenia models. The psychotic condition induced by most of these agents can, however, be clearly distinguished from schizophrenia. A striking exception is the amphetamine group of agents, because they are capable of reproducing very faithfully the picture of paranoid schizophrenia (see Snyder *et al.*, 1974). Therefore, the mode of action of amphetamine is of special interest in the present context and, fortunately, it is at least partly understood. It has been shown that amphetamine even in low dosage is capable of releasing central (and peripheral) catecholamines and that its central stimulant action is prevented by pretreatment with α-methyltyrosine. The data indicate that amphetamine acts by releasing catecholamines from a small pool which is immediately dependent upon the synthesis of new catecholamine molecules. The failure of an inhibitor of dopamine-β-hydroxylase to prevent amphetamine-induced excitation suggests that dopamine is involved in this action, although a contributory role of noradrenaline cannot be ruled out (for review, see Carlsson, 1970). It has been shown in experiments on human subjects that the euphoriant action of amphetamine can be prevented by α-methyltyrosine pretreatment (Jönsson *et al.*, 1971). Whether this enzyme inhibitor is capable of preventing amphetamine psychosis, remains to be elucidated. However, it seems probable that the psychotic action is related to central stimulation and thus depends upon catecholamine release.

Paranoid delusions during treatment of Parkinsonian patients with L-dopa have also been reported, although this side effect appears to be less frequent than the confusion-delirium type of mental disturbance (Goodwin *et al.*, 1971).

These observations on amphetamine and L-dopa support an involvement of catecholamines in at least a certain type of schizophrenia.

The Possible Role of GABA in Schizophrenia

Baclophen (lioresal, Ciba: β-(-4-chlorophenyl)-γ-aminobutyric acid), is a derivative of GABA capable of penetrating through the blood-brain barrier. In a preliminary study, Frederiksen

TABLE 4
Reduction of Thioridazine Dosage and Plasma Level Made Possible by the
Simultaneous Administration of α-Methyltyrosine
(1-3 Trials on Each Patient)

Patient no.	Thioridazine dose			Thioridazine plasma level			Homovanillic acid CSF level		
	I**	II	III	I	II	III	I	II	III
1	94	75	85	–	76	75	–	88	81
2	60	30	50	–	32	48	–	83	100
3	87	73	73	–	70	64	–	0	91
4	–	33	58	–	4	48	–	71	77
5	–	83	–	–	61	–	–	89	–
6	–	70	–	–	68	–	–	86	–
7	74	–	–	–	–	–	–	–	–
8*	98.5	–	–	–	–	–	–	–	–
Median	74			64			85		

* Chlorpromazine instead of thioridazine   ** Trial number

investigated the action of this drug in schizophrenic patients. The drug was superimposed on the previous treatment with neuroleptics, which had been only partially successful in these cases. In most of the patients a marked improvement was seen setting in within a few days of baclophen treatment. In particular, the autism and the thought disorder improved with a partial apparent re-integration of the personality. Many of the patients said they could think and read more easily, and they became more communicative. Hallucinations did not disappear but were less intense and appeared more remote. In some patients psychotic symptoms disappeared altogether. Phenothiazine medication could be reduced or discontinued. In fact, the tolerance to phenothiazines seemed to be reduced by the drug, causing complaints of rigidity, which disappeared after reducing the phenothiazine dosage (Frederiksen, 1975).

The idea that deficiency in GABA may play a role in schizophrenia has been put forward (Roberts, 1972; Stevens et al., 1974). Similar considerations formed the basis of Frederiksen's trial, even though the mode of action of baclophen has not yet been established (Birkmayer, 1972; Davidoff and Sears, 1974).

These speculations and observations on the possible role of GABA in schizophrenia are very interesting and will no doubt stimulate basic and clinical research in this area. It may be recalled that an intimate, mutually antagonistic relationship appears to exist between dopamine- and GABA-carrying neuronal pathways, at least in the striatum, and that deficiency of the latter transmitter might well have the same effect as hyperactivity of the former (Okada et al., 1971; Kim et al., 1971; Andén and Stock, 1973b). Also, it may be recalled that paranoid delusions and other schizophrenia-like symptoms may occur in Huntington's chorea, in which a deficiency of the striatal GABA pathway has been detected (Perry et al., 1973; Bird et al., 1973). Baclophen has been tried in Huntington's chorea, and some slight improvement was reported (Andén et al., 1973).

In rats we have observed actions of baclophen on behaviour, somewhat similar to those of a neuroleptic agent such as haloperiodol (Fig. 7) (Ahlenius et al., 1975). Thus amphetamine-induced loss of discrimination was restored by baclophen. However, baclophen, unlike haloperidol, did not antagonise amphetamine-induced hypermotility and did not *per se* disrupt conditioned behaviour.

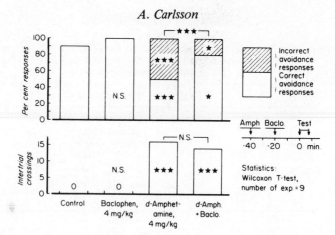

Fig. 7. Loss of discrimination ability after treatment with dexamphetamine and restoration of correct performance by baclophen. (Reproduced by Ahlenius *et al.*, 1975.)

Rats were trained as described in the legend of Fig. 6.

Note. Amphetamine appeared to block the discrimination ability completely, while preserving the responsiveness to the conditioned stimulus. It thus acted similarly to L-dopa as shown in Fig. 6. Baclophen restored this ability almost completely, as did haloperidol in the experiment shown in Fig. 6. There are, however, two distinct differences between baclophen and haloperidol: the former drug, unlike the latter, does not antagonise the hypermotility induced by amphetamine, and does not inhibit responding when given alone.

$P < 0.01$
$P < 0.05$ $\Big\{$ Wilcoxon *T*-test; the values shown are medians.

Thus the profile of baclophen appears to be clearly different from that of classical antipsychotic agents, as assessed both clinically and experimentally. In addition, differences in chemical structure suggest a different point of attack. Future work will decide whether baclophen interacts with GABA or some other neurohumoral transmitter. Moreover, the clinical effect of baclophen in schizophrenia remains to be established in controlled studies.

Concluding Remarks

An intimate relationship appears to exist between schizophrenic symptomatology and the activity of central dopamine receptors in the sense that an activation of these receptors leads to production or aggravation and an inhibition to alleviation of schizophrenic symptoms. The receptors involved appear to be located somewhere in the dopamine-rich limbic regions of the brain. It seems logical to suggest that dopaminergic mechanisms are fundamentally involved in the schizophrenic disturbance. This does not necessarily mean that dopaminergic mechanisms are primarily disturbed in schizophrenia. The primary disturbance may well reside in a functionally related system, e.g. a GABA system.

Nevertheless, it seems reasonable to predict that continued analysis of central dopaminergic and related systems will ultimately lead to the disclosure of the fundamental mechanisms underlying schizophrenia.

References

AGHAJANIAN, G.K. and BUNNEY, B.S. (1974) Pre- and postsynaptic feedback mechanisms in central dopaminergic neurons. In *Frontiers in Neurology and Neuroscience Research 1974*. (Seeman, P. and Brown, G.M., eds.) The University of Toronto Press, Toronto, pp. 4-11.

AHLENIUS, S., CARLSSON, A. and ENGEL, J. (1975) Antagonism by baclophen of the d-amphetamine-induced disruption of a successive discrimination in the rat. *J. Neural Transmission* **36**, 327-333.

AHLENIUS, S. and ENGEL, J. (1971) Behavioural effects of haloperidol after tyrosine hydroxylase inhibition. *European J. Pharmacol.* **15**, 187-192.

AHLENIUS, S. and ENGEL, J. (1973) On the interaction between pimozide and α-m
Pharmac. **25**, 172-174.

AHLENIUS, S. and ENGEL, J. (1975) Antagonism by haloperidol of the *L*-DOPA-induced disruption of a successive discrimination in the rat. *J. Neural Transmission* **36**, 43-49.

ANDÉN, N.-E. (1972) Dopamine turnover in the corpus striatum and the limbic system after treatment with neuroleptic and anti-acetylcholine drugs. *J. Pharm. Pharmac.* **24**, 905-906.

ANDÉN, N.-E. (1973) Catecholamine receptor mechanisms in vertebrates. In *Frontiers in Catecholamine Research* (Usdin, E. and Snyder, S., eds.) Pergamon Press, Oxford, pp. 661-665.

ANDÉN, N.-E., BUTCHER, S.G., CORRODI, H., FUXE, K. and UNGERSTEDT, U. (1970) Receptor activity and turnover of dopamine and noradrenaline after neuroleptics. *European J. Pharmacol.* **11**, 303-314.

ANDÉN, N.-E., CARLSSON, A., DAHLSTRÖM, A., FUXE, K., HILLARP, N.-Å. and LARSSON, K. (1964) Demonstration and mapping out of nigro-neostriatal dopamine neurons. *Life Sci.* **3**, 523-530.

ANDÉN, N.-E., CARLSSON, A. and HÄGGENDAL, J. (1969) Adrenergic mechanisms. *Annu. Rev. Pharmacol.* **9**, 119-134.

ANDÉN, N.-E., DALÉN, P. and JOHANSSON, B. (1973) Baclofen and lithium in Huntington's chorea. *Lancet* **July 14**, 93.

ANDÉN, N.-E. and STOCK, G. (1973a) Effect of clozapine on the turnover of dopamine in the corpus striatum and in the limbic system. *J. Pharm. Pharmac.* **25**, 346-348.

ANDÉN, N.-E. and STOCK, G. (1973b) Inhibitory effect of gammahydroxybutyric acid and gammaaminobutyric acid on the dopamine cells in the substantia nigra. *Naunyn-Schmiedeberg's Arch. Pharmacol.* **279**, 89-92.

BERTLER, Å. and ROSENGREN, E. (1959) Occurrence and distribution of dopamine in brain and other tissues. *Experientia* **15**, 10.

BIRD, E.D., MACKAY, A.V.P., RAYNER, C.N. and IVERSEN, L.L. (1973) Reduced glutamic-acid-decarboxylase activity of post-mortem brain in Huntington's chorea. *Lancet* **May 19**, 1090-1092.

BIRKMAYER, W. (ed.) (1972) Spasticity – a topical survey. Hans Huber Publishers, Bern.

BIRKMAYER, W. and HORNYKIEWICZ, O. (1961) Der L-3,4-Dioxyphenylalanin (=DOPA)-Effekt bei der Parkinson-Akinese. *Wien. Klin. Wschr.* **73**, 787-788.

CARLSSON, A. (1959) The occurrence, distribution and physiological role of catecholamines in the nervous system. *Pharmacol. Rev.* **11**, 490-493.

CARLSSON, A. (1965) Drugs which block the storage of 5-hydroxytryptamine and related amines. In *5-Hydroxytryptamine and Related Indolealkylamines* (Erspamer, V., ed.) Springer Verlag, Heidelberg, pp. 529-592.

CARLSSON, A. (1970) Amphetamine and brain catecholamines. In *Proceedings of the Mario Negri Institute for Pharmacological Research, Milan, Italy* (Costa, E. and Garattini, S., eds.) Raven Press, New York, pp. 289-300.

CARLSSON, A. (1974a) Antipsychotic drugs and catecholamine synapses. *J. psychiat. Res.* **11**, 57-64.

CARLSSON, A. (1974b) Receptor-mediated control of dopamine metabolism. Paper read at Workshop on *"Pre- and Postsynaptic Receptors"*, Annual ACNP Meeting, Puerto Rico.

CARLSSON, A. (1975) The effect of neuroleptic drugs on brain catecholamine metabolism. In *Antipsychotic Drugs, Pharmacodynamics and Pharmacokinetics* (Sedvall, G., Uvnäs, B. and Zotterman, Y., eds.) Pergamon Press, in press.

CARLSSON, A. FALCK, B. and HILLARP, N.-Å. (1962) Cellular localisation of brain monoamines. *Acta physiol. scand.* **56**, *Suppl. 196*, 1-28.

CARLSSON, A. and HILLARP, N.-Å. (1956) Release of adrenaline from the adrenal medulla of rabbits produced by reserpine. *Kgl. Fysiogr. Sällsk. Lund Förh.* **26**, 8.

CARLSSON, A. and LINDQVIST, M. (1963) Effect of chlorpromazine or haloperidol on formation of 3-methoxytyramine and normetanephrine in mouse brain. *Acta pharmacol. et toxicol.* **20**, 140-144.

CARLSSON, A., LINDQVIST, M. and MAGNUSSON, T. (1957) 3,4-Dihydroxyphenylalanine and 5-hydroxytryptophan as reserpine antagonists. *Nature (Lond.)*, **180**, 1200.

CARLSSON, A., LINDQVIST, M. and MAGNUSSON, T. (1960) On the biochemistry and possible functions of dopamine and noradrenaline in brain. In *Ciba Symposium on Adrenergic Mechanisms* (Vane, J.R., Wolstenholme, G.E.W. and O'Connor, M., eds.) J. & A. Churchill Ltd, London, pp. 432-439.

CARLSSON, A., LINDQVIST, M., MAGNUSSON, T. and WALDECK, B. (1958) On the presence of 3-hydroxytyramine in brain. *Science* **127**, 471.

CARLSSON, A., PERSSON, T., ROOS, B.-E. and WÅLINDER, J. (1972) Potentiation of phenothiazines by α-methyltyrosine in treatment of chronic schizophrenia. *J. Neural Transmission* **33**, 83-90.

CARLSSON, A., ROOS, B.-E., WÅLINDER, J. and SKOTT, A. (1973) Further studies on the mechanism of antipsychotic action: Potentiation by α-methyltyrosine of thioridazine effects in chronic schizophrenics. *J. Neural Transmission* **34**, 125-132.

CARLSSON, A., ROSENGREN, E., BERTLER, Å. and NILSSON, J. (1957) Effect of reserpine on the metabolism of catecholamines. In *Psychotropic Drugs* (Garattini, S. and Ghetti, V., eds.) Elsevier Publ. Co., Amsterdam, pp. 363-370.

DAHLSTRÖM, A. and FUXE, K. (1964) Evidence for the existence of monoamine-containing neurons in the central nervous system. *Acta physiol. scand.* **62**, *Suppl. 232*, 1-55.

DAHLSTRÖM, A. and FUXE, K. (1965) Evidence for the existence of monoamine neurons in the central nervous system. *Acta physiol. scand.* **64**, *Suppl. 247*, 1-85.

DAVIDOFF, R.A. and SEARS, E.S. (1974) The effects of Lioresal on synaptic activity in the isolated spinal cord. *Neurology* **24**, 957-963.

EHRINGER, H. and HORNYKIEWICZ, O. (1960) Verteilung von Noradrenalin und Dopamin (3-Hydroxytyramin) im Gehirn des Menschen und ihr Verhalten bei Erkrankungen des Extrapyramidal Systems. *Klin. Wschr.* **38**, 1236-1239.

FREDERIKSEN, P.K. (1975) Baclofen in the treatment of schizophrenia. *Lancet* **1**, 702-703.

FUXE, K. and ANDÉN, N.-E. (1966) Studies on central monoamine neurons with special reference to the nigro-neostriatal dopamine neuron system. In *Biochemistry and Pharmacology of the Basal Ganglia* (Costa, E., Coté, L.J. and Yahr, M.D. eds.) Raven Press, New York, pp. 123-129.

GERSHON, S., HEIKIMIAN, L.J., FLOYD, A. Jr. and HOLLISTER, L.E. (1967) Methyl-p-tyrosin (AMT) in schizophrenia. *Psychopharmacologia* **11**, 189-194.

GOODWIN, F.K., MURPHY, D.L., BRODIE, H.K.H. and BUNNEY, W.E. (1971) Levodopa: alterations in behaviour. *Clin. Pharm. Ther.* **12**, 383-396.

GREENGARD, P. (1974) Molecular studies on the nature of the dopamine receptor in the caudate nucleus of the mammalian brain. In *Frontiers in Neurology and Neuroscience Research 1974* (Seeman, P. and Brown, G.M., eds.) The University of Toronto Press, Toronto, pp. 12-15.

JACKSON, D.M., ANDÉN, N.-E. and DAHLSTRÖM, A. (1975) A functional effect of dopamine in the nucleus accumbens and in some other dopamine-rich parts of the rat brain. *Psychopharmacologia* (Berl.), in press.

JÖNSSON, L.E., ÄNGGÅRD, E. and GUNNE, L.M. (1971) Blockade of intravenous amphetamine euphoria in man. *Clin. Pharm. Ther.* **12**, 889-896.

KIM, J.S., BAK, I.J., HASSLER, R. and OKADA, Y. (1971) Role of γ-aminobutyric acid (GABA) in the extrapyramidal motor system. 2. Some evidence for the existence of a type of GABA-rich strionigral neurons. *Exp. Brain Res.* **14**, 95-104.

MAY, P.R.A. (1968) Anti-psychotic drugs and other forms of therapy. In *Psychopharmacology A Review of Progress 1957-1967* (Efron, D.H., ed.) U.S. Government Printing Office, Washington, pp. 1155-1176.

NYBÄCK, H. and SEDVALL, G. (1970) Further studies on the accumulation and disappearance of catecholamines formed from tyrosine-¹⁴C in mouse brain. Effect of some phenothiazine analogues. *European J. Pharmacol.* **10**, 193-205.

OKADA, Y., NITSCH-HASSLER, C., KIM, J.S., BAK, I.J. and HASSLER, R. (1971) Role of γ-aminobutyric acid (GABA) in the extrapyramidal motor system. 1. Regional distribution of GABA in rabbit, rat, guinea pig and baboon CNS. *Exp. Brain Res.* **13**, 514-518.

PERRY, T.L., HANSEN, S. and KLOSTER, M. (1973) Huntington's chorea. *New Engl. J. Med.* **288**, 337-342.

ROBERTS, E. (1972) A hypothesis suggesting that there is a defect in the GABA system in schizophrenia. *Neurosci. Res. Progr. Bull.* **10**, 468-480.

SEDVALL, G., FYRÖ, B., NYBÄCK, H., WIESEL, F.-A. and WODE-HELGODT, B. (1974) Mass fragmentometric determination of homovanillic acid in lumbar cerebrospinal fluid of schizophrenic patients during treatment with antipsychotic drugs. *J. psychiat. Res.* **11**, 75-80.

SHORE, P.A., SILVER, S.L. and BRODIE, B.B. (1955) Interaction of reserpine, serotonin and lysergic acid diethylamide in brain. *Science* 122, 284-285.

SNYDER, S.H., BANERJEE, S.P., YAMAMURA, H.I. and GREENBERG, D. (1974) Drugs, neurotransmitters, and schizophrenia. *Science* 184, 1243-1253.

STEVENS, J., WILSON, K. and FOOTE, W. (1974) GABA blockade, dopamine and schizophrenia: Experimental studies in the cat. *Psychopharmacologia (Berl.)* 39, 105-119.

WÅLINDER, J., SKOTT, A., CARLSSON, A. and ROOS, B.-E. (1975) Potentiation by α-methyltyrosine of thioridazine effects in chronic schizophrenics: a long-term trial using double-blind cross-over technique. To be published.

Drug-induced Psychoses and their Relationship to Schizophrenia

KENNETH DAVISON

Introduction

In this review the term *drug* refers to any exogenous chemical substance which alters brain function. Most drugs, either directly or via withdrawal effects, induce a psychic reaction displaying features of Bonhoeffer's "exogenous reaction syndrome" (delirium, acute confusional state) characterised by impairment of consciousness, indicated clinically by disturbance of memory, orientation and awareness[1] e.g. barbiturates, alcohol, atropine.

The psychoses to be reviewed are not of this type but rather those which are distinguished by a minimal or absent impairment of consciousness and at least a superficial resemblance to the group of naturally occurring psychoses we term schizophrenia.

The clinical features of schizophrenia are listed by a WHO committee[2] as follows:

In the presence of clear consciousness:

(1) Unmistakeable change of personality or accentuation of schizoid traits.
(2) Autism – withdrawal.
(3) Thought disorder – bizarre statements, abnormal syntactical, grammatical and other linguistic usages; incapacity to pursue a sustained train of thought; use of private symbols.
(4) Shallow or incongruous affect.
(5) Hallucinations and delusions.
(6) Behaviour anomalies – peculiarities of posture, gesture and movement (catatonia).

After drug ingestion features 1, 2 and 6 are insufficiently specific to be used as diagnostic criteria. The drug-induced psychoses to be reviewed are therefore those which include features 3, 4 or 5 singly or in combination, with the all-important condition of the retention of clear consciousness. The degree of resemblance of the psychoses to "true" schizophrenia will be discussed later. At this point it is intended merely to give a general impression of the type of mental state under consideration.

A wide variety of drugs has been reported to induce psychoses of this nature. As it is impossible to analyse in detail every such report, it is proposed to list the main groups of drugs which have been inculpated and review in detail selected groups which are of particular interest or significance in relation to the possible aetiology of schizophrenia. The following list (Table 1) is taken from Brune[3] with a few additions by the present author.

105

TABLE 1

Exogenous substances reported to have induced psychoses[*]

Psychotomimetic drugs
    LSD
    Mescaline
    Psilocybin
    Cannabis

CNS stimulants
    Amphetamines, Methylphenidate ('Ritalin')
    Appetite suppressants – diethylpropion ('Tenuate', 'Apisate'), phenmetrazine ('Preludin')
    Ephedrine, propylhexedrine ('Benzedrex'), mephentermine.
    Cocaine[9,10]

CNS depressants
    Ethyl alcohol
    Barbiturates[8,11,12]
    Bromides[5,6,7,13,14]
    Chloral hydrate[15]
    Opium[16]
    Paraldehyde[17,18]
    Anti-histamines – diphenhydramine[19,20]
    'Mandrax' (Methaqualone+diphenhydramine)[21]
    Anti-convulsants – diphenylhydantoin,[22] sulthiame,[23] ethyl-methyl-succinamide,[24]
                    phenylacetylurea[25]

Organic solvents and anaesthetics
    Acetylene[26]
    Chloroform[27]
    Ether[28,29]
    Carbon disulphide[30]
    Trichloroethylene[31,32]
    Nitrous oxide[33]
    Petrol (gasoline)[34,35]

Anti-infective agents
    Anti-TB drugs – isoniazid, cycloserine, ethionamide[36]
    Anti-malarial drugs – atebrine,[37] mepacrine,[38] chloroquine[39,40]
    Sulphonamides[41,42]
    Penicillin[43,44,45]
    Streptomycin[46]
    Chloromycetin[47]

Cardiotherapeutic drugs
    Digitalis[48]
    Stramonium[69]
    HYDRALAZINE[49]
    Thiocyanate[50]

Metallic poisons
    Lead[51,52]
    Arsenic[53,54]
    Thallium[55,56,57]

Vegetable poisons
    Mushroom[58,59]
    Ergotism[60,61]
    Lathyrism[62,63]
    Atropine

Miscellaneous
    Disulfiram ('Antabuse')
    Nitrogen mustard[64]
    L-dopa

[*]References cited only for substances not reviewed in the text.

Many of these reports do not provide descriptions of the mental state in sufficient detail to distinguish between a delirium and a schizophrenia-like psychosis. However, there are well-documented examples of drugs which usually induce delirium producing instead a schizophreniform picture, e.g. bromides,[4,5,6,7] barbiturates.[8]

I. Psychotomimetic Drugs (Hallucinogens)

Downing[65] defined psychotomimetic drugs as substances which consistently produce changes in thought, perception and mood without causing major disturbances of the autonomic nervous system or other serious disability. Hollister[66] added to this definition the absence of intellectual or memory impairment, stupor, narcosis, excessive stimulation and addictive craving. The last criterion excludes amphetamines from this group[67] but some amphetamine derivatives qualify. Despite controversy over the addictive potential of cannabis it is conventionally included in this group.[67]

The term "psychotomimetic" carries the implication that the mental state induced by these drugs mimics naturally occurring psychoses. This is the subject of a long-standing controversy which is considered below, but for the moment it should be noted that a mental state characterised by disturbance of thought, perception and mood without impairment of intellect, memory or consciousness must bear at least a superficial resemblance to the definition of schizophrenia proposed above.

As the biochemistry of these drugs is reviewed elsewhere in this volume it will be mentioned only briefly here. Biochemistry and pharmacology of psychotomimetic drugs have been recently reviewed in detail by Brimblecombe.[67]

Psychotomimetic drugs can be classified as follows:

1. INDOLEAMINES

  (i) Lysergic acid derivatives e.g. LSD.
 (ii) Tryptamine derivatives e.g. psilocybin.
(iii) β-Carbolines e.g. harmine.
(iv) Iboga alkaloids.

2. PHENYLALKYLAMINES

 (i) Phenylethylamines e.g. mescaline.
(ii) Phenylisopropylamines – amphetamine derivatives e.g. dimethoxymethylamphetamine (DOM or "STP") (Amphetamine itself is considered below).

3. CANNABINOLS e.g. cannabis and its active components

Anti-acetylcholine (anti-cholinergic, atropine-like) drugs are also sometimes classified as psychotomimetic drugs, but as the psychoses induced by atropine[68] and drugs with atropine-like effects such as stramonium,[69] scopolamine[70] and anti-Parkinson agents,[71,72,73] despite an occasional schizophreniform quality,[74,75] are usually accompanied by impairment of consciousness, they will not be considered further here.

1. (i) LYSERGIC ACID DERIVATIVES

Lysergic acid is the nucleus of the ergot alkaloids found in the fungus Claviceps purpurea responsible for the ergot disease of rye. Lysergic acid diethylamide, known by its original laboratory code number as LSD-25, was first synthesised by Stoll and Hofmann in 1938 but its hallucinogenic properties were not recognised until 1943 when Hofmann accidentally ingested a minute quantity and experienced a typical hallucinatory reaction[76] now known as the LSD "trip". Several other lysergic acid amides have been synthesised and tested but none are as potent in hallucinogenic effect as LSD. The minimal effective dose in Man, either orally or by injection, is 0.5-1 μgm/kg.[67]

Lysergic acid amide was subsequently identified as one of the active constituents of ololiuqui, the seeds of Rivea corymbosa and Ipomoea tricolor, used in religious rites by Mexican Indians.[76]

1. (ii) TRYPTAMINE DERIVATIVES

Tryptamine itself is not psychotomimetic but its simplest alkyl derivatives N,N-dimethyl-tryptamine (DMT), N,N-diethyltryptamine (DET) and N,N-dipropyltryptamine (DPT) are.[67] DMT is one of the active constituents of cohoba, a snuff prepared from the seeds of the shrub Piptadenia in South America and the Caribbean Islands[67] but the others do not occur naturally.

Intramuscular doses in Man of 0.75-1 mgm/kg. of DMT,[77] DET[78] and DPT[79] produce intense hallucinatory reactions lasting 1-2 hours.

Tryptamine derivatives with substitution in the benzene ring of the indole nucleus also have psychotomimetic properties. N,N-Dimethyl-4-hydroxytryptamine (*psilocin*) and its phosphorylated derivative *psilocybin* induce a hallucinatory syndrome in Man in oral doses of 4-8 mgm[80] and have been isolated from the sacred mushroom Psilocybe mexicana[81] long used by Mexican Indians in religious ceremonies under the name teonanácatl.

N,N-Dimethyl-5-hydroxytryptamine (bufotenine), like DMT, is also present in cohoba snuff but there is some doubt about its psychotomimetic potency.[82] It has been found in the urine of actively psychotic schizophrenics[83] and of schizophrenic patients after amino acid loading.[84]

1. (iii) β-CARBOLINES

These include harmine, harmaline and related compounds found in various plants from which a euphoriant drink is prepared by South American Indians. There is some doubt about the psychotomimetic potency of harmine[85] but harmaline is active in Man in intravenous doses of 1 mgm/kg. and oral doses of 5 mgm/kg.[86]

1. (iv) IBOGA ALKALOIDS

These are mentioned for the sake of completeness. They have been isolated from the roots of an African shrub which is chewed for its stimulant effects. Large amounts are hallucinogenic[67] but there is some doubt about the identity of the active principle.[67]

2. (i) PHENYLETHYLAMINES

3,4,5-Trimethoxyphenylethylamine (*mescaline*) is present in various forms of Central American cactus from which mescal or peyotl is prepared and used in religious rituals. Mescaline is psychotomimetic in Man in doses of 4-8 mgm/kg.[67]

2. (ii) PHENYLISOPROPYLAMINES

These are derivatives of amphetamine (β-phenylisopropylamine or 1-phenyl-2 aminopropane) and are also structurally related to mescaline. Many have a powerful psychotomimetic action e.g. 3,4,5-trimethoxyamphetamine (TMA), 2,5-dimethoxy-4-methylamphetamine (DOM also known as "STP").[87]

3. CANNABINOLS

Cannabinols are chemically unrelated to the indoleamines and phenylalkylamines considered above. They are the active constituents of cannabis which is prepared in various forms from the Indian hemp plant Cannabis sativa, e.g. marihuana, hashish, bhang, kif, ganja. Maximum psychotropic activity is found in the sticky resin produced by the top of the plant (*hashish*), less in the stem, leaves and seeds (*marihuana*). Cannabis preparations are usually smoked but are also effective by mouth. Small amounts have a mild euphoriant or sedative effect (88) but large doses can be psychotomimetic.[89] Although many different compounds have been identified the major activity resides in the tetrahydrocannabinol (THC) fraction.[90]

Psychic Effects

ACUTE REACTIONS

The acute response to the ingestion of drugs in groups 1 and 2 in Man is generally similar. The acute LSD reaction in normal subjects, which has been observed many times[91] can be taken as the paradigm. Its effects last for 6-10 hours and are as follows:[66]

(1) *Somatic symptoms* — dizziness, weakness, tremors, nausea, drowsiness, paraesthesiae and blurred vision.
(2) *Perceptual symptoms* — altered shapes and colours, difficulty in focusing on objects, sharpened sense of hearing, synaesthesia.
(3) *Psychic symptoms* — alterations in mood, tension, distorted time sense, difficulty in expressing thoughts, depersonalisation, dream-like feelings and visual hallucinations.

These effects may be elaborated into a complicated visual and emotional experience with mystical and ecstatic qualities — the "trip" which may be enjoyable (good trip) or frightening (bad trip).

Dilated pupils, hyperreflexia, increased muscle tension, incoordination and ataxia are common physical signs. Changes in pulse rate, respiration, blood pressure, salivation and appetite are variable.[66] Tolerance develops quickly and is lost quickly. Administration to schizophrenic patients accentuates psychotic symptoms.[92]

Other hallucinogenic drugs show minor variations from this pattern. Thus *mescaline* is said to evoke visual hallucinations more often but unreality feelings and thought disorder less frequently.[92] Psilocybin,[93] DMT and DET have similar effects but a shorter duration of action than LSD or mescaline.[94]

There is wide variation in the hallucinogenic potency of these drugs. In terms of the average hallucinogenic dose of mescaline they are rated — mescaline 1, TMA 2.2-10, DOM 80-100, LSD 3-6000.[95]

THC in doses of 300-480 μgm/kg orally or 200-250 μgm/kg by smoking induces distortion of visual and auditory perception, depersonalisation and auditory and visual hallucinations.[89] Compared with LSD, THC provokes more pronounced dream-like states, euphoria and sedation but without sympathetic nervous stimulation.[96]

MODEL PSYCHOSES AND SCHIZOPHRENIA

Beringer[97] is credited with the first use of the term "model psychosis" in reference to the psychic effects of mescaline and it was subsequently applied to the acute LSD reaction.[98] It was thought that these artificially-induced mental states closely resembled the naturally occurring psychosis schizophrenia and a study of the former would enhance understanding of the latter.[99] Certainly these drugs challenged the prevailing orthodoxy that mental states secondary to drug intoxication invariably took the form of Bonhoeffer's exogenous reaction syndrome (see above).

Throughout the past two decades there has been a recurrent controversy in the literature concerning the degree of resemblance of the "model psychosis" to schizophrenia. On the one hand are those who saw an almost total identity with schizophrenia[98,100,101] even to the identification of schizophrenic Rorschach patterns;[101] on the other hand are those who rigidly reject this view.[102] Between these extremes, others accept some resemblance between the two conditions but emphasise various points of difference. Some of the differences listed by Hollister[66] are shown in Table 2.

An example of a more detailed comparison based on rating scales is shown in Table 3.[103]

As Lipton[104] points out, these older comparisons were usually made with patients suffering from chronic schizophrenia selected for their ability to co-operate. It is therefore not surprising that differences rather than similarities were highlighted. In a recent study[105] questionnaires were administered in a standard taped interview to 3 groups of 20 subjects aged 14 to 25 years comprising schizophrenic patients, subjects who had experienced an acute LSD reaction and normal controls. Analysis of the results showed that 60 per cent of the LSD group and 45 per cent of the schizophrenics had experienced visual hallucinations but the LSD group usually retained insight. There were no significant differences between the LSD and the schizophrenic group on various measures of thought disorder, motor disturbance and identity loss. Twenty-five per cent of the schizophrenic group displayed delusions as opposed to none of the LSD group and there was a higher proportion of unpleasant emotional reactions in the former. The author concludes that "the LSD and schizophrenic experiences are similar in more ways than they are different. The states are phenomenologically similar but differences exist in the affective nature of the experiences and the presence of delusions in some schizophrenic states."

TABLE 2
Comparison of model psychosis and schizophrenia (Hollister, 1968)

Psychological function	Model psychosis	Schizophrenia
Interpersonal contact	Retained	Withdrawal
Communication	Poor but concerned	Poor but apathetic
Hallucinations	Visual, pleasant or impersonal	Auditory and threatening
Suggestibility	High	Low

TABLE 3
Comparison of clinical features of acute LSD reaction and schizophrenia (Sandison, 1959)

Clinical feature	Acute LSD reaction	Schizophrenia
Memory and recall	Mild impairment	Normal
Awareness and concentration	Unimpaired	Unimpaired
Existing perceptions	Distorted or elaborated	Unaffected
Visual hallucinations	Frequent	Rare
Olfactory hallucinations	Frequent	Rare
Tactile hallucinations	Frequent	Frequent
Auditory hallucinations	Rare	Frequent
Insight	Retained	Impaired
Thought block	Frequent	Frequent
Thought disintegration	Very frequent	Very frequent
Flight of ideas	Occasional	Very frequent
Compulsive ideas	Occasional, rational	Frequent, irrational
Delusional thought	Occasional, mainly paranoid	Very frequent
Affect	Labile, anxiety, agitation	Flat, incongruous
Relationship to reality	Subjective impairment	Failure to relate to external reality
Body image distortion	Frequent	Rare
Impulsive irrational behaviour	Frequent	Frequent
Response to chlorpromazine	Affect and behaviour improved	Thought disorder and behaviour improved

This particular controversy has to some extent been overtaken by events (see below). It can, however, be concluded that *typical* model psychoses (acute reactions to LSD, mescaline or related drugs) are not identical with *typical* examples of schizophrenia, but individual features of the drug reaction are remarkably similar to some of the experiences of the more acute schizophrenic psychoses.[106,107,108]

PROLONGED PSYCHOTIC REACTIONS TO PSYCHOTOMIMETIC DRUGS

The original descriptions of the model psychosis were derived from observations on normal subjects given the drug experimentally later supplemented by the effects on neurotic patients given LSD therapeutically. Even under these relatively controlled conditions "prolonged adverse reactions" were provoked and these included psychoses. Smart and Bateman[109] reviewed 21 reports prior to June, 1967 containing details of 225 adverse reactions to LSD which are listed in Table 4.

TABLE 4
Prolonged adverse reactions to LSD (Smart and Bateman, 1967)

Adverse reaction	Number of cases
Prolonged psychotic reaction	142
Non-psychotic reaction	63
Spontaneous recurrence (Flashback)	11
Attempted suicide	19
Attempted homicide	4
Successful suicide	11
Successful homicide	1
Convulsions	6

"Prolonged psychotic reaction" therefore accounted for 63 per cent of the reported adverse reactions to LSD.

In a review of the complications resulting from 25,000 LSD administrations to about 5000 patients in the U.S.[110] psychotic reactions lasting more than 48 hours occurred at a rate of 0.8 per 1000 in experimental subjects and 1.8 per 1000 in patients receiving LSD therapeutically. In a similar review of clinical experience with LSD in Britain, Malleson[111] discovered a psychosis rate of 9 per 1000. The difference may be related to the response rate of only 70 per cent to requests for information in the U.S. study.

In Malleson's series 9 patients recovered in less than 2 weeks, 3 in 2 weeks to 3 months, 7 lasted over 3 months and 10 psychoses became chronic. The onset of the psychosis might be delayed for up to 2 months after a single dose of LSD.[112] Typical symptoms include paranoid delusions,[113,114] schizophrenia-like auditory hallucinations[115,116] and overwhelming fear.[116,117] Medication and/or hospitalisation might be needed from a few days up to several years.[109]

Smart and Bateman[109] noted that only a minority of the reported cases had pre-existing psychiatric disorder. In one series of 52 psychotic reactions it was claimed that in 77 per cent of patients the psychosis was not predictable from their previous personality structure.[109] On the other hand it is claimed that psychotic reactions are commoner in those who are already anxious[118] or have disorganised personalities.[119]

PSYCHOTIC REACTIONS TO ABUSE OF PSYCHOTOMIMETIC DRUGS

The appearance on a large scale of the repeated self-administration of hallucinogenic drugs for their mind-expanding effects, has, in effect, provided a gigantic biological experiment, the consequences of which are now being seen. Smart and Bateman[109] noted that 30-50 per cent of the prolonged psychoses in experimental or therapeutic situations occurred after a single dose of LSD. When the number of doses of LSD, or other hallucinogenic drugs, in an individual is measured in tens or hundreds[120] often of unknown potency, then unusual psychiatric reactions are to be expected.

Glass[121] distinguishes three clinical syndromes:

(i) *Acute drug reaction* in which it is claimed that an already weakened ego is overwhelmed and is unable to re-integrate when the drug effect wanes. This responds to short-term hospitalisation with supportive treatment.

(ii) A gradual shift towards projection, denial and delusional thinking and withdrawal. This is said to occur in relatively normal individuals who take drugs frequently at times of life crisis. They are said to develop alloplastic ego defences to avoid dealing with painful affect. Hospitalisation is ineffective.

(iii) Drug use in a person who is already schizophrenic.

Several authors have reported both acute and chronic paranoid psychoses.[122-126] In a series of 70 cases of adverse reactions to self-administered LSD, 14 (20 per cent) were given a diagnosis of "schizophreniform state".[126] The symptoms observed in 19 patients admitted to hospital with psychoses after LSD ingestion are listed in Table 5.[123]

TABLE 5
Symptoms observed in prolonged LSD psychoses
(Dewhurst and Hatrick, 1972)

Symptom	No. of patients displaying symptom (N=19)
Thought disorder	16
Auditory hallucinations	11
Delusions	10
Regression	8
Depression	10
Emotional lability	9
Panic reactions	9
Incongruity of affect	6
Bizarre behaviour	7
Insomnia	6
Hypomania	5
Visual hallucinations	6
Psychomotor retardation	5
Loss of time sense	7
Unreality feelings	6
Confusion	5
Apathy	3

Dewhurst and Hatrick[123] comment that the condition is difficult to distinguish from schizophrenia and in fact this was the initial diagnosis in 7 of the patients. There was no personal or family history of schizophrenia in any patient. The most striking clinical feature was the wide variety of schizophreniform, affective and psychoneurotic symptoms that could be present in a single patient.

Hays and Tilley[127] compared 15 patients with LSD psychoses of this type with 114 consecutive schizophrenic patients. There were significantly fewer auditory hallucinations and secondary delusions in the LSD group but visual hallucinations, affective flattening, catatonic symptoms, passivity phenomena and primary delusions were not significantly different. Although their conclusion is that the LSD psychosis is clinically distinguishable from schizophrenia, there is really a remarkable phenomenological resemblance between the two conditions. The most significant finding was the absence of a family history of schizophrenia in the LSD group compared to the positive family history in 33 per cent of the schizophrenia group.

Bowers[128] found that LSD psychoses usually presented the picture of a schizophreniform reaction with features predictive of a good prognosis, e.g. good pre-morbid adjustment, non-schizoid personality and acute onset.

CHRONIC PSYCHOSES

Clinicians have become increasingly familiar with an insidiously developing mental state after repeated use of LSD over a period of years, which bears a close resemblance to chronic undifferentiated schizophrenia.[88,120,129,130] Sufferers are described as withdrawn, isolated, with shallow affect, paranoid delusions and bizarre thought processes centred on religious mysticism.[120] Orientation and recent memory are usually unaffected but there may be some difficulty with distant memory. The development of this mental state can rarely be explained from knowledge of the previous social or personality state. Explanations in terms of avoidance of maturational stresses and gradual retreat from reality and affective pain have been put forward[120] but there has also been speculation about possible organic brain damage as the basis for this syndrome.[88,131]

Blacker *et al.*[132] claim that these so-called "acid-heads" are distinguished from schizophrenics by their continued involvement with people and retention of interpersonal skills, and the non-aggressive attitude and magical or mystical beliefs of these individuals are more like those of eccentric personalities than schizophrenics. There is, however, objective evidence of pathological disturbance of thinking of schizophrenic type in persistent users of hallucinogenic drugs[132] related to duration of drug use rather than type or quantity of drug ingested.[132] The most striking feature of these patients is the dramatic deterioration in all aspects of ego function compared with their condition before drug use. The only spontaneously occurring conditions with such a devastating effect are simple or undifferentiated schizophrenia or a partially controlled hebephrenic schizophrenia.

SPONTANEOUS RECURRENCES (FLASHBACKS)

Yet another clinical syndrome must be distinguished, namely the spontaneous recurrence or "flashback".[125,134] These occur after the ingestion of all the major hallucinogenic drugs, including cannabis[135] and consist of spontaneous recurrences of the hallucinatory experience weeks, months and, in one case, over a year[131] after the last ingestion of the drug and after a normal interval. Although these experiences can be frightening and bizarre, e.g. one subject had recurrent visual hallucinations of decomposing people,[125] insight is usually retained. Their occurrence is related to the frequency of drug ingestion[109],[125] but in view of the short half-life of about 3 hours for LSD in Man[66] the phenomenon cannot be due to persistence of the drug in the brain.

CANNABIS PSYCHOSES

The psychotomimetic action of Δ^9THC, the most active constituent of cannabis, is dose-dependent and has only been demonstrated experimentally after large doses.[136] Although some authors deny that clinical psychoses can be induced by cannabis ingestion[137],[138] it has been blamed for the development of a wide variety of mental disorders in Egypt and India.[139],[140] Lewis[141] comments that the latter view is not based on any satisfactory evidence.

Nevertheless, in addition to delirious reactions[142],[143] several authenticated cases of schizophrenia-like states occurring after the use of cannabis have been reported.[143-153] Paranoid-hallucinatory psychoses predominate[150] and they may persist for weeks or months[144],[147],[150] or even become permanent.[152]

Varying estimates of the frequency of these psychoses have been made. Cannabis was the direct cause of hospitalisation of 0.9 per 1000 psychiatric cases to the Brooklyn State Hospital. Of 720 hashish smokers from a U.S. Army population of 36,000 observed for a 3-year period, 3 cases of "persistent schizophrenic reaction" were noted in smokers of 10-50 gm hashish per month and 112 were noted in smokers of 25-200 gm per month but the latter group also used LSD amphetamines and alcohol.[152] The same authors also noted a fourfold increase in the incidence of schizophrenic reactions in their military population between 1967 and 1971 which they attributed to drug use, mainly cannabis. Of 38 persons aged 13-24 years, who showed adverse effects to smoking cannabis, more than twice weekly, 8 (21 per cent) developed paranoid-hallucinatory psychoses.[149]

The symptomatology of these psychoses has not been subjected to the same scrutiny as in those induced by LSD. However, there is a general resemblance to the group of "prolonged psychotic reactions" to psychotomimetic drugs described above. In addition to paranoid delusions, auditory hallucinations, catatonic symptoms and passivity feelings,[146],[151] visual hallucinations figure in several of the case reports.[146],[151],[142]

"Flashbacks" also occur[135],[142] as well as an "amotivational syndrome"[8] remarkably similar to the chronic LSD psychosis described above.

The possible aetiological relationship of cannabis use to these psychoses has been classified as follows:[150]

(i) Cannabis-induced psychosis (e.g.[146],[151])
(ii) Precipitation of a latent psychosis (e.g.[148])
(iii) Aggravation of a pre-existent psychosis.
(iv) Cannabis-withdrawal psychosis.

The validity or otherwise of these distinctions is discussed later in a general review of the relationship between drugs and their associated psychoses.

SUMMARY OF QUASI-PSYCHOTIC SYNDROMES INDUCED BY PSYCHOTOMIMETIC DRUGS

Ingestion of psychotomimetic drugs may result in:

(1) *Acute drug reaction.* This is the classical model psychosis or hallucinatory "trip". It is distinguishable from typical schizophrenia by several features but individual symptoms may resemble those seen in acute schizophreniform psychoses. They are usually of only a few hours' duration and occur in response to a single dose.

(2) *Prolonged psychotic reaction.* This is, by definition, of more than 48 hours' duration, often much longer and sometimes becoming chronic. It closely resembles schizophreniform types of psychosis but rarely displays nuclear symptoms. It can be induced by a single dose.

(3) *Chronic psychosis.* Resembles chronic undifferentiated or simple schizophrenia and related to duration of drug use.

(4) *Spontaneous recurrence (flashback).* This is a spontaneous recurrence of the experience of the acute drug reaction and therefore subject to the same distinction from schizophrenia.

MODE OF ACTION OF PSYCHOTOMIMETIC DRUGS

This is discussed elsewhere in this volume and will therefore be mentioned only briefly here. The chemical resemblance of mescaline to nor-adrenaline and of LSD and psilocybin to 5-hydroxytryptamine (serotonin), is likely to be more than coincidence.[76] The similarity in the psychic effects and the demonstration of cross tolerance between LSD and mescaline,[154,155] psilocybin[156] and DOM[67] suggests that these drugs share a common mechanism of action. There is considerable evidence, recently reviewed in detail,[67,157] to indicate that LSD and related drugs act as competitive antagonists to 5-hydroxytryptamine at central synapses, particularly the mid-brain raphe,[158] and their maximal electrophysiological effect is on the limbic system.[159]

Cannabis extracts, although having a more generally depressant action on CNS activity, produce similar effects on brain 5-hydroxytryptamine.[160]

RELEVANCE TO BIOCHEMICAL THEORIES OF SCHIZOPHRENIA

The chemical relationship of psychotomimetic drugs to cerebral neurotransmitters lead to speculation about schizophrenia being based upon the endogenous production of a psychotogenic chemical by abnormal metabolism of nor-adrenaline or 5-hydroxytryptamine.[161] From this evolved the concept of a more generalised disorder of transmethylation in schizophrenia.[162]

These hypotheses are discussed elsewhere in this volume but the point to be emphasised here is that the effects of psychotomimetic drugs provided a powerful stimulus to ideas and research into the possible biochemical substrate of schizophrenia.

II. Amphetamines and Related Substances

Amphetamine is the generic name for the racemic mixture of 1-phenyl-2 aminopropane (β-phenylisopropylamine). It was first synthesised in 1927[163] and found to have peripheral sympathomimetic and CNS stimulant properties. The d-isomer was soon isolated (dextro-amphetamine, "Dexedrine") and later a methyl derivative (methamphetamine, "Methedrine", "Pervitin"). These substances are effective orally, and produce euphoria, relieve fatigue, and enhance verbal and motor activity. The effects last several hours, tolerance develops, there is a tendency to psychological dependence and hence a risk of abuse.[164] Amphetamines have been used clinically in the treatment of narcolepsy,[165] depression and obesity.

Several anorectic drugs have been derived from amphetamine, e.g. phenmetrazine ("Preludin"), diethylpropion ("Tenuate", "Apisate"). Their central stimulant properties are attenuated but not completely absent.[166]

AMPHETAMINE PSYCHOSES

The first cases of amphetamine psychosis were reported in narcoleptics[167] although the situation is confused by the occasional spontaneous occurrence of a schizophrenia-like psychosis in narcoleptic subjects.[168] Subsequent cases were reported in individuals who were abusing amphetamines.[169,170] Connell,[170] in a classical monograph on amphetamine psychosis, reviewed 34 case reports from the literature between 1938 and 1957 and reported 42 cases of his own.

Connell described the clinical picture of amphetamine psychosis as "primarily a paranoid psychosis with ideas of reference, delusions of persecution, auditory and visual hallucinations in a setting of clear consciousness". He emphasised the absence of diagnostic physical signs and pointed out that the mental picture may be indistinguishable from acute or chronic paranoid schizophrenia and was often misdiagnosed as such. He found that the psychosis usually remitted within a week of withdrawing the drug but if it persisted in the absence of amphetamine derivatives in the urine he thought a diagnosis of schizophrenia was likely. The premorbid personalities of these patients were often unstable but the apparently well-adjusted were also affected. Schizophrenia was absent from the family histories of his patients.

These views were greeted with some scepticism at the time (e.g.[171]) but subsequent reports have amply confirmed Connell's observations.[172-177]

Identical psychoses have also been observed after the ingestion of the related stimulants ephedrine[177,178] and methylphenidate ("Ritalin")[179-182] and the appetite-suppressant drugs, phenmetrazine ("Preludin")[177,183-188] and diethylpropion ("Tenuate", "Apisate").[189-192] Even the supposedly innocuous contents of inhalers, mephentermine ("Wyamine")[193] and propylhexedrine ("Benzedrex")[194] have been implicated in the production of psychoses.

SYMPTOMS

The phenomenological similarity to paranoid schizophrenia has already been mentioned. This is borne out by the number of cases who were initially misdiagnosed as schizophrenic.[172,189,192] In at least one case a leucotomy was performed under the mistaken impression that a surreptitious drug-taker was a chronic schizophrenic.[172]

Van Praag[164] has described typical symptoms in some detail. The onset may be acute or gradual with the development of paranoid thoughts and ideas of reference. The subject becomes restless and agitated, feels threatened and begins to hear voices which confirm his suspicions. Auditory are usually more prominent than visual hallucinations. Thinking may be accelerated but the mood is more depressed and anxious than euphoric. Consciousness is not clouded and orientation remains intact.

Bell[174] analysed 14 cases of amphetamine psychosis and found delusions of persecution in 14, of external influence in 5, auditory hallucinations in 13 and visual hallucinations in 9. He thought they were distinguished from schizophrenia by the absence of thought disorder, and the greater frequency of visual hallucinations. Others have, however, reported the occurrence of thought-disorder,[173] blunting of affect[173] and all of the first-rank symptoms of Schneider.[177] The six commonest features are reported as lack of concentration, delusions of persecution, motor activity, hallucinatory behaviour, thought disorganisation, and suspiciousness.[195]

These psychoses usually develop in a setting of prolonged consumption of amphetamines in excessive quantity[164] but occasionally single doses of as little as 55 mgm amphetamine[172] and 50 mgm phenmetrazine[164] are reported to have precipitated psychoses. There is no relationship between the total amount of drug ingested and the severity of the psychosis.[185]

Typical amphetamine psychoses have been evoked experimentally by oral d-amphetamine[196,197] and intravenous methylamphetamine.[198] The oral doses varied from 20-190 mgm per day[197] to 5-50 mgm per hour[196] and the intravenous dose from 55-640 mgm. With oral administration, psychosis appeared within 1 to 5 days and with intravenous administration within 1 hour.

COURSE

Van Praag[164] proposed two criteria for diagnosis:

(1) The finding of amphetamine derivatives in the urine.[170]
(2) Spontaneous recovery within 1-2 weeks of abstinence from the offending drug.

Although the latter is the usual course of the psychosis[195,199] there are several reports of recovery taking weeks or months.[170,185,186] There is a tendency to assume that these persistent psychoses are examples of coincidental schizophrenia[170,173,174] but by analogy with the prolonged psychotic reactions to LSD there seems no reason why amphetamines should not be able to induce a prolonged psychosis. Certainly, Japanese workers, who have had a considerable experience with amphetamine psychoses, believe that some can take a chronic progressive course indistinguishable from a "true" schizophrenic defect state[200,201] possibly based on structural brain damage.[201]

MODE OF ACTION OF AMPHETAMINES

Current theories of the mechanism of action of amphetamines have recently been reviewed[202] and are as follows:

(1) Mono-amine oxidase inhibition.[203]
(2) Release of catecholamines from neuronal binding sites.[204]
(3) Inhibition of catecholamine reuptake into neurones.[205]
(4) Direct action on nor-adrenergic receptors.[206]

Method 2 above is regarded as the most probable mechanism.[202] It has been argued that release of dopamine is responsible for the stereotyped behaviour that precedes or accompanies amphetamine psychosis whereas release of nor-adrenaline provokes increased motor activity.[207]

Precipitation of psychosis has been attributed to:

(1) Production of a psychotogenic metabolite,[208] e.g. para-methoxy-amphetamine.[196]

(2) Induction of a state of cerebral over-arousal mediated via the reticular activating system.[197]

RELATIONSHIP TO SCHIZOPHRENIA

The toxic metabolite hypothesis links amphetamine psychosis to the biochemical hypothesis of schizophrenia mentioned earlier. In addition, the suggestion of cerebral over-arousal connects with the evidence, reviewed by Ban,[209] of cerebral over-arousal as an important feature of schizophrenia "close to the core of the disease".

Snyder[210] argues from the similarity of the symptoms of amphetamine psychosis and schizophrenia, the occurrence of stereotyped behaviour in both and the specific ability of phenothiazine drugs, which block dopamine receptors, to relieve them, that some disturbance of cerebral dopamine systems is involved in both disorders. From the results of animal experiments Klawans and Margolin[211] suggest that amphetamine induces dopamine receptor site hypersensitivity and this plays a role in the development of amphetamine psychosis. Furthermore they postulate that prolonged psychosis may be due to a persistent hypersensitivity outlasting the presence of amphetamine in the body. A similar pathogenesis is postulated for schizophrenia. In support of these views they cite the occurrence of dyskinetic movement disorders in chronic amphetamine use and the occurrence of both dyskinesia and schizophrenia-like psychoses in 3-6 per cent of patients receiving l-dopa treatment[212,216] and the aggravation of symptoms in schizophrenic patients by low doses of l-dopa.[217]

III. Ethyl Alcohol

ALCOHOLIC HALLUCINOSIS

Ethyl alcohol, C_2H_5-OH, is a CNS depressant and is widely consumed in various forms for its intoxicating effects. It is associated with several psychiatric syndromes but the one under review is the syndrome of auditory hallucinations which was differentiated from delirium tremens by Kraepelin, Wernicke and Bonhoeffer at the turn of the century.[218] They recorded its clinical features as active hallucinations, mainly auditory, with delusions based on the hallucinations, preservation of memory and orientation.[218] This is in contrast to delirium tremens in which visual hallucinations predominate and consciousness is clouded as indicated by disorientation in time, place or person.[218] These two disorders have been regarded as at opposite ends of a spectrum with intermediate forms occasionally observed.[219] E. Bleuler[220] thought that alcohol merely unmasked latent schizophrenic symptoms whereas Kraepelin[221] regarded alcoholic hallucinosis as a stage of the alcohol withdrawal syndrome. At that stage it was difficult to sustain the hypothesis of alcohol withdrawal as the disorder was often seen to develop during active drinking. Subsequent work,[222,223] however, established the concept of relative withdrawal during active alcohol ingestion.

SYMPTOMS

A characteristic development is the sudden awareness by the patient of unformed acoustic perceptions such as clicks, knocks and bells[224] which gradually develop into voices which criticise, threaten or command.[225] These experiences are interpreted in delusional fashion in that he feels he is surrounded by enemies, is being watched or spied upon and he may act on these beliefs.[225]

Claims are made that alcohol-induced hallucinations differ from schizophrenic hallucinations in several respects. The alcoholic variety are said to be more frequent and continuous, the voices are localised in space and emerge from a background of noises and unintelligible voices whereas the schizophrenic hallucinations are more episodic, resemble thoughts becoming audible, are localised within the body and are more intelligible.[226] Others, however, conclude that the syndrome is often clinically indistinguishable from schizophrenia.[227]

COURSE

One of the most complete follow-up studies was that of Benedetti.[228] Of 113 cases of acute alcoholic hallucinosis 90 recovered within 6 months, 13 developed into "typical schizophrenia" with symptoms such as thought disorder, autism, and grandiose delusions, and 10 developed a progressive organic dementia but this group also had multiple somatic complications. In the study of Victor and Hope[227] 68 of 76 patients recovered but in 8 subjects hallucinations persisted for weeks or months and 4 of these developed a full-blown schizophrenic picture. Persistent psychoses appear to respond to treatment with phenothiazine drugs and electroplexy.[225]

MECHANISM OF ACTION

Various mechanisms of production of a hallucinatory psychosis by alcohol have been proposed.

1. VITAMIN DEFICIENCY

Although this may co-exist, for example as peripheral neuritis, it does not appear to be the central factor.

2. REM SLEEP DEPRIVATION[229]

This is known to be related to the development of psychotic symptoms and has been proposed as a possible pathogenetic mechanism for schizophrenia.[230]

3. CEREBRAL HYPER-AROUSAL[226]

This could occur as a withdrawal effect of alcohol. It has been referred to in the section on amphetamines. Alpert and Silvers[226] found that alcoholics, but not schizophrenics, tended to hallucinate more frequently with an experimentally manipulated increase in the baseline arousal state. They thought this indicated a greater importance for arousal than REM deprivation in the genesis of hallucinosis.

RELATIONSHIP TO SCHIZOPHRENIA

Both in the U.S.A.[226] and Britain[231] heavy alcohol consumption has shown to be significantly associated with hospital admission for schizophrenia. In one of the hospitals of the Newcastle University Department of Psychological Medicine, of 331 consecutive admissions with schizophrenia, defined phenomenologically, 17 (5.1 per cent) had an extremely high alcohol consumption before the onset of the psychosis. For males only the proportion was 11.2 per cent.[231] This could indicate that alcohol abuse is an aetiological factor in schizophrenia (or a schizophrenia-like psychosis) or alternatively, that schizophrenia produces a vulnerability to alcohol abuse.[226] The view of E. Bleuler[220] that "alcoholic hallucinosis could be a mere syndrome of schizophrenia induced by alcohol" has already been mentioned. Victor and Hope[227] were quite certain that alcohol abuse could precipitate a syndrome which is clinically indistinguishable from schizophrenia and that before the appearance of the syndrome the subjects could not be considered as potential schizophrenics. Benedetti[228] emphasised the absence of a schizophrenic family history in his patients and also thought that their physique and pre-morbid personalities were not in favour of an identity with schizophrenia. In a comparison of 45 schizophrenic patients with 18 patients with alcoholic hallucinosis, Alpert and Silvers[226] found that 16 relatives of the former but only 1 relative of the latter group had received inpatient psychiatric treatment.

Schuckit and Winokur[232] compared 61 patients with alcoholic hallucinosis with 197 alcoholic patients without hallucinosis in an attempt to define a possible connection of the former with schizophrenia. Although the hallucinosis group began drinking alcohol at an earlier age and were older at the time of the study, had more previous hospital admissions and were more often unemployed or unskilled labourers, there was no difference in the frequency of previously diagnosed schizophrenia, a family history of schizophrenia, affective disorder or alcoholism between the two groups. They concluded that the study "lends no support to a theory linking alcoholism with hallucinosis to schizophrenia". Victor and Hope[227] put it more bluntly: "The concept that the schizophrenia-like illness is simply latent schizophrenia made manifest by alcohol is neither logical nor consistent with the observed facts."

The apparent paradox in these various observations is discussed, and hopefully resolved, later.

IV. Miscellaneous Drugs

In this section one drug and one group of drugs are briefly reviewed for their interesting connections with hypotheses concerning the aetiology of schizophrenia.

1. TETRAETHYLTHIURAM DISULFIDE (DISULFIRAM, "ANTABUSE")

This drug is used in the treatment of alcoholism as an aid to abstinence. Ethyl alcohol is normally metabolised within the body to acetaldehyde. Disulfiram blocks the action of aldehyde dehydrogenase leading to high blood levels of acetaldehyde after the ingestion of alcohol which clinically produces flushing, hypotension, dizziness, vomiting, collapse and eventually coma.

Liddon and Satran[233] reviewed published reports of 52 disulfiram-induced psychoses. Some of these were delirious states but a psychosis without delirium was recognised. However, they regarded only one case as showing symptoms of paranoid schizophrenia.[234] In a more recent review Knee and Razani[235] regarded 21 cases as clinically schizophrenic and 9 as showing acute schizophrenic episodes. The reported incidence of psychosis varies from 2 to 20 per cent of those taking the drug[233] and it is claimed that the incidence has declined since the recommended dose was reduced. Psychosis is particularly likely to follow the combination of disulfiram with metronidazole ("Flagyl"), a drug which is supposed to suppress the taste for alcohol.[236]

The link with schizophrenia is provided by the effect of disulfiram in inhibiting the action of dopamine-β-hydroxylase, leading to a reduction in the conversion of dopamine to nor-adrenaline. Stein and Wise[237,238] postulate that in schizophrenia a pathological gene leads to a marked reduction in the activity of dopamine-β-hydroxylase or in the capacity to induce the enzyme under stress. This results in a mixture of dopamine and nor-adrenaline being stored in nor-adrenergic terminals of the brain reward system. Release of dopamine into the synaptic cleft permits the formation of toxic amounts of 6-hydroxydopamine which damages the binding capacity and eventually the structural integrity of the nor-adrenergic terminal. The alleged resulting progressive damage to the nor-adrenergic reward mechanism is regarded as responsible for the fundamental symptoms and long-term downhill course of schizophrenia. It is suggested that phenothiazine drugs exert their therapeutic effect by blocking the entry of 6-hydroxydopamine into the nor-adrenergic terminal.

2. ANTI-CONVULSANT DRUGS

Reynolds[239] proposed that the schizophrenia-like psychoses that occur in epileptic patients[168] are in fact precipitated by the action of anti-convulsant medication. He postulated that the effect was mediated via disturbances in folic acid and vitamin B_{12} metabolism which have been identified particularly with phenobarbitone, diphenylhydantoin and primidone.[239]

This interesting hypothesis has never really been substantiated.[240] However, it is of considerable interest that the metabolism of folic acid and B_{12} is related to transmethylation. Folic acid acts as an acceptor and donor of single carbon units and is required for the synthesis of methyl groups and ultimately methionine. Vitamin B_{12} also acts as a co-enzyme in the transfer of methyl groups in the formation of methionine.[241] S-Adenosylmethionine which is involved in the latter reaction is the active methyl donor in the transmethylation of amines and has a central role in the transmethylation hypothesis of schizophrenia.[242]

More recently Levi and Waxman[243] have further elaborated this hypothesis by linking with it an alleged low incidence of cancer in schizophrenia and the need for methionine for the growth of malignant tissues. They postulate that in schizophrenia there is a deficiency of methionine adenosyltransferase or its co-factors and suggest a trial of replacement therapy with S-adenosylmethionine.

DRUG-PSYCHOSIS RELATIONSHIPS

The question that arises is whether the drug

(1) Induces a schizophrenic reaction in an individual who would not otherwise have developed a psychosis.
(2) Precipitates a psychosis in a predisposed personality harbouring a latent psychotic tendency.
(3) Aggravates or accompanies a pre-existing schizophrenia.[8,150]

In apparent support of hypotheses (2) and (3) are those studies which suggest a non-specific action of drugs on the occurrence of mental disorders in general and schizophrenia-like psychoses in particular.

Dubé and Handa[244] surveyed an Indian population of 16,725 and found the prevalence of mental illness in the drug users (6.8 per cent) to be roughly double that in the non-users (3.6 per cent). Alcohol users had a mental disorder rate of 2.2 per cent, cannabis users 10.6 per cent and users of combinations of drugs 16.25 per cent. The prevalence of drug use in psychotic patients was 9.84 per cent and in psychoneurotic patients 1.91 per cent. According to diagnosis 13.69 per cent of schizophrenic patients, 16.22 per cent of patients with manic-depressive psychosis, 5.38 per cent of organic psychotic patients and 2.2 per cent of the normal population were drug users.

Breakey *et al.*[245] compared the drug-taking history for LSD, mescaline, cannabis and amphetamines in 46 young schizophrenics and 46 controls. Surprisingly the proportion of drug users was the same in each group, but the "schizophrenics" had used a wider variety of drugs in greater amounts before the onset of the psychosis. Drug-using "schizophrenics" had an onset of psychosis 4 years earlier than non-drug user "schizophrenics" and had better premorbid personalities. Unfortunately, the sample was too small to allow a family history comparison. The results were thought to indicate some precipitating role of drug abuse in the onset of schizophrenia. As the schizophrenic group was, however, selected on phenomenological criteria the possibility exists that it was a heterogenous mixture of true schizophrenia and drug-induced psychoses.

The problem for hypothesis (1) is that only a minority of drug-takers develop a psychosis and this has yet to be satisfactorily explained. The only objective measure of predisposition to schizophrenia is the genetic loading as indicated by the incidence of schizophrenia in the first-degree relatives of a large series of patients with appropriate correction for age. Unfortunately, so far the genetic evidence concerning drug-induced psychoses remains at the anecdotal level. Most observers, however, agree that a family history of schizophrenia is usually absent.[170,226,227,228]

Personality disposition is difficult to quantify but again the general view, with a few exceptions[148,175,246] is that pre-schizophrenic personalities are uncommon[170,112,197,227,228,109,186,185] and the type of personality disorder usually encountered is the unstable sociopathic type. Reference in the literature to a precipitation of a latent schizophrenia[125] seems to be a theoretical assumption based on the circular argument that a psychosis can only develop when there is a predisposition to it. Until the nature of the predisposition can be identified this is not a helpful argument.

Stone[8] proposes a multifactorial assessment of predisposition to psychosis after drug use utilising the presence or absence of four variables which are assumed to have some predisposing effect. He designates these, P (psychological factors), C (constitutional factors), O (organic factors) and G (genetic predisposition). This is a useful method of describing a clinical situation but it remains to be seen whether it has any predictive value. Stone concludes that although predisposing factors can often be identified, psychoses are also occurring after drug use in quite normal people but he is unable to estimate how large a proportion of the cases seen are of this type.

Such evidence as there is therefore seems to indicate that these psychoses are mostly induced by the drugs in individuals who are not in any recognisable way predisposed to develop schizophrenia (hypothesis (1)) although cases do occur according to the other two hypotheses. Clearly more work is needed to identify the clinical, social, genetic and biochemical features which distinguish those who respond to drugs with a psychosis and those who do not.

Wharton[247] suggests that the predisposition may not be to develop schizophrenia but rather an abnormal sensitivity to or defect in the metabolism of the drug which may be genetically determined. This is an interesting speculation for which there is, as yet, no supporting evidence.

GENERAL HYPOTHESES OF DRUG ACTION

Specific hypotheses of the action of each drug have been discussed earlier. Here hypotheses common to all the drugs reviewed will be discussed.

Brune,[3] by analogy with somatically-determined schizophrenia-like psychoses, proposes that an endogenous type of psychosis occurs as a result of an exogenous toxin when the metabolic disturbance interferes only with the function of the limbic system, an area which represents the anatomical substrate of behaviour,[248] and has been specifically connected with the pathogenesis of true schizophrenia.[249] He suggests that this can occur when the limbic system has a lower threshold to the action of the drug than the other functional systems of the brain. He cites LSD and other psychotomimetic drugs which evoke electrophysiological activity predominantly in the hippocampus and amygdala[159] and the neurotransmitters 5-hydroxy-tryptamine (serotonin), dopamine and nor-adrenaline are concentrated mainly in this area.[250] Brune suggests that if additional cerebral structures are involved the exogenous reaction syndrome will appear. This hypothesis would account for those drug-induced psychoses seen with drugs which usually produce delirious states.

Another possible psychotogenic mechanism common to the drugs reviewed is the induction of a state of cerebral hyperarousal either directly as with LSD[91] and amphetamines[174] or by withdrawal of a depressant effect, as with alcohol.[226] This is not necessarily an alternative to biochemical hypotheses as arousal is mediated by cerebral amines.[251] Sophisticated elaborations of this hypothesis have been put forward by Szara[252] and Winters and Wallach[253] both for drug-induced states and true schizophrenia. The important role of cerebral hyperarousal in the latter has already been mentioned and is fully reviewed by Ban.[209]

Some workers have argued for organic brain damage as the common factor in the production of drug-induced psychoses.[8] Conversely there is evidence that structural brain lesions have widespread effects on cerebral amine metabolism.[254] The author has reviewed the schizophrenia-like psychoses associated with organic brain disease[168] and concluded that they usually occur in individuals without genetic loading for schizophrenia and the site of the brain lesion is more important than the predisposition of the patient in the genesis of the psychosis, lesions in the diencephalic region of the brain being particularly significant.

THE SCHIZOPHRENIA CONCEPT

The production by drugs, and organic brain lesions, of psychoses which are often phenomenologically indistinguishable from schizophrenia but differing in their genetic loading, personality and course, leads inevitably to the view that schizophrenia is purely a descriptive term for a syndrome which can be the end-result of many aetiological factors.[255,256] An attempt to integrate drugs and organic brain disorders into current views of the aetiology of schizophrenia is portrayed in Fig. 1 which was originally published by the author in 1969.[168] Idiopathic schizophrenia requires a genetic predisposition whereas drugs and certain brain lesions act beyond this point in the aetiological chain and produce directly the brain

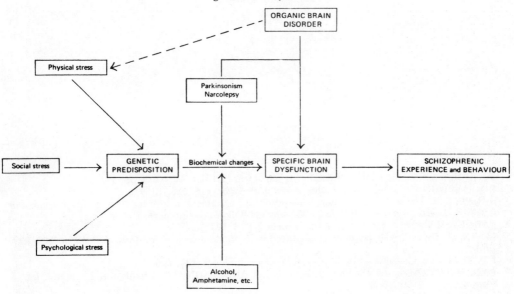

Fig. 1. Organic brain disease and drugs in the aetiology of schizophrenia.

dysfunction which results in the schizophrenic experience.

It is now almost 40 years since the British psychiatrist, Mapother[257] stated: "like epilepsy, schizophrenia is the name of a syndrome and the idiopathic variety is merely the commonest among many". This reviewer firmly believes that, also like epilepsy, an understanding of the symptomatic psychoses will enhance our knowledge of the idiopathic variety. That is the justification for this review.

References

1. BONHOEFFER, K. Die exogene Reaktionstypen. *Arch. Psychiat. Nervenkr.* 58, 58, 1917.
2. Report of WHO Study on Schizophrenia. *Amer. J. Psychiat.* 115, 685, 1959.
3. BRUNE, G.G. The somatically determined psychoses. Chapter 3 in *Biochemistry, Schizophrenias and Affective Illnesses*, Himwich, H.E. (ed.) Williams and Wilkin Co. Baltimore, 1971.
4. CARNEY, M.W.P. Five cases of bromism. *Lancet* 2, 523, 1971.
5. LEVIN, M. Transitory schizophrenias produced by bromide intoxication. *Amer. J. Psychiat.* 103, 229, 1946.
6. LEVIN, M. Bromide hallucinosis. *Arch. gen Psychiat. (Chic.)* 2, 429, 1960.
7. POZUELO-UTANDA, J., CRAWFORD, D.C. and ANDERSON, J.C. Bromism and epilepsy. *Int. J. Neuropsychiat.* 2, 90, 1966.
8. STONE, M.H. Drug-related schizophrenic syndromes. Ibid. 11, 391, 1973.
9. JACOBI, A. Die psychische Wirkung des Cokains in ihrer Bedeutung für die Psychopathologie. *Arch. Psychiat.* 79, 383, 1927.
10. KRAEPELIN, E. Delirium, Halluzinose and Dauervergiftung. *Mschr. Psychiat.* 54, 43, 1923.
11. DÖRRIES, H. and LANGELÜDDEKE, A. Weitere Beobachtungen über Phanodormpsychosen und Phanodormsucht. *Z. Neurol.* 154, 658, 1936.
12. ISBELL, H., ALTSCHUL, S., KORNETSKY, C.H., EISENMAN, A.J., FLANARY, H.G. and FRASER, H.F. Chronic barbiturate intoxication. *Arch. Neurol. Psychiat (Chic.)* 64, 1, 1950.
13. GEIGER, W. Über Brompsychosen. *Nervenarzt* 26, 99, 1955.
14. LEVIN, M. Bromide psychoses: four varieties. *Amer. J. Psychiat.* 104, 798, 1948.
15. MARGETTS, E. L. Chloral delirium. *Psychiat. Quart.* 24, 278, 1950.
16. COHEN, S. The toxic psychoses and allied states. *Amer. J. Med* 15, 813, 1953.
17. NOTHASS, M. Paraldehydpsychosen. *Allg. Z. Psychiat.* 76, 826, 1921.
18. PROBST, M. Über Paraldehyddelir. *Mschr. Psychiat.* 14, 113, 1903.
19. NIGRO, S.A. Toxic psychosis due to diphenhydramine hydrochloride. *J.A.M.A.* 203, 301, 1968.
20. SACHS, B.A. The toxicity of Benadryl: report of a case and review of the literature. *Ann. Int. Med.* 29, 135, 1948.
21. ROMAN, D. Schizophrenia-like psychosis following "Mandrax" overdose. *Brit. J. Psychiat.* 121, 619, 1972.
22. GLASER, G.H. Diphenylhydratoin toxicity. In *Anti-epileptic Drugs.* Woodbury, D.M., Penry, J.K. and Schmidt, R.P. (eds.), Raven Press, New York, 1972.
23. GARLAND, H. and SUMNER, D. Sulthiame in treatment of epilepsy. *Brit. med. J.* 1, 474, 1964.
24. FISCHER, M., KORSATIJAER, G. and PEDERSEN, E. Psychotic episodes in Zarandan treatment. *Epilepsia.* 6, 325, 1965.
25. GIBBS, F.A. Ictal and non-ictal psychiatric disorders in temporal lobe epilepsy. *J. nerv. ment. Dis.* 113, 522, 1951.
26. SIOLI, F. Gewohnkeitsmissbrauch der Inhalationsnarkotika. *Mschr. Psychiat.* 68, 551, 1928.
27. HEILBRUNN, G., LIEBERT, E. and SZANTO, P. Chronic chloroform poisoning. *Arch. Neurol.* (Chic.) 53, 68, 1945.
28. HART, E. An address on ether-drinking. *Brit. med. J.* 2, 885, 1890.
29. SAUVET, D. Selbstebeobachtungen in Ätherausch. *Am. méd. psychol.* 10, 467, 1847.
30. HERZIG, E. Schwefelkohlenstoffpsychosen. *Z. Neurol. Psychiat.* 33, 185, 1916.
31. STEPHENS, J.A. Poisoning by accidental drinking of trichloroethylene. *Brit. med. J.* 218, 1945.
32. TODD, J. Trichlorethylene poisoning with paranoid psychosis and Lilliputian hallucinations. Ibid. 1, 439, 1954.
33. ZADOR, J. Das Lachgas (N_2O) – Rausch in seines Bedeutung für Psychiatrie und Neurologic. *ARCH. Psychiat.* 84, 1, 1928.
34. KNABENHAUS, P.J. Psychische Symptome bei Vergiftungen mit modernen gewerblichen Lösungmitten. *Schweiz. Arch. Neurol. Psychiat.* 49, 129, 1942.
35. RAWKIN, J.C. Psychopathologie der gewerblichen Massenvergiftung. *Z. Neurol.* 127, 407, 1930.

36. WALLACH, M.B. and GERSHON, S. Psychiatric sequelae to tuberculous chemotherapy. In *Psychiatric complications of medical drugs*. Shader, R.I. (ed.), p. 201. Raven Press, New York, 1972.
37. GREIBER, M.F. Psychoses associated with the administration of atabrine. *Amer. J. Psychiat.* 104, 306, 1947.
38. PERK, D. Mepacrine psychosis. *J. Ment. Sci.* 93, 756, 1947.
39. MUSTAKALLIO, K.K., PUTKONEN, T. and PIHKANEN, T.A. Chloroquine psychosis. *Lancet* 2, 1387, 1962.
40. KABIR, S.M.A. Cloroquine psychosis. *Trans. Roy. Soc. Trop. Med. Hyg.* 63, 549, 1969.
41. GARVIN, C.F. Complications following the administration of sulphanilamide. *J.A.M.A.* 113, 288, 1939.
42. PEARSON, M.M. and BURNSTINE, M.D. Psychoses precipitated by sulphanilamide. Report of 2 cases. *New Int. Clin.* 3, 246, 1939.
43. COHEN, S. Psychosis resulting from penicillin hypersensitivity. *Amer. J. Psychiat.* 111, 699, 1955.
44. KLINE, C.L. and HIGHSMITH, L.R.S. Toxic psychosis resulting from penicillin hypersensitivity. *Ann. Int. Med.* 28, 1057, 1948.
45. UTLEY, P.M., LUCAS, J.B. and BILLINGS, T.E. Acute psychotic reactions to aqueous procaine penicillin, *South. Med. J.* 59, 1271, 1966.
46. POROT, M. and DESTAING, F. Streptomycine et troubles mentaux. *Ann. méd. psychol.* 108, 47, 1950.
47. PERREAU, O. and BEYLE, T. Psychoses par chloromicetine en T.B.C. *Bull. Soc. Med. Hop.* 65, 1401. 1949.
48. KING, T.T. Digitalis delirium. *J. Amer. Clin. Chem. Ass.* 1, 314, 1949.
49. MOSER, M., SYNER, J., MALITZ, S. and MATTINGLY, T.W. Acute psychosis as a complication of hydrallazine therapy in essential hypertension. *J.A.M.A.* 152, 1329, 1953.
50. BARNETT, J.H.M., JACKSON, M.V. and SPAULDING, W.B. Thiocyanate psychosis. *J.A.M.A.* 147, 1554, 1951.
51. KEHRER, F. Über Abstinenzpsychosen bei chronischen Vergiftungen (Saturnismus USW) *Z. Neurol.* 3, 472, 1910.
52. SCHRÖDER, P. Beitrag zur Lehre von den Intoxikationspsychosen. *Allg. Z. Psychiat.* 63, 714, 1906.
53. MERTENS, H.G. Zur Klinik und Pathogenese der Salvarsanschäden am Nervensystem. *Deutsch. Z. Nervenbeilk.* 161, 135, 1949.
54. SCHMIDT, W. Psychose und Polyneuritis bei Arsenvergiften durch arsenhaltigen Honig. *Nervenarzt* 26, 95, 1955.
55. AMLER, G. and MEIER-EWART, K. Zum Problem der Thalliumpsychose. *Arch. Psychiat. Nervenkr.* 196, 349, 1957.
56. SCHÜTZLER, H. and KREUTSCH, E. Fehldiagnosen und psychiatrische Komplikationen bei Thalliumvergiftungen. *Nervenarzt.* 22, 90, 1951.
57. SCHEDIFKA, R. Psychische Dauerschädigung nach Thalliumvergiftungen. Ibid. 36, 81, 1965.
58. LEONHARDT, W. Über Rauschzustände bei Pantherpilzvergiftungen. Ibid. 20, 181, 1949.
59. MARX, N. Intoxikationspsychose durch Pilzvergiftung. *Allg. Z. Psychiat.* 79, 369, 1923.
60. SIEMENS, F. Psychosen bei Ergotismus. *Arch. Psychiat.* 108, 366, 1880.
61. LEONHARD, K. Behandlungserfolge mit Atropin und Ergotamin bei Manischen und Melancholischen. *Arch. Psychiat.* 97, 290, 1932.
62. FAUST, C. 3 Fälle von Lathyrismus. *Deutsch. Med. Wschr.* 72, 122, 1947.
63. MERTENS, H.G. Zur Klinik des Lathyrismus. *Nervenarzt.* 18, 493, 1947.
64. ROSWIT, B. and PISETSKY, J.E. Toxic psychosis following nitrogen mustard therapy. *J. nerv. ment. Dis.* 115, 356, 1952.
65. DOWNING, D.F. In *Psychopharmacological Agents*. Gordon, M. (ed.), p. 555. Academic Press, London and New York. 1964.
66. HOLLISTER, L.E. *Chemical Psychoses*. Charles C. Thomas, Springfield, Ill. USA, 1968.
67. BRIMBLECOME, R.W. Psychotomimetic drugs: biochemistry and pharmacology. *Adv. Drug Res.* 7, 165, 1973.
68. WELBOURNE, R.B. and BUXTON, J.D. Acute atropine poisoning. *Lancet* 2, 211, 1948.
69. GOWDY, J.M. Stramonium intoxication. Review of symptomatology in 212 cases. *J.A.M.A.* 221, 585, 1972.
70. ULLMAN, K.C. and GROH, R.H. Identification and treatment of acute psychotic states secondary to the usage of over-the-counter sleeping preparations. *Amer. J. Psychiat.* 128, 1244, 1972.
71. PORTEOUS, H.B. and ROSS, D.N. Mental symptoms in Parkinsonism following benzhexol therapy. *Brit. med. J.* 2, 138, 1956.
72. STEINBRECHER, W. Akinetonpsychosen. *Dtsch. med. Wschr.* 83, 1399, 1958.
73. STEPHENS, D.A. Psychotoxic effects of benzhexol hydrochloride (Artane). *Brit. J. Psychiat.* 113, 213, 1967.
74. Di GIACOMO, J.N. Toxic effect of stramonium simulating LSD trip. *J.A.M.A.* 204, 265, 1968.
75. MATIAR-VAHR, H. Über eine durch Akineton ausgelöste Psychose schizophrener Prägung. *Nervenarzt* 32, 473, 1961.

76. HOFMANN, A. The discovery of LSD and subsequent investigations on naturally occurring hallucinogens. In *Discoveries in Biological Psychiatry.* Ayd, F.J. and Blackwell, B. (eds.), Ch. 7, Lippincott, Philadelphia, 1970.

77. SAI-HALÁSZ, A. The effect of antiserotonin on the experimental psychosis induced by dimethyltryptamine. *Experientia* 18, 137, 1962.

78. BOSZORMENYI, Z., DER, P. and NAGY, T. Observations on the psychotogenic effect of N-N Diethyltryptamine. *J. Ment. Sci.* 105, 171, 1959.

79. SZÁRA, S. and HEARST, E. The 6-hydroxylation of tryptamine derivatives: a way of producing psychoactive metabolites. *Ann. N.Y. Acad. Sci.* 96, 134, 1962.

80. HOFMANN, A., HEIM, R., BRACK, A., KOBEL, H., FREY, A.J., OTT, H. and TROXLER, F. Psilocybin and psilocin. Two psychotropically active principles of Mexican hallucigenic fungus. *Hlev. Chim. Acta.* 42, 1557, 1959.

81. HOFMANN, A., HEIM, R., BRACK, A. and KOBEL, H. Psilocybin ein psychotroper Wirkstoff aus dem mexicanisch Rauschpilz Psilocybe mexicana Heim. *Experientia* 14, 107, 1958.

82. TURNER, W.G. and MERLIS, S. Effect of some indolealkylamines in man. *Arch. Neurol. Psychiat.* 81, 121, 1959.

83. TANIMUKAI, H., GINTHER, R., SPAIDE, J. and HIMWICH, H.E. Psychotomimetic indole compounds in the urine of schizophrenics and mentally defective patients. *Nature*, 216, 490, 1967.

84. TANIMUKAI, H., GINTHER, R., SPAIDE, J., BUENO, J.R. and HIMWICH, H.E. Bufotenin (5-hydroxy-N, N-dimethyl-tryptamine) in urine of schizophrenic patients. *Life Sci.* 6, 1697, 1967.

85. TURNER, W.G., MERLIS, S. and CARL, A. Concerning theories of indoles in schizophrenigenesis. *Amer. J. Psychiat.* 112, 466, 1955.

86. NARANJO, C. In *Ethnopharmacologic Search for Psychoactive drugs,* Efron, D.H., Holmstedt, B. and Kline, N.S. (eds.), p. 291. Public Health Service Pub. No. 1645, 1967.

87. SHULGIN, A.T. Psychotomimetic amphetamines: methoxy-3,4-dialkoxyamphetamines. *Experientia* 20, 366, 1964.

88. McGLOTHLIN, W.H. and WEST, L.J. The marihuana problem: an overview. *Amer. J. Psychiat.* 125, 370, 1968.

89. ISBELL, H. Clinical pharmacology of marihuana. *Pharmacol. Rev.* 23, 337, 1971.

90. MECHOULAM, R. and GAONI, Y. A total synthesis of dl-Δ'-tetrahydrocannabinol, the active constituent of hashish. *J. Amer. Chem. Soc.* 87, 3273, 1965.

91. FUJIMORI, M. and ALPERS, H.S. Psychotomimetic compounds in Man and Animals. In *Biochemistry, Schizophrenias and Affective Illnesses.* Himwich, H.E. (ed.), p. 361. Williams and Wilkins Co. Baltimore, 1970.

92. HOCH, P.H., CATTELL, J.P. and PENNES, H.H. Effects of mescaline and lysergic acid (d-LSD-25). *Amer. J. Psychiat.* 108, 579, 1952.

93. ISBELL, H. Comparison of the reactions induced by psilocybin and LSD-25 in man. *Psychopharmacologia,* 1, 29, 1959.

94. SZARA, S. The comparison of the psychotic effect of tryptamine derivatives with the effects of mescaline and LSD-25 in self-experiments. In *Psychotropic Drugs,* Garattini, S. and Ghetti, V. (eds.), p. 460. Elsevier, Amsterdam, 1957.

95. SHULGIN, A.T., SARGENT, T. and NARANJO, C. Structure-activity relationships of one-ring psychotomimetics. *Nature* 211, 537, 1969.

96. HOLLISTER, L.E., RICHARDS, R.K. and GILLESPIE, H.K. Comparison of THC and synhexyl in man. *Clin. Pharmacol. Therap.* 9, 783, 1968.

97. BERINGER, K. Der. Meskalinrausch. *Monogr. Gesamtgeb. Neurol. v. Psychiat.* 49, 1, 1927.

98. BERCEL, N.A., TRAVIS, L.E., OLINGER, L.B. and DREIKURS, E. Model psychoses induced by LSD-25 in normals. *Arch. Neurol. Psychiat.* 75, 588, 1956.

99. JARVIK, M.E. Comparison of drug-induced and endogenous psychoses in Man. In *Proc. 1st. Internat. Cong. Neuropharmacology,* p. 172. Elsevier, London, 1959.

100. KRILL, A.E., WIELAND, A.M. and OSTFELD, A. The effect of two hallucinogenic agents on human retinal function. *Arch. Ophthal.* (Chic.) 64, 723, 1960.

101. RINKEL, M., DeSHON, H.J., HYDE, R.W. and SOLOMON, H.C. Experimental schizophrenia-like symptoms. *Amer. J. Psychiat.* 108, 572, 1952.

102. BLEULER, M. Comparison of drug-induced and endogenous psychoses in Man. In *Proc. 1st Internat. Cong. Neuropharmacology,* p. 161. Elsevier, London, 1959.

103. SANDISON, R.A. Ibid., p. 176, 1959.

104. LIPTON, M.A. The relevance of chemically-induced psychoses to schizophrenia. In *Psychotomimetic Drugs,* Efron, D.H. (ed.), p. 231. Raven Press, New York, 1970.

105. YOUNG, B.G. A phenomenological comparison of LSD and schizophrenic states. *Brit. J. Psychiat.* 124, 64, 1974.

106. CHAPMAN, J. The early symptoms of schizophrenia. Ibid. 112, 225, 1966.

107. McGHIE, A. and CHAPMAN, J. Disorders of attention and perception in early schizophrenia. *Brit. J. Med. Psychol.* **34**, 103, 1961.
108. SILVERMAN, J. Perceptual and neurophysiological analogues of "experience" in schizophrenia and LSD reactions. In *Schizophrenia, Current Concepts and Research*, Siva Sankar, D.V. (ed.), p. 182. PJD Publications Ltd. New York, 1969.
109. SMART, R.G. and BATEMAN, K. Unfavourable reactions to LSD: A review and analysis of the available case reports. *Canad. med. Assoc. J.* **97**, 1214, 1967.
110. COHEN, S. Lysergic acid diethylamide: side effects and complications. *J. nerv. ment. Dis.* **130**, 30, 1960.
111. MALLESON, N. Acute adverse reactions to LSD in clinical and experimental use in the United Kingdom. *Brit. J. Psychiat.* **118**, 229, 1971.
112. HATRICK, J.A. and DEWHURST, K. Delayed psychosis due to LSD. *Lancet* **2**, 742, 1970.
113. COHEN, S. A classification of LSD complications. *Psychosomatics* **7**, 182, 1966.
114. RINKEL, M. and DENBER, H.C.B. Chemical concepts of psychosis. McDowell Oblensky Inc. New York, 1958.
115. ROBINS, E., FROSCH, W.A. and STERN, M. Further observations on untoward reactions to LSD. *Amer. J. Psychiat.* **124**, 393, 1967.
116. UNGERLEIDER, J.T., FISHER, D.D., GOLDSMITH, S.R., FULLER, M. and FORGY, E. A statistical survey of adverse reactions to LSD in Los Angeles County. Ibid. **125**, 352, 1968.
117. SUB-COMMITTEE ON NARCOTICS ADDICTION. The dangerous drug problem. N.Y. Med. **22**, 241, 1966.
118. BRIDGER, W.H. The interaction of stress and hallucinogenic drug action: implications for a pathophysiological mechanism in schizophrenia. In *Schizophrenia: Current Concepts and Research*, Siva Sankar, D.V. (ed.), p. 470. PJD Publications, New York, 1969.
119. DITMAN, K.S., TIETZ, W., PRINCE, B.S., FORGY, E. and MOSS, T. Harmful aspects of the LSD experience. *J. nerv. ment. Dis.* **145**, 464, 1968.
120. GLASS, G.S. and BOWERS, M.B. Jr. Chronic psychosis associated with long-term psychotomimetic drug abuse. *Arch. gen. Psychiat.* **23**, 97, 1970.
121. GLASS, G.S. and BOWERS, M.B. Jr. Psychedelic drugs, stress and the ego. *J. nerv. ment. Dis.* **156**, 232, 1973.
122. BEWLEY, T.H. Adverse reactions from the illicit use of Lysergide. *Brit. med. J.* **3**, 28, 1967.
123. DEWHURST, K. and HATRICK, J.A. Differential diagnosis and treatment of LSD induced psychosis. *Practitioner* **209**, 327, 1972.
124. KLEBER, H.B. Prolonged adverse reactions from unsupervised use of hallucinogenic drugs. *J. nerv. ment. Dis.* **144**, 308, 1967.
125. ROSENTHAL, S.H. Persistent hallucinosis following administration of hallucinogenic drugs. *Amer. J. Psychiat.* **121**, 238, 1964.
126. UNGERLEIDER, J.T., FISHER, D.D. and FULLER, M. The dangers of LSD. *J.A.M.A.* **197**, 389, 1966.
127. HAYS, P. and TILLEY, J.R. The differences between LSD psychosis and schizophrenia. *Canad. Psychiat. Assoc. J.* **18**, 331, 1973.
128. BOWERS, M.B. Jr. Acute psychosis induced by psychotomimetic drug abuse. I. Clinical findings. *Arch. gen. Psychiat.* **27**, 437, 1972.
129. COHEN, S. and DITMAN, K.S. Prolonged adverse reactions to LSD. Ibid. **8**, 475, 1963.
130. FROSCH, W.A., ROBINS, E.S. and STERN, M. Untoward reactions to LSD resulting in hospitalisation. *New Eng. J. Med.* **273**, 1235, 1965.
131. McGLOTHLIN, W.H., ARNOLD, D.O. and FREEDMAN, D.X. Organicity measures following repeated LSD ingestion. *Arch. gen. Psychiat.* **21**, 704, 1969.
132. BLACKER, K.H., JONES, R.T., STONE, G.C. and PFEFFERBAUM, D. Chronic users of LSD: The "acid-heads". *Amer. J. Psychiat.* **125**, 341, 1968.
133. TUCKER, G.T., QUINLAN, D. and HARROW, M. Chronic hallucinogenic drug use and thought disturbance. *Arch. gen. Psychiat.* **27**, 443, 1972.
134. HOROWITZ, M.J. Flashbacks: recurrent intrusive images after the use of LSD. *Amer. J. Psychiat.* **126**, 565, 1969.
135. KEELER, M.H., REIFLER, C.B. and LIPTZIN, M.B. Spontaneous recurrences of marijuana effect. *Amer. J. Psychiat.* **125**, 384, 1968.
136. ISBELL, H., GORODETZSKY, C.W., JASINSKI, D., CLAUSSEN, V., SPULAK, F. and von KARTE, F. Effects of THC in man. *Psychopharmacologia* **2**, 184, 1967.
137. ALTMAN, H. and EVENSON, R.C. Marijuana use and subsequent psychiatric symptoms: a replication. *Comprehens. Psychiat.* **14**, 415, 1973.
138. GRINSPOON, L. Marihuana. *Int. J. Neuropsychiat.* **9**, 488, 1970.
139. DHUNJIBHOY, J.E. A brief resumé of the types of insanity commonly met with in India, with a full description of "Indian hemp insanity" peculiar to the country. *J. ment. Sci.* **76**, 254, 1930.
140. WARNOCK, J. Insanity from hasheesh. *J. ment. Sci.* **49**, 96, 1903.

141. LEWIS, A. A review of the international clinical literature. Appendix I. In *Cannibis*. Report by the Advisory Committee on Drug Dependence. H.M.S.O., London, 1968.
142. CHOPRA, G.S. and SMITH, J.W. Psychotic reactions following cannabis use in East Indians. *Arch. gen. Psychiat.* **30**, 24, 1974.
143. TALBOTT, J.A. and TEAGUE, J.W. Marihuana psychosis. *J.A.M.A.* **210**, 299, 1969.
144. ALLENTUCK, S. and BOWMAN, K.M. Psychiatric aspects of Marihuana intoxication. *Amer. J. Psychiat.* **99**, 248, 1942.
145. BERNHARDSON, G. and GUNNE, L.-M. 46 cases of psychosis in cannabis abusers. *Internat. J. Addict.* **7**, 9, 1972.
146. DAVISON, K. and WILSON, C.H. Psychosis associated with cannabis smoking. *Brit. J. Addict.* **67**, 225, 1972.
147. GEORGE, H.R. Two psychotic episodes associated with cannabis. *Brit. J. Addict.* **65**, 119, 1970.
148. KLEE, G.D. Marihuana psychosis. A case study. *Psychiat. Quart.* **43**, 719, 1969.
149. KOLANSKY, H. and MOORE, W.T. Effects of marihuana on adolescents and young adults. *J.A.M.A.* **216**, 486, 1971.
150. KEUP, W. Psychotic symptoms due to cannabis abuse. *Dis. Nerv. Syst.* **31**, 119, 1970.
151. PERNA, D. Psychotogenic effect of marihuana. *J.A.M.A.* **209**, 1085, 1969.
152. TENNANT, F.S. and GROESBECK, J. Psychiatric effects of hashish. *Arch. gen. Psychiat.* **27**, 133, 1972.
153. THACORE, V.R. Bhang psychosis. *Brit. J. Psychiat.* **123**, 225, 1973.
154. BALESTRIERI, A. and FONTANARI, D. Acquired and crossed-tolerance to mescaline, LSD-25 and BOL-148. *Arch. gen Psychiat.* **1**, 279, 1959.
155. ISBELL, H., WOLBACH, A.B., WIKLER, A. and MINER, E.T. Cross-tolerance between LSD and psilocybin. *Psychopharmacologia*, **2**, 147, 1967.
156. HOLLISTER, L.E. Clinical, biochemical and psychologic effects of psilocybin. *Arch. Intern. Pharmacodyn. Ther.* **130**, 42, 1961.
157. BRAWLEY, P. and DUFFIELD, J.C. The pharmacology of hallucinogens. *Pharmacol. Rev.* **24**, 31, 1972.
158. AGHAJANIAN, G.K., SHEARD, M.H. and FOOTE, W.E. LSD and Mescaline: comparison of effects in single units in the midbrain raphe. In *Psychotomimetic Drugs*, Efron, D.H. (ed.), p. 165. Raven Press, New York, 1970.
159. CHAPMAN, L.F., WALTER, R.D., ADEY, W.R., CRANDALL, P.H., RAND, R.W., BRAZIER, M.A.B. and MARKHAM, C.H. Altered electrical activity of human hippocampus and amygdala induced by LSD-25. *Physiologist* **5**, 118, 1962.
160. TRUITT, E.B. and ANDERSON, S.M. Biogenic amine alteration produced in the brain by tetrahydrocannabinols and their metabolites. *Ann. NY. Acad. Sci.* **191**, 68, 1971.
161. SMYTHIES, J.R. Introduction to Amines and Schizophrenia. Himwich, H.E., Kety, S.S. and Smythies, J.R. (eds.), Pergamon Press, London, 1967.
162. KETY, S.S. Current biochemical approaches to schizophrenia. *New Eng. J. Med.* **276**, 325, 1967.
163. ALLES, G.A. The comparate physiological actions of dl-phenylisopropylamines. *J. Pharmacol.* **32**, 121, 1927.
164. van PRAAG, H.M. Abuse of, dependence on and psychoses from anorexigenic drugs. In *Drug-induced Diseases*, Vol. 3. Meyler, L. and Peck, H.M. (eds.), p. 281. Excerpta Medica, Amsterdam, 1968.
165. DANIELS, L.E. A symptomatic treatment for narcolepsy. *Proc. Staff. Meet. Mayo Clinic.* **5**, 299, 1930.
166. MODELL, W. Status and prospect of drugs for over-eating. *J.A.M.A.* **173**, 1131, 1960.
167. YOUNG, D. and SCOVILLE, W.B. Paranoid psychosis in narcolepsy and the possible danger of benzedrine treatment. *Med. Clin. N. Amer.* **22**, 637, 1938.
168. DAVISON, K. and BAGLEY, C. Schizophrenia-like psychoses associated with organic disorders of the CNS: a review of the literature. In *Current Problems in Neuropsychiatry*. Herrington, R.N. (ed.), p. 113. Headley, Ashford, Kent.
169. HERMAN, M. and NAGLER, S.H. Psychoses due to amphetamine. *J. nerv. ment. Dis.* **120**, 268, 1954.
170. CONNELL, P.H. Amphetamine Psychoses. Maudsley Monograph No. 5. Chapman and Hall, London, 1958.
171. SLATER, E. Review of Connell (1958). *Brit. med. J.* **1**, 488, 1959.
172. BEAMISH, P. and KILOH, L.G. Psychosis due to amphetamine consumption. *J. ment. Sci.* **106**, 337, 1960.
173. ANGRIST, B.M. and GERSHON, S. Psychiatric sequelae of amphetamine use. In *Psychiatric complications of medical drugs*. Shader, R.I. (ed.), p. 175. Raven Press, New York, 1972.
174. BELL, D.S. Comparison of amphetamine psychosis and schizophrenia. *Brit. J. Psychiat.* **111**, 701, 1965.
175. ELLINWOOD, E.H. Jr. Amphetamine psychosis. I. Description of the individuals and process. *J. nerv. ment. Dis.* **144**, 273, 1967.
176. McCONNELL, W.B. Amphetamine substances in mental illnesses in Northern Ireland. *Brit. J. Psychiat.* **109**, 218, 1963.

177. PANSE, F. and KLAGES, W. Klinisch-psychopathologische Beobachtungen bei chronischem Missbrauch von Ephedrin und verwandten Substanzen. *Arch. Psychiat. Nervenkr.* **206**, 69, 1964.
178. HERRIDGE, C.F. and A'BROOK, M.F. Ephedrine psychosis. *Brit. med. J.* **2**, 160, 1968.
179. LUCAS, A.R. and WEISS, M. Methylphenidate hallucinosis. *J.A.M.A.* **217**, 1079, 1971.
180. McCORMICK, T.C. Jr. and McNEEL, T.W. Acute psychosis and ritalin abuse. *Texas State J. Med.* **59**, 99, 1963.
181. SPENSLEY, J. Folie à deux with methylphenidate psychosis. *J. nerv. ment. Dis.* **155**, 288, 1972.
182. SPENSLEY, J. and ROCKWELL, D.A. Psychosis during methylphenidate abuse. *New Eng. J. Med.* **286**, 880, 1972.
183. ANANTH, J.V. Repeated episodes of phenmetrazine psychosis. *Canad. med. Assoc. J.* **105**, 1280, 1971.
184. BETHELL, M.F. Toxic psychosis caused by Preludin. *Brit. med. J.* **1**, 30, 1957.
185. EVANS, J. Psychosis and addiction to phenmetrazine (Preludin). *Lancet* **2**, 152, 1959.
186. MENDELS, J. Paranoid psychosis associated with phenmetrazine addiction. *Brit. J. Psychiat.* **110**, 865, 1964.
187. SIMMA, K. Über Preludin-Halluzinose. *Wien. klin. Wschr.* **72**, 441, 1960.
188. WITTSTOCK, P. Schizophrenie-ämliche exogene Psychose bei Preludin-Sucht. *Nervenarzt.* **38**, 39, 1967.
189. CLEIN, L.J. and BENADY, D.R. A case of diethylpropion addiction. *Brit. med. J.* **2**, 456, 1962.
190. JONES, H.J. Diethylpropion dependence. *Med. J. Aust.* **1**, 267, 1968.
191. KUENSSBERG, E.V. Diethylpropion psychosis. *Brit. med. J.* **2**, 729, 1962.
192. WHITLOCK, F.A. and NADORFI, M.I. Diethylpropion and psychosis. *Med. J. Aust.* **2**, 1097, 1970.
193. ANGRIST, B.M., SCHWEITZER, J.W., GERSHON, S. and FRIEDHOFF, A.J. Mephentermine psychosis: misuse of the Wyamine inhaler. *Amer. J. Psychiat.* **126**, 1315, 1970.
194. ANDERSON, E.D. Propylhexedrine (Benzedrex) psychosis. *N.Z. Med. J.* **71**, 302, 1970.
195. JÖNSSON, L.-E. and GUNNE, L.-M. Clinical studies of amphetamine psychosis. In *Amphetamines and related compounds*, Costa, E. and Garattini, S. (eds.), p. 929. Raven Press, New York, 1970.
196. ANGRIST, B.M. and GERSHON, S. The phenomenology of experimentally induced amphetamine psychosis – preliminary observations. *Biol. Psychiat.* **2**, 95, 1970.
197. GRIFFITHS, J.D. CAVANAGH, J.H. and OATES, J.A. Psychosis induced by the administration of d-amphetamine to human volunteers. In *Psychotomimetic Drugs*, Efron, D.H. (ed.), Raven Press, New York, 1970.
198. BELL, D.S. The experimental reproduction of amphetamine psychosis. *Arch. gen. Psychiat.* **29**, 35, 1973.
199. JÖNSSON, L.E. and SJÖSTRÖM. A rating scale for evaluation of the clinical course and symptomatology in amphetamine psychosis. *Brit. J. Psychiat.* **117**, 661, 1970.
200. SANO, I. and NAGASAKA, C. Über chronische Weckaminsucht bei Japan. *Fortsch. Neurol. Psychiat.* **24**, 391, 1956.
201. YOSHIMOTO, C. Psychopathologische Studien der Weckaminpsychose. *Folia psychiat-neurol. Jap.* **13**, 174, 1959.
202. CALDWELL, J. and SEVER, P.S. The biochemical pharmacology of abused drugs. 1. Amphetamines, cocaine and LSD. *Clin. Pharmacol. Ther.* **16**, 625, 1974.
203. RUTLEDGE, C.O. The mechanism by which amphetamine inhibits oxidative deamination of norepinephrine in brain. *J. Pharmacol. Exp. Therap.* **171**, 181, 1970.
204. STEIN, L. Self-stimulation of the brain and the central stimulant action of amphetamine. *Fed. Proc.* **23**, 836, 1964.
205. BURN, J.H. *The Principles of Therapeutics*, p. 130. C.C. Thomas. Springfield, Ill. 1957.
206. VANE, J.R. *Adrenergic Mechanisms*, p. 356. Churchill, London, 1960.
207. ELLINWOOD, E.H. Jr., SUDILOVSKY, A. and NELSON, L.M. Evolving behaviour in the clinical and experimental amphetamine (model) psychosis. *Amer. J. Psychiat.* **130**, 1088, 1973.
208. ÅNGGÅRD, E., JÖNSSON, L.-E., HOGMARK, A.-L. and GUNNE, L.-M. Amphetamine metabolism in amphetamine psychosis. *Clin. Pharm. Therap.* **14**, 870, 1973.
209. BAN, T.A. *Recent advances in the biology of schizophrenia*, p. 92. C.C. Thomas. Springfield, Ill. 1973.
210. SNYDER, S.H. Amphetamine psychosis. A "model" schizophrenia mediated by catecholamines. *Amer. J. Psychiat.* **130**, 61, 1973.
211. KLAWANS, H.L. and MARGOLIN, D.I. Amphetamine-induced dopaminergic hypersensitivity in guinea pigs. *Arch. gen. Psychiat.* **32**, 725, 1975.
212. GOODWIN, F.K. Psychiatric side effects of levodopa in man. *J.A.M.A.* **218**, 1915, 1971.
213. GOODWIN, F.K. Behavioural effects of L-DOPA in Man. In *Psychiatric complications of medical drugs*. Shader, R.I. (ed.), p. 149. Raven Press, New York, 1972.
214. MURPHY, D.L. L-Dopa, behavioural activation and psychopathology. *Res. Publ. Ass. Ment. Dis.* **50**, 472, 1972.
215. CELESIA, G.G. and BARR, A.N. Psychosis and other psychiatric manifestations of levodopa therapy. *Arch. Neurol.* **23**, 193, 1970.
216. JENKINS, R.B. and GROH, R.H. Mental symptoms in Parkinsonian patients treated with L-Dopa. *Lancet* **2**, 177, 1970.

217. YARYURA-TOBIAS, J.A. and MERLIS, S. Levodopa and schizophrenia. *J.A.M.A.* **211**, 1857, 1970.
218. GROSS, M.M., HALPERT, E. and SABOT, L. Toward a revised classification of the acute alcoholic psychoses. *J. Nerv. ment. Dis.* **145**, 500, 1968.
219. VICTOR, M. and ADAMS, R.D. Effects of alcohol on the nervous system. *Res. Publ. Ass. Ment. Dis.* **32**, 526, 1953.
220. BLEULER, E. *Textbook of Psychiatry*, p. 635. Dover, New York, 1951.
221. KRAEPELIN, E. and LANGE, J. *Psychiatrie*, 9th ed., Thieme. Leipzig, 1927.
222. ISBELL, H., FRASER, H.F. and WILKER, A. An experimental study of the etiology of "rumfits" and delirium tremens. *Quart. J. Stud. Alcohol.* **16**, 1, 1955.
223. MENDELSON, J.H. and LaDOU, J. Experimentally induced chronic intoxication and withdrawal in alcoholics. Part I. Background and experimental design. Ibid. **2** (suppl) 1, 1964.
224. SARAVAY, S.M. and PARDES, H. Auditory elementary hallucinations in alcohol withdrawal psychosis. *Arch. gen. Psychiat.* **16**, 652, 1967.
225. SLATER, E. and ROTH, M. *Clinical Psychiatry*, p. 402. Baillière, Tindall and Cassell, 1969.
226. ALPERT, M. and SILVERS, K.N. Perceptual characteristics distinguishing auditory hallucinations in schizophrenia and acute alcoholic psychoses. *Amer. J. Psychiat.* **127**, 298, 1970.
227. VICTOR, M. and HOPE, J.M. The phenomenon of auditory hallucinations in chronic alcoholism. *J. Nerv. ment. Dis.* **126**, 451, 1958.
228. BENEDETTI, G. Die Alkoholhalluzinosen, Thieme, Stuttgart, 1952.
229. GROSS, M.M., GOODENOUGH, D., TOBIN, M., HALPERT, E., LEPORE, D., PERLSTEIN, A., SIROTA, M., DIBIANCO, J., FULLER, R. and KISHNER, I. Sleep disturbances and hallucinations in the acute alcoholic psychoses. *J. nerv. ment. Dis.* **142**, 493, 1966.
230. DEMENT, W.C. Recent studies on the biological role of rapid eye movement sleep. *Amer. J. Psychiat.* **122**, 404, 1965.
231. McCLELLAND, H.A. Personal communication. 1975.
232. SCHUCKITT, M.A. and WINOKUR, G. Alcoholic hallucinosis and schizophrenia. A negative study. *Brit. J. Psychiat.* **119**, 549, 1971.
233. LIDDON, S.C. and SATRAN, R. Disulfiram (Antabuse) psychosis. *Amer. J. Psychiat.* **123**, 1284, 1967.
234. SHAW, I.A. The treatment of alcoholism with tetraethylthiuram disulfide in a State mental hospital. *Quart. J. Stud. Alcohol.* **12**, 576, 1951.
235. KNEE, S.T. and RAZANI, J. Acute organic brain syndrome: a complication of disulfiram therapy. *Amer. J. Psychiat.* **131**, 1281, 1974.
236. ROTHSTEIN, E. and CLANCY, D.D. Toxicity of disulfiram combined with metronidazole. *New Eng. J. Med.* **280**, 1006, 1969.
237. STEIN, L. and WISE, C.D. Possible etiology of schizophrenia: progressive damage to the noradrenergic reward system by endogenous 6-hydroxy-dopamine. In *Neurotransmitters Res. Publ. Ass. ment. Dis.* **50**, 298, 1972.
238. STEIN, L. Neurochemistry of reward and punishment: some implications for the etiology of schizophrenia. *J. Psychiat. Res.* **8**, 345, 1971.
239. REYNOLDS, E. Epilepsy and schizophrenia. Relationship and biochemistry. *Lancet* **1**, 398, 1968.
240. SNAITH, R.P., MEHTA, S. and RABY, A.H. Serum folate and vitamin B_{12} in epileptics with and without mental illness. *Brit. J. Psychiat.* **116**, 179, 1970.
241. WOODS, D.D., FOSTER, M.A. and GUEST, J.R. In *Transmethylation and Methionine Biosynthesis*. Shapiro, S.K. and Schlenk, F. (eds.), p. 138. Chicago, 1965.
242. BALDESSARINI, R.J. In *Amines and Schizophrenia*. Himwich, H.E., Kety, S.S. and Smythies, J.R. (eds.), p. 199. Pergamon Press, Oxford, 1967.
243. LEVI, R.N. and WAXMAN, S. Schizophrenia, epilepsy, cancer, methionine and folate metabolism. *Lancet* **2**, 11, 1975.
244. DUBÉ, K.C. and HANDA, S.K. Drug use in health and mental illness in an Indian population. *Brit. J. Psychiat.* **118**, 345, 1971.
245. BREAKEY, W.R., GOODELL, H., LORENZ, P.C. and McHUGH, R.P. Hallucinogenic drugs as precipitants of schizophrenia. *Psychological Medicine,* **4**, 255, 1974.
246. GLICKMAN, L. and BLUMENFIELD, M. Psychological determinants of "LSD reactions". *J. nerv. ment. Dis.* **145**, 79, 167.
247. WHARTON, R.N. A commentary on drug-related schizophrenic syndromes. *Inter. J. Psychiat.* **11**, 438, 1973.
248. MACLEAN, P.D. Contrasting functions of limbic and neocortical systems of the brain and their relevance to psychophysiological aspects of medicine. *Amer. J. Med.* **25**, 611, 1958.
249. TORREY, E.F. and PETERSON, M.R. Schizophrenia and the limbic system. *Lancet* **2**, 942, 1974.
250. CARLSSON, A. The occurrence, distribution and physiological role of catecholamines in the nervous system. *Pharmacol. Rev.* **11**, 490, 1959.
251. Leading article – Amines, alerting and effect. *Lancet* **1**, 1237, 1968. ·
252. SZARA, S. Hallucinogenic amines and schizophrenia. In *Amines and Schizophrenia*, Himwich, H.E., Kety, S.S. and Smythies, J.R. (eds.), p. 181, Pergamon Press, London, 1967.

253. WINTERS, W.D. and WALLACH, M.B. Drug induced state of CNS excitation: a theory of hallucinosis. In *Psychotomimetic Drugs*. Efron, D.H. (ed.), p. 193. Raven Press, New York, 1970.
254. MOORE, R.Y. Brain lesions and amine metabolism. *Internat. Rev. Neurobiol.* **13**, 67, 1970.
255. BELLAK, L. Toward a unified concept of schizophrenia. An elaboration of the multiple factor psychosomatic theory of schizophrenia. *J. nerv. ment. dis.* **121**, 60, 1955.
256. COBB, S. Thoughts on schizophrenia. *Amer. J. Psychiat.* **120**, 707, 1964.
257. MAPOTHER, E. Mental symptoms associated with head-injury. *Brit. med. J.* **2**, 1055, 1937.

On the Biochemistry and Pharmacology
of Hallucinogens

K. FUXE, B.J. EVERITT, L. AGNATI, B. FREDHOLM and G. JONSSON

Hallucinogens are also called phantastica, psychotomimetics or psychodelics. These terms are to a large extent synonymous, and this class of compounds is characterised by their ability to cause a change of reality while still allowing recall. It should be pointed out that true hallucinations are rare events. According to most authors the main families of hallucinogens are as follows:

(1) d-LSD and derivatives.
(2) Psilocybine, psilocin and other indolalkylamines such as dimethyltryptamine (DMT) and 5-methoxy-DMT. Psilocybine and psilocin are found in the teonanacatl mushroom of Mexico. DMT and 5-methoxy-DMT are found in a number of South American snuffs.
(3) Mescaline and other hallucinogenic phenylethylamines such as trimethoxy-amphetamines, p-methoxy-amphetamine (PMA) and 4-methyl,2,5-methoxy-amphetamine (DOM). Mescaline stems from the peyotl. the cactus Anhalonium lewinii, found in Mexico.

Anticholinergic drugs such as atropine, scopolamine and ditrane are also known to cause hallucinations, but they cause a delusional state (disorientation) associated with amnesia rather than recall and therefore represent a special group of hallucinogens.

A special group is also the group of amphetamines. Thus, after chronic treatment with large doses of amphetamine a paranoid psychosis can develop (Griffith et al., 1970; Snyder, 1972) which may resemble paranoid schizophrenia.

The great interest in these groups of compounds is due to the fact that they can produce in man a psychotic state that resembles acute schizophrenia (Bowers and Freedman, 1966). It has been pointed out, however, that it is difficult to demonstrate the fundamental symptoms of schizophrenia such as thought disorder, blunted affect, withdrawal and autistic behaviour (Hollister, 1968) after treatment with e.g. d-LSD. But there is no doubt that a better understanding of the mechanism of action of hallucinogens will improve our understanding of schizophrenia and of the neuronal systems that may be mainly involved in the schizophrenia process. It may be mentioned that tryptamine exists in brain and also the N-methylating enzymes (Wyatt et al., 1974a). Thus, under certain conditions substrate and enzyme can be brought together and an hallucinogenic compound DMT formed. Recently, it has been claimed that DMT is found in the cerebrospinal fluid of certain types of schizophrenic patients (Christian et al., 1975). One problem with this hypothesis is, however, that tolerance has been shown to develop to d-LSD, psilocybine, DMT and mescaline both in normal and in schizophrenic patients (Chessick et al., 1964), and therefore the chronic nature of the disease cannot be explained. It may be speculated, however, that supersensitivity has developed at certain receptor sites in the brain and therefore tolerance to the psychotic actions of the

135

hallucinogens will not develop. Also, it has been reported that tolerance does not develop to many effects of DMT (Wyatt *et al.* 1974). For further information on hallucinogens, see books edited by Efron (1970) and by Smythies (1970).

The present article will mainly deal with d-LSD and the hallucinogenic indolealkylamines and phenylethylamines and their actions on central 5-hydroxytryptamine (5-HT) and catecholamine (CA) systems. The major interest for many years has been focused on the 5-HT systems which seem very sensitive to the actions of these hallucinogens (Freedman, 1961; Rosecrans *et al.*, 1967; Andén *et al.*, 1968; Aghajanian *et al.*, 1968).

Central 5-HT neurons

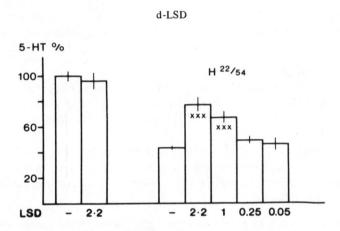

Fig. 1. *The effect of d-LSD on the H22/54 induced 5-HT depletion in whole brain.*

The animals received d-LSD i.p. and 15 min later H22/54 was given (500 mg/kg, i.p., 3 h before killing). The second dose was given 2 h after the first injection. On the x-axis the treatments are given. On the y-axis the 5-HT contents (means ± s.e.m., 4 rats) are shown expressed in per cent of untreated group means. Student's t-test. xxx: p<0.005. All comparisons were made with H22/54 alone group. From Andén *et al.*, 1968.

As seen in Fig. 1, d-LSD reduces the depletion of brain 5-HT after tryptophan hydroxylase inhibition using α-propyldopacetamide (H 22/54; Andén *et al.*, 1968). These results suggest a reduction of 5-HT turnover by d-LSD, since the 5-HT stores were not affected as measured 3 h after d-LSD. In these experiments d-LSD was given 15 min before H 22/54. Similar results have also been observed when d-LSD was given at the same time as H 22/54 (Table 1). In this study relatively high doses of d-LSD were used. However, recently it has also been possible to observe a reduction of 5-HT turnover using a dose of 40 µg/kg of d-LSD twice (Fig. 10). It should be noted that the non-hallucinogenic LSD derivatives methysergide and 2-Br-d-LSD did not cause a reduction of 5-HT turnover. In order to establish the mechanism for this reduction of 5-HT turnover, the effects of d-LSD were studied on the extensor reflex activity of the acutely spinalised rat, which is highly dependent on 5-HT receptor activity (Andén, 1968). It was found that d-LSD increased this reflex and did so independently of presynaptic 5-HT stores, since the effects were not diminished by pretreatment with reserpine and α-propyldopacetamide (Andén *et al.*, 1968). As seen in Table 2 doses of d-LSD as low as 20 µg/kg can increase the extensor

TABLE 1
The effect of d-LSD on the H22/54 induced
whole brain 5-HT depletion

The rats were given d-LSD (1 mg/kg, i.p.) at the same time as the inhibitor
H 22/54 (α-propyldopacetamide, 500 mg/kg, i.p.). The rats were killed
1, 2 or 3 h later. Means ± s.e.m (4 rats/group) are shown in per cent of
the control group mean value (411 ± 4 ng/g, 12 rats). Student's t-test was
used for statistical analysis (Corrodi and Fuxe, unpublished data).

Treatment	Time	5-HT
	h	%
No drug treatment		100 ± 3.7
d-LSD	1	96 ± 7.5
H 22/54	1	74 ± 3.4
d-LSD + H 22/54	1	88 ± 4.4 [x]
No drug treatment		100 ± 3.7
d-LSD	2	92 ± 8.3
H 22/54	2	55 ± 3.4
d-LSD + H 22/54	2	101 ± 3.4 [xxx]
No drug treatment		100 ± 3.7
d-LSD	3	95 ± 2.7
H 22/54	3	43 ± 2.4
d-LSD + H 22/54	3	65 ± 6.3 [xx]

x: $p < 0.05$;   xx: $p < 0.02$;   xxx: $p < 0.001$.
All comparisons have been made with respective H 22/54 group.

hindlimb reflex activity, suggesting a high affinity of d-LSD for the postsynaptic spinal 5-HT
receptor. The non-hallucinogenic compounds methylsergide and 2-Br-LSD did not increase the
reflex activity. In view of these findings on postsynaptic 5-HT receptor activity, it was
suggested by Andén, Corrodi, Fuxe and Hökfelt (1968) that d-LSD was a postsynaptic 5-HT
receptor agonist and that the reduction of 5-HT turnover was the consequence of a nervous
feedback elicited by the 5-HT receptor stimulation leading to a reduction of nervous impulse
flow and consequently of a slowing of 5-HT turnover (Fig. 2). Simultaneously it was shown by
Aghajanian *et al.* (1968) that low i.v. doses (threshold dose: 10 μg/kg) of d-LSD caused a rapid
and uniform slowing of firing rate in the nuc. raphe dorsalis which is built up of 5-HT cell
bodies. These results were therefore in good agreement. It is not likely that a direct inhibition
of 5-HT release is responsible for the reduction of 5-HT turnover by d-LSD, since inhibition by
d-LSD of ^{3}H-5-HT release *in vitro* induced by field-stimulation is only seen with high
concentrations of d-LSD (Fig. 2, Chase *et al.*, 1967; Farnebo and Hamberger, 1971).
    Recently Aghajanian's group has made the important discovery that presynaptic 5-HT
receptors on the 5-HT raphe cells (Fig. 2) are more sensitive to the action of d-LSD than the
postsynaptic 5-HT receptors in the ventral part of the lateral geniculate body and other parts of
the forebrain (Haigler and Aghajanian, 1974). Therefore, they propose that the main action of

TABLE 2
The effect of hallucinogens on the extensor
hindlimb reflex activity of the acutely
spinalised rat

The spinal cord transection was made in the midthoracic region 2-3 h before testing. The strength of the extensor reflex was semiquantitatively estimated on coded animals. 4 = very strong; 3 = strong; 2 = medium; 1 = weak; 0.5 = very weak. N = 4−5. Statistical analysis was made according to the Quantile test (Conover, 1971).

Treatment	Dose mg/kg	Strength of the extensor reflex			
		Mediane	Range	Sample size	Significance
Normal males					
d-LSD	0.02	1.5	(1−2)	4	p=0.06
	0.08	2	(2−2.5)	4	p=0.06
Psilocybine	0.1	0	(0−0.5)	4	NS
Psilocybine	1	2	(1.5−2.5)	4	p=0.6
DMT	1	1.5	(1−1.5)	4	p=0.6
5-Methoxy-DMT	1	2.5	(2−2.5)	4	p=0.6
DOM	1	2	(1.5−2)	5	p<0.03
Mescaline	5	0	(0−0.5)	4	NS
TMA-2	1	0.125	(0−0.5)	4	NS
TMA-2	5	0.5	(0.25−0.5)	4	p=0.6
Ovariectomized female rats					
d-LSD	0.02	1.5	(1−1.5)	5	p<0.03
Psilocybine	1	2.5	(2−2.5)	5	p<0.03
5-Methoxy-DMT	1	1.5	(1−2.5)	5	p<0.03
3,5-Methoxy-4-methyl-phenylethyl-amine	0.5	1	(0.5−1.2)	5	p<0.03

d-LSD is on presynaptic 5-HT receptors and thus that reduction of brain 5-HT release and receptor activity is mainly responsible for the pharmacological and hallucinogenic effects of d-LSD. It is known from the study of Haigler and Aghajanian (1974) that 5-HT inhibits firing rate of neurons in the nuclei that it innervates. Therefore, a release of inhibition would be the neurophysiological event that triggers the behavioural and mental consequences of d-LSD according to these workers.

Recent studies in our laboratory by Everitt, Fuxe and Hökfelt (1975) on the effect of d-LSD on sexual behaviour also indicate that d-LSD in low doses preferentially activates presynaptic 5-HT receptors. 5-HT pathways are known to inhibit sexual behaviour (Meyerson, 1964). Thus,

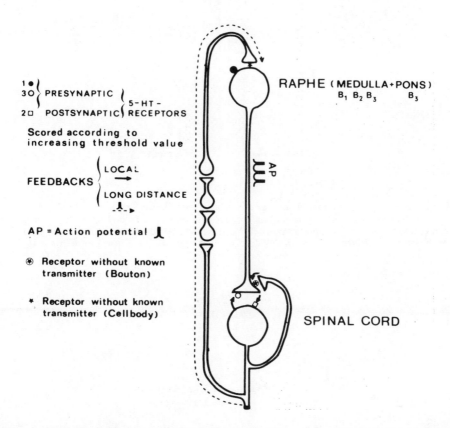

Fig. 2. *Schematic illustration of postsynaptic and two types of presynaptic 5-HT receptors in the bulbospinal 5-HT systems and possible feedback mechanisms.*

The 5-HT raphe cell groups B1-B3 are found mainly within the nuc. raphe pallidus, nuc. raphe obscurus and nuc. raphe magnus (see Dahlström and Fuxe, 1964). Local feedback (→) can involve several mechanisms. There may exist presynaptic 5-HT receptors on the 5-HT boutons (o) which inhibit 5-HT release.

There may exist axo-axonic contacts with an associated receptor (Ⓧ). GABA may here be the transmitter. Furthermore, transsynaptic feedback may also occur. Thus, a substance, e.g. prostaglandin (Hedquist, 1973) may be released on postsynaptic stimulation to reduce 5-HT release.

The long-distance or nervous feedback involves a chain of neurons with unknown numbers of nerve cells finally ending on the 5-HT cell bodies. The transmitter is unknown (*). It has been shown by Aghajanian and coworkers (1974) that there probably also exists presynaptic 5-HT receptors on the cell bodies (●). It is not known if their receptors are innervated by indolamine containing nerve terminals or if they are simply controlled by 5-HT leaking out from the cell bodies or dendrites. These receptors are more sensitive to d-LSD than the postsynaptic 5-HT receptors. The presynaptic 5-HT receptor on the bouton, however, appear to be the least sensitive to d-LSD, since high concentration of d-LSD are necessary in order to inhibit 5-HT release from brain slices *in vitro* using field stimulation (Chase *et al.*, 1967; Farnebo and Hamberger, 1971).

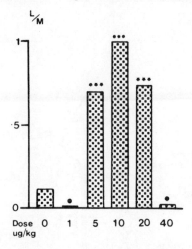

L/M

Dose 0 1 5 10 20 40
ug/kg

Fig. 3. *The effects of d-LSD on lordosis behaviour of estrogen primed, ovariectomised rats.*
    The rats were treated daily with estrogen (2 μg/kg/day). On the x-axis the dose of d-LSD is shown. On the y-axis the median of the lordosis mount ratio (L/M) is shown. All d-LSD injections were made 12 min before observation. Mann-Whitney U-test was used in the statistical analysis. From Everitt *et al.*, 1975.

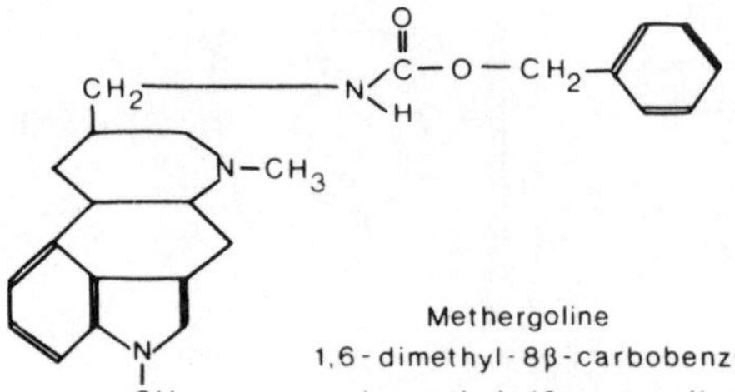

Methergoline
1,6 - dimethyl - 8β - carbobenzyloxy -
aminomethyl - 10 - α - ergoline

Fig. 4. *Formula of methergoline*

as seen in Fig. 2, d-LSD in doses of 10-20 μg/kg increases sexual behaviour in the ovariectomised estrogen primed female rat, whereas in doses of 40 μg/kg and above an inhibition of sexual behaviour is observed. The question, however, still remains whether the hallucinogenic property of d-LSD is related mainly to its effects on presynaptic or on postsynaptic 5-HT receptors. It should be remembered that in the spinal cord the postsynaptic 5-HT receptors may be as sensitive to d-LSD as the presynaptic 5-HT receptors on the raphe cells. Likewise there may also exist in the brain, e.g. the cortex cerebri, postsynaptic 5-HT receptors that are very sensitive to d-LSD. It should also be pointed out that electrical stimulation of the raphe nuclei and treatment with d-LSD both will enhance responsivity to sensory stimuli (Aghajanian *et al.*, 1970b). This is well illustrated by the failure of habituation to repeated stimuli after both d-LSD and electrical stimulation of the 5-HT cell bodies. Thus, here d-LSD mimics the effects of 5-HT released onto postsynaptic receptors.

    A stereospecific high-affinity d-LSD binding (4×10^{-9} M, half-saturation) has recently been demonstrated in a number of brain regions (Bennett and Aghajanian, 1974; Snyder and Bennett, 1975), which seems to be associated with a *postsynaptic* 5-HT receptor rather than with a presynaptic 5-HT receptor. In view of the fact that 5-HT had a 100 times higher affinity for the 5-HT than for the d-LSD binding sites and that similar results were obtained with other tryptamines, it was suggested that d-LSD is bound to a different configuration of the 5-HT receptor than 5-HT. Thus, it might be a partial agonist binding both to the "agonist" and "antagonist" conformation of the 5-HT receptor. In these studies the finding was made that the

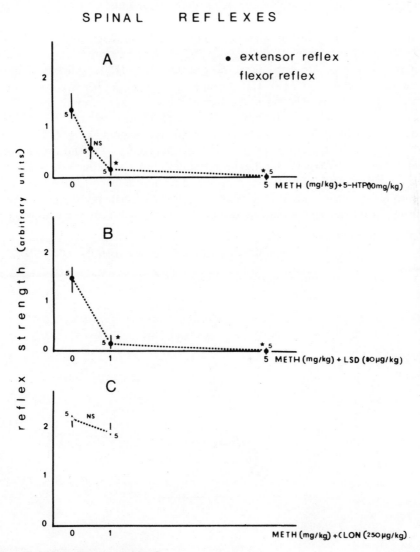

Fig. 5. *Effect of methergoline on spinal reflexes*
On the x axes the doses of methergoline (i.p.) are given. On the y axes the median values of the reflex strength observed in five trials after each treatment are given. Each median value is reported with its semiquartile deviation. Numbers represent number of rats. In Fig. A methergoline (i.p., 3 h earlier) is shown to block in a dose response pattern the extensor reflex increase seen after treatment with 5-HTP (10 mg/kg, iv) following nialamide (100 mg/kg, i.p. 2 h earlier). Statistical analysis according to treatments versus control non-parametrical procedure (α = .049). In Fig. B the interaction on extensor reflex activity between methergoline (i.p., 30 min earlier) and d-LSD (80 μg/kg, i.p.) is reported. Statistical analysis according to treatments versus control non-parametrical procedure (α = .049). In Fig. C the interaction on flexor reflex activity of methergoline (i.p., 30 min earlier) and clonidine (250 μg/kg, i.p.) is reported. Statistical analysis according to Slippage test.

non-hallucinogenic 2-Br-LSD was as potent a displacer of 5-HT and d-LSD binding as was d-LSD. In contrast, it is well-known that 2-Br-LSD is only weakly active on the raphe cells and does not reduce 5-HT turnover (Aghajanian *et al.*, 1968; Andén *et al.*, 1968). These results can therefore be interpreted to suggest that the psychodelic effects of d-LSD are due to actions on presynaptic 5-HT autoreceptors. On the other hand, it should be pointed out that 2-Br-LSD *in vivo* has not been found to exert any effects on the postsynaptic 5-HT receptors in the spinal cord and in behaviour tests it does not mimic the effects of d-LSD or 5-HTP.

In order to solve the problem whether mainly pre- or postsynaptic 5-HT receptors are involved there exists at least one possibility.

Thus, it seems necessary to develop central postsynaptic 5-HT receptor blocking agents. If the hypothesis of Aghajanian *et al.* (Haigler and Aghajanian, 1974) is correct, such a drug should cause hallucinations, whereas if the hypothesis of Andén, Corrodi, Fuxe and Hökfelt (1968) is correct, it should be an antidote against the psychodelic effects of d-LSD and related hallucinogens. Recently we have obtained evidence that methergoline (Fig. 4) can block at least some postsynaptic 5-HT receptors without affecting dopamine (DA) and noradrenaline (NA) receptors (Fuxe *et al.*, 1975a). Thus, it has been found to block the effects of 5-HTP and d-LSD on extensor reflex activity without affecting the clonidine induced increase in flexor reflex activity which is dependent on NA receptor activity (Fig. 5). Furthermore, there seems to be an increase in 5-HT turnover without any certain effects on brain NA and DA turnover (Figs. 6, 7,

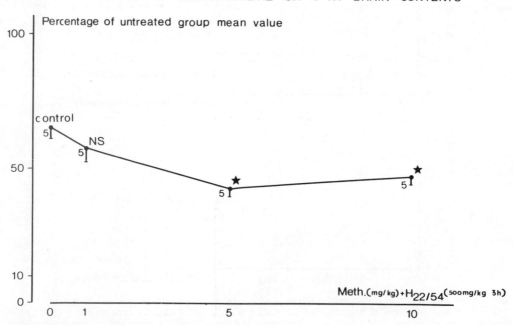

Fig. 6. *Effect of methergoline on 5-HT brain contents*

On the x axis the methergoline (meth.) doses (i.p.) after tryptophane (meth. was given 15 min earlier) hydroxylase inhibition are given (H22/54, 3 h, i.p.) on the y axis the 5-HT brain contents are given in per cent of untreated group mean value. Mean values with respective standard deviation and sample size are plotted.

The statistical analysis was performed according to treatments vs control non-parametrical procedure (experimentwise error α = .05). An asterisk marks the treatments significantly different from the control. NS = not significant.

EFFECT OF METHERGOLINE ON NA BRAIN CONTENTS

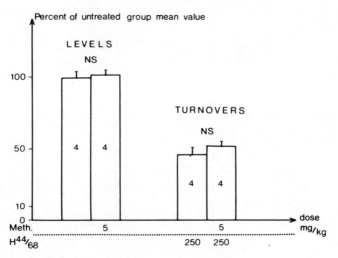

Fig. 7. *Effect of methergoline (meth.) on NA brain contents*
On the x axis the different treatments (i.p. injections) are given. Meth. was injected 30 min before H44/68 (250 mg/kg, i.p., 4 h). On the y axis the NA brain contents are given in per cent of the untreated group mean value. Each mean is reported with its standard deviation; sample sizes are given inside each bar. Methergoline treated groups were compared with the respective control groups (Mann-Whitney U test). NS = not significant.

EFFECT OF METHERGOLINE ON H^{44}/$_{68}$ INDUCED CA FLUORESCENCE DISAPPEARANCE

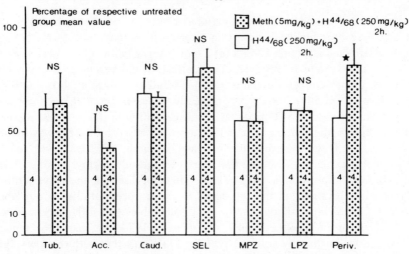

Fig. 8. *Effect of methergoline on H44/68 induced CA fluorescence disappearance in brain*
On the x axis the different treatments (i.p. injections) are given. Meth. was given 15 min before H44/68 (250 mg/kg 2 h). On the y axis the fluorescence disappearance values are given in per cent of the respective untreated group mean value. For the statistical analysis see Fig. 4.
Tub. = Tuberculum; Acc. = Accumbens; Caud. = Caudatus; SEL = Subependymal layer; MPZ = Medial palisade zone; LPZ = Lateral palisade zone; Periv. = Periventricular posterior hypothalamus.

SPONTANEOUS OVERFLOW

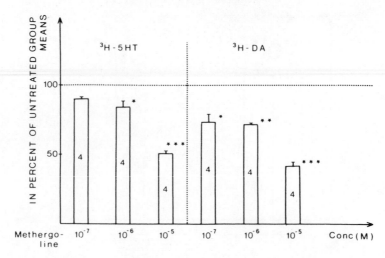

Fig. 9. *Effect of methergoline on the spontaneous release of ³H-5-HT and ³H-DA from cortical neostriatal slices of untreated rats*

The slices were preincubated for 30 min in a Krebs-Ringer buffer at 37°C containing the isotope. Methergoline was then added and incubation continued for another 30 min. Afterwards the slices were taken for liquid scintillation counting (see Farnebo and Hamberger, 1971).

On the x-axis the concentrations of methergoline are shown. On the y-axis the remaining amount of ³H-5-HT and ³H-NA present in the slices (cpm/slice) is shown expressed in per cent of untreated group mean value (12 experiments, means ± s.e.m.). The sample size is shown in the bars. Student's t-test was used in the statistical analysis. x: p<0.05; xx: p<0.01; xxx: p<0.001.

8). These results are in agreement with the functional results and can be explained on the basis of a selective 5-HT receptor blockade occurring after methergoline. The 5-HT, NA and DA stores are largely unaffected although a trend for a reduction of whole brain 5-HT stores and of DA stores in the limbic system is observed. These effects could be due to a direct action of methergoline on the uptake-storage mechanism of 5-HT and DA, since as shown in Fig. 9, the spontaneous overflow of ³H-5-HT and ³H-DA is clearly increased by methergoline but only in high concentrations in the case of 5-HT (10⁻⁵ M). In agreement with the view that methergoline can block 5-HT receptors, the reduction of 5-HT turnover caused by d-LSD was found to be counteracted (Fig. 10). It is true that the increases of brain 5-HT turnover found after methergoline could be explained also on the basis of blockade of presynaptic brain 5-HT receptors which on activation reduce 5-HT release when localised on the nerve terminal and reduce firing rate when localised on the cell body. However, recent studies in our laboratory have shown that a ³H-LSD specific binding (5-HT displaceable), which is associated with the postsynaptic 5-HT receptor (Bennett and Aghajanian, 1974) is markedly reduced by methergoline, even more so than by cold d-LSD (Fig. 11). Consistent with this view, then, was the finding that methergoline (50 μg/kg) caused a marked enhancement of sexual behaviour. However, at doses of 500 μg/kg and 1 mg/kg this effect of methergoline progressively disappeared – a phenomenon analogous to the effects of hallucinogens on sexual behaviour described herein. This may be explained by the fact that methergoline also binds to the presynaptic 5-HT receptor (see above), which will cause an increase in the firing rate in 5-HT neurons and, thus, more 5-HT will be released to compete with methergoline at the

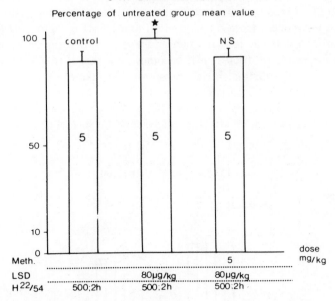

Fig. 10. *Interaction between methergoline (meth.) and d-LSD on 5-HT brain contents*
On the x axis the different treatments (i.p. injections) are given. Meth. was injected 1 h before H22/54 (500 mg/kg, i.p. 2 h). d-LSD was given i.p. 5 min before and 1 h after H22/54 in a dose of 40 μg/kg. On the y axis the 5-HT brain contents are given in per cent of the untreated group mean value. Each mean is reported with its standard deviation. Sample size is given within each bar. For the statistical analysis see Fig. 2: experimentwise error α = .10.

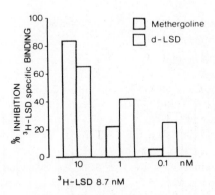

Fig. 11. *Effect of various concentrations (0.1-10 nM) of methergoline and d-LSD on the* in vitro *binding of* [3]*H-LSD (8.7 nM, 15 min at +37°C) to homogenate from rat cerebral cortex according to the technique of Bennett and Aghajanian (1975)*
Each column represents the mean of 3 determinations expressed as per cent inhibition of control "specific" ^{3}H-LSD binding (= 5-HT displaceable).

postsynaptic receptor site. Clearly this possibility must be investigated further. In addition d-LSD may be a partial 5-HT agonist (Snyder and Bennett, 1975) and therefore may bind also the "antagonist" conformation of the 5-HT receptor. As an antagonist methergoline therefore may be more capable of antagonising the binding of d-LSD to the postsynaptic 5-HT receptor than of 5-HT itself. However, it may be that methergoline also has some intrinsic activity, although this was not evident from the studies on spinal 5-HT receptor activity. This would be an alternative explanation to the lack of effect on sexual behaviour in higher doses.

Against this background of discussion it becomes clear that it should be very interesting to test methergoline in schizophrenia. If hallucinogenic LSD-like compounds or indolamines are formed in certain types of schizophrenias, methergoline certainly should antagonise their actions at postsynaptic 5-HT receptor sites and therefore also alleviate the schizophrenic symptoms provided that this site of attack is crucial for their mental actions.

HALLUCINOGENIC INDOLAMINES

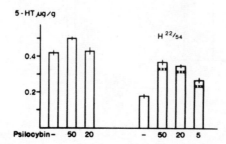

Fig. 12. *The effect of psilocybine on the H22/54 induced 5-HT depletion in whole brain*
The rats received psilocybine (i.p.) 15 min before H22/54 (500 mg/kg. i.p., 3 h before killing). On the x-axis the treatments are shown. On the y-axis the 5-HT contents (means ± s.e.m., 4 rats) are shown expressed in per cent of untreated group means. Student's t-test. xxx: p<0.005. All comparisons were made with H22/54 alone group. From Andén *et al.*, 1971.

PSILOCYBINE

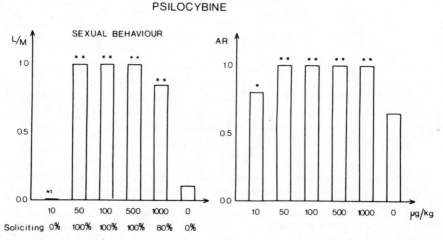

Fig. 13. *The effects of psilocybin on the sexual receptivity of castrate, estrogen-treated (1 μg/kg/day) female rats*
Psilocybin was given i.p. in a volume of 1 cc/rat 10 min before testing. Saline was administered identically to controls. L/M = number of lordoses ÷ number of mounts by male. AR = number of male mounts ÷ number of mounts + refused mounting attempts, i.e. female's acceptance ratio. NS = not significant. x: p<0.05; xx: p<0.01: Mann-Whitney 'U' test.

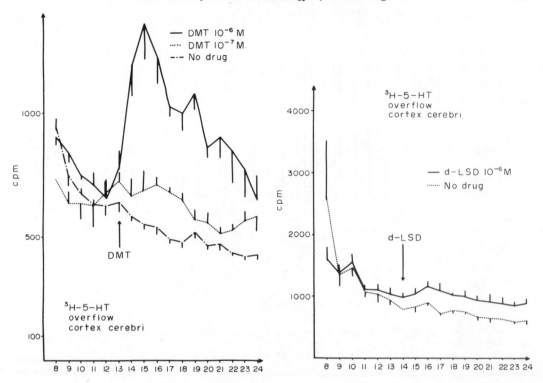

Fig. 14. *The effects of DMT and d-LSD on the spontaneous tritium overflow from* ^3H-*5-HT labelled cortical* slices
    Superfusion of cortical slices from nialamide pretreated rats (100 mg/kg, 2 h before killing). The *slices* were preincubated with ^{3}H-5-HT (10^{-6} M) and then superfused. The effect of DMT (10^{-6}-10^{-7} M) (A) or of d-LSD (10^{-6} M) (B) is shown. On the x-axis the time in min is shown. On the y-axis the tritium effect (cpm/5 min) is given (means ± s.e.m.; 3 experiments). A marked increase in overflow is observed after 10^{-6} M of DMT; whereas no effect is observed after d-LSD.

    It has been shown that psilocybine (Fig. 12), DMT and 5-methoxy-DMT all can reduce 5-HT turnover, increase postsynaptic spinal 5-HT receptor activity (Table 2) and reduce firing rate in 5-HT pathways (Andén *et al.*, 1971; Aghajanian *et al.*, 1970a; Fuxe *et al.*, 1972). This latter action is probably due to a direct action of the indolamines on presynaptic 5-HT receptors localised on the 5-HT cell bodies which seem to be preferentially sensitive to the hallucinogenic indolamines. Thus, these indolamines seem to act on the 5-HT neurons in the same way as d-LSD. In agreement with the neurophysiological results of Aghajanian's group, it has recently been observed in our laboratory (Everitt and Fuxe, to be published) that psilocybine in doses down to at least 50 μg/kg markedly enhanced sexual behaviour (Fig. 13), whereas in doses above 1 mg/kg inhibition of sexual behaviour appeared, probably due to the onset of agonistic actions of psilocybine on postsynaptic 5-HT receptors. As seen in Table 2 a marked increase of extensor hindlimb reflex activity is seen with 1 mg/kg of psilocybine.
    Some of the indolamines such as DMT differ from d-LSD in being able to cause a marked release of extragranular stores of 5-HT as seen in Fig. 14. There is a marked increase in the ^{3}H-5-HT overflow when DMT (10^{-6} M) is added to the superfusing medium. Such an effect is not observed after d-LSD. As seen in Fig. 15, 1 mg/kg of DMT and 5-methoxy-DMT did not

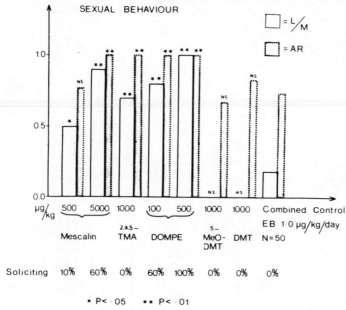

Fig. 15. *The effects of hallucinogenic drugs on the sexual receptivity of castrate, estrogen-treated (1 μg/kg/day) female rats*
   All drugs were given i.p. in a volume of 1 cc/rat 10 min before testing. Saline was administered identically to controls. Abbreviations as for Fig. 13.

enhance sexual behaviour. The reason is that at this dosage these drugs already increase brain postsynaptic 5-HT receptor activity. Thus, in a dose of 100 μg/kg both DMT and 5-methoxy-DMT increase sexual behaviour.

HALLUCINOGENIC PHENYLETHYLAMINES

In man the most potent one appears to be 2,5-methoxy-4-methyl-amphetamine (DOM, STP) as shown by Snyder *et al.* (1967). This compound and p-methoxy-amphetamine has been found to have similar effects on central 5-HT mechanisms as d-LSD and psilocybine. Thus, there is a reduction of 5-HT turnover (Fig. 16) and an increase in postsynaptic spinal 5-HT receptor activity (Andén *et al.*, 1974; Table 2). However, in Aghajanian's study (Aghajanian *et al.*, 1970a), he only found a reduction of firing rate in a ventral subgroup of the nuc. raphe dorsalis after DOM whereas d-LSD and psilocybine caused a uniform reduction of firing rate. Again recent studies on sexual behaviour suggest that DOM and 2,5-methoxy-4-methyl-phenylethylamine (see Fig. 15) can markedly enhance sexual behaviour in doses of 100-500 μg/kg, pointing to a potent action of these drugs on presynaptic 5-HT receptors. The trimethoxy-phenylethylamines such as mescaline and trimethoxy-amphetamines such as 2,4,5-trimethoxy-amphetamine (TMA-2) differ from the other hallucinogenic drugs so far studied in causing no certain reduction of 5-HT turnover (mescaline, Andén *et al.*, 1974) and in having little effect on spinal postsynaptic 5-HT receptor activity (Table 2). On the other hand, they enhance sexual behaviour in doses of 0.5-5 mg/kg (see Fig. 15, Everitt and Fuxe, to be published), and in the dose of 25 mg/kg mescaline inhibits sexual behaviour. Also mescaline has been shown to inhibit firing rate in the ventral group of cells in nuc. raphe dorsalis, an effect

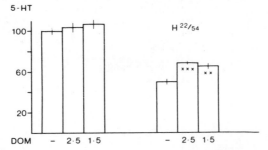

Fig. 16. *The effect of 2,5-dimethoxy-4-methylamphetamine (DOM) on the H22/54 induced 5-HT depletion in whole brain*
DOM was given i.p. 15 min before H22/54 (500 mg/kg, i.p., 3 h before killing) and the second dose 90 min after the first dose. On the x-axis the treatments are given. On the y-axis the 5-HT contents are shown (means ± s.e.m., 6-9 experiments) in per cent of untreated group means (0.30 μg/g, 9 rats).
The statistical analysis was made according to Student's t-test. xxx: $p<0.001$; xx: $p<0.01$. All comparisons were made with the H22/54 alone group. From Andén *et al.*, 1974.

which seems to be due to an indirect action (Haigler and Aghajanian, 1973). Therefore, it may still be that mescaline and related compounds could also act via a 5-HT mechanism although indirectly.

As seen from the above, the major families of hallucinogenic drugs have potent actions on central 5-HT receptors, where they appear to act as agonists at both pre- and postsynaptic 5-HT receptor sites. The so-called presynaptic 5-HT receptors certainly are preferentially activated by the hallucinogens, as elegantly demonstrated by Aghajanian's work and also indicated in the present behavioural work (Everitt *et al.*, 1975; Everitt and Fuxe, to be published). It still remains to be established, however, whether the pre- or postsynaptic 5-HT receptors mainly mediate the hallucinogenic actions and if in addition other receptors may be involved. It is hoped that by correlating hallucinogenic potency with enhancing and inhibitory effects on sexual behaviour and with effects on high-affinity d-LSD and 5-HT binding to postsynaptic 5-HT receptors, it may be possible to solve this problem. It should be pointed out, however, that if the hypothesis of Aghajanian is correct, hallucinations should only be observed in the low dose range, and with higher doses the hallucinations should be counteracted due to the onset of agonistic actions also at postsynaptic 5-HT receptor sites. To our knowledge such findings are not available at the present time.

Effects on Central DA Neurons

With the discovery that ergot drugs such as ergocornine, 2-Br-α-ergocryptine (CB 154) and ergometrine could stimulate DA receptors (Hökfelt and Fuxe, 1972; Corrodi *et al.*, 1973; Fuxe *et al.* 1974; Pijnenburg *et al.*, 1973) it became of interest also to study other ergots such as d-LSD on DA receptors. However, it was known from previous work that d-LSD, and also other hallucinogenic indolamines such as psilocybine and DMT did not reduce whole brain DA turnover as shown in the tyrosine-hydroxylase inhibition model (Andén *et al.*, 1968, 1971). Pieri and Pieri (1974) were the first to observe that d-LSD induced rotational behaviour in rats with unilateral 5,6-HT induced degeneration of ascending monoamine pathways suggesting that d-LSD can be a DA agonist. In May 1974 at a meeting on dopaminergic mechanisms (Fuxe *et al.*, 1975b) we reported that d-LSD could activate supersensitive DA receptors, since rotational

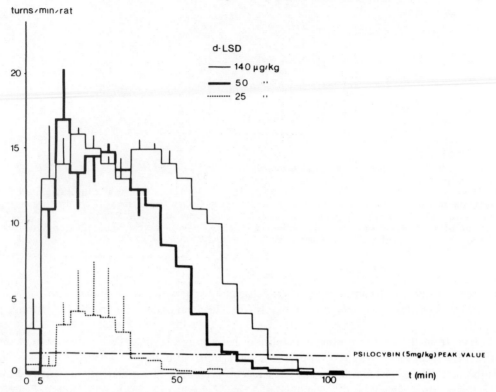

Fig. 17. *The effect of d-LSD on rotational behaviour in rats with a unilateral 6-OH-NA induced degeneration of the ascending DA neurons*
    The rats (4) received 6-OH-DA (8 µg/4 µl) into the substantia nigra as described by Ungerstedt (1968) several months before the experiments started. On the x-axis the time in min after the d-LSD (i.p.) is shown. On the y-axis turns/min/rat are shown for every 5 min and expressed as means ± s.e.m. The psilocybine (5 mg/kg, i.p.) peak value is indicated by the horizontal line above the x-axis.

behaviour occurred towards the innervated side (Fig. 17) in rats with a unilateral 6-OH-DA induced degeneration of the ascending pathways (Ungerstedt and Arbuthnott, 1970). It should be noted that d-LSD is active in doses down to 10 µg/kg and that psilocybine and DOM were without effects. As seen from the dose-effect curves in Fig. 18 the affinity of d-LSD for the supersensitive DA receptor is at least as high as that of apomorphine and higher than that of other ergot drugs known to be DA receptor agonists. In view of the fact that the maximally observed peak effects (turns/min/rat) after d-LSD on rotational behaviour were not different from those of apomorphine, it may also be that d-LSD is a relatively full agonist on *supersensitive* DA receptors. The possibility should be considered that a supersensitivity change in some DA receptors can occur in the schizophrenic brain. If so, there is no doubt that endogenously formed hallucinogens of the d-LSD type would have one of their major actions on the DA receptors of such a pathologically diseased brain. In view of the lack of effect of d-LSD on whole brain DA turnover noted in our previous work it was postulated that d-LSD had marked effects exclusively on supersensitive DA receptors, where its potency mimicked that of apomorphine. However, it has been reported that d-LSD is a partial DA agonist on the basis of studies on adenylate cyclase activity (Pieri *et al.*, 1974; von Hungen *et al.*, 1974; Da

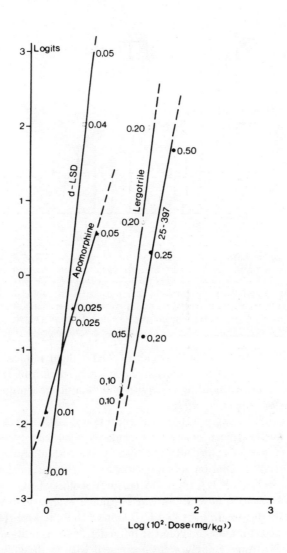

Fig. 18. *Dose-effect curves of DA receptor agonists on rotational behaviour*
On the x-axis the log of 100 times the dose in mg/kg is shown. (Each dose was multiplied by 100 in order to avoid decimal figures so that negative log could be avoided.) On the y-axis the logits are shown. Logit = ln P/I-P, where P is the proportion (E/Emax) of the max effect (Emax) observed after the dose used. At the respective points the doses are given in mg/kg. The effect was the mean peak activity (4 rats) found after i.p. administration of the DA agonist. All injections were made i.p. Lergotrile = 2 chloro-6-methyl-ergoline-8β -acetonitrile; 25-397 = 9,10 didehydro-6-methyl-8β-(2-pyridylthiomethyl)-ergoline.

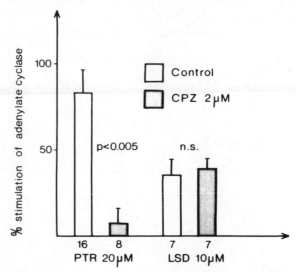

Fig. 19. *The effect of d-LSD and a DA receptor agonist (5 R, 8 R)-8-(4-p-methoxyphenyl-1-piperazinylmethyl)-6-methylergolene (PTR) on the adenylate cyclase activity in the nuc. accumbens-tuberculum olfactorium region of untreated rats and their interaction with chlorpromazine*
  The adenylate cyclase activity was determined in homogenates in triplicates principally according to Kebabian *et al.* (1972). On the x-axis the treatments and number of experiments are shown. On the y-axis the per cent stimulation of adenylate cyclase is given (means ± s.e.m.). Student's t-test.

Prada *et al.*, 1975). The latter workers have also found a slight reduction of DA turnover as revealed in the tyrosine-hydroxylase inhibition model. A reduction of HVA levels and of DA outflow in perfusates of caudatus using the push-pull cannula technique as also observed in doses of 0.2-1 mg/kg (Da Prada *et al.*, 1975).

  In the present article it has been possible to confirm that d-LSD is a DA receptor agonist also on the normally sensitive DA receptor in experiments on adenylate cyclase activity (Fig. 19). Furthermore, d-LSD may have a high affinity also to the "normally sensitive" DA receptor since the increase in cAMP formation was not blocked by chlorpromazine in a concentration that clearly blocked the actions of DA and a DA receptor agonist of the ergot type (Fig. 19).

  In view of this work we have now performed a regional analysis on the effect of d-LSD (1 mg/kg) on DA turnover. As seen in Fig. 20 d-LSD alone did not reduce the DA turnover in any of the DA systems studied. In order to avoid the influence of the simultaneous activation of the 5-HT receptors by d-LSD, some animals were pretreated with methergoline (5 mg/kg). As seen in Fig. 20 a significant retardation appeared in the islandic DA system of the neostriatum whereas no other significant changes were observed although a clearcut trend for reduction of DA turnover now appeared in the subcortical limbic system. The explanation for this relative lack of effect of d-LSD on DA turnover may be that d-LSD is a partial DA agonist. Thus, it might act as an antagonist at the postsynaptic DA receptor and as an agonist at the presynaptic DA receptor on the cell body. In agreement, apomorphine but not d-LSD (0.1 mg/kg) has been found to increase GABA turnover in the striatum, limbic system and in the A9-A10 area (Perez de la Mora *et al.*, 1975).

  After a low dose (0.03 mg/kg) of d-LSD, however, a preliminary analysis of limbic cortical DA turnover suggests a slowing of amine turnover in the DA islands of the entorhinal cortex. Further work is necessary to elucidate if these findings may reflect an important agonistic action of d-LSD on some cortical DS receptors.

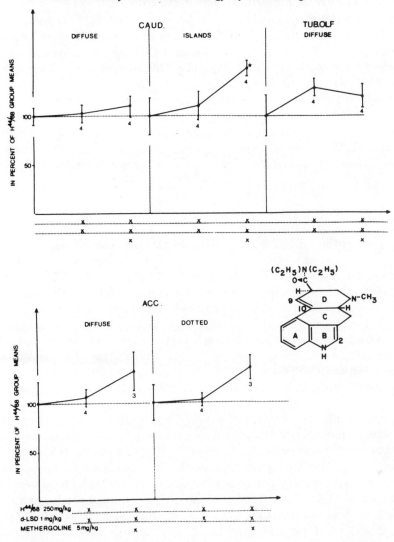

Fig. 20. *The effect of d-LSD with or without methergoline on the H44/68 induced DA fluorescence disappearance in various DA systems of the limbic system and the neostriatum*

d-LSD was given i.p. 15 min before H44/68 (250 mg/kg, i.p., 2 h before killing). Methergoline was given i.p. 1 h before d-LSD. The DA fluorescence in nuc. caudatus (caud.) in tuberculum olfactorium (tub. olf.) and nuc. accumbens (acc.) was measured with the help of quantitative microfluorimetry (see Einarsson *et al.*, 1975).

On the x-axis the treatments are shown. On the y-axis the DA fluorescence values are expressed in per cent of the H44/68 group mean value (means ± s.e.m.). The sample size is shown at the respective points. Student's t-test. x: p<0.05. All comparisons are made with the respective H44/68 group.

It should be pointed out, however, that 5 mg/kg of mescaline, psilocybine and DOM did not show signs of activating the supersensitive DA receptors. On the other hand, d-LSD is more potent than the latter three drugs in its ability to activate both DA and 5-HT receptors. It may be mentioned that DA receptor blocking agents can counteract d-LSD induced psychosis (Isbell and Logan, 1957).

Ergocornine is another compound which is both a DA and 5-HT receptor agonist (Fuxe *et al.*, 1974; Corrodi *et al.*, 1975). If the above is true, ergocornine should thus have a high hallucinogenic potency similar to that found after d-LSD. To our minds such information is as yet not available. The work on ergocornine and d-LSD also give the important indication that the DA and 5-HT receptors may be similar.

In conclusion, d-LSD has a potent action on supersensitive DA receptors, to which it has a high affinity as revealed in the dose-effect curves (Fig. 18) and in competition experiments with DA antagonists in studies on rotational behaviour. d-LSD may also have a high affinity for the normally sensitive DA receptors, where it seems to act as a partial DA receptor agonist as revealed in studies on adenylate cyclase activity. These effects may be related to its hallucinogenic potency.

Summary

A large number of studies suggest that d-LSD and hallucinogenic indolamines and phenylethylamines have important actions on central 5-HT neurons resulting in reduction of 5-HT turnover. The presynaptic 5-HT receptor localised on the 5-HT cell body seems to be more sensitive than the postsynaptic 5-HT receptor as revealed in neurophysiological studies by Aghajanian's group and in studies on sexual behaviour (Everitt and Fuxe, to be published). Thus, in very low doses the hallucinogenic drugs caused a marked enhancement of sexual behaviour, probably by activating presynaptic 5-HT receptors on the cell bodies, leading to reduced firing rate and subsequently reduced 5-HT release. The 5-HT pathway is known to inhibit sexual behaviour (Meyerson, 1964). It is not yet established if the hallucinogenic property of the compounds is mainly related to the activation of pre- or postsynaptic 5-HT receptors.

In the present article the discovery of a central postsynaptic 5-HT receptor blocking agent without blocking effects on DA and NA receptors is also reported. Thus, methergoline seems to have this quality. It increases 5-HT turnover without affecting DA and NA turnover. Furthermore, it blocks the actions of d-LSD and 5-HTP in the spinal cord without affecting the responses to clonidine. Methergoline also in low doses increases sexual behaviour and markedly reduces the specific high affinity binding of ^{3}H-d-LSD. This and similar compounds will be highly valuable tools in the evaluation, if indeed activation of 5-HT receptors is mediating the hallucinogenic actions of psychodelic drugs. It will also help to establish if mainly pre- or postsynaptic 5-HT receptors are involved.

Recent evidence by several groups suggest that d-LSD is a partial DA receptor agonist as revealed in studies on the adenylate cyclase activity. The present work on adenylate cyclase indicates that d-LSD may have a high affinity for the DA receptor. The behavioural work on supersensitive DA receptors using the rotometer model also suggests that d-LSD has a high affinity for this receptor, since the dose-effect curve shows an ED_{50} of 0.025 mg/kg similar to that obtained with apomorphine. The maximal peak effects are not different from those obtained with apomorphine, and therefore it may be that d-LSD is a relatively full agonist in supersensitive DA receptors. The failure of d-LSD to cause any changes of DA turnover in various DA systems in doses of 1-2 mg/kg may be due to the fact that d-LSD is a partial DA agonist and a 5-HT receptor agonist. Thus, 5-HT neurons may also control DA neuronal activity and after methergoline pretreatment d-LSD reduces DA turnover in the islandic system of the neostriatum.

As postulated by other groups (Da Prada *et al.*, 1975) the actions of d-LSD on DA receptors could contribute to its hallucinogenic potency and in view of the present findings particularly if a supersensitive change has occurred in the DA receptors. DA receptor agonists used in the treatment of Parkinson's disease such as ET495 have also been shown to cause psychotic reactions in predisposed Parkinsonian patients.

It should be pointed out that potent hallucinogens such as psilocybine and DOM appear to lack effect on supersensitive DA receptors. Therefore, the hallucinogens probably act mainly via 5-HT receptors (see above).

Acknowledgements

This work has been supported by a grant (04X-715) from the Swedish Medical Research Council and by a grant (MH 25504) from the National Institutes of Mental Health and by grants from M. Bergvall's Foundation and Karolinska Institute's funds.

References

ANDÉN, N.-E. (1968) Discussion of serotonin and dopamine in the extra-pyramidal system. *Advan. Pharmacol.* **6A**, 347.

ANDÉN, N.-E., CORRODI, H., FUXE, K. and HÖKFELT, T. (1968) Evidence for a central 5-hydroxytryptamine receptor stimulation by lyseric acid diethylamide. *Br. J. Pharmac.* **34**, 1.

ANDÉN, N.-E., CORRODI, H. and FUXE, K. (1971) Hallucinogenic drugs of the indolealkylamine type and central monoamine neurons. *J. Pharmacol. Exp. Ther.* **179**, 236.

ANDÉN, N.-E., CORRODI, H., FUXE, K. and MEEK, J.L. (1974) Hallucinogenic phenylethylamines: Interactions with serotonin turnover and receptors. *Eur. J. Pharmac.* **25**, 176.

AGHAJANIAN, G.K., FOOTE, W.E. and SHEARD, M. (1968) Lysergic acid diethylamide: Sensitive neuronal units in the midbrain raphe. *Science* (Washington) **161**, 706.

AGHAJANIAN, G.K., FOOTE, W.E. and SHEARD, M.H. (1970a) Action of psychotogenic drugs on single midbrain raphe neurons. *J. Pharmacol. Exptl. Ther.* **171**, 178.

AGHAJANIAN, G.K., SHEARD, M.H. and FOOTE, W.E. (1970b) LSD and mescaline: Comparison of effects on single units in the midbrain raphe. In *Psychotomimetic drugs* (D.H. Efron, ed.), Raven Press, New York, p. 165.

BENNETT, J.L. and AGHAJANIAN, G.K. (1974) D-LSD binding to brain homogenates: Possible relationship to serotonin receptors. *Life Sci.* **15**, 1935.

CHASE, T., BREESE, G. and KOPIN, I. (1967) Serotonin release from brain slices by electrical stimulation: Regional differences and effect of LSD. *Science* (Washington) **157**, 1461.

CHESSICK, R., HAERTZEN, C. and WIKLER, H. (1964) Tolerance to LSD-25 in schizophrenic subjects. *Arch. Gen. Psychiat.* **10**, 653.

CHRISTIAN, S. and CORBETT, L. Paper presented at Willow Point Symposium, USA, April 1975.

CONOVER, W.J. (1971) *Practical non-parametric statistics.* Publ. J. Wiley, New York, p. 104.

CORRODI, H., FUXE, K., HÖKFELT, T., LIDBRINK, P. and UNGERSTEDT, U. (1973) Effect of ergot drugs on central catecholamine neurons: evidence for a stimulation of central dopamine neurons. *J. Pharm. Pharmacol.* **25**, 409.

CORRODI, H., FARNEBO, L.-O., FUXE, K. and HAMBERGER, B. (1975) Effect of ergot drugs on 5-Hydroxytryptamine neurons: Evidence for 5-hydroxytryptamine release or 5-hydroxytryptamine receptor stimulation. *Eur. J. Pharmac.* **30**, 172.

DAHLSTRÖM, A. and FUXE, K. (1964) Evidence for the existence of monoamine containing neurons in the central nervous system. I. Demonstration of monoamines in the cell bodies of brain stem neurons. *Acta Physiol. Scand.* **62**, *Suppl.* **232**, 1.

DA PRADA, M., SANER, A., BURKARD, W.P., BARTHOLINI, G. and PLETSCHER, A. (1975) Lysergic acid diethylamide: Evidence for stimulation of cerebral dopamine receptors. *Brain Res.* **94**, 67.

EFRON, D.H. (ed.). *Psychotomimetic Drugs* (1970), Raven Press, New York.

EINARSSON, P., HALLMAN, H. and JONSSON, G. (1975) Quantitative microfluorimetry of formaldehyde induced fluorescence of dopamine in the caudate nucleus. *Med. Biol.* **53**, 15.

EVERITT, B.J., FUXE, K. and HÖKFELT, T. (1975) Serotonin, catecholamines and sexual receptivity of female rats. Pharmacological findings. *J. Pharmacol.* (Paris) **6**, 3, 269.

FARNEBO, L.-O. and HAMBERGER, B. (1971) Drug-induced changes in the release of ^{3}H-monoamines from field stimulated rat brain slices. *Acta Physiol. Scand.* **371**, 35.

FREEDMAN, D.X. (1961) Effects of LSD 25 on brain serotonin. *J. Pharmacol. Exp. Ther.* **134**, 160.

FUXE, K., HOLSTEDT, B. and JONSSON, G. (1972) Effects of 5-methoxy-N,N-dimethyltryptamine on central monoamine neurons. *Eur. J. Pharmacol.* **19**, 25.

FUXE, K., CORRODI, H., HÖKFELT, T., LIDBRINK, P. and UNGERSTEDT, U. (1974) Ergocornine and 2-Br-α-ergocryptine. Evidence for prolonged dopamine receptor stimulation. *Med. Biol.* **52**, 121.

FUXE, K., AGNATI, L. and EVERITT, B. (1975a) Effects of methergoline on central monoamine neurons. Evidence for a selective blockade of central 5-HT receptors. *Neuroscience Letters.* In press.

FUXE, K., AGNATI, L., CORRODI, H., EVERITT, B.J., HÖKFELT, T., LÖFSTRÖM, A. and UNGERSTEDT, U. (1975b) Action of dopamine receptor agonists in forebrain and hypothalamus: Rotational behaviour, ovulation, and dopamine turnover. *Adv. in Neurology* **9** (D.B. Calne, T.N. Chase and A. Barbeau, eds.), Raven Press, New York.

GRIFFITH, J.D., CAVANAUGH, J.H. and OATES, J.A. (1969) Psychosis induced by the administration of d-amphetamine to human volunteers. In *Psychotomimetic Drugs* (D.H. Efron, ed.), Raven Press, New York, p. 287.

HAIGLER, H.J. and AGHAJANIAN, G.K. (1973) Mescaline and LSD: Direct and indirect effects on serotonin-containing neurons in brain. *Eur. J. Pharmac.* **21**, 53.

HAIGLER, H.J. and AGHAJANIAN, G.K. (1974) Lysergic acid diethylamide and serotonin: a comparison of effects on serotonergic neurons and neurons receiving a serotonergic input. *J. Pharmacol Exp. Ther.* **188**, 688.

HEDQVIST, P. (1973) Aspects on prostaglandin and α-receptor mediated control of transmitter release from adrenergic nerves. In *Frontiers in Catecholamine Res.* (E. Usdin and S. Snyder, eds.), Pergamon Press, New York, p. 583.

HOLLISTER, L.E. (1968) *Chemical Psychoses*, Springfield.

HUNGEN VON, K., ROBERTS, S. and HILL , D.F. (1974) LSD as an agonist and antagonist at central dopamine receptors. *Nature* (Lond.) **252**, 588.

HOKFELT, T. and FUXE, K. (1972) On the morphology and the neuroendocrine role of the hypothalamic catecholamine neurons. *Int. Symp. Munich*, pp. 181-223 (Karger, Basel).

ISBELL, H. and LOGAN, C.R. (1957) Studies on the diethylamide of lysergic acid (LSD-25). *Arch. Neurol. Psychiat. (Chic.)* **77**, 350.

KEBABIAN, J.W., PETZGOLD, G.L. and GREENGARD, P. (1972) Dopamine-sensitive adenylate cyclase in caudate nucleus of rat brain, and its similarity to the "dopamine receptor". *Proc. nat. Acad. Sci. (Wash.)* **69**, 2145.

MEYRERSON, B.J. (1964) Central nervous monoamines and hormone-induced estrous behaviour in the spayed rat. *Acta Physiol. Scand. Suppl.* **241**, 1.

PEREZ DE LA MORA, M., FUXE, K., HÖKFELT, T. and LJUNGDAHL, Å. (1975) Effect of apomorphine on the GABA turnover in the DA cell group rich area of the mesencephalon. Evidence for the involvement of an inhibitory gabaergic feedback control of the ascending DA neurons. *Neuroscience Letters.* In press.

PIERI, L. and PIERI, M. (1974) Drug-induced rotation in rats after unilateral intracerebral injection of 5,6-dihydroxytryptamine (5,6-DHT). *Experientia (Basel)* **30**, 696.

PIERI, L., PIERI, M. and HAEFELY, W. (1974) LSD as an agonist of dopamine receptors in the striatum. *Nature (Lond.)* **252**, 586.

PIJNENBERG, A.J.J., WOODRUFF, G.N., ROSSUM, van J.M. (1973) Ergometrine induced locomotor activity following intracerebral injection into the nucleus accumbens. *Brain Res.* **59**, 289.

ROSECRANS, J.A., LOVELL, R.A. and FREEDMAN, D.X. (1967) Effects of lysergic acid diethylamide on the metabolism of brain 5-hydroxytryptamine. *Biochem. Pharmacol.* **16**, 2001.

SMYTHIES, J.R. (1970) The mode of action of psychotomimetic drugs. In *Neurosci. Res. Progr. Bulletin*, **8**, 1.

SNYDER, S.H. (1973) Amphetamine psychosis: A "model" schizophrenia mediated by catecholamines. *Am. J. Psychiat.* **130**, 61.

SNYDER, S.H., FAILLACE, L. and HOLLISTER, L. (1967) 2,5-Dimethoxy-4-methylamphetamine (STP): A new hallucinogenic drug. *Science*, **158**, 669.

SNYDER, S.H. and BENNETT, J.P. Jr. (1975) Biochemical identification of the postsynaptic serotonin receptor in mammalian brain. In *Pre- and Postsynaptic receptors* (E. Usdin and W.E. Bunney, Jr. eds.), Publ. Marcel Dekker, Inc. (New York), p. 191.

UNGERSTEDT, U. (1968) 6-Hydroxy-dopamine induced degeneration of central monoamine neurons. *Eur. J. Pharmac.* **5**, 107.

UNGERSTEDT, U. and ARBUTHNOTT, G. (1970) Quantitative recording of rotational behaviour in rats after 6-hydroxydopamine lesions of the nigro-striatal dopamine-system. *Brain Res.* **24**, 485.

WYATT, R.J., GILLIN, J.C., KAPLAN, J., STILLMAN, R., MANDEL, L., AHN, H.S., VANDENHEUVEL, W.J.A. and WALKER, R.W. (1974) N,N-Dimethyltryptamine – A possible relationship to schizophrenia? In *Serotonin – New Vistas, Adv. Biochem. Psychopharm.* (E. Costa, G.L. Gessa and M. Sandler, eds.), **11**, 299.

Neuroleptic Drugs

The Drug Approach to Therapy.
Treatment of Acute Schizophrenia

CARLO L. CAZZULLO

I. Guides to Classification

The need for prompt and, as far as possible specific, intervention in acute psychotic states is supported by an increasing amount of experience, not only in psychiatry, but coming also from other fields, such as neurology and medicine. As Arnhoff[1] has pointed out, with the increased development of outpatient facilities, families are now, more than in the past, compelled to deal with acute psychotic states. The institution of appropriate treatment, not necessarily in hospital, depends on the early recognition of the salient features of such acute psychotic states in the medical history and current life situation of the patient.

Although attempts were made in the past to classify acute schizophrenia in terms of the main descriptive features,[2] there is little agreement in the recent literature as to the clinical criteria that should be used. This is shown also by the heterogeneity of the descriptive data reported by different authors, owing apparently to their using different criteria in characterising this illness. It is therefore somewhat surprising that publications dealing with the treatment of acute schizophrenia do not always give a detailed description of the symptoms of the patients, who are often described only as "acute schizophrenics" newly admitted to the hospital.

The international Draft Glossary (WHO[3]), which devotes a whole section (No. 295) to schizophrenia, defines acute schizophrenic episodes as

schizophrenic disorders (other than those listed in the preceding forms, which define general characteristics of schizophrenia and in particular those of the various subtypes: simplex, hebephrenic, catatonic and paranoid), in which there is a dream-like state with slight clouding of consciousness and perplexity. External things, people and events may become charged with personal significance for the patient. There may be ideas of reference and emotional turmoil. In many cases remission occurs within a few weeks or months.

Under this heading are included: acute schizophrenia (undifferentiated), acute schizophrenic attack, schizophrenic episode (acute), oneirophrenia, and schizophreniform psychosis (confusional type). Particular attention should be paid to the outcome criteria given near the end of section 295, where it is stated that a diagnosis of schizophrenia "should not be restricted to conditions running a protracted, deteriorating or chronic course". This statement, and the earlier reference to early recovery in the acute forms of schizophrenia, express views developed in recent years, which are somewhat different from those of Kraepelin,[4] E. Bleuler,[5] H. Ey[6] and others who thought of schizophrenia as taking a constant progressive course. Divergent views about the nature of acute schizophrenia, depending on the use of structural[7] or evolutional criteria,[5] are reflected also in the descriptions given in the WHO Draft Glossary.

A survey of the literature suggests the need to consider carefully the relation of acute schizophrenia to other related forms of mental illness. These include:

161

(1) *Schizo-affective psychosis,* first described by Kasanin[8] in 1933 as a psychosis of acute onset with prominent affective features, in which characteristics of schizophrenia occur together with manic-depressive symptoms. It is described also as "mixed psychosis".

(2) *Psychogenic or reactive psychosis,* recently described as "Third psychosis" by McCabe. (9) The characteristics commonly described are: acute onset related to precipitating factors (emotional stress); affective disorders (depression, anxiety) not associated with endogenous depression; premorbid personality not schizoid; lack of autism; delusions of self-depreciation or persecution and ideas of reference; sometimes hallucinations and slight mental confusion.

(3) *Acute episodes of manic-depressive psychosis.* There is an increasing body of evidence that many patients given a diagnosis of acute schizophrenia actually suffered from affective illness, since they failed to satisfy the rigorous criteria for schizophrenia. (10-14) The presence of prominent symptoms of psychotic depression or mania must be taken as definitive, even when non-systemised paranoid delusions are present.

Most important from the point of view of differential diagnosis is the relation of acute schizophrenia to the whole group of primary affective disorders.[15-17] This is important also with respect to the new methods of pharmacological treatment, which may help in diagnostic and prognostic assessment. The wide variation in diagnostic criteria in different countries is indicated by the gross differences in admission rates for schizophrenia and for manic-depressive illness. As Kendell[18] pointed out in 1971, the admission rate for schizophrenia in the New York mental hospitals is double that in London, whereas for mania the difference is even greater in reverse. Consistent with this finding is the observation that many cases originally diagnosed as "schizophrenia" are later rediagnosed as "manic-depressive illness", and vice versa.[19,20] Such variations in diagnosis are understandable in view of our ignorance of the underlying etiological factors in schizophrenia. The variation in diagnostic criteria may be related to Beck's[21] concept of a "spectrum" mental illness extending from schizophrenia at one extreme to manic-depressive illness at the other, with schizo-affective psychoses in between. On this basis reactive (or psychogenic) psychoses could perhaps be placed opposite to toxic, with infective and traumatic psychoses on either side.

These views are mentioned here since special care is needed in defining the acute phases of schizophrenia; but it must be recognised that, from the original statement of Bleuler,[5] which is still operative also in Chinese psychiatry, and from Schneider's[7] identification of "first-rank symptoms", to the more recent enumeration of symptoms through rating scales, a great deal of work has been done. The biometric investigations of Carpenter *et al.*[22] (a and b) on twelve main symptoms of schizophrenia in the International Pilot Study of Schizophrenia (IPSS) of WHO is an example of these recent trends in research. The criteria obtained in this way provide, not so much a description of schizophrenia as a means of developing co-operative research in different countries.

The main criteria used to establish the picture of acute schizophrenia may be described in the following terms:

Chronological: concerning the rapidity of the clinical onset (implying a sudden, more or less complete disruption of the personality), or the transience of the course, which may be from a few weeks to six months.[23]

Structural: presuming that discriminative symptoms of schizophrenia associated with disturbances of consciousness at various levels can be recognised.

Qualitative: relating to the strength and violence of the symptoms.

Evolutional: relating to the probable outcome, which may tend towards recovery (remitting schizophrenia), chronicity (process schizophrenia) or remission with recurrent acute attacks.

II. Assessment and Treatment

A better clinical therapeutic approach can be achieved if consideration is given to other aspects besides symptoms and the course of the illness: these include the premorbid personality, age, the impact of stresses (and their significance), social and family factors (both genetic and psychodynamic), biological background and response to treatment.

At the start, acute schizophrenia is characterised by an abrupt impairment of vigilance and a disturbance of consciousness of varying intensity (changes in sleep-wakefulness rhythm, and mental confusion), with behavioural abnormalities (excitement, catatonic stupor) and withdrawal from reality (derealisation, depersonalisation), as well as cognitive and psychosensory disturbances (delusions and hallucinations). It may be hard to identify the basic symptoms of schizophrenia at this stage, but generally they become evident as the more florid features fade away.

Although some general guidelines for therapy can be suggested, the actual treatment must be chosen and adjusted to suit each individual patient, keeping in mind the factors already mentioned. The two major influences, pharmacodynamic and psychodynamic, reciprocally influence each other; but at certain phases of treatment either the one or the other will predominate. In the treatment of a patient with acute schizophrenia the aim is to encourage him to develop helpful relationships with his environment and with his doctor, and to enable him to improve his verbal and practical behavioural performance. Pharmacological treatment may be regarded also as a non-verbal approach to the thinking and cognitive processes of the patient.

(a) FIRST PHASE

In the first phase of treatment evidence of a metabolic abnormality may be detected, such as a disturbance of salt and water balance, abnormal protein metabolism and acidosis, slight hyperazotemia or adrenal hormonal impairment. There may be a disturbance associated with abnormal eating behaviour. The therapeutic approach is therefore directed towards correcting any metabolic derangement. Treatment is mainly concerned with rehydration by perfusion with natural or synthetic plasma and detoxication by perfusion with properly adjusted solutions of lactates, glutamic acid esters, glycuronic acid derivatives and vitamins. This kind of treatment is also useful for controlling possible acute allergic or similar reactions to psychotropic drugs, and it may reduce the effects of abnormal retention of drugs in the tissues (liver, kidney, central nervous system). In this respect laboratory findings have been applied successfully to clinical practice by the introduction of adenosine triphosphate (ATP) to protect against neuronal damage by reserpine or chlorpromazine, and of a sodium salt of aescine (Reparil) to prevent the toxic effects of some benzodiazepine derivatives and MAO inhibitors when given in high doses by intravenous injection.[25],[26]

Clearly changes in metabolic balance (or signs of a hidden septic focus) are more likely to be found in cases where an exogenous factor is involved, and which therefore are not cases of acute schizophrenia; but the prompt recognition of their features assists the differential diagnosis. This also applies to acute psychoses due to hallucinogenic drugs. Diagnostic problems are to be expected, especially when facilities for toxicological investigation are not available, in conditions such as the acute paranoid reaction induced by cocaine.[27]

The impressive body of biochemical research in schizophrenia, relating to biogenic amines,[28] plasma proteins[29] and neurotransmitters, especially dopaminergic receptors, is becoming increasingly important for the better understanding of pharmacological mechanisms of action as well as the pathophysiology of the psychoses.[30] So far as the platelet mono-amine oxidase is concerned, normal values were found in acute schizophrenia.[31] Sachar *et al.*,[32] who studied endocrinological factors in patients with acute schizophrenic reactions, reported high levels of plasma cortisol which decrease within a few days, either when anxiety decreases or, in some cases, as the psychosis becomes more organised and structured. A further rise in plasma cortisol may occur again in the period of anxious depression following the remission of delusions. The study of hormonal changes in acute and subacute schizophrenia promises to be helpful in connection with the programme of comprehensive treatment described later (second phase).

Disturbances of the sleep-wakefulness cycle are a prominent feature of the acute phase. Severe and persistent insomnia, especially in the first part of the night, may be related to hallucinative or delusional activity, and to bizarre or hyperactive behaviour. Some of these phenomena have been associated with a lack of dreaming sleep (D-state deprivation), altered sleep patterns, or a disturbance of REM sleep.[33] In the treatment of sleep disturbances neuroleptics with high sedative properties such as chlorpromazine (100-200 mg a day) should be preferred to haloperidol, which is contraindicated in view of its reported activating properties.[34,35] The administration in the evening of benzodiazepines such as flurazepam, which have no side-effects on the EEG sleep pattern, permits the neuroleptic dosage to be reduced.

Psychotropic drugs

The major therapeutic goal in the first phase is to decrease the psychotic symptoms as quickly as possible, using drugs with high pharmacodynamic activity. The most powerful phenothiazines are the most suitable, especially those with an aliphatic side-chain (chlorpromazine, levomepromazine), some piperidines (thioridazine, trifluoperazine) and piperazine derivatives (fluphenazine, perphenazine). The piperazines are more likely to cause extrapyramidal side-effects. Other powerful drugs are haloperidol (among the butyro-phenones), clothiapine[36] and, more recently introduced, clozapine.

Oral as well as parenteral administration is suggested, using gradually increasing divided doses, so as to obtain an effective response with the lowest possible amount. Chlorpromazine and levomepromazine are suitable for reducing agitation and excitement. In treating confusional states haloperidol and/or chlorpromazine together with piperidine derivatives are the first choice. For catatonic stupor, phenothiazines such as thioridazine, perphenazine, trifluoperazine or haloperidol may be suggested. It is noticeable, however, that the drug chosen often depends on the personal experience and faith of the therapist, or on suggestions from the producers. A survey carried out at several different centres by the N.I.M.H. in 1964 showed that three different types of phenothiazines (chlorpromazine, thioridazine and fluphenazine) were in fact equally effective in the treatment of acute schizophrenia.[37]

Special care is needed in using psychotropic drugs on some schizophrenics who have certain somatic conditions. Some young patients, mainly females and catatonics, show autonomic lability.[24] Also patients with leptosomatic body-build, signs of impaired pituitary function and disturbed autonomic function (profuse perspiration, blueness of hands and feet), as well as others with signs of adrenogenital syndrome, may react with serious symptoms of intolerance such as severe neurodysleptic crises or acute hypotension, during the course of treatment with chlorpromazine or haloperidol.[38] We have sometimes seen an incipient sinus tachycardia made worse by neuroleptics such as phenothiazines or, in a lesser degree, by haloperidol. Haloperidol appears to be contraindicated in cases with symptoms of organic pathology of the central nervous system. To reduce such concomitant symptoms, and to avoid the side-effects of drugs, it is advisable that in very acute schizophrenia the treatment should not be restricted to the psychotropic drugs. The use of protective preparations such as ATP, ADP (adenosine diphosphate), cocarboxylase, liver extracts and injectable corticosteroids should also be considered. The excessive use of drugs designed to control extrapyramidal side-effects can, as Hollister[39] has emphasised, produce an extra pathology.

(b) SECOND PHASE

As Detre and Jarecki[40] have observed, at about six to eight days after the onset of acute schizophrenia a second phase begins. By this time the management of the acute symptoms will have allowed any incidental accessory features to clear up and the therapeutic strategy must deal, not just with target symptoms, but rather with the target syndrome that may emerge.[26] Moreover pharmacotherapy must develop a psychodynamic meaning in the doctor-patient and in the doctor-patient-family relationship. The acceptance and active participation of the members of the family in the treatment must come from the doctor, and from his deep convictions and understanding, which the patient and the family take in through his general behaviour and the psychotherapeutic or rational nature of the prescriptions he applies. The more the patient is made aware of and taught about the real properties of the drugs and their relevance to his personal problems, the more he will be able to mobilise his defence mechanisms and avoid the two extremes of complete rejection or too-eager acceptance, as an expression of underlying aggression. Usually there is a fleeting appearance of certain clusters of symptoms before the picture takes the form of one of the well-known types of hebephrenic, catatonic, paranoid or, more rarely, simple schizophrenia. The therapeutic approach can be better managed and validated by making use of various tests and rating scales, and especially the Rorschach test. Drugs are often used singly, but when this is done care is needed to avoid going on increasing the dosage until very high levels (1000-1200 mg chlorpromazine, or 40-60 mg haloperidol) are reached, if the expected effect is not obtained. If this should be the case, the drug first tried should be replaced by another with similar indications but of a different chemical type (e.g. fluphanazine replaced by haloperidol, clopentixol or clothiapine). In any case with some drugs, such as clopenthixol, the difference between the therapeutic and toxic levels is relatively small.

The use of combinations of two or more psychotropic drugs is widespread in clinical practice and occurs in at least two-thirds of the patients so treated, as reported in many text-books.[42-44] In this connection it is necessary to consider qualitative and quantitative restrictions imposed on their use by drug interactions, some of which can be useful (as combining tricyclic drugs with phenothiazines), but which are more often dangerous.[45] Thus the combination of MAO inhibitors with halogen-containing or piperazine-type phenothiazines, or with imipramine, can cause severe neuronal damage or damage to liver cells.[26,46] On the positive side, according to some authors there is the possibility of combining two neuroleptics, such as chlor-promazine and haloperidol, so as to obtain a stronger action,[42,43,47] and this may allow a reduction in dosage and facilitate adaptation to changes in symptoms, especially the so-called "transit syndromes".

Strategy of relating treatment to changes in symptoms

One must be aware of likely changes in the pattern of symptoms during treatment in the first and second phases of acute schizophrenia. Thus affective features may change in form and in intensity. There may be an intensification of the initial pattern, such as a deepening of withdrawal to the point of emotional anxiety not yet organised into an appropriate defence mechanism. Again, there may be an emergence of depressive features, which often become more intense as delusions and hallucinations are removed and the patient comes into contact with reality in becoming aware of his situation. Under these conditions it is better to give imipramine or amitryptiline to patients on phenothiazines, or nortryptiline to those on butyrophenones.[48] During the second phase the treatment of affective symptoms may be important and by adding a benzodiazepine or promazine it may be possible to achieve a more balanced control of anxiety and a better response to psychotherapy.[49]

Naturally there are difficult situations, as in states of psychomotor impairment (catatonic or simple schizophrenia) in which treatment with chlorpromazine or haloperidol is unsatisfactory. Treatment with a disinhibiting drug (sulpiride or dimethylimipramine), or according to some authors a few applications of electroshock (ECT), may then be tried.[44] Patients with acute schizophrenia of paranoid type, usually given phenothiazine and haloperidol, may develop delusions of self-identification which are particularly hard to control, and in that case further administration of an incisive thioxanthene (clopenthixol) may be suggested. Consideration must be given, not only to the dosage level, but also to the duration of each form of drug treatment. Thus some phenothiazines, such as chlorpromazine and fluphenazine, are effective in controlling the psychotic symptoms in hebephrenic forms of acute schizophrenia, but too high doses given for too long a time may result in impairment of affective and psychomotor functions and so interfere with the patient's ability to establish satisfactory interpersonal relations. It should be noted that in young patients who develop a psychosis of hebephrenic type at or before puberty, there occurs in a high proportion of cases a concomitant blockage of the hypothalmic-pituitary-gonadal axis, which may get worse during intensive treatment with neuroleptic drugs. Since the patients are at the stage of maturation of the endocrine system, the balance is disturbed. For biological as well as psychological reasons it is therefore necessary to introduce simultaneous controlled treatment with a preparation of human chorionic gonadotrophin.[50] For hebephrenics who are apathetic and withdrawn, sulpiride, a drug with disinhibiting and stabilising properties, has been used with success. When there have been one or more previous episodes of acute schizophrenia, the previous experience must be considered with respect to both the pharmacological and the psychotherapeutic treatment given. In a collaborative investigation Levine[51] found that the effectiveness of high-dosage chlorpromazine or trifluoperazine depended on the type of phenothiazine medication the patient had been receiving hitherto. In patients who had been receiving piperazine phenothiazines, trifluoperazine was no more effective, while patients who had been on a non-piperazine phenothiazine just prior to treatment gave no greater response when treated with chlorpromazine.

Reviewing the results of a large controlled investigation, Cole and Davis[52] concluded that the more active phenothiazines act specifically in correcting the symptoms of schizophrenia, and their action cannot be regarded only as a superficial or placebo effect. A similar conclusion was reached by Prien *et al.*[53] in the area of social adaptation. Recent research on dopaminergic transmission has shown that the phenothiazines and butyrophenones which are most effective clinically have the common property of being powerful inhibitors of dopaminergic transmission in the mesolimbic system, whereas other phenothiazine derivatives less effective in treating schizophrenia lack this property and have little action on the adenylate cyclase enzyme concerned.[54,55] Yet it is known that individual patients show a considerable specificity in their reaction to different neuroleptics, so that some patients can be regarded as "responders" to a particular drug, while other patients are not. Drug resistance seems to be a result either of biological factors influencing the drug metabolism or, more likely, of genetically determined characteristics of the cell membranes.[56,57]

During the second phase, which continues for one or two months, there is increasing freedom to carry out a progressive, but constantly supervised, decrease in the dosage, especially of the anticholinergic drugs. The use either of long-acting drugs (pimozide, fluspirilene, fluoperidol, etc.) or slow-release drugs (fluphenazine decanoate) has been proposed[58,59] but the initial doses should be carefully adapted to the needs of the individual patient.[60]

Psychotherapeutic and environmental aspects

The care of the acute psychotic patient in a protective environment, without making him too dependent or isolated from the external world, raises special problems. Under-stimulation is as undesirable as over-stimulation, which can lead to a strengthening of autistic phantasies and paranoid ideas, with consequent excitement. Since the psychotic symptoms tend to distort and limit communication, psychotherapy should be limited to brief supportive contacts in which doctor and patient discuss only the most immediate and concrete problems. In this type of verbal exchange it may also be possible to give the patient a plausible explanation of the pharmacological treatment, so reducing the sense of remoteness engendered by the psychosis on the one hand and the environment on the other.

When the symptoms have improved and the patient has established a reasonably good contact with his environment, he should be helped to examine the conflicts and stresses operative both at the time and in the period just before the acute onset of the psychosis.[40] This can proceed only gradually, step by step. The doctor should make himself available as much as possible and should be ready to tolerate interruptions in their relationship depending on the mental state of the patient. Especially at this stage the patient should be encouraged to develop a sense of belonging, by constant presence of relatives, members of the staff (doctors, nurses) and other patients. The patient must never be thought of as an individual in isolation, but as belonging to a group which must be induced as soon as possible to cooperate in a reciprocal relationship. In this way the optimum conditions for pharmacological treatment can also be achieved.

III. Prognostic Aspects

The possibility of detecting prognostic features, which is hard enough in schizophrenia as a whole, is harder still in the case of acute schizophrenia, in which precise analytical and biometric information is relatively scarce. However there are some factors of predictive value, both in a positive and in a negative sense, that appear to be of general application in the different types of schizophrenia. Thus evidence of a "schizoid type of pre-morbid personality", in the words of Astrup *et al.*[61,62] or of "pre-morbid personality with schizoid adjustment", as expressed by Vaillant,[63-66] is associated with mental deterioration in a high proportion (80 per cent) of cases. The same may be said for similar features in the family history, even if their presence is not unanimously agreed. Some authors believe there is a greater likelihood of a patient developing psychotic episodes of a type similar to those in his relatives.[61] On the other hand other authors claim a better prognosis for schizophrenia if there is a tendency to affective psychoses in the family.[63,65]

The acute onset and short duration of the psychotic episodes are in themselves favourable features. In fact only 20 per cent of acute cases show symptoms of mental deterioration compared with 85 per cent of those with acute onset but in whom the course is that of process schizophrenia without recurrent relapses.[61] Vaillant[23,63] who reviewed 16 reports on cases of schizophrenia of good prognosis studied over a long period of time, formulated seven indices for favourable prognosis: acute onset, absence of previous autistic personality, family history of affective psychoses, and certain curious clinical features such as the intensity of confusional state, extent of affective features, the fear of death and the importance of precipitating factors. In follow-up studies of a large number of cases continued over a period of 20 years (a period in which new kinds of treatment were introduced), Astrup *et al.*[61,62] obtained evidence agreeing with that of Langfeld,[67] that the use of psychotropic drugs reduces the risk of chronicity and reduces the extent of deterioration, in comparison with shock therapies. In a more recent controlled investigation in which drug and placebo treatment were administered randomly to a group of acute schizophrenics of good prognosis on Vaillant's criteria, Evans *et al.*[64] found that patients receiving phenothiazines obtained earlier remission than those on placebo treatment. The impact of various factors influencing outcome was analysed in the reports of Strauss and Carpenter[68,69] who carried out research for predicting outcome based on the systems theory concept of "linked open systems". They suggest that multiple etiologies need to be considered for psychiatric disability; and outcome and its prediction in schizophrenia appear to depend on several different semi-independent factors.

A single factor such as duration of previous hospitalisation, past unemployment or poor capacity for social relationships, as also the pattern of symptoms, can give by itself only an approximate indication of outcome. Treatment can also be inadequate if focused on only one causal factor. It may be concluded that, although drugs may be useful in reducing the symptoms of schizophrenia, a purely pharmacological treatment could be inadequate unless supported by programs of individual and social therapy.

References

1. ARNHOFF, F.N. Social consequences of policy toward mental illness. *Science,* **188**, 1277, 1975.
2. WYRSCH, J. Ueber akute schizophrener Züstände. *Abh. Neur.* H. 82, Karger, Basel, 1937.
3. WORLD HEALTH ORGANIZATION, Draft Glossary, Geneva, 1970.
4. KRAEPELIN, E. Psychiatrie. *Siebente auflage.* II Band. Ambrosius, Leipzig, 1904.
5. BLEULER, E. *Dementia praecox or the group of schizophrenias.* (Transl. by Zinkin J.), Int. Univ. Press., New York, 1952.
6. EY, H. Les problèmes cliniques des schizophrénies. *Evol. Psychiat.* **1**, 149, 1958.
7. SCHNEIDER, K. Psychopathologie clinique. Nauwelaerts, Louvain, 1957.
8. KASANIN, H. The acute schizo-affective psychoses. *Am. J. Psychiat.* **13**, 97, 1933.
9. McCABE, M.S. Reactive psychoses. *Acta Psychiat. Scand., Suppl. 259,* 1975.
10. GURLAND, B.J. and FLEISS, J.L. Cross national study of diagnosis of the mental disorders: some comparisons of diagnostic criteria from the first investigation. *Am. J. Psychiat.* **125** (Suppl.) 30, 1969.
11. BALDESSARINI, R.J. Frequency of diagnoses of schizophrenia versus affective disorders from 1944 to 1968. *Am. J. Psychiat.* **127**, 759, 1970.
12. LIPKIN, K.M., DYRUD, J. and MEYER, G.G. The many faces of mania. *Arch. Gen. Psychiat.* **22**, 262, 1970.
13. COHEN, S.N., ALLEN, N.G., POLLIN, W. and HRUBEC, Z. Relationship of schizo-affective psychosis to manic depressive psychosis and schizophrenia. *Arch. Gen. Psychiat.* **26**, 539, 1972.
14. TAYLOR, M.A., GAZTANAGA, P. and ABRAHMS, R. Manic depressive illness and acute schizophrenia; a clinical family history and treatment response study. *Am. J. Psychiat.* **131**, 678, 1974.
15. WINOKUR, G., CLAYTON, P.J. and REICH, T. Manic depressive illnesses. Mosby Co., St. Louis, 1969.
16. PERRIS, C. A study of cycloid psychoses. *Acta Pyschiat. Scand. Suppl. 253,* 1974.
17. CAZZULLO, C.L. Predictive factors in diagnosis and treatment of manic depressive psychoses. In *Psihofarmakologija* 3, Bohacek, M., Miholivocic, J. (eds.), 155. Medicinska Naklada, Zagreb, 1974.
18. KENDELL, R.E. Psychiatric diagnosis in Britain and the United States. *British J. Hospital Medicine,* **6**, 147, 1971.
19. LEHMANN, H.E. Schizophrenia IV: Clinical features. In *Comprehensive textbook of Psychiatry,* Freedman, A.M., Kaplan, H.J. (eds.), William and Wilkins, Baltimore, 1967.
20. OLLERENSHAW, D.P. The classification of the functional psychoses. *Brit. J. Psychiat.* **122**, 517, 1973.
21. BECK, A.T. Depression. Clinical, experimental and theoretical aspects. Staples Press, London, 1967.
22a. CARPENTER, W.T. Jr., STRAUSS, J.S. and BARTKO, J.J. Flexible system for the diagnosis of schizophrenia: A report from the W.H.O. International pilot study of schizophrenia. *Science,* **182**, 1275, 1973.
22b. CARPENTER, W.T. Jr., STRAUSS, J.S. Cross-cultural evaluation of Schneider's first-rank symptoms of schizophrenia. A report from: International pilot study of Schizophrenia. *Am. J. Psychiat.* **131**, 682, 1974.
23. VAILLANT, G.E. An historical review of the remitting schizophrenias. *J. Nerv. Ment. Dis.* **138**, 48, 1964.
24. CAZZULLO, C.L. Biological and clinical studies on schizophrenia related to pharmacological treatment. In *Recent Advances in Biological Psychiatry,* Wortis, J. (ed.), V., p. 114, Plenum Press, New York, 1963.
25. CAZZULLO, C.L. and TERRANOVA, R The role of ATP upon reserpin neuronal action. First Int. Congr. of Neuro-psychopharmacology 15, Elsevier Pub. Co., Amsterdam, 1959.
26. CAZZULLO, C.L. New Trends in Psychopharmacology. Proc. IV World Congress of Psychiatry. *Excerpta Medica Int. Congr. Series n.150,* 308, 1967.
27. POST, R.M. Cocaine psychoses. A continuum model. *Am. J. Psychiat.* **132**, 225, 1975.
28. FRIEDHOFF, A.J. Biogenic amines and schizophrenia. In *Biological Psychiatry.* Mendels, J. (ed.), p. 113, J. Wiley & Sons, New York, 1973.
29. FROHMAN, C.E. Plasma protein and schizophrenia. In *Biological Psychiatry,* Mendels, J. (ed.), p. 131, J. Wiley & Sons, New York, 1973.
30. IVERSEN, L.L. Dopamine receptors in the brain. *Science,* **188**, 1084, 1975.

31. WYATT, R.J., BELMAKER, R. and MURPHY, D. Low platelet monoamine oxidase and vulnerability to Schizophrenia. In *Genetics and Pharmacopsychiatry*, Mendlewicz, J. (ed.), p. 38, Karger, Basel, 1975.
32. SACHAR, E.J. Endocrine factors in psychopathological states. In *Biological Psychiatry*, Mendels, J. (ed.), p. 175, J. Wiley & Sons, New York, 1973.
33. HARTMANN, E.L. The biochemistry and pharmacology of the D-state (dreaming sleep). *Exp. Med. Surg.* 27, 105, 1969.
34. SINGH, M.M. and SMITH, J.M. Sleeplessness in acute and chronic schizophrenia. Response to haloperidol and antiparkinsonian agents. *Psychopharmacologia*, 29, 21, 1973.
35. ITIL, T.M., GANNON, P., HSU, W. and KLINGENBERG, H. Digital computer analysed sleep and resting EEG during haloperidol treatment. *Am. J. Psychiat.* 127, 462, 1970.
36. JACOBSON, L., NOREIK, M.B., PERRIS, C. and RAPP, W. A controlled trial of clothiapine and chlorpromazine in acute schizophrenic syndromes. *Acta Psychiat. Scand. Suppl. 255*, 55, 1974.
37. COLE, J.O. Phenothiazine treatment in acute schizophrenia. *Arch. Gen. Psychiat.* 10, 246, 1964.
38. CAZZULLO, C.L. and BRAMBILLA, F. Fonction surrenalienne et interaction hypophyso-surrenale dans la schizophrénie. *C.R. LV Congr. Med. Al. Neurol. Langue Franç.*, 226, Masson, Paris, 1962.
39. HOLLISTER, L. Combinations of Psychotropic drugs. In *Advances in Neuropsychopharmacology*, Vindr, O., Votava, Z., Bradley, P.B. (eds.), p. 407, North Holland Pub. Co., 1971.
40. DETRE, T.P. and JARECKI, H.G. *Modern psychiatric treatment*. Lippincott, Philadelphia, 1971.
41. BARAHONA-FERNANDES, H.J., CAZZULLO, C.L., COCCHI, A., DENBER, H.C.B., FREYHAN, F.A., KLERMAN, G.L., KÖKNEL, Ö., LEVINE, J., SAARMA, J., SARTESCHI, P., VINAR, O. and WITTENBORN, J.R. Therapeutic problems. In *The Neuroleptics*, Bobon, D.P., Jansenn, P.A., Bobon, J. (eds.), p. 148, Karger, Basel, 1970.
42. KIELHOLZ, P. Psychiatrische Pharmakotherapie in klinik und Praxis. Huber, Bern, 1965.
43. DENIKER, P., GINESTET, D. *Neuroleptiques*. In *Enciclop. Méd. Chir.*, B 20, 2, 1973.
44. FINK, M. and ITIL, T. Schizophrenia. VI Organic treatment. In *Comprehensive Textbook of Psychiatry*, Freedman, A.M., Kaplan, H.J. (eds.), p. 661, William and Wilkins, Baltimore, 1972.
45. GARATTINI, S. and MORSELLI, P.L. *Interazioni tra i farmaci*. Ferro, Milano, 1973.
46. CAZZULLO, C.L., DE MARTIS, D. and VANNI, F. Significato terapeutico del la applicazione di associazioni psicofarmacologiche. *Atti Convegni Farmitalia. Aggiornamenti in Psiconeurofarmacologia*, p. 126, Minerva Medica, Torino, 1966.
47. SUTTER, J.M. and SCOTTO, J.C. Quelques aspects prometteurs de la chimiothérapie psychotrope. *Thérapeutique Sem. Hôp. Suppl. 45*, 866, 1969.
48. RIZZO, C., quoted by Garattini, S., Morselli, P. In *Integrazioni fra i farmaci*, Ferro, Milano, 1973.
49. SARTESCHI, P., MURATORIA, A. and SIMONETTI, C. Aggiornamenti sui risultati terapeutici dei neurolettici minori. Atti Convegni Farmitalia. *Aggiornamenti in psiconeuro farmacologia*, p. 72, Minerva Medica, Torino, 1966.
50. BRAMBILLA, F., CAZZULLO, C.L. and PENATI, G. Les hormones et la schizophrénie. Problèmes actuels d'endocrinologie et de nutrition. Série 18, 273, Expansion Scientifique, Paris, 1974.
51. LEVINE, J. Therapeutic problems. *The Neuroleptics*, Bobon, D.P., Janssen, P.A.J., Bobon, J. (eds.), p. 151, Karger, Basel, 1970.
52. COLE, J.O. and DAVIS, J.M. Drug treatment of schizophrenia. In *Schizophrenia*, Bellak. L. (ed.), p. 171, Grune and Stratton, New York, 1971.
53. PRIEN, R., LEVINE, J. and COLE, J.O. High dose trifluoperazine therapy in chronic schizophrenia. *Am. J. Psychiat.* 126, 305, 1969.
54. KEBANIAN, J.W., PETZOLD, G.L. and GREENGARD, P., quoted by Meltzer, H.Y. (55).
55. MELTZER, H.Y., SACHAR, E.J. and FRANTZ, A.G. Serum prolactin levels in newly admitted psychotic patients. *Neuropharmacology of monoamines and their regulatory enzymes*, p. 229, Usdim, New York, 1974.
56. CAZZULLO, C.L., BRAMBILLA, F. and MANGONI, A. Drug resistance and biological clinical factors in the response of schizophrenic patients to chlorpromazine. *Riv. Sper. Freniat.* 4, 723, 1973.
57. SMERALDI, E., SACCHETTI, E. and BELLODI, personal communication, 1975.
58. CHIEN, C. and COLE, J.O. Depot phenothiazine treatment in acute psychosis: a sequential comparative clinical study. *Am. J. Psychiat.* 130, 13, 1973.
59. ROPERT, R., LEVY, L. and ROPERT, M. Problèmes posés par les essais d'emploi des néuroleptiques à action prolongée (Nap) dans les syndromes psychiatriques aigus. *Ann. Med. Psychol.* 1, 259, 1973.
60. AYD, F.G. The depot fluphenazines; a reappraisal after ten years of clinical experiences. *Am. J. Psychiat.* 132, 491, 1975.
61. ASTRUP, C. and NOREIK, K. Functional psychoses: diagnostic and prognostic models. Charles C. Thomas Pub., Springfield, Ill., 1966.
62. NOREIK, K., ASTRUP, C., DALGARD, A.S. and HOLMBOE, R. A prolonged follow-up of acute schizophrenic and schizophreniform psychoses. *Acta Psychiat. Scand.* 43, 432, 1967.
63. VAILLANT, G.E. Prospective prediction of schizophrenic remission. *Arch. Gen. Psychiat.* II, 509, 1964.
64. EVANS, J.R., RODNICK, E.H., GOLDSTEIN, M.J. and JUDD, L.L. Premorbid adjustment, phenotiazine treatment, and remission in acute schizophrenics. *Arch. Gen. Psychiat.* 27, 487, 1972.

65. McCABE, M.S. Reactive psychoses. *Acta Psychiat. Scand., Suppl. 259*, 1975.
66. FAIBISH, G.M. and POKORNY, A.D. Prediction of long-term outcome in schizophrenia. *Dis. Nerv. Syst.* **33**, 304, 1972.
67. LANGFELDT, G. Diagnosis and prognosis of schizophrenia. *Proc. R. Soc. Med.* **53**, 1047, 1960.
68. STRAUSS, J.S. and CARPENTER, W.T. Jr. The prediction of outcome in schizophrenia. I. Characteristics of outcome. *Arch. Gen. Psychiat.* **27**, 739, 1972
69. STRAUSS, J.S. and CARPENTER, W.T. Jr. The prediction of outcome in schizophrenia. II. The relationship between predictor and outcome variables: a report from the W.H.O. International Pilot Study of Schizophrenia. *Arch. Gen. Psychiat.* **31**, 37, 1974.

Acknowledgment. I am very indebted to Prof. R. Spiazzi, Dr. Anna Cazzullo, Dr G. Fornari and Dr. G. Spoto for valuable help in the preparation of the manuscript.

The Drug Approach to Therapy. Long-term Treatment of Schizophrenia

I. MUNKVAD, R. FOG and P. KRISTJANSEN

For centuries it has been known that drugs can influence mind and behaviour, but only in recent years have we obtained a more systematic understanding of the pharmacological and biochemical basis of this influence – an understanding which is essential for the development of a rational system of drug therapy. Developments in psychopharmacology have been rapid in the past two decades. Before the early 1950s the drugs available for the treatment of psychotic patients were very limited, and only very few patients, including the schizophrenics on long-term treatment, were able to benefit from them.

The so-called psychopharmacological era in psychiatry started in 1952 when Delay, Deniker and Harl published a paper on "4560 RP", later called "Largactil" or chlorpromazine.[1] This paper contained almost everything that is known about the drug as to its clinical and side effects, and today it can be regarded as one of the classical contributions to psychopharmacology.

Etiology of Schizophrenia

Since the etiology and pathogenesis of the schizophrenic disease processes are unknown, we can treat only the symptoms and not the causes of the condition. Evidence from several laboratories including our own indicates, however, that the neurotransmitter dopamine plays a role in pathophysiology of the schizophrenias.[2] From a pharmacological point of view it is significant that all known antipsychotic drugs to a greater or lesser extent have antidopaminergic properties as a common trait.

Neuroleptics inhibit stereotyped behaviour such as the sniffing, licking and biting, induced in the rat by amphetamine or aporphine, but at the same time they may stimulate other activities such as grooming, rearing or running. The fact that the neuroleptics act specifically in inhibiting the stereotyped behaviour induced by amphetamine makes it likely that they inhibit the nigro-striatal dopaminergic system which is activated by amphetamine. This view is supported by further biochemical and anatomical evidence. The two characteristic actions of neuroleptic drugs, in inhibiting stereotyped behaviour and in inducing catalepsy in the rat, may be used to define the group of drugs effective in the treatment of schizophrenia. Their efficacy in treating psychotic patients may also give some indication of the mechanisms involved in the psychosis.

Classification of Antipsychotic Drugs

The antipsychotic drugs – the so-called neuroleptics – can be classified in several different ways, from a chemical, pharmacological or clinical point of view. The chemical classification is

174   *I. Munkvad, R. Fog and P. Kristjansen*

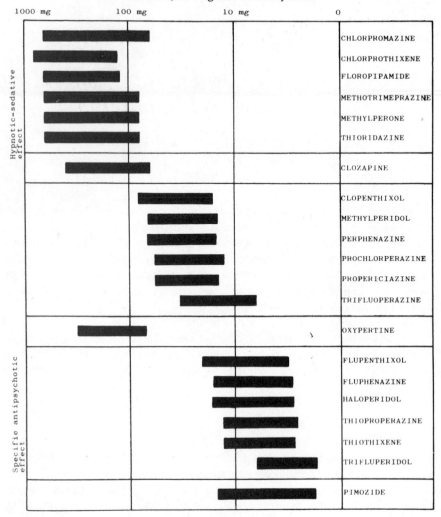

Fig. 1.

of limited value clinically and much the same can be said of several pharmacological systems of classification. Two form of clinical classification will be mentioned here.

The first one, worked out by one of the co-authors of this paper,[3] distinguishes the neuroleptics given in high doses, with sedative properties, from those given in low doses, which have more specific antipsychotic properties (Fig. 1). Many other neuroleptics could be added to the list, but the above-mentioned are those in common use in Scandinavian countries.

The model of Bobon and Collard[4] deserves special attention and some details of this model will be given here (Fig. 2). As seen from the properties of the neuroleptics described by the authors, both clinical and pharmacological effects are included in the model, and it is often possible to use a clinical analysis (identifying the main symptoms in the schizophrenic patients) in order to select the drug of choice for the individual patients. This method has special relevance to the long-term treatment of schizophrenics of various types with different clinical symptoms.

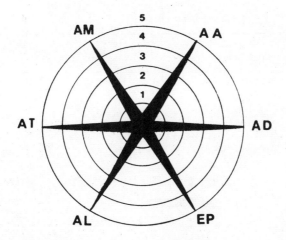

Type of effect		Intensity of effect	
AT	ataraxie	0	nil or reverse
AM	antimanic	1	very weak
AA	antiautistic	2	weak
AD	antidelusional	3	moderate
EP	extrapyramidal	4	potent
AL	adrenolytic	5	very potent

The revised Liege clinical physiognomy of neuroleptics (BOBON J. *et al.*,

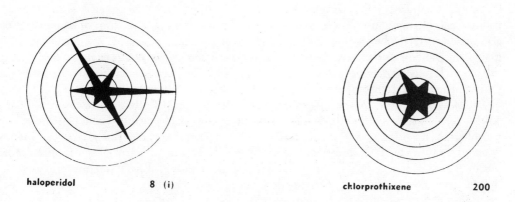

haloperidol   8 (i)   chlorprothixene   200

Next to the WHO international non-proprietary or generic names is the daily dosage in mg for a 70 kg adult acute psychotic inpatient ; (i) — injectable.

Fig. 2.

LONG – ACTING NEUROLEPTICS

(modified from Ayd)

GENERIC NAMES	ROUTE OF ADMINISTRATION	MEAN LENGTH OF ACTION (WEEKS)	CURRENT USUAL DOSAGE RANGE	
PENFLURIDOL	ORAL	1	10–40	MG
FLUSPIRILENE	I.M.	1	2–10	MG
FLUPENTHIXOL DECANOATE	I.M.	3	20–80	MG
FLUPHENAZINE ENANTHATE	I.M.	2	25–100	MG
FLUPHENAZINE DECANOATE	I.M.	3	12,5–50	MG
PERPHENAZINE ENANTHATE	I.M.	1–2	50–200	MG
PIPOTHIAZINE UNDECYLENATE	I.M.	2	100–150	MG
PIPOTHIAZINE PALMITATE	I.M.	4	50–300	MG

Fig. 3.

General Rules for Long-term Treatment

Generally a specific antipsychotic drug, given in lower doses, is the drug of choice for the long-term treatment of schizophrenia, and it is often possible to give such a drug as maintenance therapy only once a day – perhaps in the evening. This form of administration is also easier to remember for out-patients and easier for them to accept. We must never forget that many patients fail to take their tablets regularly and this is one reason for unsatisfactory treatment results. It has been reported that up to 45 per cent of schizophrenic out-patients cannot be relied on to take their medication after discharge from hospital.[5]

Drugs given as a depot and long-acting drugs deserve special attention in the case of those schizophrenic patients who refuse medication or are unreliable medication takers. Long-acting neuroleptics are listed in Fig. 3. Generally it is an advantage, as mentioned above, to use low doses of a more specific antipsychotic drug in the long-term treatment of schizophrenia and if possible only one drug should be prescribed for each patient. Psychopharmacology-cocktails should generally be avoided, with the reservation that sometimes it is necessary to give an unspecific neuroleptic drug for sleeping disorders and also during periods of exacerbation of the psychosis.

Antiparkinsonian Treatment

Reversible extrapyramidal reactions are unfortunately common during treatment with neuroleptic drugs.[7] The overall incidence in 3755 patients is shown in Fig. 4. The routine administration of antiparkinsonian drugs for neurological side-effects should be avoided because of a possible antagonistic effect of such drugs against the antipsychotic action of the neuroleptics. Animal experiments from several laboratories, including our own, have demonstrated such an effect, and it has been shown that the concentration of chlorpromazine in the plasma decreases when antiparkinsonian treatment is given.[8,9] Clinical investigations, among others those of Haase and co-workers as early as in 1965, underline this statement.[10-11] It is also more economical if antipsychotic drugs are given only once a day and if (unnecessary) antiparkinsonian drugs are avoided.[12] It is quite unnecessary and therefore a mistake to combine an antipsychotic drug with an antiparkinsonian drug right from the start of the treatment, as is customary for many psychiatrists. If neurological side-effects are seen during the treatment they can be relieved by reducing the dosage of antipsychotic drug or, if necessary, by administering an antiparkinsonian drug *for a short period only.*[13] It is incorrect to say that symptoms of acute dystonia (called "dyskinesia", as distinct from "tardive dyskinesia", in the U.S.A. and some other countries), if seen during long-term treatment, should be treated immediately by intravenous injection of an antiparkinsonian drug such as biperiden or procyclidin. One of the main principles in all long-term treatment is to give a dosage of an antipsychotic drug of such a structure and in such a way that psychotic symptoms are reduced as much as possible, while at the same time the patient experiences no neurological side-effects. Sometimes this is a difficult act of balance, but often it is possible.

DRUG-INDUCED
EXTRAPYRAMIDAL REACTIONS:

OVERALL INCIDENCE IN 3,775 PATIENTS

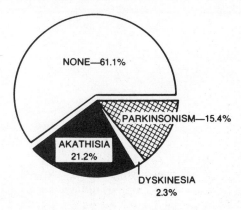

Fig. 4.

Tardive Dyskinesia in Relation to Long-term Treatment

Too high doses of neuroleptics for too long a period can provoke so-called tardive dyskinesia, often reversible but sometimes irreversible — a serious problem in long-term treatment. The syndrome consists of coordinated, involuntary, stereotyped and rhythmic movements of choreiform type in various groups of muscles — especially the facial, mandibular and lingual muscles.

Antiparkinsonian drugs tend to accentuate the symptoms of tardive dyskinesia and should be discontinued at once. The only relevant corrective treatment is to give drugs with antidopaminergic properties such as pimozide or tetrabenazine. There is a clear and rational pharmacological background for this statement. The treatment of tardive dyskinesia with drugs that either inhibit the uptake of dopamine by the dopamine granules in the nerve endings (tetrabenazine, reserpine) or increase the sensitivity of the receptor membrane to dopamine (haloperidol, pimozide), has been tried for a decade with good results. Many psychiatrists have tried hitherto to treat tardive dyskinesia with antiparkinsonian drugs — in our opinion a mistake and of no value to the patient.

Some recent investigations in our laboratories have shown a cell reduction of up to 20 per cent in the corpus striatum in rats receiving perphenazine enanthate (3.4 mg/kg) every 2 weeks for 12 months (no reduction was found in the cortex). The experiments continue with other doses of perphenazine, and with younger and older animals for different periods. Other neuroleptics will also be investigated. These results are only mentioned in relation to the problem of tardive dyskinesia and in order to underline the possibility that too high doses of neuroleptics for too long a period may perhaps be dangerous clinically in view of the risk of causing organic brain damage.

Results of Treatment

Evaluation of the outcome of long-term treatment of schizophrenia is difficult. Many papers of varying quality reporting controlled and uncontrolled studies have been published. Kline, however, in 1967 reported figures which illustrate a dramatic change in the total population of the mental hospitals since the introduction of antipsychotic drugs (Fig. 5). In the 1920s, 60 per cent of schizophrenic patients were expected to remain hospitalised indefinitely and only 20 per cent made a good social remission.[16] In a study by Brown and co-workers[17] published in 1966 (a 5-year follow-up) it was found that 11 per cent were still hospitalised while 56 per cent had recovered socially.

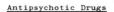

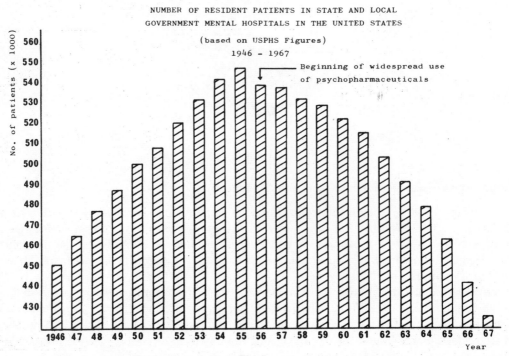

Fig. 5.

Pharmacological treatment has in several studies[18] been compared with other forms of treatment, including group psychotherapy and individual psychotherapy, and most investigators conclude that pharmacotherapy is superior to other forms of treatment. Nevertheless it should never be forgotten that other kinds of treatment — psychotherapy, occupational therapy, social care, etc. are important adjuncts to psychopharmacological treatment.

The optimum duration of the continued maintenance of psychopharmacological treatment is a controversial question and Chapman and co-workers reviewed this problem in 1975.[19] It is relevant that we are dealing only with the treatment of symptoms: pharmacotherapy cannot cure schizophrenia. As pointed out by Lehmann,[20] there is no way of determining which patients are likely to have or to have had spontaneous remissions, so that we have to accept either the continuous administration of unnecessary drugs to a certain proportion of schizophrenic patients, or the risk of possible relapse. Hogarty and co-workers[18] reported a relapse rate of 72.5 per cent after 12 months for patients on placebo, and a rate of 32.6 per cent for those on chlorpromazine. Generally the risk of relapse is at least twice as great in patients not on maintenance treatment as in those on active drug treatment. On the other hand it has been stated that 25 per cent of newly admitted schizophrenic patients do well without drug treatment, and there is suggestive evidence that some schizophrenic patients may actually do better without antipsychotic drugs.[21] In our laboratory Schiørring has shown in animal experiments that neuroleptics may disrupt social interaction, and, therefore, it is suggested that neuroleptics in certain cases may increase autism rather than ameliorating it.[22] In our opinion it is quite legitimate to interrupt long-term treatment, and periods without medication can be recommended if it is possible to observe the patients carefully during these periods. Lehmann[23] is of the same opinion, mainly in view of the risk of tardive dyskinesia, and he discusses drug holidays lasting from a few days to 4 weeks, pointing out that longer interruptions may involve the risk of relapse or deterioration of the patient's condition.

New Drugs and Drugs of the Future

Of great pharmacological and clinical interest is a fairly new drug, clozapin, which has a new type of chemical structure and an unusual pharmacological profile[24] (Fig. 6). In our experience it acts clinically as a strong antipsychotic drug — especially against psychotic

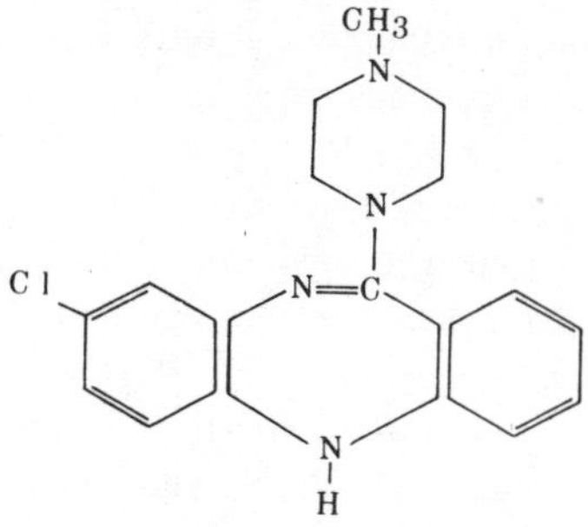

CLOZAPINE

Fig. 6.

aggressive behaviour. In relation to long-term treatment it is important that it does not induce so-called extrapyramidal side-effects, but it influences autonomic functions and causes sedation, which is most pronounced during the first 2 weeks of treatment.

In ordinary screening tests in animals this drug (a dibenzodiazepine derivative) does not exert an antagonistic effect against apomorphine-induced stereotypies and it has only a weak antiamphetamine effect. However, recent experiments in our laboratories[25] have shown that direct bilateral microinjection of clozapine into the corpus striatum of rats inhibits amphetamine-induced stereotypies and induces catalepsy. Clozapin, like other neuroleptics used clinically, therefore does have an antidopaminergic action, although a weak one. Investigators in a number of pharmacological research centres are interested in this drug, especially in view of its lack of extrapyramidal side-effects, and they are trying to find derivatives without the sedative properties and without its autonomic side-effects.

In summary, the ideal antipsychotic drug would be one which antagonises psychotic behaviour, but does not affect normal behaviour, i.e. that it either alone or together with other treatments will not only eliminate psychotic behaviour, but also replace psychotic behaviour by normal behaviour. New antipsychotic drugs with different chemical structures and unusual pharmacological properties may perhaps throw new light on the biological background of the schizophrenic processes, and psychiatrists working in the clinical field should keep aware of this problem.

Discussion

The above-mentioned so-called "rules" are generally applicable for the long-term treatment of schizophrenic patients, but naturally there are exceptions. Some patients feel better on a more sedative "high dosage" drug — and it should be pointed out that it may be impossible initially to pick out the drug of choice for the individual patient. It is therefore an advantage for the psychiatrist working in the field of psychopharmacology to have an armamentarium of drugs at his disposal. A flexible attitude towards drug administration is of benefit to the schizophrenic patient on long-term treatment.

We do not agree with pharmacologists who claim that all neuroleptics are of equal value, whatever the schizophrenic symptoms may be.[26] In the case of out-patients it must be said that sedation is seldom of any benefit to the patient (even if there are some patients who do not feel unwanted sedation on nonspecific drugs) and in our experience successful resocialisation is more frequently obtained with out-patients who are treated with a more specific antipsychotic "low-dosage" drug. Hitherto it has not been possible to assert that the more specific drugs in lower doses are less toxic than drugs given in higher doses (especially in the CNS), but it has been claimed that until now no verified case of persistent dyskinesia has been reported in patients treated exclusively with a depot neuroleptic (perphenazine as depot treatment was not included in the investigation).[27] It is assumed that the lower concentrations in the plasma and CNS are responsible for this observation. On the same basis some investigators recommend "drug-holidays",[28] the lowest possible dosage of the given neuroleptic and in this connection, only if absolutely necessary, antiparkinsonian treatment for shorter periods.

A special pharmacological phenomenon, neuroleptic-induced supersensitivity of the "synaptic events", described amongst others by Møller Nielsen,[29] might perhaps be used clinically by giving neuroleptics for limited periods, interrupted by drug-free intervals. Investigations of such treatments are being planned in our department.

References

1. DELAY, J., DENIKER, P. and HARL, J. Utilisation en therapeutique d'une phenothiazine d'action centrale elective (4560 RP). *Annales Medico-Psychologiques,* **110**, 112-117, 1952.
2. RANDRUP, A. and MUNKVAD, I. Evidence indicating an association between schizophrenia and dopaminergic hyperactivity in the brain (Conference on schizophrenia, London, September 1971). *Ortemolecular Psychiatry*, **1**, 2-7, 1972.
3. KRISTJANSEN, P. Scandinavian standpoint on the Liège classification of neuroleptics. *Acta psychiat. belg.* **74**, 462-469, 1974.
4. COLLARD, J. The main clinical classifications of neuroleptics. *Acta psychiat. belg.* **74**, 447-461, 1974.
5. BLACKWELL, B. Drug deviation in psychiatric patients. In *The future of pharmacotherapy*, ed. by Ayd, F.J. (International drug therapy newsletter, Baltimore, 1973), pp. 17-31.
6. AYD, F.J. *The future of pharmacotherapy* (International drug therapy newsletter, Baltimore, 1973).
7. AYD, F.J. Neuroleptic-induced extrapyramidal reactions. Incidence, manifestations and management. *Ibid.*, pp. 77-88.
8. FOG, R. On stereotypy and catalepsy: Studies on the effect of amphetamines and neuroleptics in rats (Thesis). *Acta neurol. scand.* **48**, 1-66 (suppl. 50), 1972.
9. LADER, M. Personal communication, in press.
10. HAASE, H.-J. Neuroleptika, Tranquilizer und Antidepressiva in Klinik und Praxis. Düsseldorf, pp. 31-66, 1966.
11. LEHMANN, H.L. The somatic and pharmacologic treatments of schizophrenia. In *Strategic intervention in schizophrenia* (ed. by Cancro, Fox and Shapiro, Behavioural publications, New York, 153-185, 1974).
12. DI MASCIO, A. Changing patterns of psychotropic drugs in Massachusetts Mental Hospitals. *Psychopharmacol. Bull.* **10**, 24-27, 1974.
13. Ibid.
14. FOG, R. and PAKKENBERG, H. Combined nitoman-pimozide treatment of Huntington's Chorea and other hyperkinetic syndromes. *Acta Neurol. Scand.* **46**, 249-251, 1970.
15. PAKKENBERG, H., FOG, R. and NILAKANTAN, B. The long-term effect of perphenazine enanthate on the rat brain. *Psychopharmacologia (Berl.)* **29**, 329-336, 1973.
16. HASTINGS, D.W. Follow-up results in psychiatric illness. *Amer. J. Psychiat.* **114**, 1057-1066, 1958.
17. BROWN, G.W., BONE, N., DALISON, B. and WING, J.K. Schizophrenia and social care. London: Oxford University Press, p. 232, 1966.
18. HOGARTY, G.E., GOLDBERG, S.C. and the collaborative study group. Drug and sociotherapy in the aftercare of schizophrenic patients: one year relapse rates. *Arch. Gen. Psychiat.* **28**, 54-65, 1973.
19. CHAPMAN, L.J., CAMERON, R., COCKE, J.G. and PRITCHETT, Th. Effects of phenothiazine withdrawal on proverb interpretation by chronic schizophrenics. *J. of Abnormal Psychology* **84**, 24-29, 1975.
20. LEHMANN, H.L. The somatic and pharmacologic treatments of schizophrenia. In *Strategic intervention in schizophrenia* (ed. by Cancro, Fox and Shapiro, Behavioural publications, New York, 153-185, 1974).
21. LEVINE, J. Guidelines for the conduct of clinical trials. *Psychopharmacol. Bull.* **10**, 70-91, 1974.
22. SCHIØRRING, E. Social isolation and other behavioural changes in a group of three vervet monkeys (Cercopithecus) produced by single, low doses of amphetamine. *Psychopharmacologia,* **26**, 117, suppl. 1972.
23. LEHMANN, H.L. The somatic and pharmacologic treatments of schizophrenia. In *Strategic intervention in schizophrenia* (ed. by Cancro, Fox and Shapiro, Behavioural publications, New York, 153-185, 1974).
24. GERLACH, J., KOPPELHUS, P., HELWEG, E. and MONRAD, A. Clozapine and Haloperidol in a single blind cross-over trial. Treatment of schizophrenia, therapeutic and biochemical aspects. *Acta psychiat. scandinav.* **50**, 410-424, 1974.
25. FOG, R. Neuroleptic action of clozapine injected into various brain areas in rats. *Int. Pharmacopsychiat.* **10**, 89-93, 1975.
26. GOLDBERG, S. Prediction of response to antipsychotic drugs. In *Psychopharmacology: a review of progress 1957-1967*, Ed. Efron, Washington: Govt. Printing Office 1968.

27. AYD, F.J. Neuroleptic-induced extrapyramidal reactions. Incidence, manifestations and management. *Ibid.*, pp. 77-88.
28. LEHMANN, H.L. The somatic and pharmacologic treatments of schizophrenia. In *Strategic intervention in schizophrenia* (ed. by Cancro, Fox and Shapiro), Behavioural publications, New York, 153-185, 1974..
29. MØLLER NIELSEN, I. Biochemical vs. clinical physiognomy of neuroleptics, with special reference to their sedative and antipsychotic effects. *Acta psychiat. belg.* 74, 473-484, 1974.

Neuroleptic Drugs. Chemical versus Biochemical Classification

A. PLETSCHER and E. KYBURZ

The term "neuroleptic drug" was originally created on the basis of clinical observations on human subjects treated with chlorpromazine and other phenothiazines. These drugs showed a new type of profile characterised in principle by antipsychotic action in schizophrenia, disturbances of extrapyramidal motor activity (hypokinesia, rigidity and tremor) and sedation without hypnosis. Subsequently, other chemical classes of compounds with neuroleptic properties were developed, and a multiplicity of biochemical effects of these drugs were described.

This paper deals mainly with neuroleptics which are not reserpinelike. An attempt will be made to analyse the following questions:

(1) Do the neuroleptics exhibit common chemical features and can these drugs be grouped into chemical subclasses relating to their clinical profile?

(2) Are there biochemical properties characteristic of all neuroleptics and can the drugs be grouped into biochemical subclasses connected with their clinical profile?

(3) What relation exists between the chemical and the biochemical classification of the neuroleptics?

1. Chemical Classification

Neuroleptics differ widely in their origin, molecular size, structure and physico-chemical properties. They range from the rather simple benzamide derivatives like sulpiride to the pentacyclic compounds like butaclamol. The various chemical classes of neuroleptics are shown in Table 1.

Another important distinction may be made between rigid (pentacyclics) and semirigid molecules (tricyclics with piperazine side-chain) and those with a high degree of freedom (tricyclics with mobile aliphatic side-chain, butyrophenones).

Several attempts have been made to find common structural features for the many active compounds of all the different classes. This presentation deals with two approaches: a formal, purely structural and a more biologically oriented one, whereby more emphasis will be put on the latter.

1.1. FORMAL STRUCTURAL APPROACH

It has been proposed by Fielding and Lal (1974) that all neuroleptic molecules of the tricyclic, butyrophenone, diarylbutylamine and benzamide classes may be assembled according to a general scheme as shown in Fig. 1. In fact, all the derivatives of these classes possess a

TABLE 1
Chemical classification of neuroleptics

1. Pentacyclics			(+)−Butaclamol
2. Tricyclics	(a) Dibenzo	−thiazepines	Clothiapine
		−thiepines	Octoclothepine
		−diazepines	Clozapine
		−oxazepines	Loxapine
	(b) Thioxanthenes		Chlorprothixene
			Flupentixol
	(c) Phenothiazines		Chlorpromazine
			Thioridazine
			Fluphenazine
3. Butyrophenones			Haloperidol
			Spiroperidol
4. Diarylbutylamines			Pimozide
5. Benzamides			Sulpiride
6. Indoles			Molindone

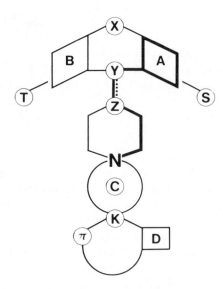

Fig. 1. General scheme of neuroleptic molecules of the tricyclic butyrophenone, diarylbutylamine and benzamide classes (Fielding and Lal, 1974).

common, almost superimposable portion. It consists of a meta- or para-substituted aromatic ring attached to a chain of four atoms bearing a tertiary amino group at its end (Fig. 2) (Janssen, 1973). However, the formal approach is unsatisfactory because it fails to accommodate two classes of compounds represented by molindone and (+)-butaclamol (Fig. 2) whose neuroleptic properties are beyond doubt.

Formal structural correlation

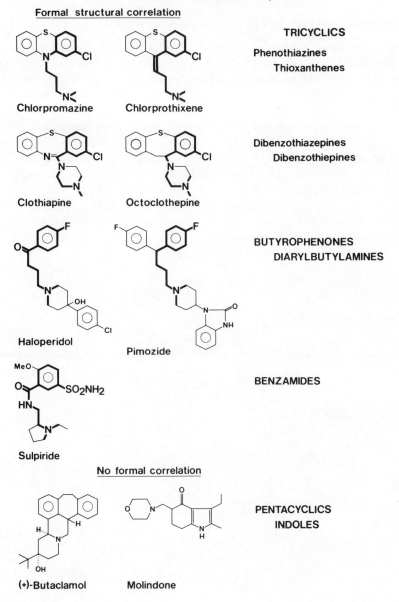

TRICYCLICS

Phenothiazines
Thioxanthenes

Chlorpromazine   Chlorprothixene

Dibenzothiazepines
Dibenzothiepines

Clothiapine   Octoclothepine

BUTYROPHENONES
DIARYLBUTYLAMINES

Haloperidol
Pimozide

BENZAMIDES

Sulpiride

No formal correlation

PENTACYCLICS
INDOLES

(+)-Butaclamol   Molindone

Fig. 2. Formal structural correlation of neuroleptics.

1.2. BIOLOGICALLY ORIENTED APPROACH

The outstanding common biological property of neuroleptics is their reversible interference with the dopaminergic system, e.g. with pre- and postsynaptic dopamine (DA) receptors (see below). Therefore, it appears reasonable to postulate that neuroleptics and the dopaminergic agonist dopamine must exhibit the same structural features. In the following, this hypothesis will be analysed in some detail.

1.2.1. *Configuration of dopamine in its biologically active form*

Indirect evidence about the conformation of DA in its biologically active form stems from the study of compounds which contain the DA structure in a fixed conformation, e.g. the potent striatal DA agonist (R)-apomorphine (Corrodi and Hardegger, 1955). An inspection of the Dreiding model of (R)-apomorphine shows that in this molecule the side-chain of DA exhibits trans-conformation and is extended nearly in the same plane as the aromatic ring except for a rotation of approximately 35° about the bond connecting the side-chain with the aromatic ring (angle τ) (Fig. 3). The X-ray analysis of DA-hydrochloride has demonstrated that the trans-configuration is also present in the solid state, but with an angle τ of 90° (Bergin and Carlström, 1968). Moreover, the trans-configuration is preferred in solutions of the hydrochloride (Bustard and Egan, 1971).

Another important feature of the agonist molecules is probably the distance between the N-atom and the centre of the aromatic ring. According to the Dreiding models of trans-DA and (R)-apomorphine, this distance corresponds to approximately 5.1 Å, which is close to a precise calculation from crystallographic data (Horn *et al.*, 1975).

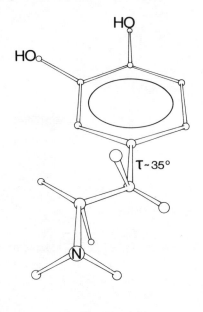

Dopamine

Fig. 3. Dopamine in the conformation present in (R)-apomorphine. (Receptor-conform)

1.2.2. *Neuroleptics as antagonists of dopamine*

In order to explain their interaction with the DA receptor, neuroleptics may be postulated to fulfil the same minimal configurational requirements as DA. This means the presence of at least one aromatic ring and a basic centre in similar relative position and distance as previously discussed. These conditions are on the one side more general than those of the formal approach (where the number of atoms between the aromatic ring and the N-atom is determined as 4), on the other side more strict because of possible stereochemical implications. In the following, it will be analysed whether the above mentioned criteria can be applied to the different classes of neuroleptics.

1.2.2.1. *Pentacyclics.* A neuroleptic with a completely rigid structure has recently been discovered which proved most suitable for the present considerations. It is the pentacyclic dibenzo(a,d) cycloheptene derivative butaclamol (Bruderlein *et al.*, 1975). This compound does not conform to the formal approach and also differs from other neuroleptics because it shows high activity, although it does not bear a substituent on the aromatic rings. Inspection of the Dreiding models shows that butaclamol has the required aromatic ring and the N-atom built in at the correct distance (5.1 Å) and in a suitable relative position, the angle τ (approximately 20°) (Fig. 4) being smaller than in apomorphine. It is particularly interesting that only the

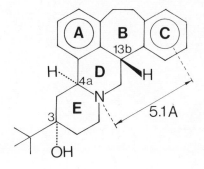

Fig. 4. (+)-Butaclamol

(+)-form, but not the (−)-enantiomer of butaclamol shows marked neuroleptic activity. This stereospecificity of action is in accordance with that exhibited by the agonist apomorphine (only active in the (R)-configuration) (Saari *et al.*, 1973).

The absolute configuration of (+)-butaclamol has been shown to be 3S, 4aS, 13bS (Fig. 4) (Miller *et al.*, 1975). A comparison of the Newman projections of the essential parts of (R)-apomorphine and those of (+)-butaclamol shows a good stereochemical agreement which is not the case for (−)-butaclamol (Fig. 5). It is also possible to superpose the

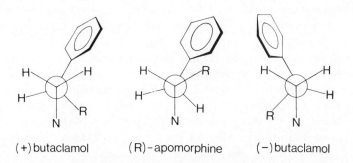

(+)butaclamol   (R)-apomorphine   (−)butaclamol

Fig. 5. Steric comparison of essential parts of (R)-apomorphine and the butaclamol enantiomers.

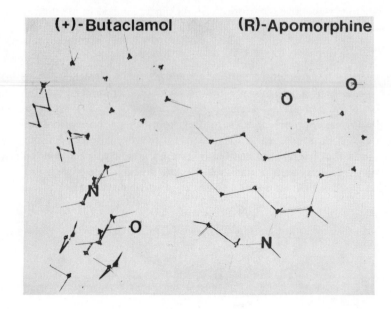

Fig. 6. Superposition of (R)-apomorphine and (+)-butaclamol.

hydroxyl-substituted ring and the N-atom of (R)-apomorphine with ring C and the N-atom respectively of (+)-butaclamol (Fig. 6). The practically flat (R)-apomorphine molecule lies then approximately in the plane of ring C, while the rest of the (+)-butaclamol molecule is almost perpendicular to this plane. This means that ring C and the N-atom of (+)-butaclamol are free to adhere to a hypothetical "receptor" in the same way as in (R)-apomorphine, since the bulky part would not interfere.

These considerations support the choice of (R)-apomorphine as a model of the DA conformation apt to biological interactions (1.2.1).

1.2.2.2. *Piperazine-substituted tricyclics.* This class of neuroleptics (2a of Table 1) which includes clothiapine, octoclothepine and clozapine has a semi-rigid structure. The models show a somewhat increased distance (about 5.4 Å) between the aromatic ring and the N-atom. However, since many representatives of this class are highly active, it can be assumed that this distance is compatible with the requirements for antagonistic activity. Through rotation of the piperazine ring and adjustment of the thiepine ring it is possible to adapt the position of the more distant N-atom in respect to the substituted aromatic ring in such a way that they approximately reach the same relative position as in (R)-apomorphine.

In the case of clozapine only the unsubstituted aromatic ring reaches the correct distance to the N-atom. In contrast, in the other tricyclic neuroleptics the aromatic ring with the correct distance to the N-atom is substituted. Since experience shows that a properly placed substituent enhances the antagonistic activity, clozapine would be expected to be a weak antagonist, which is indeed the case. In this class there are no publications showing a stereospecificity of the biological action (Jilek *et al.*, 1973).

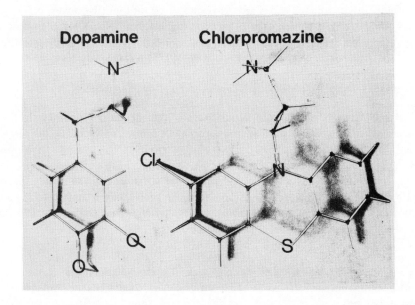

(a)

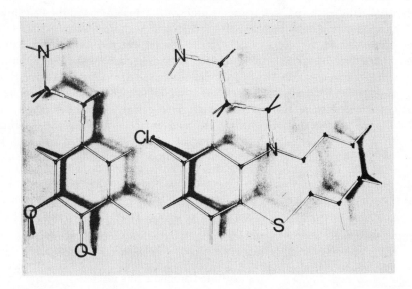

(b)

Fig. 7. (a) Preferred adaptation of chlorpromazine to the postulated (receptor-conform) conformation of dopamine. (b) Alternative adaptation.

1.2.2.3. Thioxanthenes. It is well known that in the thioxanthene class the Z-isomers, in which the N-atom is placed closer to the substituted aromatic ring, are the active ones. The side-chain of the thioxanthenes has many possibilities of rotation. However, chlorprothixene may be accommodated in a similar way to chlorpromazine (see below), but it fits less well, the distance being approximately 6 Å. A similar distance of 5.8 Å for Z-flupenthixole (Post *et al.*, 1975) and 6.2 Å for Z-chlorprothixene (Horn *et al.*, 1975) has recently been verified by X-ray analysis in the solid state.

1.2.2.4. Phenothiazines. These compounds have a high degree of mobility. In the case of chlorpromazine, there are two ways of superimposing DA in the configuration postulated above (Figs. 7a and 7b). The situation where the m-hydroxy group of DA overlays the sulphur atom of chlorpromazine (Fig. 7a) seems preferred for steric reasons. In this respect, Horn and Snyder (1971) reached the same conclusion by comparing the structures of DA and chlorpromazine determined by X-ray crystallographic analysis. However, their study is limited to the solid state and therefore to the trans-rotamer of DA with $\tau = 90°$ (Bergin and Carlström, 1968) which is not necessarily that to be expected at the site of action.

1.2.2.5. Butyrophenones and diarylbutylamines. The butyrophenones remain a difficult case. The butyrophenone moiety can be adapted to DA in its postulated conformation, since the buryrophenone molecule is flexible enough. However, then the position of the F-atom, e.g. in haloperidol, would not correspond to that of the substituent present in the tricyclic class. The same situation most likely exists in the diarylbutylamine series which possesses two aromatic rings and thus resembles more the tricyclics. However, since there are potent antagonists with a distance between the N-atom and the aromatic ring attaining 6 Å (see above), it could be conceived that the phenylpiperidine moiety of haloperidol and the benzimidazolone moiety of pimozide may also be involved in a receptor interaction (distance 5.5 Å). This dual aspect has been studied by Koch (1974) who found marked similarities between the 3-dimensional structures of the phenothiazine and butyrophenone derivatives. From this study it seems more likely that the side-chain of the phenothiazine derivatives corresponds to that of the butyrophenones and diarylbutylamines and that therefore the butyrophenone and the diphenylmethane moieties are the essential ones. Interestingly, as models show, there is a considerable correspondence between haloperidol and butaclamol. When the fluorinated ring lies on ring C of butaclamol, a complete overlap of the piperidine rings and their hydroxyl groups may be reached while the p-chlorphenyl moiety of haloperidol takes the place of the tertiary butyl group of butaclamol.

1.2.2.6. Benzamides. The benzamide class could be taken in support of the view expressed in the previous paragraph since it resembles the butyrophenone moiety without the piperidino side-chain. The relatively small effect of sulpiride (compared to the butyrophenones) (Tagliamonte *et al.*, 1975) on DA turnover may, *inter alia*, be connected with the very low partition coefficient of the drug.

1.2.2.7. Indoles. In this class molindone has been chosen as an example. As already mentioned, the formal approach cannot be applied to this drug. However, the distance between the pyrrol ring (which is taken as the aromatic centre) and the N-atom is correct. In addition,

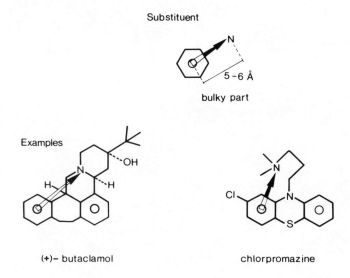

Fig. 8. Minimal structural and steric requirements for neuroleptics.

the rotation of the side-chain may enable the molecule to adopt the required stereochemical configuration.

1.2.2.8. *Conclusion.* The analysis of the different classes of neuroleptics shows that, based on the biological approach, minimal structural and steric requirements valid for all active compounds can be established. These are (Fig. 8):

(a) presence of an aromatic ring (possibly substituted),
(b) distance of 5-6 Å between the centre of the aromatic ring and a N-atom,
(c) position of the bulky part of the molecule to the right of a vector departing from the centre of the aromatic ring towards the N-atom, provided the orientation of the molecule is such that the N-atom lies below the plane of the aromatic ring,
(d) position of an eventual substituent on the aromatic ring to the left of this vector.

These requirements are necessary but not sufficient for determining the activity of a compound as a DA antagonist. Other structural features, such as the nature of the bulky part, the substituent on the aromatic ring and the side-chain attached to the N-atom, influence the biological activity. At the present moment it is hardly possible to establish general rules regarding these additional features. Since the chemical classification is based on analogies with DA, the structural and steric features outlined above are probably essential for the affinity of the molecules for the DA receptor. The additional structural elements may be of importance for determining whether a compound is a DA receptor agonist or antagonist, and they also may be crucial for the biological profile of agonists and antagonists. The proposed biologically oriented approach of a chemical classification of neuroleptics is thus far from being complete, has the advantage, however, of including all the neuroleptics presently known.

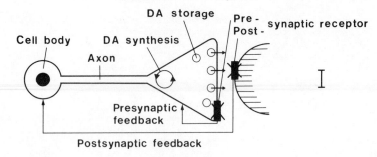

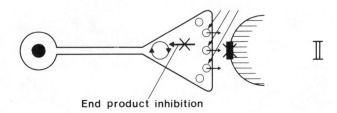

Fig. 9. Two theories on the mechanism how neuroleptics enhance dopamine (DA) turnover.
I: Primary blockade (X) by neuroleptics of pre- and/or postsynaptic DA receptors leading to a positive feedback.
II: Primary enhancement by neuroleptics of DA release from presynaptic DA storage vesicles ($\downarrow\downarrow\downarrow$) leading to a removal of end product inhibition.

2. Biochemical Classification

2.1. ACTION ON DOPAMINERGIC SYSTEMS

There is general agreement that a prominent feature of all types of neuroleptics is their effect on cerebral dopaminergic systems, especially those of the nigrostriatum and the mesolimbic forebrain. All neuroleptics cause a marked enhancement of the DA turnover (Ref. see Bartholini and Pletscher, 1972; Lippmann and Pugsley, 1975) and an inhibition of the DA-stimulated adenylate cyclase in the striatum and limbic system where cyclic adenosine-5'-monophosphate (c-AMP) is thought to be a second messenger for the postsynaptic action of the transmitter DA (Brown and Makman, 1973; Clement-Cormier, 1974; Karobath and Leitich, 1974; Iversen *et al.*, 1975; Lippmann *et al.*, 1975) (Table 2). Thereby, in contrast to reserpine, they do not markedly decrease the content of endogenous cerebral DA. The mechanism of neuroleptics in enhancing the DA turnover is not yet completely clear. An attractive hypothesis postulates that this enhancement results from a primary blockade of DA receptors which would disinhibit a feedback mechanism leading to an enhanced presynaptic DA release and synthesis. It seems that two types of feedback mechanisms are operating: one local, presynaptic, and another neuronal, postsynaptic (Fig. 9). However, the relative importance of these two feedbacks is not fully clear. DA-stimulated adenylate cyclase has been claimed to be related with the DA receptor (Kebabian *et al.*, 1972), and therefore inhibition of the enzyme might also indicate DA receptor blockade. Whether adenylate cyclase shows an exclusive postsynaptic localisation (as thought until recently) or whether it is also localised presynaptically remains to be further investigated.

TABLE 2
Increase in rat striatum or telediencephalon of homovanillic acid (HVA) in percent of untreated controls (= 100) (Pletscher, 1975b) and inhibition of dopamine (DA)-stimulated adenylate cyclase in striatal homogenates of rat by neuroleptic drugs. The K_i-values for DA-stimulated adenylate cyclase were taken from the work of Íversen et al. (1975) which is referred to for experimental details and further information.

Drug	Chemical class	Cerebral HVA in % (drug dose in mg/kg)	DA-stimulated adenylate cyclase K_i (nM)
Chlorpromazine	Phenothiazines	316 ± 7 (5)	48.0
Chlorprothixene	Thioxanthenes	310 ± 17 (10)	37.0*
Haloperidol Spiroperidol	Butyrophenones	353 ± 6 (0.25)	95.0
Pimozide	Diarylbutylamines	276 ± 29 (50)	140.0
Clozapine	Dibenzodiazepines	243 ± 7 (20)	170.0
(+)–Butaclamol	Benzocycloheptapyrido isoquinolizine	400 (0.2)†	8.8
Molindone	Oxoindoles	213 ± 22 (50)	
Sulpiride	Benzamides	232 ± 24 (100)	
Imipramine	Dibenzazepines	91 ± 8 (10)	
Diazepam	Benzodiazepines	83 ± 8 (5)	
Meprobamate	Propandiols	115 ± 8 (50)	
Phenobarbital	Barbiturates	100 ± 17 (50)	

* Z-isomer
† taken from Lippmann et al. (1975)

According to this hypothesis the enhanced turnover of DA and the inhibition of the DA-stimulated adenylate cyclase would reflect the blockade of pre- and/or postsynaptic DA receptors which is thought to be causally connected with the antipsychotic and extrapyramidal effects of neuroleptic drugs.

Recently, two somewhat different hypotheses explaining the action of neuroleptics have been put forward. The first postulates that the acceleration of DA turnover by neuroleptics (similar to the acceleration caused by reserpine) is at least in part due to a direct enhancement of DA release from presynaptic terminals (possibly by a primary action on the DA storage process) which by a removal of end product inhibition would lead to an increased activity of tyrosine hydroxylase (Seeman and Lee, 1974) (Fig. 9). According to this view, the increase of DA turnover is probably not a direct consequence of DA receptor blockade. A parallelism between the latter and the enhancement of presynaptic DA release may exist.

The second hypothesis claims that neuroleptics block the presynaptic coupling between the nerve impulse and the neurosecretion of DA by interfering with the Ca^{++}-influx in presynaptic nerve terminals. This blockade of impulse-secretion may elicit a neuronal feedback activation as a compensatory mechanism leading to an enhanced DA turnover in the nigrostriatal neurons at rest (Seeman and Lee, 1975).

Whatever the exact mechanism may be by which neuroleptics enhance the DA turnover, this enhancement shows a fair parallelism with the antipsychotic and extrapyramidal effects of the drugs. The same is true for the neuroleptic-induced inhibition of DA-stimulated adenylate cyclase (Iversen *et al.*, 1975; Snyder *et al.*, 1974a). Quantitative discrepancies between the biochemical actions (especially the relatively weak *in vitro* effect of butyrophenones on DA-stimulated adenylate cyclase) and the clinical effects may be due to differences in the regional distribution of the neuroleptics in the brain *in vivo* and to different relative potencies of the drugs with regard to pre- and postsynaptic receptor blockade *in vivo* (Iversen *et al.*, 1975). Also other actions of neuroleptics (clozapine and thioridazine), e.g. blockade of acetylcholine receptors, seem to be able to modify the clinical manifestations of DA receptor blockade (see below).

In conclusion, biochemical effects typical for neuroleptic drugs are (a) enhancement of DA turnover, which probably results from blockade of pre- and/or postsynaptic DA receptors, and (b) inhibition of DA-stimulated adenylate cyclase, which is possibly a direct manifestation of postsynaptic DA receptor blockade. Evidence (although not conclusive) exists that the antipsychotic and extrapyramidal effects of neuroleptic drugs are causally related with DA receptor blockade in the mesolimbic system and the striatum respectively (Andén and Stock, 1973; Matthysse, 1973; Stevens, 1973).

2.2. ACTION ON OTHER NEURONAL SYSTEMS

Besides a blocking action on DA receptors neuroleptics show other properties which are probably connected with the neuroleptic profile in man. In this regard, their effect on acetylcholine and noradrenaline (NA) neurons are of main importance.

2.2.1. *Acetylcholine neurons*

Based on clinical and pharmacological observations it has been shown that neuroleptic drugs have a central antiacetylcholine action and that the intensity of this effect varies with the individual drug. Recently, techniques have been developed to quantitatively estimate the affinity of various neuroleptics to muscarinic sites of the brain. The criterium of this affinity was the interference in brain homogenates or in brain membrane preparations of the various neuroleptics with radioactive markers (e.g. 3-quinuclidinylbenzylate and N-2'-chloroethyl-N-propyl-2-aminoethylbenzylate) thought to specifically bind to muscarinic receptors (Miller and Hiley, 1974; Snyder *et al.*, 1974b). It remains to be proven whether this interference strictly reflects the central anticholinergic potency of neuroleptic drugs. However, since the data presently available on the central anticholinergic activity of neuroleptics do not contradict this hypothesis, its maintenance seems to be reasonable at the present time.

The results of the binding experiments showed considerable differences between the various neuroleptic drugs regarding their affinity for muscarinic sites of the brain. For instance, the affinity of thioridazine and clozapine was 2 to 3 orders of magnitude higher than that of fluphenazine and haloperidol, whereas chlorpromazine had an intermediate position (Table 3). In contrast, with regard to the inhibition of DA-sensitive striatal adenylate cyclase, clozapine (Table 2) and thioridazine (Iversen, 1975) were relatively weak compared to other neuroleptics. It can therefore be assumed that the neuroleptics show considerable differences in their anticholinergic properties and that the potency of their anticholinergic action does not parallel that of DA receptor blockade.

What is the importance of the anticholinergic effect for the neuroleptic profile of a drug? Good evidence exists that in the striatum there is a complex interaction between cholinergic and dopaminergic influences (Ref. see Bartholini *et al.*, 1973; Pletscher, 1975a). For instance, a

TABLE 3

Relative affinities of some neuroleptic drugs for muscarinic cholinergic receptors in rat brain and rank order of extrapyramidal side effects in man.

Drug	Relative affinity	Extrapyramidal side effects (rank order)*
Clozapine	385	5
Thioridazine	67	4
Chlorpromazine	10	3
Fluphenazine	0.8	2
Haloperidol	0.2	1

*1 means most, 5 least side effects.

For more information see Snyder *et al.* (1974b) wherefrom these data have been taken.

decrease in the dopaminergic or an increase in the cholinergic activity is thought to lead to disturbances of extrapyramidal motricity as seen in Parkinson's syndrome (Bartholini *et al.*, 1973). Therefore, it has been speculated that the incidence of extrapyramidal side effects due to a neuroleptic drug might not only be connected with its DA receptor-blocking effect, but also with the extent of its anticholinergic action. In fact, there seems to be a good inverse correlation between the anticholinergic effect of a neuroleptic drug (measured by its affinity to central muscarinic sites) and its effect on extrapyramidal motricity (Miller and Hiley, 1974; Snyder *et al.*, 1974b). For instance, drugs like thioridazine and clozapine which, as indicated above, are strongly anticholinergic have been reported to cause very little extrapyramidal side effects, whereas the opposite is true for various butyrophenone derivatives devoid of a marked anticholinergic action.

Based on experimental biochemical evidence, the action of neuroleptics is assumed to involve cholinergic mechanisms to a less extent in the limbic system than in the striatum (Andén, 1972; Lloyd *et al.*, 1973). Furthermore, it has been speculated that the effects of neuroleptic drugs on extrapyramidal motricity and their antipsychotic action are due to DA receptor blockade in the striatum and the mesolimbic system respectively (see above). This may explain why anticholinergic drugs (and possibly the anticholinergic component of some neuroleptics) counteract the adverse effect of neuroleptics on extrapyramidal motricity without interfering with their antipsychotic action.

Although this hypothesis remains to be confirmed, the present experimental evidence indicates that the anticholinergic action of neuroleptic drugs seems to be of importance in determining the clinical profile, especially with regard to disturbance of extrapyramidal motricity. The interference of the neuroleptics with the cholinergic system of the striatum might thus be an additional criterium for the biochemical classification of these drugs.

2.2 2. *Noradrenaline neurons*

Neuroleptics also enhance the cerebral NA turnover, probably by a feedback mechanism due to primary blockade of NA receptors (Ref. see Keller *et al.*, 1973). There is no parallelism,

A. Pletscher and E. Kyburz

TABLE 4

Potency of neuroleptic drugs in increasing
the content of 3-methoxy-4-hydroxyphenyl-
ethylene glycol (MOPEG) in brain of rats
and approximate daily doses in µmoles of
these neuroleptics in man.

Compound	ED_{25} MOPEG Rat	Daily dose in man
Methiothepine	1	4 – 35
Haloperidol	6	3 – 20
Clozapine	18	300 – 1800
Thioridazine	27	250 – 1500
Chlorpromazine	35	140 – 550
Pimozide	140	2 – 15

ED_{25} = dose in µmoles/kg increasing the MOPEG concentration by 25 per cent over control values (Keller *et al.*, 1973).

however, between the enhancement of NA and DA turnover. Thus, for instance, in the rat chlorpromazine is much more potent (about 20 times) than clozapine in increasing the content of homovanillic acid (HVA) in the striatum and the limbic system (indicating an enhanced DA turnover) (Pletscher, 1975b), whereas chlorpromazine is less potent than clozapine in enhancing the NA turnover (as measured by an increase in cerebral 3-methoxy-4-hydroxyphenylethylene glycol, a main NA metabolite) (Table 4). Furthermore, haloperidol shows an over 100 times higher potency than clozapine in enhancing cerebral DA turnover (Pletscher, 1975b), but is only about 6 times more potent in increasing NA turnover (Table 4). These and other findings indicate that blockade of NA receptors by neuroleptics does not parallel the interference of the drugs with DA receptors.

The question whether blockade of NA receptors influences the clinical profile of neuroleptic drugs cannot be answered with certainty. However, evidence exists that blockade of NA receptors may be connected with the sedative component of neuroleptic drugs (Fuxe *et al.*, 1970). Thus, activation of noradrenergic brain systems such as the dorsal ascending NA pathway is thought to lead to increased alertness and, on the other hand, depression of such systems may result in sedation. There is indeed a certain relation between the sedative effect of a neuroleptic drug and its action on NA turnover (Ref. see Keller *et al.*, 1973). For instance, drugs like methiothepine, clozapine and thioridazine, which have a relatively marked sedative component, increase the cerebral NA turnover in relatively low doses compared to the clinical dose. On the other hand, compounds like haloperidol and pimozide, showing little sedation, activate the NA turnover in relatively high doses compared to the clinical dose (Table 4). Furthermore, butaclamol, which accelerates the turnover of NA much less markedly than that of DA, does not seem to cause overt sedation in man (Lippmann and Pugsley, 1975). Chlorpromazine takes an intermediate position (Table 4).

Therefore, it may reasonably be assumed that the intensity of sedation caused by a neuroleptic drug reflects the degree of NA receptor blockade induced by this drug. Although this hypothesis remains to be further substantiated, a tentative subclassification of the neuroleptic drugs according to their blocking effect on NA receptors and thus their enhancing action on NA turnover may also be justified.

2.3 CONCLUSION

Based on the knowledge presently available regarding the biochemistry of neuroleptics, it seems possible to establish a tentative classification of these drugs which shows a fair relation to their clinical effects. Thus, the enhancement of DA turnover as described above (probably a consequence of DA receptor blockade) appears to be a typical biochemical feature of the neuroleptics as a group which correlates reasonably well with their antipsychotic activity. A finer differentiation within the group of neuroleptics seems possible on the basis of their action on NA turnover and their central anticholinergic activity. Thus, blockade of NA receptors is likely to be at least in part responsible for the sedative effect, and the central anticholinergic action may be inversely related with disturbances of extrapyramidal motricity. Accordingly, a drug which changes the pattern of DA metabolism as outlined above may be predicted with some probability to exert antipsychotic activity. Additional blockade of NA receptors seems to add a sedative component, whereas an additional strong central anticholinergic effect may be clinically manifested by a relative lack of extrapyramidal disturbances. This hypothetical biochemical classification, however, remains to be substantiated. It may also be further extended in the future (e.g. in relation to other transmitters) with increasing knowledge on the biochemical action of the neuroleptics.

3. Relation Between Chemical and Biochemical Classification

The biochemical classification of the neuroleptics as a group is based on the enhancement by the drugs of the cerebral DA turnover which probably results from a blockade of DA receptors. For the chemical classification the structural and steric analogy of the neuroleptics with DA in its receptor-conform configuration (as for instance present in apomorphine) seems to be a reasonable approach. Therefore, both classifications have a common denominator.

However, the structural and steric features chosen for the proposed chemical classification represent only minimal requirements which probably determine the affinity of the compounds for the DA receptor. Other properties of the molecules for which no general rule has been established as yet might determine and/or modify the clinical profile. This classification therefore allows some prediction as to whether a given compound is a potential neuroleptic candidate. However, it seems very difficult at the present time to establish a general chemical classification which would correspond to the various components of the clinical profile of a neuroleptic, e.g. antipsychotic action, sedation, disturbance of extrapyramidal motricity. In contrast, the biochemical classification shows some relation to this profile. Thus, the enhancement of the cerebral DA turnover correlates reasonably well with the antipsychotic activity. Furthermore, the effect of neuroleptics on cerebral NA turnover and cholinergic mechanisms probably has some predictive value regarding the intensity of sedation and disturbance of extrapyramidal motricity respectively caused by the drugs in man.

4. Summary

The proposed chemical classification of all the neuroleptic drugs presently available is based on their structural and steric analogy with dopamine (DA) in its receptor-conform configuration (as, for instance, present in (R)-apomorphine). The features they have in common include: presence of an aromatic ring, distance of 5-6 Å between its centre and a N-atom, position of the bulky part of the molecule and of an eventual aromatic ring substituent to the right and the left respectively of a vector departing from the centre of the aromatic ring in direction of the N-atom. The biochemical classification is based on the enhancing action of neuroleptics on cerebral DA and noradrenaline (NA) turnover (probably a consequence of blockade of DA and NA receptors respectively) as well as on their interference with cerebral cholinergic mechanisms. The chemical classification shows less relation to the clinical activity than the biochemical classification. In fact, the former is only based on minimal structural and steric requirements which may be responsible for the affinity of the drugs for the DA receptor, whereas other features of the molecules possibly determine their clinical profile. The biochemical classification of neuroleptics has a reasonable predictive value with regard to their antipsychotic and sedative effect as well as to their action on extrapyramidal motricity.

Acknowledgement

We thank Dr. W. Oberhänsli, Department of Physics, F. Hoffman-La Roche & Co. Ltd., Basel, for advice regarding the physico-chemical part of this work.

References

ANDÉN, N.E. (1972) Dopamine turnover in the corpus striatum and the limbic system after treatment with neuroleptic and antiacetylcholine drugs. *J. Pharm. Pharmac.* **24**, 905-906.

ANDÉN, N.E. and STOCK, G. (1973) Effect of clozapine on the turnover of dopamine in the corpus striatum and the limbic system. *J. Pharm. Pharmac.* **25**, 346-348.

BARTHOLINI, G. and PLETSCHER, A. (1972) Drugs affecting monoamines in the basal ganglia. In *Advances in Biochemical Pharmacology*, vol. 6, pp. 135-148, Raven Press, New York.

BARTHOLINI, G., STADLER, H. and LLOYD, K.G. (1973) Cholinergic-dopaminergic interregulations within the extrapyramidal system. In *Advances in Neurology*, vol. 3, p. 233 (Calne, D.B., ed.), Raven Press, New York.

BERGIN, R. and CARLSTRÖM, D. (1968) The crystal structure of dopamine hydrochloride. *Acta Cryst.* **B 24**, 1506.

BROWN, J.H. and MAKMAN, M.H. (1973) Influence of neuroleptic drugs and apomorphine on dopamine sensitive adenylate cyclase of retina. *J. Neurochem.* **21**, 477-479.

BRUDERLEIN, F.T., HUMBER, L.G. and VOITH, K. (1975) Neuroleptic agents of the benzocycloheptapyridoisoquinoline series. Syntheses and stereochemical and structural requirements for activity of butaclamol and related compounds. *J. Med. Chem.* **18**, 185.

BUSTARD, T.M. and EGAN, R.S. (1971) The conformation of dopamine hydrochloride. *Tetrahedron* **27**, 4457.

CLEMENT-CORMIER, Y.C., KEBABIAN, H.W., PETZOLD, G.L. and GREENGARD, P. (1974) Dopamine-sensitive adenylate cyclase in mammalian brain: a possible site of action of antipsychotic drugs. *Proc. Natn. Acad. Sci. U.S.A.* **71**, 1113-1117.

For the absolute configuration of (R)-apomorphine see:

CORRODI, H. and HARDEGGER, E. (1955) Die Konfiguration des Apomorphins und verwandter Verbindungen. *Helv. chim. Acta* **38**, 2038.

FIELDING, S. and LAL, H. (1974) *Neuroleptics*, Futura, New York.

FUXE, K., HÖKFELT, T. and UNGERSTEDT, U. (1970) Morphological and functional aspects of central monoamine neurons. *Int. Rev. Neurobiol.* **13**, 93-126.

HORN, A.S. and SNYDER, S.H. (1971) Chlorpromazine and dopamine: conformational similarities that correlate with the antischizophrenic activity of phenothiazine drugs. *Proc. Natn. Acad. Sci. U.S.A.* **68**, 2325.

HORN, A.S., POST, M.L. and KENNARD, O. (1975) Dopamine receptor blockade and the neuroleptics, a crystallographic study. *J. Pharm. Pharmac.* **27**, 553.

IVERSEN, L.L., HORN, A.S. and MILLER, R.J. (1975) Structure-activity relationships for agonist and antagonist drugs at pre- and postsynaptic dopamine receptor sites in brain. In *Pre- and Postsynaptic Receptors* (Usdin, E. and Bunney, W.E., eds.), pp. 207-243. Marcel Dekker, New York.

JANSSEN, P.A.J. (1973) *Int. Encycl. Pharm. Therap.* **1**, Sect. 5, 37.

JÌLEK, J.O., SÌNDELÁŘ, K., POMYKÁČEK, J., HOREŠOVSKÝ, O., PELZ, K., SVÁTEK, E., KAKÁČ, B., HOLUBEK, J., METYŠOVÁ, J. and PROTIVA, M. (1973) New synthesis of 8-chloro-10-(4-methylpiperazino)-10,11-dihydrodibenzo[b,f]thiepin and related compounds. *Collection Czechoslov. Chem. Comm.* **38**, 115.

KAROBATH, M. and LEITICH, H. (1974) Antipsychotic drugs and opamine stimulated adenylate cyclase prepared from corpus striatum of rat brain. *Proc. Natn. Acad. Sci. U.S.A.* **71**, 2915-2918.

KEBABIAN, J.W., PETZOLD, G.L. and GREENGARD, P. (1972) Dopamine-sensitive adenylate cyclase in caudate nucleus of rat brain and its similarity to the "dopamine receptor". *Proc. Natn. Acad. Sci. U.S.A.* **69**, 2145-2149.

KELLER, H.H., BARTHOLINI, G. and PLETSCHER, A. (1973) Increase of 3-methoxy-4-hydroxyphenylethylene glycol in rat brain by neuroleptic drugs. *Europ. J. Pharmac.* **23**, 183-186.

KOCH, M.H.J. (1974) The conformation of neuroleptic drugs. *Molec. Pharmac.* **10**, 425.

LIPPMANN, W. and PUGSLEY, T.A. (1975) The effect of butaclamol hydrochloride, a new neuroleptic drug, on catecholamine turnover. *Pharmac. Res. Comm.* **7**, 371-385.

LIPPMANN, W., PUGSLEY, T.A. and MERKER, J. (1975) Effect of butaclamol and its enantiomers upon striatal homovanillic acid and adenyl cyclase of olfactory tubercle in rats. *Life Sci.* **16**, 213-224.

LLOYD, K.G., STADLER, H. and BARTHOLINI, G. (1973) Dopamine and acetylcholine neurons in striatal and limbic structures: effect of neuroleptic drugs. In *Frontiers in Catecholamine Research* (Usdin, E. and Snyder, S.H., eds.), pp. 777-779. Pergamon Press, New York.

MATTHYSSE, S. (1973) Antipsychotic drug action: a clue to the neuropathology of schizophrenia? *Fed. Proc.* **32**, 200-205.

MILLER, R.J. and HILEY, C.R. (1974) Antimuscarinic properties of neuroleptics and drug induced Parkinsonism. *Nature* **248**, 596-597.

MILLER, R.J., HORN, A.S. and IVERSEN, L.L. (1975) Effect of butaclamol on dopamine-sensitive adenylate cyclase in the rat striatum. *J. Pharm. Pharmac.* **27**, 213.

PLETSCHER, A. (1975a) Biochemical and pharmacological aspects of Parkinson's syndrome: a short review. In *Parkinson's Disease* (Birkmayer, W., ed.). Editiones Roche, Basel, in press.

PLETSCHER, A. (1975b) Interference of antipsychotic drugs with cerebral monoamine turnover. In *Antipsychotic Drugs, Pharmacodynamics and Pharmacokinetics* (Sedvall, G., ed.). Pergamon Press, Oxford, in press.

POST, M.L., KENNARD, O. and HORN, A.S. (1975) Stereoselective blockade of the dopamine receptor and the X-ray structures of α and β-flupenthixol. *Nature* **256**, 342.

SAARI, W.S., KING, S.W. and LOTTI, V.J. (1973) Synthesis and biological activity of (6aS)-10,11-dihydroxyaporphine, the optical antipode of apomorphine. *J. Med. Chem.* **16**, 171.

SEEMAN, P. and LEE, T. (1974) The dopamine-releasing actions of neuroleptics and ethanol. *J. Pharmac. exp. Ther.* **190**, 131-140.

SEEMAN, P. and LEE, T. (1975) Antipsychotic drugs: direct correlation between clinical potency and presynaptic action on dopamine neurons. *Science* **188**, 1217-1219.

SNYDER, S.H., BANERJEE, S.P., YAMAMURA, H.I. and GREENBERG, D. (1974a) Drugs, neurotransmitters and schizophrenia. *Science* **184**, 1243-1252.

SNYDER, S.H., GREENBERG, D. and YAMAMURA, H.I. (1974b) Antischizophrenic drugs and brain cholinergic receptors. *Arch. Gen. Psychiat.* **31**, 58-61.

STEVENS, J.R. (1973) An anatomy of schizophrenia. *Arch. Gen. Psychiat.* **29**, 177-179.

TAGLIAMONTE, A., DE MONTIS, G., OLIANAS, M., VARGIU, L., CORSINI, G.U. and GESSA, G.L. (1975) Selective increase of brain dopamine synthesis by sulpiride. *J. Neurochem.* **24**, 707-710.

SESSION 5

Physiological and Psychological Findings

Novel Neurophysiological Findings in Schizophrenia

TURAN M. ITIL

I. Introduction

Although Berger (1931) and, later, Davis (1940) reported that the majority of schizophrenic patients have low voltage, desynchronised, fast EEGs without noticeable alpha rhythm, referred to as "choppy" activity (Davis, 1940), these findings have not been confirmed by the majority of investigators. In contrast to Berger and Davis, who were concerned with the "normal" variations of the EEG pattern, the investigators who challenged their findings were involved with "abnormal" EEG findings in describing the EEG pattern of schizophrenia. Depending on the investigator, 18-60 per cent of the EEGs of schizophrenics were reported as "abnormal". As a final conclusion, it was decided that no "pathognomonic" EEG patterns of schizophrenics exist and the electroencephalogram is useful only to diagnose the organicity in psychiatric patients.

In recent years, however, with the application of quantitative methods of EEG analysis, various investigators have claimed the presence of significant differences between the EEG patterns of schizophrenics and those of normal control groups (Goldstein *et al.*, 1965; Kennard and Schwartzmann, 1957; Volavka *et al.*, 1966). Using thiopental activation, we have been able to demonstrate that schizophrenic patients indeed have EEG patterns different from those of patients with endogenous depression (Itil, 1964). As described by Berger and Davis, schizophrenics showed less alpha activity and more fast beta waves than did depressive patients. Because the question of whether schizophrenic patients have EEG patterns different from those of normals has never been satisfactorily answered, we have conducted a series of studies in the last ten years using quantitative analysis of the EEG, and particularly computerised EEG (CEEG).

II. EEG in Adult Schizophrenics

Concerning the variety of shortcomings of the previous studies, such as the problem of the diagnosis of schizophrenia, the interference by therapeutic procedures in studies utilising the spontaneous EEG pattern, the failure to use control groups, the lack of standard EEG evaluation, and the failure to use quantitative techniques, we conducted a large study comparing the EEG patterns of 100 chronic schizophrenic patients with a group of 100 normal subjects who were matched according to age, sex and social status. Patients would, according to every criterion and every diagnostic school, be accepted as schizophrenic. They were drug-free a minimum of 2 weeks and up to 17 weeks, so that the interference by "organic" therapeutic procedures was minimised. The records were evaluated by conventional visual (eyeball) evaluation (however, this was done in a blind fashion so that the electroencephalographer did not know which record belonged to a schizophrenic and which to a normal), as well as using quantitative methods, such as analog frequency analyser and digital computer period analysis.

A. RESTING EEG FINDINGS

1. *Visual Evaluation*

Both statistical methods (analysis of variance and two-sample t-test) demonstrated that schizophrenics have significantly $(P < .01)$ more fast beta waves (over 20 cps) and more generalised dysrhythmic pattern than normal volunteers, while they showed significantly $(P = .01-.05)$ less alpha activity (10-13 cps), occipito-frontal synchronisation, rhythmical activity, and alpha and beta burst. Normal volunteers revealed a higher amplitude and more sleep-like patterns than schizophrenics.

2. *Analog Frequency Analyser Data*

Analog frequency analyser data demonstrated that schizophrenics showed a significantly higher power in slow and very fast frequencies but low power in alpha bands $(P = .05-.01,$ analysis of variance and two-sample t-test) as compared with normals.

3. *Digital Computer Period Analysis*

The digital computer period analysis data demonstrated that the schizophrenic patient had significantly (analysis of variance and two-sample t-test) more slow delta waves (1.3-3.5 cps, $P < .05$) and significantly more superimposed high frequency waves (40-50 cps in the first derivative) $(P < .01)$ than normal volunteers. On the other hand, schizophrenics showed significantly less 13-20 cps activity (in the primary wave analysis) and significantly more over 20 cps activity (in the first derivative measurements, all at $P < .01$ level of significance).

4. *Discrimination of Schizophrenics from Normals*

Multiple discriminant analysis showed that the group of schizophrenic patients could be clearly differentiated from the normal group, based on all three methods of analysis (at the level of $P < .005$ significance). When we tried to classify each subject retrospectively as schizophrenic or normal, based on the coefficients of discriminant analysis, we observed that the classification based on the combination of visual analysis, power spectrum and digital computer period analysis was most reliable (87 of 100 normals were classified as normals (Itil *et al.*, 1972a)).

B. STABILITY INVESTIGATIONS

With the question of whether the previous findings, which were the result of a single EEG recording, might be due to chance, we conducted CEEG investigations in one group of schizophrenics at weekly intervals and in another group of schizophrenics at monthly intervals.

Both groups were matched with the normal control subjects.

It was established that the differences between the CEEG profiles of schizophrenics and control subjects were almost identical to those seen in our previous studies. Most strikingly, it was found that the differences between schizophrenics and the controls were almost the same when the recordings were done at weekly intervals or at monthly intervals. The results of these investigations indicated that the EEG patterns of chronic adult schizophrenics are different from those of a matched group of normals, and these differences were stable when the recordings were done at weekly or monthly intervals (Itil *et al.*, 1974).

C. COMPUTER ANALYSED SLEEP EEG

Based on the digital computer "sleep print" method (Itil and Shapiro, 1968), it was demonstrated that schizophrenics have marked variability in the total sleep profile from one night to another (Itil *et al.*, 1972b). In contrast to control subjects, the schizophrenics exhibited a late onset of spindle sleep, high variable sleep stages, a short duration of different sleep stages, an increase in the awakening period, a marked attenuation of deep sleep stages, and an obvious reduction of well formed sleep cycles. The automated classified sleep stages, based on the digital computer "sleep print" method, showed that schizophrenics indeed have a statistically significant shorter deep-sleep stage and longer awakening periods than normal controls whether the sleep was classified based on a simple three sleep-stage classification, five sleep-stage classification, or a nine sleep-stage classification.

III. Computer EEG in Schizophrenic Children

The CEEG analysis of a group of psychotic children (the majority were diagnosed as schizophrenic) and a matched group of normal children demonstrated that the CEEG profiles of both groups were significantly ($P < .01$, discriminant analysis) different. Psychotic children are characterised by more slow waves (3.5-5.5 cps) and more high frequency waves (above 20 cps in the primary wave measurements and above 30 cps waves in the first derivative measurements) than the control group of subjects.

Also, the visual evoked potential investigations demonstrated that psychotic children showed significantly different responses to visual stimuli from those of a matched group of normal children. Psychotic children were characterised by shorter latencies and lower amplitudes in visual evoked potential measurements (Itil *et al.*, 1974).

IV. CEEG Finding in Children at "high risk" for Schizophrenia

All EEG studies in schizophrenia have been carried out hitherto in patients in whom the illness was already manifested. This approach has the weakness of being a "retrospective" study model. The "prospective" approach in schizophrenia research, as demonstrated by Mednick and Schulsinger (1965) in their "High-risk" studies, has a variety of advantages, such as the absence of interference by some epiphenomenon as a consequence of the illness or the effects of somatic therapeutic procedures, and even the EEG recording was done after a drug-free or "washout" period. Based on these considerations, we accepted the invitation of Drs. Mednick and Schulsinger to conduct neurophysiological investigations in the group of "high-risk" children who were studied in Copenhagen. The results of the preliminary investigations, based

Turan M. Itil

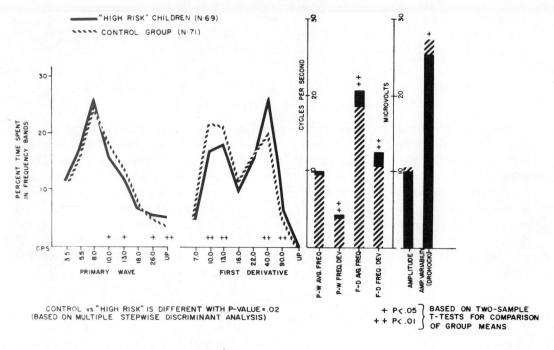

COMPUTERIZED EEG PROFILES OF "HIGH RISK" CHILDREN AND MATCHED CONTROLS
(BASED ON DIGITAL COMPUTER PERIOD ANALYSIS)
EEG LEAD· T₄-P₄

IAPR/402

Fig. 1. In the abscissa computer EEG measurements: in the ordinates the mean values of 69 "high-risk" children and 71 controls. As seen, "high-risk" children have more slow and fast activities and less fast alpha waves than controls in primary wave and first derivative measurements. They have more frequency deviation, high average frequency and less amplitude variability in the EEG than those of control group children. Differences between the two groups were at the level of statistical significance in various CEEG measurements.

on only 31 high-risk children and 50 normal controls, were most interesting: according to the results of the CEEG, the "high-risk" children showed more slow delta waves (1.3-3.5 cps), more fast beta activity (about 18 cps), high average frequencies, less alpha activity and less average absolute amplitude than that of the control group (Itil *et al.*, 1974).

In the meantime, we completed the analysis of the total group of 69 "high-risk" children with an extremely well matched control group of 71 children. The results of the analysis confirmed the preliminary findings. "High-risk" children, in contrast to the control group, were characterised by an increase of very slow and, particularly, very fast beta waves in both primary wave and first derivative measurements, and a decrease of alpha activities in the 10-13 cps range (Fig. 1). High-risk children had significantly higher average frequencies in the first derivative, and higher frequency deviations in the primary wave and first derivative measurements than those of control subjects. High-risk children showed significantly less amplitude variability. Both groups could be differentiated significantly ($P < .01$, discriminant analysis) from each other by CEEG measurements (Fig. 2). The difference between "high-risk" children and the

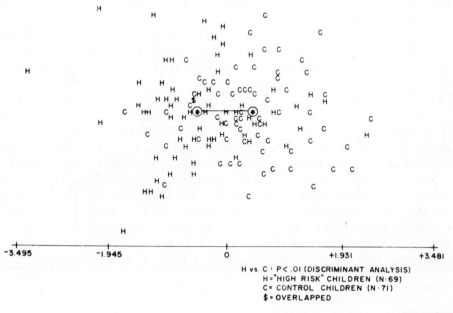

DISCRIMINATION OF "HIGH RISK" CHILDREN FROM CONTROLS
BASED ON COMPUTER EEG PERIOD ANALYSIS
(PLOT BASED ON THE 1st AND 2nd CANONICAL VARIABLES USING SIGMA VALUES)
(CEEG LEAD: $T_4 - P_4$)

H vs. C : P < .01 (DISCRIMINANT ANALYSIS)
H = "HIGH RISK" CHILDREN (N : 69)
C = CONTROL CHILDREN (N : 71)
$ = OVERLAPPED

IAPR/401

Fig. 2. Based on discriminant analysis, the two groups could be differentiated at the level of $P < .01$ significance.

control group could be established in the EEG recordings from all 8 recording leads. The striking difference between the two groups was the increase of slow activities in primary wave measurements, and particularly the increase of very fast activities in both the primary wave and first derivative measurements in high-risk children. The activities from 8-16 cps were significantly decreased in high-risk children, in comparison to the controls, at the level of statistical significance (t-test).

In order to determine the distribution of the subjects with high frequency beta activity and slow alpha waves, all subjects were ranked according to the presence of the amount of these activities. It was observed that more subjects in the control group had a higher percentage of 10-13 cps alpha waves than in the "high-risk" children. More subjects showed a lesser percentage of alpha activity in the high-risk group than in the control subjects. The average of the number of subjects with a higher percentage of alpha waves in control group was more than that of the high-risk children and the difference was at the level of statistical significance ($P < .01$, two-sample t-test). In contrast, more subjects in the high-risk group showed a higher percentage of very fast beta activity (40-90 cps in first derivative) than did the control group. The difference between the two groups was at the level of statistical significance ($P < .01$, two-sample t-test).

V. Summary and Conclusion

When we compare the CEEG findings of adult schizophrenics, psychotic children, and children of schizophrenic parents (high risk to become schizophrenic), we established the most striking findings: in all three groups, the control subjects had less slow waves, but particularly more alpha and less very fast beta activity than the "sick" groups and the "high-risk" group. Average frequencies and the variabilities of the average frequencies in the primary wave and in the first derivative measurements of the "sick" and "high-risk" groups were higher than the control groups. Both amplitude and amplitude variability were lower in the high-risk children and in psychotic children than the control group. (Also in adult schizophrenics the amplitude variability was less than in the control group.)

Out of the various parameters, low voltage, high variability (desynchronisation) and high frequency cerebral biopotentials are the most predominant measurements by which schizophrenic adults and schizophrenic children can be differentiated from the control subjects. Since these types of EEG patterns were also found in subjects who are not yet schizophrenic (high-risk children for schizophrenia) one could hypothesise that "desynchronised" high frequency EEG activity may be the electrophysiological representation of the genetic predisposition for schizophrenia (Itil, 1974). Clearly additional exogenous and/or endogenous factors may be responsible for the eventual clinical manifestations of the schizophrenic illness.

In this framework, it is important to point out that the "schizophrenic" CEEG profiles are very similar to those seen after hallucinogenic compounds (after LSD and particularly after Ditran). All drugs effective in schizophrenia (major tranquilisers or neuroleptics) produce

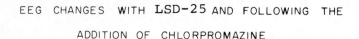

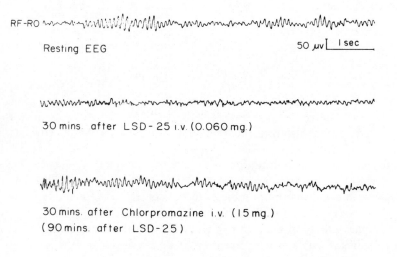

Fig. 3. Thirty minutes after 60 mcg of LSD-25, a decrease of alpha waves, increase of fast activity, and decrease of amplitudes were seen. Thirty minutes after 15 mg chlorpromazine, changes induced by LSD-25 were reversed.

changes opposite to those induced by LSD (Fig. 3). The CEEG profiles of neuroleptics are almost in an opposite direction to those seen in schizophrenic subjects. The increase of slow waves, but particularly a significant decrease of fast alpha and very fast beta activity, are characteristic changes induced by neuroleptic compounds (Itil, 1975).

Based on these findings, one could postulate that adult and child schizophrenics and children with a high risk for schizophrenia may have a "hyper-vigilant" state associated with low voltage desynchronised fast EEG pattern. This state may be the result of a genetically-determined imbalance between dopaminergic and cholinergic activities (Friedhoff, 1973) which can be temporarily corrected by the administration of neuroleptics (major tranquilisers).

Since only 10-15 per cent of the "high-risk" group of children will eventually become schizophrenic (Mednick and Schulsinger, 1965), it is important to define this group among the high-risk children. If our hypothesis is valid, we will expect to find more significant differences in neurophysiological patterns between the high-risk children who eventually will become schizophrenics and those who will not. The early prediction of schizophrenia, based on a neurophysiological model, certainly has far-reaching implications in understanding the pathophysiology of schizophrenia, but, more important, in applying preventative treatment for this illness. If the low voltage, desynchronised, high frequency beta pattern does contribute to the development of the clinical manifestations of schizophrenia, the modification of these patterns in early childhood could prevent the outbreak of the actual illness. As demonstrated above, all neuroleptic drugs will indeed counteract the "schizophrenic" EEG pattern. Therefore, theoretically it could be possible to transform the high frequency beta EEG's of high-risk children for schizophrenia to slower waves, and through this modification it could be possible to prevent the outbreak of the clinical manifestation of schizophrenia. Despite the theoretical attraction of these thoughts, their practical application would be rather difficult. As known, all neuroleptic drugs produce side-effects when administered chronically, particularly in the form of neurological disorders, some of them, such as tardive dyskinesia, are irreversible. On the other hand, it is to be noted that some of the behavioural modification techniques, such as alpha training, meditation and yoga, do produce slow alpha waves and decrease fast activities, producing EEG patterns similar to those of chronically administered neuroleptics. If our findings are confirmed concerning the "specificity" of the high frequency beta activity and the lack of alpha pattern in schizophrenia, certain behavioural modification techniques may be applied in "high-risk" children to modulate the fast beta EEGs to slow alpha EEGs to prevent the clinical manifestation of schizophrenia. Another possibility is to develop natural substances and/or the body's own substances which are able to decrease fast beta activity in the EEG. These kinds of substances could not only be helpful in preventing the actual manifestation of the syndrome, but also could be effective in the causal treatment of schizophrenic illness.

References

BERGER, H. (1931) Uber das Electro-Enzephalogramm des Menschen (part 3). *Arch Psychiatr Nervenkr.* **94**, 16-37.

DAVIS, P.A. (1940) Evaluation of the electroencephalograms of schizophrenic patients. *Am. J. Psychiatry* **96**, 851-860.

GOLDSTEIN, L., SUGERMAN, A.A., STOLBERG, H., MURPHREE, H.B. and PFEIFFER, C.C. (1965) Electrocerebral activity in schizophrenics and nonpsychotic subjects: Quantitative EEG amplitude analysis. *Electroencephalog. Clin. Neurophysiol.* **19**, 350.

KENNARD, M.A. and SCHWARTZMAN, A.F. (1957) A longitudinal study of electroencephalographic frequency patterns in mental hospital patients and normal controls. *Electroencephalog. Clin. Neurophysiol.* **9**, 263.

VOLAVKA, J., MATOUSEK, M. and ROUBICEK, J. (1966) EEG frequency analysis in schizophrenia. *Acta Psychiat. Scand.* **42**, 237.

ITIL, T.M. (1964) *Elektroencephalographische Studien bei endogenen Psychosen und deren Behandlung mit psychotropen Medikamenten unter besonderer Berücksichtigung des Pentothal-Elektroencephalogramms*, Ahmet Sait Matbaasi, Istanbul.

ITIL, T.M., SALETU, B. and DAVIS, S. (1972a) EEG findings in chronic schizophrenics based on digital computer period analysis and analog power spectra. *Biol. Psychiatry* **5**, 1-13.

ITIL, T.M., SALETU, B., DAVIS, S. and ALLEN, M. (1974) Stability studies in schizophrenics and normals using computer-analysed EEG. *Biol. Psychiatry* **8**, 3, 321-335.

ITIL, T. and SHAPIRO, D. (1968) Computer classification of all-night sleep EEG (sleep prints). In Gastaut, H., Lugaresi, E., Berti Ceroni, G. and Coccagna, G. (eds.), *The Abnormalities of Sleep in Man*. Bologna: Aulo Gaggi, pp. 45-53.

ITIL, T.M., HSU, W., KLINGENBERG, H., *et al.* (1972b) Digital computer analysed all-night sleep EEG patterns (sleep prints) in schizophrenics. *Biol. Psychiatry* **4**, 3-16.

ITIL, T.M., HSU, W., SALETU, B. and MEDNICK, S. (1974) Computer EEG and auditory evoked potential investigations in children at high risk for schizophrenia. *Am. J. Psychiatry* **131**, 8, August, pp. 892-900.

MEDNICK, S.A. and SCHULSINGER, F. (1965) Children of schizophrenic mothers. *Bulletin of the International Association of Applied Psychology* **14**, 11-27.

ITIL, T.M. (1974) *Computerised EEG Findings in Schizophrenia and Effects of Neuroleptic Drugs, Biological Mechanisms of Schizophrenia and Schizophrenia-like Psychoses*, Hisatoshi Mitsuda and Tetsuo Fukuda (eds.), Igaku Shoin Ltd. Tokyo, pp. 196-207.

ITIL, T.M. (1975) Electroencephalography in psychiatry. In *Psychopharmacological Treatment, Theory and Practice*, (ed.) Herman C.B. Denber, Marcel Dekker, Inc., New York.

FRIEDHOFF, A.M. (1973) Biogenic amines and schizophrenia. In *Biological Psychiatry*, ed. by Mendels, J. Philadelphia, John Wiley and Sons, pp. 113-129.

Basic Logico-mathematical Structures in Schizophrenia

IGNACIO MATTE BLANCO

I. Types of Symptoms in Schizophrenia

In this paper it is intended to show that the many different symptoms that have been described in schizophrenia are all an expression of certain basic thinking and feeling processes and mental structures, which can be seen to operate also in various other kinds of human thinking, feeling and behaving. They can be identified by the use of certain logico-mathematical ideas.

The symptoms of schizophrenia may be divided into two main categories:

(a) *Continuity disturbances*, which involve changes in the *course* of the mental performance or the theme under consideration. These occur also in other conditions and are not specific for schizophrenia, but they must be mentioned here since they are frequently observed. They may be classified according to the scheme shown on p. 212.

(b) *Structural disturbances*, which are disturbances of the normal organisation or pattern of thinking, feeling and behaving, are more characteristic of schizophrenia. Symptoms of this type are discussed in detail in the following section (Part II), and the distinguishing features of "bi-logical structures" in schizophrenics are studied in Part IV after first considering the notion of bi-logical structure.

II. Manifestations of Schizophrenia Viewed in the Light of Symbolic Logic

1. FOREWORD

I shall now study the manifestations of schizophrenia in terms of continuity and structural disturbances, and the latter in terms of two principles of logic which I first formulated in 1956 (Matte Blanco, 1959a, 1959b). I have discussed at length elsewhere (especially Matte Blanco, 1975) the conceptual and practical meanings and implications of this formulation, and here I shall only give an outline of the principles and their corollaries.

I came to these principles after further research in schizophrenia, and then realised that they could account for all the characteristics of the unconscious described by Freud. For a time, surprising though it now seems to me, I was puzzled and uneasy at this coincidence. I gradually saw that this was no mere coincidence, but simply the consequence of the fact that schizophrenia has an intimate relation to these characteristics. Subsequent studies led me to see both unconscious and schizophrenic manifestations as the result of the interaction between two modes of being which are constantly seen in man.

In previous papers on schizophrenia I have formulated these principles in terms of

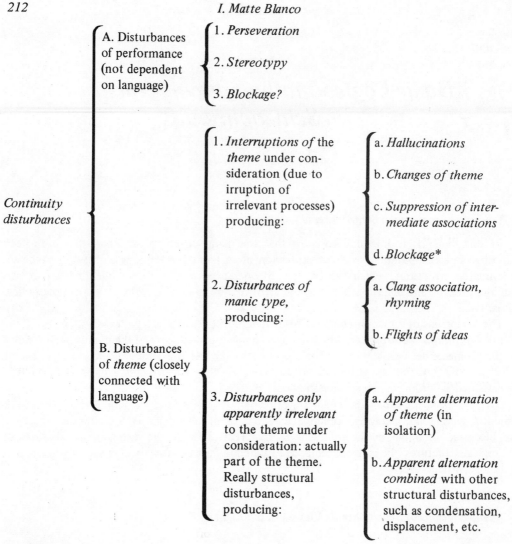

Continuity disturbances

A. Disturbances of performance (not dependent on language)
- 1. *Perseveration*
- 2. *Stereotypy*
- 3. *Blockage?*

B. Disturbances of *theme* (closely connected with language)
- 1. *Interruptions of* the *theme* under consideration (due to irruption of irrelevant processes) producing:
  - a. *Hallucinations*
  - b. *Changes of theme*
  - c. *Suppression of intermediate associations*
  - d. *Blockage**
- 2. *Disturbances of manic type,* producing:
  - a. *Clang association, rhyming*
  - b. *Flights of ideas*
- 3. *Disturbances only apparently irrelevant* to the theme under consideration: actually part of the theme. Really structural disturbances, producing:
  - a. *Apparent alternation of theme* (in isolation)
  - b. *Apparent alternation combined* with other structural disturbances, such as condensation, displacement, etc.

* Blockage appears here because in some cases it results from the sudden irruption of a theme which causes the patient to stop, as happens to a normal person who suddenly remembers something. It is included also above, with a question mark, since it is possible that at times blockage may be an expression of nervous inhibitions which are not relevant in themselves to the disturbance of continuity.

schizophrenic thinking. Here I shall, instead, formulate them in terms of the unconscious, for the reasons just explained. In Part IV the same concepts will be put in terms of the two modes of being. I hope that this explanation will enable the reader to follow the arguments more easily.

2. THE PRINCIPLES AND THEIR CONSEQUENCES OR COROLLARIES

It is essential for a proper understanding to keep in mind that (a) *both principles are formulated in terms of bivalent logic and both act in the midst of bivalent-logical structures,* (b) Principle I is, so to speak, the representant of ordinary scientific bivalent, or Aristotelian, logic in the logic of the unconscious, and (c) Principle II describes in terms of bivalent logic the violations of this logic.

The principles. I shall now quote from a previous work (Matte Blanco, 1975):

I. *The unconscious treats an individual thing (person, object, or concept) as if it were a member or element of a set or class which contains other members; it treats this class as a subclass of a more general class, and this more general class as a subclass or subset of a still more general class, and so on.*

We may call this the *principle of generalisation.* It is a very general principle which *frequently* is applied according to another principle which predicates it:

I_1. *In the choice of classes and of higher and higher classes the unconscious shows a preference for those propositional functions which in one aspect constitute increasing generality and in others keep particular characteristics of the individual thing from which they started.*

In other words, from all the possibilities of generalisation an individual thing offers, it chooses some and abstains from choosing others. Because of this, there frequently remain in the general class, as finally formulated, characteristics of the individuality of the thing from which the generalisation started.

The second principle is formulated thus:

II. *The unconscious treats the converse of any relation as identical with the relation. In other words, it treats asymmetrical relations as if they were symmetrical.*

To quote an example: If John is the brother of Peter, the converse is; Peter is the brother of John. The relation which exists between them is symmetrical, because the converse is identical with the direct relation. But if John is the father of Peter, the converse is; Peter is the son of John. In this case the relation and its converse are not identical. This type of relation which is always different from its converse is called asymmetrical. What the second principle affirms is that the unconscious tends to treat any relation as if it were symmetrical. In the example given: if John is the father of Peter, then Peter is the father of John. In Aristotelian logic this is absurd: in the logic of the unconscious it is normal as we shall see in a moment.

We may call this the *principle of symmetry.* It represents the most formidable departure from the logic upon which all the scientific and philosophical thinking of mankind has been based. We see it constantly in operation in schizophrenic and unconscious thinking. From it follow several consequences which are:

II_1. *When the principle of symmetry is applied there cannot be succession.*

This is an inevitable conclusion if asymmetrical relations are barred.

II_2. *When the principle of symmetry is applied the part is necessarily identical to the whole.*

A page of a given book is a part of the book, an arm is a (proper) part of a given body. If the principle of symmetry is applied then the relation "the arm is part of the body" implies its converse: "the body is part of the arm". In the same way that time disappears, there is also no place for any difference between the proper part and the whole.

Three examples of II_2 may be mentioned:

II_{2a}. *When the principle of symmetry is applied, all members of a set or of a class are treated as identical to one another and to the whole set or class, and are therefore interchangeable with respect both to the propositional function which defines the class and also with respect to all the propositional functions which differentiate them.*

In Aristotelian logic each member of a class fully expresses the propositional function of the class, but it also expresses other propositional functions as well, and it is in these other propositional functions that the members of a class are different from one another. But if the principle of symmetry is applied this is no longer so. To give an example: Francisco may be an element of the class of Chileans and so may Juan; this means that both satisfy the propositional function which defines or determines the class. But Francisco is also a member of a number of other classes, such as for instance the class of tall people, of blue-eyed people, of those with an I.Q. of 120, etc. Juan, on the other hand, may or may not be an element of these classes and also is an element of various classes to which Francisco does not belong. The difference between them can be described precisely in terms of these propositional functions which they do not have in common. If Juan were an element of *all* the classes to which Francisco belongs, then there would be no difference whatsoever between them. But if the principle of symmetry is applied it is sufficient that both are elements of one class to be identical. In scientific logic this is absurd.

When we see II_{2a} at work in manifestations of the unconscious or in schizophrenia we soon realise that no distinction is made between the individual and the class, so that one stands for the other. Seen from the outside, in terms of bivalent logic, this looks as though the individual is treated as if it were a class. We can describe this as a corollary of II_{2a} in the following way:

II_{2aa}. *The unconscious does not know individuals but only classes or propositional functions which define the class and, therefore, treats individuals as though they were propositional functions.*

Owing to the fact that the logic of the unconscious is a mixture of bivalent logic and the logic resulting from the principles described here, the class or the propositional function is not treated by the unconscious as a pure abstraction, as in logic, but

II_{2aaa}. *Classes or propositional functions are treated as having characteristics of individuals: they are like a "magnified" or "generalised" individual.*

II_{2aa} and II_{2aaa} are both expressions of a hybrid, a "bi-logical" system, which will be discussed in Part IV.

A second example of II_2 is:

II_{2b}. *When the principle of symmetry is applied, certain classes whose propositional functions are of the type* p *and not-*p *and which, therefore, are empty by definition, may be treated as not empty.*

The third example of II_2 can be formulated as follows:

II_{2c}. *When the principle of symmetry is applied there can be no relations of contiguity between the parts of a whole.*

This is most important if applied to material objects. Take for instance the pages (parts) of a book: if the whole book is contained in each page, there can be no relation of contiguity between the pages. The same can be said of any material object, because our conception of material objects contains contiguity as an essential element.

3. CHARACTERISTICS OF THE UNCONSCIOUS IN THE LIGHT OF THESE PRINCIPLES

Absence of time. If no asymmetrical relations are available no succession is possible. Hence absence of time. Note, however, that in order to speak of absence of time it is necessary for a certain amount of bivalent logic to be present; otherwise no discourse would be possible and no distinction between anything and anything else.

Displacement. Let us take the example of a schizophrenic woman who was cured at our University Psychiatric Clinic and who called me "papa". This can be described as a displacement from the notion of father to that of director. Now, according to principle I, the class of fathers and that of directors are both subclasses or subsets of the set of authorities. According to II_2 and II_{2a} both are identical. This and nothing else is what *always* characterises every example of displacement.

Replacement of external by psychical reality. This is an example of displacement. Both are treated as subsets of a larger set (I) and then, according to II_{2a}, treated as identical.

Exactly the same thing is true of what in the literature on schizophrenia has been called "the literal interpretation of metaphor". The man who put a rudder on his behind in order to find his way in life was (implicitly) applying I and II_{2a} (see also Part IV).

Lack of mutual contradiction and of negation. The first is the consequence of I, the formation of a wider class formed by all p and not-p; and of II_{2b}, making both subsets identical. When p equals not-p, it follows that not-p is "filled" with that which it negates, i.e. that no negation is possible.

Condensation. This suggests the formation of more inclusive sets, which contain as subsets the various sets that are the constituents of the condensation in question: principle I. Then principle II is applied and only one whole results, which is equal to any and all of its parts.

4. SCHIZOPHRENIC STRUCTURAL THINKING DISTURBANCES

It appears that every one of the schizophrenic thinking disturbances can be understood in a manner which is both simpler and more precise than that in which they are usually described, if they are considered in terms of continuity and structural disturbances, and mostly in terms of the latter. This is what I now shall try to show.

Displacement. This has already been considered.

Paralogia, para-answer, metonymic distortion. Although the *definitions* of Kraepelin and Cameron refer to practically the same process, the *examples* given by the former correspond to at least two different types of disturbances:

(a) In one type the patient knows the exact answer and gives the impression that he is intentionally making a ridiculous reply. This is, for instance, the case with a patient who, when asked his age, answered that he was one day old. This reply obviously represents, not a structural disturbance but one of the continuity of the theme and corresponds to B_{1b} in our classification of *continuity disturbances*: the patient is just changing the theme because, for whatever reason, he just does not give the right answer, which he actually knows. He does not, however, stray entirely from the point: he remains in the general area of the question by replacing the right answer by one which bears some relation to it. This gives the impression that although he is deliberately avoiding the answer, he does so by conforming to I (generalisation to a wider subject or class) and II_{2a} (choice of one member of this class and treating it as identical to that which constitutes the right answer).

(b) The second meaning of the term corresponds to what Kraepelin calls *displacement-paralogia*. The examples he gives are obvious applications of our principles. For instance, when one of his patients says that he is completely headless on the date, meaning that he does not know the date, he is obviously going from "knowing the date" to "having it in the head", and then according to II$_2$ treating the head as equal to the date; hence not knowing the date equals being headless on the date.

Something similar can be said of the other examples he gives. Cameron's illustrations can also be shown to be essentially an application of our principles. To take the shortest of them, his "case 7 thinks that his body makes a shadow 'because it hides the part of the light that is used for full room capacity or area capacity which you intervene' ".

This, like the other examples, is a beautiful illustration of a process of thinking which in some ways is surprising, because the schizophrenic seems so easily to follow the principles in question, whereas one would find it hard to apply them if one wanted to construct artificially a piece of thinking conforming to them. "The part of the light that is used for full room capacity" may be translated: the part of the light that, had it been allowed to enter the room, would have filled this room with light to its utmost (full) possibility (capacity). But the phrase employed by the patient says that this part of the light is used *for* (full) room capacity, which implies the equality between the light that fills the room and the capacity of the room to be filled, that is, between the content and the container (II). Hence the strangeness to normal thinking.

Area capacity is employed as identical to room capacity. This may simply be an imprecision of the type which is frequently seen in ordinary language; it amounts to making a surface identical to a volume (I and II$_{2a}$). The word "intervene" as a substitute to intercept is clearly an example of the use of I and II$_{2a}$ combined: it corresponds to a class which includes both "intercept" and "intervene" as members; such would be for instance the class of all disturbing actions.

Put more generally: the analysis of the various examples of metonymic distortion reveals the following components: (a) various disturbances of continuity, especially changes of the theme and suppression of intermediate associations; (b) condensation; (c) various applications of our two principles.

So, we may say in conclusion that *paralogia and metonymic distortion do not constitute simple mechanisms, but represent a mixture of continuity and structural disturbances, and that the structural disturbances expressed in them are all expressions of I and II.*

I must add, however, that in the analysis of the examples given in the literature one must sometimes (as in the last case) take into consideration the fact that when a process of thinking conforms to our two principles and to all their consequences, it undergoes changes which need further study: e.g. *grammar cannot be the same in this type of logic, so it must be adapted to make it serve the new purposes, with the result that new structures of phrases make their appearance.* I believe this may be the clue to most if not all of the peculiarities of paralogia and metonymia which do not become immediately clear with the help of our principles.

Derailment. It is impossible to analyse all the examples given by Kraepelin because they are presented in a summary fashion and we do not have any intermediate links or comments from the patient which would permit an interpretation. I shall, however, make a few observations on them. Kraepelin quotes the case of a patient who was asked the date and answered "perhaps we will have Australia". The author himself remarks that "he derailed from the line (or succession) of the years to that of the parts of the earth". This is exactly an example of I and II$_{2a}$ combined. When a patient expressed the unpleasant influence of the male nurse by saying that he had imposed or "oppressed" on him the tax burden, obviously he also was making an application of I and II$_{2a}$. And similar considerations apply to the other examples quoted by

Kraepelin. In fact, it can even be said that *his conception of derailment corresponds exclusively or almost exclusively to our two principles*, only they are not explicit but implicit in it.

Literal interpretation of metaphor; use of symbols. A little reflection shows, as already discussed in Section 3, that *this symptom represents I and II$_{2a}$ combined, and nothing else.* In fact there is such a coincidence between the symptom and the principles that it may be asked what is the advantage of replacing one by the others. The answer is easily given by saying that, while the symptom only describes a behaviour, our principles do the same and more because they show that this behaviour is not arbitrary but has a logic of its own; which represents a deeper understanding of it.

Tendency to generalisation. This just corresponds to I. In the literature this symptom is almost the opposite of the preceding one, and in this sense it becomes difficult to understand why the patient follows two opposing procedures. There is no opposition if we view the whole thing as a unity in terms of our two principles and if we remember that generalisation is frequently seen as a step previous to the application of II.

Condensation. We have already discussed this.

Alteration of time relations. According to II$_1$ succession disappears. This is exactly the characteristic of this schizophrenic disturbance. So our principle describes this symptom, but furnishes a deeper understanding of it.

Alteration of space relations. We see that patients affirm that (a) a person is several persons at the same time. This is similar to condensation and may be explained along similar lines; (b) a person may be in several places at the same time. With the disappearance of contiguity, which, we have seen, follows from II, there is no contradiction, because it is the concept of contiguity that conditions the exclusion between parts, as can be seen from the consideration of a whole and its parts: each part is, to our usual logic, separated from every other and in a different position in space; to "symmetrical logic", in contrast, the whole is in each part, hence the whole may be considered to be in different places. Similar considerations can be applied to our present problem. All this presupposes the simultaneous use of two logics: a "bi-logical" reasoning.

Asyndesis. The essence of this concept consists of "thinking in clusters" "formed by loosely connected" elements. Cameron's description represents a progress in understanding because it establishes a relation among elements which previously appeared unrelated. But the expressions "thinking in clusters" and "loosely connected elements" leave us very uncertain and vague about the type of relation. Our formulation gives a precise meaning to the word "cluster", by establishing that it is a more general class (concept) which contains several subclasses. The expression "loosely connected" may then be interpreted, according to the case or example in question, either as the wider class considered together with the subclasses just alluded to, or as the identification of these subclasses, owing to their satisfying the particular propositional function which defines the class, with no consideration of the propositional functions which differentiate one subclass from the others.

In the examples of asyndesis given by Cameron one of the most frequent traits observed is the complete neglect of causality, which leads to the confusion between cause and effect. This follows from II, (if *a* causes *b*, *b* causes *a*; hence, if the principle of symmetry is applied there can be no causality), and in consequence the term "because" has no meaning in such type of thinking. This is exactly what we observe in asyndesis. To take an example from Cameron, the wind blows owing to velocity, to loss of air, or evaporation of water: all show the lack of distinction between cause and effect. In other words, "because" is not employed in these examples as expressing a cause-effect relation.

We may also observe how an ascent is made to higher classes and then all members are treated as identical. This can be seen from the case of the patient who said that the wind blows "because it howls, lack of cooperation with the rain and sun". We see here the process just mentioned acting together with lack of causality.

I should like to make a similar remark here to that already made about metonymic distortion and paralogia: it is possible that some aspects of asyndetic thinking are the consequence of a new structure of thinking and language, resulting from the interaction between bivalent logic and the logic which conforms to the principles we have mentioned. It also is possible that this different atmosphere provides the ground for the development of the different types of causal relationships studied by Piaget in children, and which Cameron has found in asyndetic thinking. In this respect Piaget's observation that adult logic is born as a result of the necessity to influence and convince others represents an interesting suggestion to consider in the study of the relations between both types of logic.

5. DISTURBANCES OF AFFECT IN THE LIGHT OF THIS FORMULATION

We must mention first a series of non-specific subjective disturbances, such as excitability, exaltation, depression, or indifference. The so-called affective dementia, on the other hand, does not correspond to a precise unitary disturbance, but is rather a description, made from a wide external viewpoint, of a complex process whose nature cannot be understood if it is not studied in its component parts.

In contrast, there are some affective disturbances in schizophrenia which correspond to basic manifestations of this illness. We may mention, with M. Bleuler, the following:

1. *Loss of the capacity for affective modulation*, which results in an *affective stiffness* and in *abrupt or sudden passages from one affect to another.*

2. *Parathymia*, whose essential characteristic is the dissociation between the type of affect and the type of stimulus that provokes it. For instance, the stimulus which normally should provoke joy provokes sadness or anger; and vice versa.

3. *Paramimia*, that is, the dissociation between the affect and the ways in which it is expressed in its totality. The patient may show, for instance, signs of joy and at the same time cry plaintively.

4. Finally, the *loss of unity within the affect itself and/or its manifestations.* As an example Bleuler mentions the case of a woman patient who killed her son, whom she dearly loved as a son while at the same time hated as a husband. After this event she fell for several weeks into a state in which she cried with her eyes and laughed with her mouth. One of my patients simultaneously expressed severe rejection and reverence towards his mother in the following phrase: "the canaille, the perverse Rosalind, my ex-mother, may her soul rest in peace."

If we consider these more genuinely schizophrenic, affective disturbances, we can immediately see that there is an intimate relation between the last three, which can be viewed ultimately as a manifestation of the same phenomenon. We could define it as *the union of the opposed*, a true process of *condensation*, which in parathymia is referred to what normally would appear as a contrast between stimulus and affect, in paramimia to the contrast between the various external manifestations of the affect; and in the loss of unity to both the previous ones, together with the fusion in a new unity – affective and expressive unity – of contradictory affects. In the end it would probably be more accurate to consider all three manifestations as only one, and describe this as an *affective condensation*. We know that in normal adult life we do not observe these strikingly visible condensations because a more harmonious unity is reached. When this contrast between schizophrenia and so-called normality is considered, it seems that the old concept of E. Stransky (1904, 1909, 1929) of intra-psychic ataxia, so much discussed in by-gone days and finally almost forgotten, is an accurate description of these and other schizophrenic manifestations.

Now condensation can be understood with the help of the principles of generalisation and symmetry; we have already seen that it shows the formation of more general classes, in accordance with the principle of generalisation. To refer to one of the examples given above, love and hate may be treated as elements or subsets of a larger set. Then, and in accordance with the principle of symmetry, both subsets are treated as identical and, therefore, as interchangeable. Hence the strange impression produced by schizophrenics when they treat (more or less implicitly or explicitly) love and hate as if they were identical and deal with them as though they were a unity. And this is probably the most basic aspect of schizophrenic affectivity as such.

When the affective atmosphere of the schizophrenic is considered from this point of view, it becomes understandable that loss of affective modulation, stiffness of affects and the sudden passage from one affect into another is inevitable. For there cannot be distinctions of the modulation if there are no distinctions between the affects. The subtlety of expression presupposes the subtlety of differentiation. In a whole or ensemble or set which contains everything, the affective contact must necessarily be of a different type, rather one of diffuse, all-permeating atmospheres, and these made of contradictory affects, instead of sharp contacts in "points" or small "zones" of affects. The contacts are thus of a more "global" quality and the individual becomes "immersed" or "wrapped" in a given atmosphere. The sudden changes can be understood as flashes of "asymmetrisation" in the midst of a world immersed in the "symmetrical unity". Note that the sense given here to the expression "symmetrical unity" corresponds to the corollary of the principle of symmetry according to which the part is treated as equal to the whole. From this it follows that any part contains all the potentialities of the whole: there is no division into parts, no heterogeneity, but precisely a "symmetrical unity".

6. ALTERATIONS OF THE "ERLEBEN" OR EXPERIENCING OF THE SELF

In this group of disturbances, so fundamental in schizophrenia, the problem of space is clearer. Numerous alterations of the Erleben have been described and perhaps Storch's monograph (1922 [1924]) still represents the most detailed and comprehensive account of them. The descriptions given in the literature on the subject convey the distinct impression of an amorphous and disorderly conglomerate, where no leading thread is clearly visible, even though one also has the intuitive impression that there is something that might permit an ordering which could faithfully mirror reality. I shall now make an effort to find the distinctive features of this hidden order.

I shall start by an enumeration of the facts. The patient, as M. Bleuler remarks, elaborates the impressions of the external world in a new manner, both intellectually and emotionally. In conformity with the distinction between somato-psychic, auto-psychic and allo-psychic depersonalisation, it may be said that in a greater or in a lesser degree he feels either his body, his own person or the outer world to be strange. His body and his person are changed; he feels in a different form, he may be "possessed", "concentrated" (as a patient said), hypnotised, controlled by mysterious contraptions. The world is strange and full of meanings. People look at each other, make gestures which refer to him; his thoughts are not free. Specially relevant here are the observations made along the anthropological-existential orientation, among which I mention in particular those described by Kuhlenkampf (1953). The patient does not feel any longer sure within himself, in his psychical "habitation" (Wohn). The walls of his psychical abode no longer constitute, so to speak, an impenetrable defence, but are full of cracks and holes, all of which prevent the individual from defending his own privacy.

Another large group of these disturbances refers to what has been called the "limits of the self". Not only the self can be wounded and invaded, but also its own limits have become indistinct and imprecise. This is shown among other things, in the transitivistic and impersonation symptoms: something that happens to the patient also happens to the others, and vice versa. It is immediately apparent that the eight symptoms which K. Schneider considers of "first-rank importance" in the diagnosis of schizophrenia all have to do with the loss of privacy and with the external control of intimate psychical happenings, with the sole exception of the delusional perception; even in this latter, however, we usually come across the same problem, because the symptom generally refers to talks about the patient or messages to him, all of which also have to do with the loss of privacy.

Furthermore, the patient may identify himself with any object, be inside other beings, be possessed by others or be several persons at the same time.

Is there anything in common between the components of this great variety of pathological manifestations? A careful study definitely shows that there is, and that if we succeed in discovering it, then all this apparent chaos and lack of connection becomes ordered, and the meaning of the disturbance becomes apparent. In fact, it can be said that the *central theme of all these multiple disturbances which frequently are gathered under the not sufficiently precise term of "depersonalisation", is single, that is, space, or to be more precise, the relations of contiguity, which are fundamental to this concept.* In other words, the careful study of the disturbances of the *Erleben* shows *in each case* that the patient becomes aware, though not in these words, that these relations are altered, and are in a greater or lesser degree of dissolution. Normally, when *a* is to the right of *b*, then *b* is to the left of *a*; when *a* is above *b*, then *b* is below *a*. When I am in a given place, nobody else can be there at the same time. But if this condition is not fulfilled, when, in accordance with the principle of symmetry, somebody can be on my right, and I can at the same time be on his right, and he can be outside and inside me; my limits in relation to him no longer count as limits. He can invade me, get into my own abode and be the master there. A chair or a piece of wood can play host to my identity, and someone else's identity can be inside me. My thinking is "inside" the thinking of another because no separation between things exists any longer. The feelings, thoughts and actions of others happen in me because there is no contiguity, and no separation between self and not-self. And (here is an important point) if they happen in me, then, in a certain sense, I am controlled.[1] To be sure, all this "reasoning" presupposes the conception that psychical and material reality are the same thing; we have already considered this question. It must also be kept in mind that the strange and disturbing feeling of invasion of one's own privacy would not be possible if the patient did not have, so to speak, an asymmetrical observation point from which to contemplate these symmetrical happenings: he would then be submerged in symmetry and would not be able to establish the differences. In other words, coming back to E. Bleuler's old notion, we could not understand various happenings in schizophrenia without the "double bookkeeping". As we shall see in Part IV, this is precisely what characterises bi-logical structures.

It may be asked what the process is that results in the loss of contiguity relations. If one

---

[1] Note that when somebody feels controlled because he feels that the limits between self and not-self have disappeared, he is using a typical "bi-logical reasoning" (see Part IV): he is "reading" his symmetrical experience of dissolution of limits in asymmetrical terms: "my limits have been damaged and destroyed because I have been invaded".

leaves open the issue of cause, to concentrate only on accurate description, this process is understandable in terms of our principles, as already seen.

Conclusion. It is evident that *in the disturbances of the Erleben the patient witnesses a most disturbing process of dissolution of asymmetry; he is invaded in a greater or lesser degree, according to the case, by a devastating application of the principle of symmetry. The most varied manifestations of depersonalisation, referred to by patients, represent simply descriptions of symmetrical thinking as seen from the point of view of somebody who preserves intact or only partially impaired the capacity to establish asymmetrical relations.* It is, in general, a process of grasping symmetry with the help of asymmetry − a "bi-logical" experience − even if at times it would seem that the patient adopts, so to speak, symmetry, and makes it his own point of view, though always preserving some "asymmetrical" vantage point, however small, that is alien to it.

If looked at in this way, the large chapter of schizophrenic disturbances of the *Erleben* becomes clear.

7. THE ROLE OF THE TENDENCY TO HEAL

When studying schizophrenic manifestations we frequently observe some products which can only be understood in terms of both the pathological disturbances and the tendency to circumscribe these disturbances and/or defend oneself against them in various other ways. This has been pointed out by various authors, and it should be kept in mind whenever we study individual cases.

8. THE PRINCIPLE OF VON DOMARUS

Von Domarus' explicit formulation is that while the logician accepts identity only upon the basis of identical *subjects*, the paralogician does so on the basis of identical *predicates*, or from the similar nature of adjectives. Taken at its face value this phrase is ambiguous for the following reasons: it employs the term "identity" in two different meanings: (a) identity of predicates in which both the logician and the paralogician agree (in his example both agree that stags and certain indians are swift), and therefore it cannot be made the basis for the concept of identity in which both differ, and (b) identity of subjects, where the difference lies. So there are here two meanings of identity, one in which both agree and one in which they disagree. To avoid ambiguity the phrase would have to be modified to run something as follows: the logician accepts identity of subjects upon the basis of identical subjects whereas the paralogician also accepts identity of subjects upon the basis of identical predicates or adjectives. But put in this way the first part is superfluous.

The problem may be solved by considering how we define a subject. It is clear that we do so in terms of a series of predicates. In a whimsical story people were invited to see an extraordinary animal which was not a cat but had the head, the eyes, the mouth, the colour, the legs, etc., of a cat. What could it be? The answer was: a she-cat. In logical terms, a cat and a she-cat differ in one predicate: sex; if they did not, they would be identical.

Then there is the problem of meaning of identity of predicates. In the example of identity of predicate given by the author both the logician and the paralogician agree. But this would not always be the case. In one of our examples, a patient was attacked, and her arm was attacked; but the arm also attacked; there was, obviously as the consequence of the application of the principle of symmetry, an identity of predicates which a logician would not accept: the identity between attacking and being attacked. So it seems exact to say that von Domarus employs the term identity, even in the case of predicates, to mean what the logician accepts as such. The paralogician coincides at times with the logician, but at other times does not.

After all these considerations we may now rephrase or reformulate von Domarus' findings *in his own terms*, but avoiding the imperfections mentioned above. We could then say that whereas the logician accepts identity of subjects on the basis of actual or real identity of *all* the predicates that define a subject, the paralogician does so on the basis of actual or real identity of only one of these predicates. It then becomes easy to see that corollary II_{2a} of the principle of symmetry corresponds exactly to the principle of von Domarus, only it is expressed in terms not of predicates but of propositional functions. Put briefly, if two "things", whatever they may be, have one propositional function in common, then they are identical to the class defined by this function and hence, *in bivalent or Aristotelian logic*, identical to one another (a typical bi-logical reasoning). The advantages of this alternative formulation are several. To speak of predicates may become ambiguous; it is always easy to rephrase any statement by making the subject predicate and the predicate subject. This may be done in bivalent-logical thinking and is *always* done by the principle of symmetry (note that the results are not necessarily identical in both cases, because, if it is a question of an asymmetrical relation, in bivalent-logical thinking one must change the relation to make the subject predicate and vice versa). *What really matters in any case is the relation between something and something else:* this seems to be the starting point of all logic (Matte Blanco, 1975).

Furthermore, so far as I can see, von Domarus' principle does not enable us to consider cases where the question of identity of subjects is not at stake. For example A is the father of B implies, according to the principle of symmetry, that B is the father of A. Here the question of identity is not at stake: only that of paternity. In bivalent logic this implication is absurd because the relation father is asymmetrical. On the other hand, neither in bivalent nor in symmetrical logic does the statement mean that A is identical to B. Note also that neither in *this* application of the principle of symmetry nor in bivalent logic is somebody his own father. The whole question of bi-logic is at stake here.

On the other hand, as the principle of von Domarus is a corollary of the principle of symmetry, both would be equivalent if it could be shown that the converse is also true, as happens with the not-defined concepts or starting points of bivalent logic, for instance with p incompatible with q on the one hand and not-p and p or q on the other. Personally I have not been able to find a way to show that the principle of symmetry is a corollary of the principle of von Domarus.

A great deal more could be said about this subject but I must stop here, saying as a conclusion that von Domarus' principle represents a very important approximation to the reality of schizophrenia but is not a sufficiently general and precise formulation. On the other hand, it is a corollary of the principle of symmetry.

9. THE QUESTION OF CONCRETE THINKING IN SCHIZOPHRENIA

This is also an interesting subject which I must touch upon very rapidly. In a very summary fashion I may say that the description of concrete thinking found in the literature always reveals that there is a triple process in what has been called concrete thinking: (a) as some authors have pointed out, there is a clear process of abstraction which connects apparently unconnected things. On close inspection this turns out to be I in action; (b) once this is done, any element of the general class is treated as identical to any other; an application of II; (c) a concrete object is chosen as a *representant* of the equivalence class formed by all the classes that are elements of the larger class arrived at in (a). This is the same procedure that abstract algebraists employ when they choose 1/2 as representant of the equivalence class formed by 1/2, 2/4, 3/6, 4/8 ..., in which any element is equivalent to any other, but 1/2 is usually chosen to represent the whole class.

10. A BRIEF COMMENT AND CONCLUDING REMARKS

At this point it seems convenient to pause and try to recapitulate our findings in order to place them in their proper perspective. In what may be considered a synthetic all-round view of the alterations in schizophrenia, Manfred Bleuler (1975) writes:

> In schizophrenia the whole personality appears, and this gives it its name, loosened, split, deprived of its natural harmony, which exteriorises in equal measure in the scattering, the parathymia and depersonalisation."[2]

In terms of the ideas put forward here we may say that so-called loosening or splitting corresponds to an invasion of, or increase in symmetrical relations in territories where normally these do not exist or appear in a lesser degree, or at least are not so obvious. I submit that the classical term "splitting" is hardly appropriate to what is observed in this respect. It seems that what happens in schizophrenia is precisely the contrary, namely the formation of more inclusive classes or sets, to which the principle of symmetry is applied: as a result, everything becomes a transparent, unstructured, colossal unity. By saying this I do not wish to question the name of schizophrenia because much militates in its favour: first of all, because of its being so intimately linked to the history of the disease, even if it seems inappropriate to describe the invasion of symmetry, a venerable inaccuracy is in this case better than an accurate innovation. But the notion of splitting, if inaccurate in the sense just mentioned, can be considered to refer to the "double bookkeeping", which could be described as a form of splitting. Anyway, what seems important is to keep in mind the new meanings which we may now include under the old name.

We may consider the interesting fact that in thinking, affectivity and in *Erleben* we have found the same logical characteristics. Assuming that our findings are correct, we conclude that this is no mere coincidence but the expression of a more intimate unity, as pointed out by M. Bleuler.

It may too easily be objected that the view of schizophrenia presented here is a partial one, and, even if it corresponds to reality, only gives an account of one part of this reality. The answer to this objection is that *a careful and detailed study of all the literature on schizophrenic symptomatology from Kraepelin and Bleuler onwards, shows unmistakeably that the central themes of the descriptions of symptoms given by various authors are precisely those which I have tried to formulate here*; and that everything that is covered by such descriptions is also covered in a more simple and more basic way by the formulation proposed here. Therefore, a thorough familiarity with this line of approach will considerably increase our understanding of schizophrenia and facilitate contact with the patient.

III. Subsequent Studies. The Two Modes of Being and the Bi-logical Structures

After the preceding formulation I have continued to study the subject and have come to

---

[2] The same phrase is found already in the 9th edition (1955) while it is not present in the Spanish translation (1924) of the 3rd edition, which was written by E. Bleuler.

what I believe to be a wider and more precise view, of which I shall now briefly discuss several aspects.

1. THE PRINCIPLE OF SYMMETRY AND LOGIC

Put in short sentences, the principle of symmetry cannot be formulated if a classical logical system is not available. Occidental thinking employs a two-valued logic: bivalent logic. It is in terms of simply bivalent logic that the principle of symmetry is formulated. Put in another way, *the principle of symmetry describes in terms of bivalent logic the violations of this logic which are observed in schizophrenia and in unconscious manifestations.*

2. THE TWO MODES OF BEING IN MAN

The result of the application of the principle of symmetry is a homogenisation and a unification or identification of concepts which in themselves are different if seen in terms of bivalent logic. *This happens at the "point" where the principle is applied.* For instance, in an example given, a schizophrenic patient said he has exchanged cells with his father. Put in a proposition: "my father begets me" implies: "I beget my father". The fact that no asymmetrical relation is allowed at this point of the (logical) process of thinking results in that to be "giving life" (begetting) does not correspond to "being given life" (being begotten) but to "giving life" (begetting). There is, here, no division or differentiation of roles but, on the contrary, a homogenisation or unification of them.

If the principle of symmetry is applied to a more ample "zone" of a discourse — for example to the class of mothers — the result is the same in essence but more devastating in its results. Whereas in the first case what was "homogenised" was only the begetting of *this* father and the being begotten of *this* son, *leaving all the rest intact*, in the second example, instead, the *same process* of unification or homogenisation appears much more radical in its results, as a consequence of its being applied to a larger "zone": the class of mothers. It then happens that any mother is identical to the whole class and to any other mother: "*a* is included in the class of mothers" implies "the class of mothers is included in *a*".

Finally, in a last type of example one arrives at the whole world as a homogeneous indivisible reality: "*a* is part of the world" implies, if we treat the relation part-whole as symmetrical, that "the world is part of *a*". As this holds for any *a*, the result is that any *a* is the whole world and identical to any other *a*.

In other words, *the principle of symmetry puts a total, absolute end to the possibility of logic-thinking in any "zone" of thinking-logic where it is applied.* For this reason we may say that *within its radius of action the principle of symmetry dissolves all logic: it is antilogical.* It is obvious that it has no antilogical intentions, but only effects. We may more accurately say that *the principle of symmetry is a logical way of describing an aspect of man which is completely alien to logic: an alogical component of man.*

If we study the essential structural aspects of schizophrenic manifestations and the characteristics of unconscious processes we find that all of them constitute examples of *different degrees* of this process of unification and homogenisation; conversely, we could say that an "original" state of indivision may be divided in a greater or lesser degree, according to the greater or lesser action of the dividing process. We may now consider all these cases in their ensemble. When we do so we begin to understand that there is not only in schizophrenia but in all normal human beings, an aspect which tends to treat reality as though it were homogeneous and indivisible. This aspect contrasts with the thinking-logical aspect of man, which tends to distinguish things from one another.

The result of these observations can be expressed by saying that there are in man two modes of being in the world. I shall now try to formulate this in terms of some general propositions or principles.

The new principles. I. There is a psychical mode of being in man which appears as if it were — or can be described or characterised by saying that it is — a homogeneous, indivisible totality. Alternatively formulated:

There is a psychical aspect of man which appears as if it were a homogeneous indivisible reality or totality.

There are psychical manifestations in man which can be characterised by saying that reality is seen by them as though it were a homogeneous indivisible reality or totality.

As a corollary:

Ic. This homogeneous, indivisible totality is also shown by the fact that it makes no distinction between self and not-self. In other words, on account of its own nature, such a distinction cannot be made. Hence the self and all other persons are one and the same thing, and there are no individuals.

II. There is a psychical mode of being in man which can be described or characterised by saying that it treats or conceives or "views" or "lives" all reality (including its own reality) as though it were divisible or formed by parts. In other words we get to know this mode of being by its expressions or manifestations: both physical and psychical reality are treated as though they were divisible into parts.

Just as we have referred to the first mode of being as a homogeneous, indivisible totality, we might, correspondingly, call this mode *the dividing, heterogenic mode of being.* It is to be noted that whereas the first was called indivisible, this is not called divisible but dividing; and whereas the first was called homogeneous, this is not called heterogeneous but heterogenic. In other words, this second mode is characterised in terms of its (psychical) activity with respect to reality — either its own or external reality; whereas the first was characterised in terms of being and not of activity. . .

III. All human psychical manifestations are the result of the interaction, co-operation and/or any other type of relationship between both modes of being.

The relation between this new formulation and the formulation in terms of the principle of generalisation and symmetry. An analysis of this new formulation easily shows (Matte Blanco, 1975) the following: (a) that the older one in terms of the principle of generalisation and symmetry can be deduced from the new one and vice versa; (b) that the characteristics of the system unconscious described by Freud can also be explained in terms of the new formulation. In other words, we may say that from a logical point of view both formulations are equivalent. The new one, however, opens up meaningful perspectives which were not clearly visible in the formulation in terms of the principle of symmetry.

3. THE CONCEPT OF BI-LOGIC AND BI-LOGICAL STRUCTURES

The formulation of the two modes of being in man opens the way to the understanding of a great variety of phenomena, normal and pathological. For a better use of these possibilities of understanding it seems convenient to start by clarifying the concepts of bi-logic and bi-logical structures.

Symmetrical logic and bi-logic. I hope that the previous considerations have shown that the principle of symmetry, or the description of the homogeneous indivisible reality, points to an aspect of man which is completely and irrevocably alien to logic. This does not take anything away from another fact, namely that with the help of this principle we have been able to describe the "aberrant" behaviour of the system unconscious and of schizophrenic patients. It is evident that such a behaviour is not chaotic, but that, on the contrary, it conforms to certain laws. Otherwise we could not identify it except by saying that no structure, no order of whatever kind is visible in it; and obviously this is not the case, for instance, with displacement, replacement of external by psychical reality, paralogia, metonymic distortion, depersonalisation, parathymia etc.: *we are able to describe such manifestations in a way which permits their recognition and definition.* In the previous section I have studied them in terms of the principles of generalisation and symmetry and we could equally well describe them in terms of the interaction of our first two new principles. Therefore, the question arises: if this is neither chaos nor a form of bivalent logic, what is it?

The answer seems to lie in the following considerations. The application of the principle of symmetry makes impossible any logical structure, and thinking, *in the zone where it is applied.* I have already given various examples. On the other hand, if applied at a certain point or zone of a given logical structure, the result is a combination of bivalent logic and homogeneity which has quite distinct characteristics of its own. It is a new order which is recognisable and definable. To give some new examples, a schizophrenic woman had a delusion connected with the hospital experience of having had some blood taken from her arm for some tests. She felt that she was being stolen from and that the person who had taken the blood should be tried for an assault. At times she said that the man, whom she called the owner of the needle, should be tried for attacking her arm and at times she said that her arm should be tried. It was obvious that "the owner of the needle attacks the arm" implied "the arm attacks the owner of the needle": an application of the principle of symmetry.

The same woman said sometimes, not that blood had been taken from her arm but that her arm had been taken from her, obviously identifying the blood, part of the arm, with the whole arm.

Let us consider a case from the literature. Storch (1922 [1924] p. 10) mentions that a patient saw a door opening and commented with anxiety: "the animals are eating me", in German: "da fressen mich die Thüren"; in German the word "doors" (Thüren) has a similar sound to the word "animals" (Tieren); on account of this similarity of sound, in this case the use of "Thüren" probably represents a condensation. But also the similarity between an opening door and an opening mouth is obvious and represents a clear process of reasoning: both are constituted by two parts which separate at one end while remaining together at the other. Thus to go from an opening door to opening jaws implies going first to the class of "objects made of two parts which separate at one end while remaining together at the other end" (principle of generalisation), and then treating both members of this class as identical (principle of symmetry).

A process of this kind entails the simultaneous use of bivalent logic and of the principle of symmetry; it is incomprehensible if both are not considered together: bivalent logic interacting with something alien to it but which we describe in terms of logic, in order to show the violations of logic it entails. Our description could be called *the description of a limited logical disorder.*

As the understanding of this point is essential to the conception put forward here, I shall try to explain it further. Bivalent logic is or pretends to be a self-contained system of logic. When the principle of symmetry is in action we witness, within its "radius", the appearance of something alien to logic even if we describe it in terms of logic: the homogeneous indivisible mode. In other words, if we take a piece of bivalent-logical reasoning and at a certain stage in it "add" a "drop" or "small dose" of "homogeneity-indivision", a disorder arises immediately. In the case of the schizophrenic who exchanged cells with his father this disorder leads to establishing the (implicit) identity or "homogenisation-indivision" between begetting and being begotten.[3] This is, obviously, a violation – *through homogenisation-indivision* – of a bivalent-logical process. *It is a limited violation.* If we know that, *in this case*, every time we say begetting we must also mean that he who is begotten begets he who begets him, then we have delimited this disorder quite well. But the logical reasoning in question is no longer pure bivalent logic: it is a "mixture" of the latter with a "drop" of homogeneity. It has aspects or components which could not be there if bivalent logic were not available: the notions of father, son and relation between them; and these in their turn presuppose the not-defined concepts of bivalent logic and some of their consequences, such as the principle of contradiction. Now, it is this new product, this new mixture, which I call *symmetrical logic*. Owing to the (limited) introduction of homogeneity it is different from bivalent logic, but if one knows exactly where homogeneity has been introduced the results are quite understandable and predictable.

Another example would be that of the class of mothers, already mentioned. To define this class we need a number of bivalent-logical notions. If we apply the principle of symmetry *within it*, the inside becomes homogeneous but the limits of the class still remain defined in terms of bivalent logic. The result is a notion which cannot be formed with pure bivalent logic and is actually formed by using the mixture just mentioned. We may give this mixture the name of symmetrical logic. We are entitled to call it logic because it does conform to certain rules: it is not pure chaos.

A third example: to get lost in a forest or in the sea are both subclasses or subsets of a wider set: to get lost. Another subset of this set would be: to get lost in life, to have lost one's orientation and not to know what to do. If the principle of symmetry is applied to this larger set or class, then any of the subsets or subclasses just mentioned becomes identical to any other: a symmetrical logical compound, formed by notions resulting from bivalent logic ("to get lost" implies a series of logical notions) *plus* a drop of homogeneity.

We now come to the concept of bi-logic. Suppose one who is lost in life or is in danger of being lost in life decides to make a plan or a project in order to remedy or avoid this circumstance: he may then develop a series of reasonings which faithfully observe the rules of bivalent logic. But if in the middle of such reasonings he uses, as a link in the chain, the example of symmetrical logic just mentioned, he will decide to put a rudder on his behind (as a schizophrenic did), so as not to lose his way in life. This amounts to *using a link of symmetrical logic in an otherwise impeccable bivalent logical reasoning.* If we accept this link as a legitimate component of the reasoning we realise that putting on the rudder is a perfectly valid conclusion of a reasoning which in its course observes the rules of bivalent logic but which at some stage uses symmetrical logic. We can therefore correctly say that *this reasoning as a whole conforms not to one but to two different sets of logical rules: it is a form of bi-logical reasoning.*

A beautiful example of this type is the case of the patient mentioned by Bumke who consulted a dentist after being bitten by a dog. Owing to the limitation of space I leave the reader to disentangle the bi-logical reasoning involved. At this point it might be argued: why is

---

[3] Note that from the point of view of bivalent logic the fact tha A begets B and B begets A does not mean in itself the identity between begetting and being begotten. But if the principle of symmetry is applied to the set defined by the union of begetting and being begotten – which is the case here – then both are treated as identical. This means that in a fairly simple case such as that of this patient, the process in action is not so simple and entails several applications of the principle of symmetry. This leads to homogenisation.

symmetrical logic not considered a form of bi-logic? The answer: it is a composite, not of two logics but of bivalent logic and an alogical component, the homogeneous indivisible mode. The result, which is different from bivalent logic but conforms to certain rules, can legitimately be called a form of logic: symmetrical logic. But it is not bi-logic. This latter, instead, is the result of the interaction of bivalent logic and symmetrical logic, i.e. of two logics.

Bi-logical mathematical structures. An algebraic structure is a set endowed with an operation. An *n*-ary operation, for instance the binary operation of addition, is a rule which establishes a relation between two elements of a given set and a third element of the same set. For instance, in the set of all integers, $3 + 4 = 7$. Note the binary (2-ary) *operation* of addition actually is a $2 + 1 = 3$-ary *relation*, which in the example mentioned is the rule which links the numbers 3, 4 and 7. All structures so far known in mathematics conform to the rules of bivalent logic. Now, if at a certain "point" or "zone" of a given mathematical structure we apply the principle of symmetry — alternatively said: we "homogenise-undivide" that given point or zone — the result is what I propose to call *a bi-logical mathematical structure.* Most briefly mentioned, we may, for instance, consider the mathematical structure formed by the set of all integers endowed with the operation of addition. In abstract algebra this structure constitutes what is called a group, because it conforms to the so-called group axioms. Now, suppose that we "touch" this group with the "wand of homogeneity" in such a way that we make, say the number 4 equal to −4. The reader may easily verify that if this is done, then

$$\ldots -16 = -8 = 0 = 8 = 16 \ldots$$
$$\ldots -15 = -7 = 1 = 9 = 17 \ldots$$
$$\ldots -14 = -6 = 2 = 10 = 18 \ldots$$
$$\ldots -13 = -5 = 3 = 11 = 19 \ldots$$
$$\ldots -12 = -4 = 4 = 12 = 20 \ldots$$
$$\ldots -11 = -3 = 5 = 13 = 21 \ldots$$
$$\ldots -10 = -2 = 6 = 14 = 22 \ldots$$
$$\ldots - 9 = -1 = 7 = 15 = 23 \ldots \, {}^{4}$$

In other words, the additive group of all integers, after being "made homogeneous" at one point (i.e. in such a way that $4 = -4$) *and only at that point or zone*, becomes another mathematical structure known as the additive group of the congruence or residue classes mod 8. (It will be seen that such a structure is a group because it conforms to all the group axioms.) Now, in (bivalent-logical) mathematics it is said that each of the numbers written in each of the eight lines above is *equivalent* modulus 8 to any of the other numbers of the same line. In terms of the procedure followed here we may, instead, say that *if* $4 = -4$, then each of the numbers of each line above is *identical* to any of the others of the same line. Hence we can conceive the group in question as *a bi-logical group if* we see it as the result of having made $4 = -4$, that is, as the result of having "touched" the additive group of all integers with "homogeneity-indivision" just at this point and nowhere else.

If, instead, in the same additive group of all integers we make, say $7 = 8$, then a far more radical change takes place: *any number becomes identical to any other number*, as the reader may verify by himself. In such a case any sum of any number with any other number gives any number as a result. For instance:

$$7 + 8 = \ldots -4 = -3 = -2 = -1 = 0 = 1 = 2 = 3 = 4 \ldots 15 \ldots$$

---

[4] For the reader who is not used to this type of exercise: if $4 = -4$, then $4 + 1$ $(=5) = -4 + 1$ $(=-3)$, that is, 5 $= -3$; $4 + 9$ $(=13) = -4 + 9$ $(=5)$, that is, $5 = -3 = 13$. By this procedure we may construct the table above.

and the same holds for any other sum.[5] Put in other words, *each and any number is or "contains" any and all the other numbers.* We may say that the group axioms still hold in this case but instead of one result for each sum we have an infinite number of results. We may call this *the bi-logical additive group of all integers.* The reader will note that if we look at this bi-logical group in terms of our new principles it becomes obvious that in terms of our first new principle, *its* reality is homogeneous and indivisible: each and all the numbers is (are) in each and any number. In terms of our second principle this appears as an infinite set of infinite sets: the number 1 is equal to and contains any other number: an infinite set;[6] the number 2 is equal to and contains any other number: an infinite set; and so on. In the end all these infinite sets coincide: they are one infinite set which can be viewed either as only one infinite set or as an infinite number of infinite sets.

Bi-logical structures. We may try to apply the same concept of bi-logical mathematical *structures* to non-mathematical bi-logical *reasonings.* We immediately come across serious difficulties of identification of the sets and of the operations. Until a much more detailed study is carried out, our concepts will remain somewhat imprecise. But this fact need not prevent us from employing the same concepts intuitively. We may, for instance, say that if we take the example of the rudder (given above) as a whole, we can describe it in terms of a series of elements or "pieces of reasoning" and a series of relations between them, and if we remember that an *n*-ary operation is a subset of an $(n + 1)$-ary relation, then we have, *in principle*, all the elements to *conceive* the possibility of a bi-logical structure in this case, in the same way as in the case of mathematical structures.

The reader may realise that the few comments I have just made raise a series of problems. The time is not yet ripe, nor is this the moment, to tackle them in their entirety. But I believe it is permissible to use the ideas already put forward, even if in an imperfect manner. To do so will probably pave the way for a much more rigorous future formulation. I believe and hope that the next Part of this paper will justify these assertions. I shall, therefore, use the concept of bi-logical structure with the meaning just outlined.

4. INTERPRETATION OF THE PRINCIPLE OF SYMMETRY IN TERMS OF INFINITE SETS

The formulation of the two modes of being in man brings with it a curious consequence: asymmetrical or "dividing" reasoning, when confronted with the homogeneous mode, tends to consider it in terms of infinite sets. I have discussed this at length elsewhere (1975) and I shall only barely mention it here.

The set of even numbers is a subset of the set of natural numbers; it is *included* in this latter set. Yet, for each natural number there is an even number: for 1 there is 2, for 2 there is 4 and so on; in fact if we consider *n* to be the symbol of a variable which may designate any number, mathematics defines the set of even numbers by saying that it is the set of all 2*n*. Hence, for any number *n* there corresponds one and only one number 2*n*, and vice versa: a bi-univocal correspondence.

Now, in mathematics it is said that a set is infinite if and only if it can be put in bi-univocal correspondence with a proper part of itself. It is then said that in this case the (proper) part and the whole have the same *cardinal number* or *power* or *cardinality.*

[5] To verify this, use a similar procedure to that described in the previous footnote.

[6] This is so if viewed in terms of bivalent logic: for any time we have this number, 1, we also have ... −1, 0, 1, 2, ... : an infinite set.

We may now consider the homogeneous indivisible reality in terms of our dividing "eyes". We may start with the fact that at times (as we have already seen) schizophrenics and unconscious manifestations treat the part as if it were identical to the whole. This is reminiscent of an infinite set, in which the cardinal number of certain parts of it is the same as that of the whole set. But in the case we are now considering, the behaviour of the unconscious does not suggest directly a question of cardinality but the identification of the part and the whole. If, however, we consider that each of the characteristics (:elements) of a certain part, and also of a whole, can be put in bi-univocal correspondence with the series of numbers, then the numbers may be made to represent the properties both of the part and of the whole. Consequently, if we see that the part is treated as if it were identical to the whole, we may then assume, owing to the correspondence just mentioned of both part and whole with the numbers, that the part is being treated as having the same cardinal number as the whole; in other words, that the whole and the part in question are treated as infinite sets.

On the other hand, we have also seen that this identification between the part and the whole which is sometimes seen in schizophrenics and in unconscious manifestations, is a corollary of the principle of symmetry. We therefore interpret this corollary in the same terms. In other words, the symmetrical or homogeneous mode, which in itself does not have the concept of either whole or part, seems, *if looked at with the "dividing eyes" of the heterogenic mode*, to treat reality as if it were an infinite set.

This interpretation is of the utmost importance in the understanding of fundamental normal and pathological manifestations of man, as we now pass to consider very briefly.

5. EMOTION AS A BI-LOGICAL STRUCTURE, SOME PARTS OF WHICH ARE INFINITE SETS

Various characteristics of emotions make us realise that symmetrical logic is at work at the base of emotion and that, viewed from a bivalent-logical (dividing) vantage point, emotion behaves as if its objects were seen as infinite sets.

This view, which I here have outlined only very briefly, enables us to understand a great many facts of psychical life, both normal and pathological. The structure of emotion is, *as a bi-logical structure*, essentially the same as that of schizophrenic symptomatology. There are, however, some important differences which we shall consider in the next Part.

IV. Schizophrenic Bi-logical Structures

This will be a discussion of a point of view which is in its initial stages. I believe it can, and hope it will, be greatly developed. I shall consider the subject under several inter-related headings.

Normal bi-logical structures. Familiarity with the concepts outlined in the previous part of this paper opens up various possibilities of fresh understanding of the human mind. One begins to realise that the whole psychical life is a continuous interaction between the two modes of being. Mathematical thinking represents a level of almost pure asymmetrical activity, if considered as a finished product. The thinking activity of the mathematical thinker, in contrast, is a mixture of both modes. The homogeneous mode plays an important role in intellectual and artistic creations.

In general it can be said that the reciprocal modulation of both modes, i.e. the action of regulating or toning down of one mode by the other and vice versa, is essential in normal human psychical life. The assertion just made is valid in general; but it needs to be qualified or completed by the following two complementary assertions: (1) in usual or normal psychical life it seems that the homogeneous mode needs to be toned down or dissimulated more than the asymmetrical mode, for when its presence is very obvious it appears as pathological and it arouses anxiety. (2) The asymmetrical mode in a pure state, by contrast, probably appears only in mathematical reasonings, and seems to be quite alien to the psychical manifestations of every-day life. In contrast to what happens in the case of a striking presence of the homogeneous mode, the "pure" asymmetrical mode need not be dissimulated. On the other hand, if we consider the actual behaviour of people we can correctly conclude that this mode is not "held in much esteem" by the average human being. A good everyday example of this assertion is the reaction of most people to a logical reasoning which goes against their feelings of the moment: they are simply unable to follow it and are, on the whole, quite incapable of accepting that the arguments which they bring forward to reject the logical reasoning in question are not in accordance with the rules of logic. In an inconspicuous way they actually behave like people with delusions. Some years ago I pointed out that normal man is really a person with dissimulated, not obvious delusions (we could call them socio-syntonic delusions).

Put in other words: it seems that the symmetrical or homogeneous mode forms the actual basis or background of all psychical life, but its presence must be inconspicuous if one is to avoid anxiety. The asymmetrical mode, in contrast, seems like a proliferation which appears more obvious, more dominating and which, yet, seems a superimposed structure. The value that each of the modes has for the survival of man is very great, and one cannot conceive a healthy human without either of these modes. The understanding of their interaction is a vast unexplored territory.

The schizophrenic bi-logical structures. After following the arguments of this part, the reader will have become aware that the analysis of schizophrenic symptomatology made in the preceding part of this paper actually shows that this symptomatology can be seen as either an expression of symmetrical logic or as bi-logical structures. The various symptoms, on the other hand, may involve the most varied bi-logical structures.

The question, therefore, arises of whether there are some special features of schizophrenic bi-logical structures which permit their differentiation from normal bi-logical structures? I believe the answer to this question may lead to a deeper understanding of schizophrenia. I shall only put forward the very general beginning of an answer. If we compare a schizophrenic bi-logical structure, for instance the case of the rudder, or that of the man who consulted the dentist after being bitten by a dog, with a normal or fairly normal bi-logical structure, we are struck by an important difference. In schizophrenic cases one immediately sees the practical absurdity of the establishment of such identities (for instance between losing one's way in life and losing one's way in water). In normal emotion, in contrast, we tend to "understand", for instance, that a girl whose mother blatantly refuses her a few books, should feel this as a manifestation of lack of love although that may not be the true reason for the mother's action: it does not seem absurd at all. If we begin to look at the details of her reactions, however, we realise that "objectively" unwarranted generalisations and "symmetrisations" are at work and determine strong reactions which are unjustified in the actual circumstances of this girl. The differences between both cases seem to be at least the following: (1) The bi-logical process at work seems to be far more dissimulated in the normal and more sharply in contrast with bivalent logic in the case of schizophrenia. (2) In the "normal" case the attribution of certain features to the person who provokes the emotion seems to correspond to similar bi-logical processes in that person, even if such structures are not at the level of consciousness: there seems to be a "contact" between certain deep levels which are *active in both cases*. In schizophrenics, instead, the particular bi-logical process at work does not immediately or obviously seem to correspond to an active unconscious process in another person. (3) The schizophrenic frequently uses bi-logical reasonings in connection with non-personal situations, or with situations in which the aspects referring to the intimacy of persons different from the patient are not directly at stake. The case of the rudder and of the dentist are clear examples; so is that of the woman who had the delusion about her blood having been taken from her.

This latter difference must be explained. I am not trying to say that the emotional behaviour of persons connected with the patient is not concerned, but that it is not *directly* or *immediately at stake or visible* in the particular symptom, which therefore appears as bizarre. The reason for this is that owing to various displacements and other mechanisms, the connections are concealed, so that the symptom *appears* unconnected with the actual feelings of persons who have or have had something to do with the patient.

References

ARIETI, SILVANO (1955, 1974) Interpretation of Schizophrenia, New York, Robert Brunner, 1955. 2nd ed., completely revised and expanded, Basic Books Inc., New York (1974).
ARIETI, SILVANO (1966) Schizophrenic cognition. In *Psychopathology of Schizophrenia*, Grune and Stratton, New York, 1966.
ARIETI, SILVANO (1967) *The Intrapsychic self. Feeling, Cognition, and Creativity in Health and Mental Illness*, Basic Books, Inc., New York.
BLEULER, EUGEN (1911 [1950]) *Dementia Praecox or the group of Schizophrenias*. Translated from the German by J. Zinkin, International Universities Press, 1950.
BLEULER, EUGEN and MANFRED (1955, 1960, 1975) *Lehrbuch der Psychiatrie*, Springer, Berlin, 1955 (9th ed.), 1960 (10th ed.), and 1975 (13th ed.).
BLEULER, MANFRED (1972) *Die Schizophrenen Geistesstörungen im Lichte langjähriger Kranken und Familiengeschichten*, Georg Thieme Verlag, Stuttgart.
CAMERON, NORMAN (1938) Reasoning, regression and communication in schizophrenics. *Psychological Monographs*, **50**, 1, The Psychological Review Co., Ohio State University, Columbus, Ohio.
FREUD, S. (1911) Psycho-analytic notes on an autobiographical account of a case of paranoia (Dementia paranoides), *S.E.* **12**.
FREUD, S. (1915) The Unconscious *S.E.* **14**.
GRIESINGER, W. (1867 [1964]) *Pathologie und Therapie der psychischen Krankheiten*, E.J. Bonset, Amsterdam.
JASPERS, KARL (1948 [1963]) *General Psychopathology*, Translated from the German by J. Hoenig and M.W. Hamilton, The University of Chicago Press, Chicago, 1963.
JUNG, C.G. (1907 [1936]) The Psychology of Dementia praecox. *Nervous and mental disease Monograph Series* No. 3, New York.
KRAEPELIN, EMIL (1913) Psychiatrie, Ein Lehrbuch fur Studierende und Ärzte, *Achte Auflage*, Vol. III, Johann Ambrosius Barth, Leipzig.
KUHLENKAMPF, C. (1953) Uber Wahnwahrnehmungen. Ihre Interpretazion als Störung der "Wohnordnung", *Nervenarzt*, **24**, 26-331, 1953.
MATTE BLANCO, IGNACIO (1959a) A study of schizophrenic thinking: its expression in terms of symbolic logic and its representation in terms of multi-dimensional space. *Congress Report of the 2nd International Congress for Psychiatry*, Zurich, 1957, Vol. I, pp. 254-9. Reprinted in the *International Journal Psychiat.* **1**, 91-96, 1965.
MATTE BLANCO, IGNACIO (1959b) Expression in symbolic logic of the characteristics of the System Ucs, or the logic of the System Ucs, *Int. Journ. Psychoanal.* **40**, 1-5, 1959.
MATTE BLANCO, IGNACIO (1975) *The unconscious as infinite sets. An essay in bi-logic*, Duckworth, London.
MAYER-GROSS, SLATER and ROTH (1969) *Clinical Psychiatry*. 3rd ed. by Eliot Slater and Martin Roth; Baillière, Tindall and Cassell, London (1969).
SCHNEIDER, KURT (1959) *Clinical Psychopathology*. Translated from the German by M.W. Hamilton, Grune and Stratton, New York and London, 1959.
STORCH, ALFRED (1922 [1924]) *The primitive archaic forms of inner experience and thought in schizophrenia*. Translated from the German by C. Willard, Nervous and Mental Disease Publishing Co., New York, 1924.
STRANSKY, ERWIN (1904) Zur Lehre von der Dementia Praecox, *Centralblatt fur Nervenheilkunde und Psychiatrie*, **15**, 1-19, 1904.
STRANSKY, ERWIN (1909) Über die Dementia praecox. *Collection "Grenzfragen des Nerven und Seelesleben"*. Verlag von J.F. Bergman, Wiesbaden, 1909.
STRANSKY, ERWIN (1929) Zur Klinik und Kritik der Schizophrenie. *J. Psychiatr.* **46**, 1929.
VON DOMARUS, EILHARD (1925) Über die Beziehungen des normalen zum schizophrenen Denken, *Arch. Psychiat.*
VON DOMARUS, E. (1944) The specific laws of logic in schizophrenia. In *Language and thought in schizophrenia*. Ed. by J.S. Kasanin, W.W. Norton and Co., New York (1964)

Psychotherapeutic Approaches

Some Aspects of Cognitive Activities in Schizophrenics

R. TISSOT

The aim of this report is not to provide yet another assessment of the intellectual performance of schizophrenics, but rather, if possible, to grasp the structure of reasoning in such patients, or even better, the insertion of thought into reality. Clinical knowledge of the adult psychoses leads to the conclusion that the structure of thought is unaltered in schizophrenics. If schizophrenics retain the mental operations they acquired before the onset of their disease, why then are they unable to use these operations properly? Why are they unable to apply them adequately to reality?

Interesting perspectives in this field may emerge from the observation of verbal expression in these patients. Signs — in the sense de Saussure gave this word — in their *denotation* use, generally remain adequate. Schizophrenics call a spade a spade. Deviations appear in the fringe of verbal *connotations*. Thus, apart from the usual symbolic connotations of purity and virginity, the word "white" often takes on in the mind of a schizophrenic many other symbolic values more important to him than the denoted meaning. We know, since the work of Hjelmslev,[1] that a connoted message is a message of which the "significants" are made of the complete signs (significant and meaning) of another message.

In the denoted message the link between the significant and the meaning is determined arbitrarily, as described by de Saussure. It is determined by a convention, namely that of the community speaking the language in question. However, this conventional link is a stable one. According to Piaget,[2-12] earlier accommodations are retained in the present as "significants" and earlier assimilations as meanings. The significant is merely an interiorized imitation and therefore results from accommodation of the person's activities to the social milieu in which he lives. The meaning, on the other hand, results from assimilation of outer reality to the sensori-motor, and, at a later stage, to the operational schemes of the individual. However the latter may be efficient only if they represent an equilibrium between accommodation to, and assimilation of the environment. This equilibrium is responsible for the objective nature of the meaning, and at the same time for the stability of the arbitrary link between the significant and the meaning of the denotation sign.

In the connoted message, matters are somewhat different. The link between the significant (sign of the first message) and the meaning is also arbitrary, but unstable. Indeed, the construction of the meaning of connoted signs can lie anywhere between complete social determinism and complete individual, subjective determinism. In the first case it arises from complete accommodation to social habits, as for example in the colloquial expression "to hit someone on the nut"; in the second case it arises from complete assimilation of the meaning to the thought structures of the individual without accommodation, as in symbolic games, in which a stone may successively stand for a horse, a cat, a steam-engine, and so on.

In order to be adapted, biological processes must necessarily result from or comprise an equilibrium between assimilation of, and accommodation to outer reality. The partial inefficiency, the inadequacy of the mental operations of schizophrenics may be due, like those of their verbal expression, to a disturbance in this equilibrium. In terms of this hypothesis the activities of schizophrenics would continually oscillate between complete assimilation, as observed in the symbolic games of children or in dreams, and in complete accommodation, as in pure imitation, leading ultimately to total loss of meaning, as in stereotyped movements.

Is such an hypothesis open to experimental verification? It may well be, by using some of the genetic tests developed by Piaget and his school. Indeed, in Piaget's opinion, the balance between assimilation and accommodation varies for each different type of cognitive activity. In logical-mathematical thinking, accommodation has been effected and permanently fixed at the time of its genesis, through mutual assimilation of the action schemes. Once completed, its deductive application merely requires the assimilation to thought of abstract concepts, without accommodation. In contrast, in the static, figurative representation of the world, the assimilative component of action is reduced to its simplest expression, since ultimately no overall assimilative scheme is required in this activity.

On the other hand, the equilibrium has to be carefully maintained and supervised when the proposed mental operation involves the representation of space, as in the representation of movement in particular (cf. the aporiae of Zenon of Elea), or as in logical-experimental thinking (which involves the assimilation of real objects rather than indeterminate objects to the structures of thought). If this is the case, our patients would be expected to perform better in the abstract logical-mathematical tests and in tests involving the static representation of space, than in tests involving logical-experimental operations and transformed space.

Methods

In order to test our hypothesis we used various genetic tests developed by Piaget in the logical-mathematical and logical-experimental fields, as well as in the field of the static and figurative representation of space. For a detailed description the reader is referred to the original paper by Schmid-Kitsikis *et al.*[13] We applied these tests to a group of 24 schizophrenics, of which 17 suffered from the early, hebephrenic form of the disease, while the 7 others suffered from late, paranoid schizophrenia; the controls were 6 healthy individuals in the same age groups as the patients.

Results

QUANTITATIVE

The first clear-cut observation was that the degree to which the cognitive activities of schizophrenics were impaired was primarily a function of the duration of their disease. In spite of their age the paranoid schizophrenics failed to show a significant degree of impairment, except for one patient who had been ill for the last 40 years. In contrast, there was a significant difference between most results of young and older hebephrenic patients. However, since their illness started during the second or third decade of their lives, this difference may reasonably be attributed to the differences in the duration of their disease. This conclusion is supported by the fact that their performances correlated better with the latter than with their respective ages. The schizophrenic process does not immediately produce a loss of intellectual efficiency, and the loss, when it occurs, is not in proportion to the severity of the clinical symptomatology. These findings suggest that schizophrenia, which primarily impairs activities other than cognitive, only impairs the latter progressively through the development of a vicious circle, in which elapsed time plays an important part.

The second observation, which emerges from the quantitative analysis of our results, is that there is a discrepancy between the efficiency of thinking and the structure of thought. Assuming that Wechsler's test provides a valid assessment of the intellectual efficiency of our patients, our results show that, on the one hand, the efficiency of the late paranoid patients was normal (I.Q. performance 111), while on the other hand that of the hebephrenic patient was reduced, both in the younger group with an average illness duration of 7 years (I.Q. performance 93) and in the older group with an average illness duration of 30 years (I.Q. performance 80). On the contrary, in the Piagetian genetic tests, the operative levels reached by the young schizophrenics were not significantly different from those reached by the paranoid schizophrenics and controls. Only the hebephrenics with longstanding illness reached lower levels of reasoning. This statement should be somewhat attenuated in consideration of the fact that the qualitative analysis of their behaviour often speaks in favour of the preservation of those operations which they are unable to apply to reality.

These results confirm the soundness of the evolution of the clinicians' attitude toward schizophrenia over the past 50 years, and of their desire to withdraw hebephrenic schizophrenia from the category of dementias. A comparison can be made with certain neurological diseases with focal lesions, in which it seems established that the overall coordination of actual or virtual action is not impaired. Impairment of certain specific mental instruments prevents the actualisation of operations in specific fields of cognitive activity. It remains true, of course, that in aphasia or agnosia due to neurological causes, the instrumental impairment is obvious and circumscribed. What is the loss of actualization of operations in schizophrenics due to? A first clue may be provided by investigating which fields of operation are preserved and which are lost. In the control subjects the following sequence of performances was obtained, the best results being to the left and the worst to the right:

Physical causality $>$ Conservation of physical constants $>$ Formal

logical thinking $\#$

Conservation of $\begin{cases} \text{elementary logic} \\ \text{space} \\ \text{mental representation} \end{cases}$

In hebephrenic patients the sequence is different:

Conservation of physical constants $>$ Formal logical thinking $>$ space $>$
Elementary logic $>$ Mental representation $>$ Physical causality.

Is one entitled to interpret the difference as supporting our hypothesis? The latter stated that, if there is an imbalance between accommodation and assimilation, the deductive, logical-mathematical operations would be expected to suffer less impairment than operations involving the representation of space, the mobilisation of images and especially logical-experimental reasoning, since the latter calls for the assimilation of real objects to the thought process and the application of operations to objects. In this respect the conservation by our schizophrenics of the operations underlying the physical constants may seem paradoxical. However, could it not be argued that the concepts of the constancy of mass, weight and volume in the tests using changes in appearance of a lump of clay rest upon quasi-deductive operations?

At least in adults, the presence of lumps of clay is required only to illustrate concretely a situation. That the weight of the clay remains constant when it is rolled to form a sausage may well be the result of an apodictic conclusion in which logical-mathematical reasoning alone is involved. The nature of the observable is virtually immaterial. The compensation and reversibility operations are generalised from the start and apply to indeterminate objects, almost to the same extent as in the axiom which states that two quantities both equal to a third must be equal to each other. In support of this contention is the evidence that when the solubilization of sugar or the dissociation of weight and volume are involved, the performances of our patients are quite different and become equivalent to those they exhibit in the field of physical causality.

That the patients' results in some of the formal logical tests are better than in other tests of elementary logic is also very suggestive. Here we are dealing with formal tests which are only mastered quite late by children (e.g. the quantitation of probability; age 12) and which are better preserved than elementary logical tests, in particular than the easiest of these, namely the classification test, usually mastered around age 6-7. When one is dealing with the quantitation of probabilities, the nature and properties of the objects are of little importance. On the contrary, when the task is to classify geometric shapes or to arrange figures, the subject must be able to abstract some common property from the outer reality; in other words, his classification scheme must assimilate various real objects through one of their common characteristics.

QUALITATIVE

The mental operations of schizophrenia show a number of functional peculiarities:

1. Difficulty in the confrontation of logical thinking and experimental data. At times the subject loses the ability to keep the correct distance between himself and the observables (A-type deviation), while at other times he becomes unable to distanciate himself from his *a priori* line of reasoning (B-type deviation).

A-type deviation
The subject is unable to keep his distance with respect to the observables. This inability is made obvious in situations such as the following: in the triple classification test, when the subject is asked to classify geometric forms sequentially, he loses track of the given classification criterion and becomes side-tracked onto some other peculiarity of the object: in the experiment involving the solubilization of sugar, the observable (i.e. the disappearance of the sugar) becomes so coercive that it distorts the logical inferences on which the physical constants (mass, weight and volume) are based in the test with the lump of clay;
in the tests involving the representation of space and mental images the configuration presented to the patient is so coercive that it prevents his mental operations from functioning normally and impedes the mobilisation of the image, although the latter has been conceived and announced.

B-type deviation
The subject is unable to keep his distances with respect to his own *a priori* line of reasoning. Here the distance between the subject and the object is too great and results in the subject attributing too much value to his personal point of view. This behaviour leads to neglect of the object's intrinsic properties, which may result in distortion of the observables.
A first type of distortion is apparent in the tests involving elementary logic, triple classification, inclusion and overlap of classes. Each item to be classified is given a precise

meaning, as in the symbolic games of children. At other times, the choices are offered in terms of aesthetic value or surface area. When such is the case it is difficult to determine whether one is dealing with a mere predominance of the assimilation of objects to the subject's thinking or, on the other hand, with oscillation; the adherence leading to selection of the aesthetic criterion, which then assimilates the other objects.

In the formal-logical tests, particularly in quantitation of probabilities, assimilation to completely inadequate schemes of reasoning is obvious. It is expressed explicitly in terms of "forces", sometimes even in terms of magical, magnetic thinking.

In tests involving a more constraining physical system, such as the sugar solubilisation test, the test of the distinction between weight and volume, or of the mediate transmission of momentum, the *a priori* reasoning distorts the observables, even after several reruns of the experiment. As the sugar dissolves, after an initial rise, the fluid level sinks back; the heavier the object immersed in the fluid, the higher the level rises; and the intermediary spheres also move in the momentum transmission experiment. Some patients resist even the most vigorous attempts at suggestion. It is as if their reasoning was "the spheres must move, so they do". This, in effect, is a coherent apodictic (incontrovertible) reasoning, based on the same kind of foundation as the statement "cogito, ergo sum" (I am thinking; therefore I exist).

2. Discontinuity in production. This peculiarity is particularly obvious in the logical-mathematical tests. However, it does not affect all of these tests to the same degree. Nor does it affect to the same degree anticipatory reasoning and its actualisation. If a test can be carried out first in the mind and then in actual fact, discontinuity will always be less apparent in the anticipatory phase than during the effective action. Does the defect lie primarily in the programming of action and reasoning, as occurs in patients with focal prefrontal lesions or degenerative dementia? Certainly not. Patients with the latter condition are unable to infer the law governing the organisation of a temporal sequence of events. They are unable to confront the past with the present in order to anticipate the future, so that, when asked to foretell an invariable sequence of appearance of a number of colours, say red-green-green, they fail repeatedly. This test is mere child's play for a schizophrenic, as we have tested repeatedly. The difficulty for schizophrenics lies at another level.

3. A discrepancy between the anticipation of action and its actualisation and justification, the former being better than the latter. This characteristic is most probably merely a corollary of the first two.

At the risk of being considered exaggeratedly reductionistic, we feel that these three peculiarities of thinking in schizophrenics share a common denominator and at the same time support our working hypothesis.

The complete assimilation of the object to the thought process, without reciprocal accommodation of the latter, leads to distorted perception of the outer world or even to its complete anihilation. According to Piaget, such a mode of mental functioning is akin to at least two physiologic processes, i.e. dreams and symbolic games. In the latter, objects are made to take on an unlimited variety of meanings and qualities according to the particular schemes of action or thought which are brought into play. The continuity of the unfolding of schemes depends solely on their coherence. Now the latter is ensured only in mathematical thinking, which is but a particular kind of symbolic game. In mathematical thinking, coherence stems from an equilibrium between reciprocal accommodation and assimilation of the action schemes of the subject, as acquired during the process of coordination. This equilibrium is necessary and sufficient as long as the operations deal only with indeterminate objects. As soon as the operations apply to real objects, the equilibrium between assimilation of the object and accommodation to it must be continuously monitored and adjusted. Let us not forget the fruitless meanderings of conventionalism. The schizophrenic thinks best when dealing with "neutral", non-significant objects, upon which a meaning is bestowed only by the operations he applies to them. It is easier for him to imagine paired combinations of indeterminate objects than to effect such combinations with real slips of paper to be classified in real files. As he sways from predominant assimilation to predominant accommodation, he ends up with discontinuity. When accommodation predominates, as a result of the experimental situation (e.g. in particular in confrontation with spatial configurations), the schizophrenic is forced into imitation, which prevents the actualisation of the operation. Thus, when asked to draw the shadow of a circle swivelling around its diameter, he can only draw a circle and show with his hands that it is rotating. Similarly when asked to draw a sectional plane through a three-dimensional object, he describes the plane correctly in words, but is unable to draw anything else but the object as he sees it, with an additional line showing where the knife cuts it. When assimilation predominates, the observables are so distorted by thought that verification through reading of the experiment becomes impossible. When the patient oscillates between alternate predominance of assimilation and accommodation, he ends up with mutually contradictory solutions, between which he is unable to make a choice, since both of them seem to be equally correct to him.

SPECULATION

As far as we are concerned this investigation is merely a preliminary probing into a complex and very controversial field. However, it seems to throw some light on some of the characteristics of cognitive activity in schizophrenics, which are quite clearly related to the classical clinical semiology of schizophrenia. Classic descriptions of hebephrenic schizophrenia emphasise discontinuity, discordance between thought and action, perplexity and ambivalence. The term "autism", coined by Bleuler, purports to denote disruption of the normally harmonious relationship of each individual to his environment; the disruption of this harmony leads to withdrawal, retreat into one's inner world, which may alternate with attempts at complete mimicry of the environment. Admittedly, these manifestations are more obvious clinically in the emotional behaviour of schizophrenics than in their mental processes. However the chances are that, although it still remains to be ascertained, the importance of equilibrium between assimilation and accommodation in emotional schemes is at least as great as in cognitive schemes. Phenomenologically speaking, autism can be envisaged as a depersonalisation, i.e. a loss of identity as an individual. Now the corollary of identity is the distinction between subject and object. Complete assimilation annihilates the object and incorporates it into the subject, who loses the sense of his own boundaries in the process; complete accommodation, on the other hand, merges the subject into the object, which likewise loses its boundaries.

In infants, in which sensori-motor schemes are not yet coordinated, objects are merely extensions of motor activity, just as the mother is probably merely the extension of needs and desires. It does not seem unreasonable to speculate that, although schizophrenia does not entail a real loss of mental operations, it does lead to their apragmatic sterilisation (ineffectiveness) through imbalance between the ability to assimilate the environment and to accommodate to it.

It would seem well worthwhile to apply the same concept to an investigation of affectivity, in which psychosis, without causing a real loss of emotional schemes, may lead to what may be called "emotional apragmatism", i.e. athymhormia. Lastly, it should be pointed out that delusion has been so often compared with day-dreaming that its analogy to distortion of observables through over-assimilation to mental processes seems self-evident. Even the vague, ill-defined, poorly structured form which delusion takes in hebephrenics could be accounted for by the continuous oscillation of mental operations in these individuals between over-assimilation and over-accommodation.

References

1. HJELMSLEV, L. *Prolégomènes à une théorie du langage*. Editions de Minuit, collection Arguments, Paris, 1971.
2. PIAGET, J. *La naissance de l'intelligence chez l'enfant*. Delachaux et Niestlé, Neuchâtel, 1936, 7th éd. 1972.
3. PIAGET, J. et INHELDER, B. *Le développement des quantités physiques chez l'enfant*. Delachaux et Niestlé, Neuchâtel, 1941, 3rd éd., 1968.
4. PIAGET, J. *La formation du symbole chez l'enfant*. Delachaux et Niestlé, Neuchâtel, 1946, 5th éd., 1970.
5. PIAGET, J. et INHELDER, B. *La représentation de l'espace chez l'enfant*. P.U.F., collection "B.P.C.", Paris, 1948, 2nd éd., 1972.
6. PIAGET, J. et INHELDER, B. *La genèse de l'idée de hasard chez l'enfant*. P.U.F., collection "B.P.C.", Paris, 1951.
7. PIAGET, J. et INHELDER, B. *De la logique de l'enfant à la logique de l'adolescent*. P.U.F., collection "B.P.C.", Paris, 1955, 2nd éd., 1970.
8. PIAGET, J. et INHELDER, B. *La genèse des structures logiques élémentaires*. Delachaux et Niestlé, Neuchâtel, 1959, 2nd éd., 1967.
9. PIAGET, J. et INHELDER, B. *L'image mentale chez l'enfant*. P.U.F., collection "B.S.I.", Paris, 1966.
10. PIAGET, J. et INHELDER, B. *La psychologie de l'enfant*. P.U.F., collection "Que sais-je", no. 369, Paris, 1966, 5th éd., 1973.
11. PIAGET, J. *Le structuralisme*. P.U.F., collection "Que sais-je?", no. 1311, Paris, 1968, 6th éd., 1974.
12. PIAGET, J. La transmission des mouvements. *Etudes d'épistémologie génétique XXVII*, P.U.F., Paris, 1972.
13. SCHMID-KITSIKIS, E., ZUTTER, A.-M., BURNAND, Y., BURGERMEISTER, J. J., TISSOT, R., AJURIAGUERRA, J. de Quelques aspects des activités cognitives du schizophrène. *Annales médico-psychologiques, Paris*, t. 1, *133e* année, No. 2, pp. 197 à 236.

The Psychotherapeutic Approach to Schizophrenia

SILVANO ARIETI

A psychiatrist, like the present writer, who stresses a psychotherapeutic approach in the treatment of schizophrenia, is not necessarily a person who rejects *a priori* any other understanding or treatment of this disorder. I believe it is important to stress this point at first and to avoid a misunderstanding which has caused divisions and lack of collaboration in the fields of psychiatry.

Let me repeat that a psychiatrist of my orientation does not exclude a genetic component in the etiology of schizophrenia, nor is he reluctant to use drug therapy in some cases. The position of the people of my orientation is the following. At the present stage of our knowledge schizophrenia seems to be the result of a set of etiological factors, organic and psychological. It is probably enough to remove one of the two components of the set to disrupt the set and to prevent the occurrence of the disorder. If the disorder has already appeared, it seems plausible that by removing or altering one of the two components a condition will come about in which schizophrenia will no longer be possible, or if possible, will be ameliorated. Since at the present time we cannot change the genetic code of people, it seems much more promising to change the psychological factors.

Psychotherapists like myself know, of course, of the positive results obtained with drug therapy. As a matter of fact, they consider this type of treatment a useful adjunct in many cases, and as a necessary additional therapy in some others. However, whereas drug therapy removes only the symptoms, psychotherapy aims at changing the patient's attitude toward himself, people, and life in general. It aims at giving him insight about the particular ways he feels and thinks. It helps him to change his ways of interpreting and experiencing the world and himself. It attempts to undo part of the patient's past and to change his attitude toward the present and the future. Thus, although psychotherapy cannot attack the whole etiology of schizophrenia, it attacks the psychological component of the etiology.

Whereas physical therapies in psychiatry as well as in other medical fields aim at a *restitutio quo ante* (return to a premorbid condition), the psychotherapist does not consider this return a desirable goal. In fact, the so-called premorbid condition was already morbid, although in a different way. A return to a prepsychotic condition would mean to settle for the retention not only of a biological vulnerability but also of a psychological one. The potentiality for the psychosis would thus persist.

Our sponsoring of the psychotherapy of schizophrenia has additional bases. We believe that no psychiatrist could escape practising some kind of psychotherapy with schizophrenics, even if he were determined to do so. A psychiatrist, because of his particular training, may rely predominantly on phenothiazines or other neuroleptics, but cannot help making some inquiries about the origin of the patient's anguish and conflict, cannot help trying to convey to him a message of empathy and desire to be useful. The therapist's message may be as limited as his knowledge of the psychology of schizophrenia, but nevertheless it will affect the patient through a psychological medium. Although it is true that the majority of psychiatrists in most countries do not use the psychological method as much as I would like, I am gratified to see that in many psychiatric milieux some of our ways have been adopted by practically every psychiatrist. What Freida Fromm-Reichmann, other pioneers, and we, their followers, have practised had various impacts or degrees of influence on many colleagues all over the world.

I want to include also some other remarks that will disclose one aspect in which we psychotherapists are much closer to the organicists than to those who practice so-called "antipsychiatry". We do not believe that schizophrenia is not a disease but just a variety of human existence, like having blue eyes or left-handedness. In the vast majority of cases schizophrenia causes a great deal of suffering to the patient. It does not permit the patient's self-fulfilment, and in serious cases it does not even permit his survival, unless help from others is received. We do not engage just in semantic controversies on what constitutes a disease or what pertains to the medical model. Certainly if we adhere to concepts of disease and medical model which were formulated at the time of Virchow, when psychiatry had not yet gained full recognition as a science, if we base the concept of disease on undisputed evidence of cellular pathology, then we cannot call schizophrenia a disease. But to adhere to such conceptions would be like following in physics a Euclidian-Newtonian vision of the world after Einstein and Heisenberg had conceived a more inclusive system. If, in the concept of disease, we include a dysfunction of psychological mechanisms, then schizophrenia is certainly a pathological condition or disease.

In the space allotted to my presentation it will not be possible to give a detailed account of the psychotherapeutic method. I must restrict my report to a few fundamental issues, hoping that those who are interested in my approach will have access to the second edition of my book *Interpretation of Schizophrenia.*

Historical Review of the Theoretical Bases of the Main Methods

It is possible to recognise that each method adopted in the psychotherapy of schizophrenia is the clinical expression or the therapeutic realisation of one or few underlying principles held by its originator. Often the principle was deduced from the clinical experiences of the therapist; in some instances it was a preconceived theoretical view which directed the therapist to operate predominantly in certain directions.

Any review of the psychotherapy of schizophrenia must start with Freud. And yet, paradoxically, Freud, to whom we owe so much for the understanding of the regressive, restitutional, and symbolic aspects of schizophrenia, discouraged psychotherapy with schizophrenics. To be sure, he did not exclude the possibility that in the future some modified techniques would permit such an attempt (1905). Again we find that an underlying principle was at the basis of the pessimistic attitude of Freud. Freud believed that in schizophrenia there is a withdrawal of libido from the objects into the self: therefore no transference can take place, and without transference no treatment is possible.

One of Freud's first pupils, Paul Federn, attempted the treatment of schizophrenics in spite of the prevailing discouraging theories (1952). One of Federn's underlying principles was based on the concept of ego-feeling, or of an autonomous reservoir of libido in the ego. He felt that the ego of the schizophrenic is poorer, not richer in this libido, as Freud's theories implied, and that transference with the schizophrenic was possible. He attempted to establish a transference and succeeded; however, another underlying principle of Federn (of the ego boundaries) in a certain way limited his therapeutic aims. Federn felt that in the schizophrenic "the boundaries" separating the areas of the psyche (the id from the ego and the ego from the external world) are defective, so that material from the id may invade the ego and even be projected to the external world. Reversing a famous sentence of Freud, Federn said that as a result of therapy in the schizophrenic, "There where ego was, id must be". Thus he interpreted therapy with schizophrenics as a symptomatic repression of the id.

Melanie Klein and her school were also guided by an underlying principle (1948, 1955). Whereas the Freudian school assumes that the complete structure of the personality, with its division in ego, id, and superego, reaches complete development at the time of the solution of the Oedipus complex, Melanie Klein believed that this development is completed much earlier in life. According to her, the superego differentiates from the id at the same time that the ego does; furthermore, not only the superego but the ego may be the result of internalisations of objects and object-relationships — internalisations which may be traumatic.

These different views on the formation of the ego eliminate some classical differential concepts between psychoses and neuroses, the practical result being that according to Melanie Klein psychotics must be treated in the same way as neurotics; they would not require specific techniques. As far as this writer knows, this point of view is upheld now only by the adherents of the Kleinian school.

Another important group of innovators in the treatment of schizophrenia is that represented mainly by John Rosen (1947, 1953, 1962) and Marguerite Sechehaye (1951, 1956). Although their methods show important differences, they have points of contact.Their basic principle is that the world of the psychosis can be entered by the therapist. At the suggestion of Federn, Rosen called his method "direct analysis" because the therapist aims at a direct communication with the unconscious of the patient. The patient is showered or shocked with interpretations which follow the language of the unconscious. The patient feels that finally he has been understood. Often the therapist becomes or assumes the role of one of the important imaginary persons who appear in the delusional world of the patient.

Sechehaye, too, believes that the world of the psychosis can be entered by the therapist by resorting to her own method of "symbolic realisation". In her method the symbolic manifestations of the patient are not interpreted to him, but shared with him. The therapist tries to understand the patient by resorting to his intuition or to his psychoanalytic experience. He tries to grasp the patient's symbols in order to use them to establish communication and also to transform reality to a level which the patient can accept without being hurt or traumatised. With this method of presenting a reality which is altered to fit his weak ego, the patient is able to relive unsolved events or conflicts of his life and to solve them, or at least becomes able to gratify some of his primitive needs. For instance, by giving her patient Renée apples (symbolic of the maternal breast) Sechehaye allowed the patient to relive an early traumatic event and permitted her to gratify "magically" an oral need.

Sullivan (1953, 1962) and Fromm-Reichmann (1948, 1950) have instead tried to reach the patient not by entering or sharing the psychotic world. At the same time that the patient is accompanied and sustained during his psychotic journey an attempt is made to make him cope with the requirements of so-called reality. Sullivan's ideas that some degree of interpersonal relatedness is maintained throughout life by every one, including the schizophrenic, was a basic prerequisite of Fromm-Reichmann's attempts to establish transference with the psychotic. Fromm-Reichmann believed, contrary to the opinion of other psychiatrists, that the patient is not happy with his withdrawal, but is ready to resume interpersonal relations provided he finds a person who is capable of removing that suspiciousness and distrust which originated with the first interpersonal relations and made him follow a solitary path.

Fromm-Reichmann inspired many people, not only as a therapist, but also as a teacher. Many of her pupils, although maintaining her general therapeutic orientation, have made important contributions. Prominent among them are Otto Will (1970) and Harold Searles (1962, 1965).

In the second edition of my book *Interpretation of Schizophrenia* I reported on the origin and development of my therapeutic procedures with schizophrenics. The first root goes back to my work in Pilgrim State Hospital, at first as a resident and later as a staff psychiatrist from November 1941 to February 1946. During the period spent at that hospital I discovered that a few patients who resided in back buildings and had been considered hopeless would apparently recover or improve enough to be discharged, at times after many years of hospitalisation. These were considered cases of "spontaneous recovery". I was not satisfied with this explanation and looked more deeply into the matter. I soon discovered that these so-called spontaneous recoveries were not spontaneous at all, but the result of a relationship which had been established between the patient and an attendant or a nurse. I made these observations only in services of female patients, but I assumed that the same situation could take place in male services. The relationship went through two stages. In the first stage, by giving the patient special consideration and care, the nurse or the attendant had met some of her needs, no matter how primitive they were. The patient had improved somewhat and the nurse had developed attachment and deep involvement with her. The patient soon would become the pet of the nurse. In a second stage the patient had become able to help the nurse with the work on the ward. Those were war years with acute scarcity of personnel, and any help was very welcome. The patient would then be praised, and an exchange of approval, affection, and reliability was established. In this climate of exchange of warmth and concern the patient had improved to the point of being suitable for discharge. Much to my regret, however, I almost invariably observed that these formerly regressed patients would soon relapse and be readmitted to the hospital. Outside they were not able to "make it". Nevertheless, I was impressed by the fact that even an advanced schizophrenic process had proved to be reversible or capable of being favourably influenced by a human contact. I thought that perhaps methods could be devised by which we could help the patient maintain, increase, strengthen the achieved amelioration, even outside of the hospital environment.

The second root has to be traced in my psychoanalytic training at the William Alanson White Institute. There I learned much more about the role of interpersonal relations in every psychiatric condition, including schizophrenia. There I had the good fortune of having as a teacher Freida Fromm-Reichmann. She influenced and inspired me greatly. Although my therapeutic approach has developed its own basic features, it has retained some of Fromm-Reichmann's characteristics.

The relevance of thought disorders in schizophrenia has been one of my basic concerns from the beginning of my psychiatric studies. Actually the origin of such interest is much more remote in time than my reading of Eugene Bleuler's writings. It goes back to my studies of the eighteenth-century philosopher Giambattista Vico while I was in college. Vico's study of the cognitive ways in which the ancients, the primitives, children, poets, conceive the world and respond to it, fascinated me. It formed my interest in the many possible ways by which the mind faces, reconstructs, and experiences the universe. Vichian conceptions were among the best preparations for understanding the schizophrenic reality and the schizophrenic experience. Also my discovery later of the writings of the psychologist Heinz Werner helped me to evaluate the full relevance of cognition, and directed me toward a comparative developmental approach, for which Vico's writings had already prepared me.

Psychotherapy of Schizophrenia in Practice

When we are confronted with a patient who has developed a schizophrenic psychosis, we can face a vast gamut of clinical pictures which I cannot even try to mention in this brief report. However, two emerge in most cases. One is characterised by withdrawal, a withdrawal which comprehends, not a mythical withdrawal of a mythical energy, but an attitude toward the world which is the result of all the previous experiences of the patient. It is due to infinite fear of the world, infinite distrust of people, total desire to escape; and often this desire is covered up by the feeling that the world is not worth being looked at, of being contacted, not worth participating in. The other clinical picture is one of projection. A system of false beliefs possesses the patient. That's how he sees the world. The danger is there; the persecutors are plotting in a myriad of possible ways. The dangers are experienced as present and the patient lives them in agonising ways.

We know that the danger is an externalisation of an inner danger. The patient who before he became psychotic used to have a bad opinion of himself, to accuse and denigrate himself, now believes that the accusation and the denigration come from the external world. He has produced a metamorphosis through a psychotic projection. No matter how unpleasant it is to feel that people accuse him and persecute him, he no longer does that to himself. Although persecuted, he feels his spirit is free. He has succeeded in changing an inner anxiety, which produced harm to his inner self, into an external danger, which is still objectionable, but with which he can live.

In a minority of cases the psychotic metamorphosis is of a different nature. The patient becomes grandiose, megalomaniac, and immune to any danger.

How can we help the patient? First of all we must reestablish relatedness, conquer the withdrawal if it exists, and reestablish interpersonal communications.

Without establishing relatedness with the patient, no psychotherapy of schizophrenia can go beyond the initial stage. The excellent therapeutic results obtained by some authors to a large extent are the result of their ability to relate to the schizophrenic. Is this ability a mystical, irreducible, intuitional quality, as it has often been called, an innate quality that only a few privileged therapists possess? The writer feels that although there are a few talented therapists who are able to establish this relatedness almost, so to say, instinctively, this practice can be learned by many.

First of all, it must be clarified what is meant by relatedness, a concept frequently used in the interpersonal school of psychiatry. This concept does not include only the establishment of rapport or contact with the patient. It includes the classic psychoanalytic concepts of transference and countertransference, seen in their simultaneous occurrence and in their reciprocal influence. Although it includes also the psychoanalytic concept of object-relation, it does not consider such relations in a one-way direction or as an energy emanating from the individual to the object, but − at the personal level − as an interrelation between two or more individuals, almost as an I-Thou relationship in Buber's terms (1953).

Normal relatedness is based on security in interpersonal relations. Although security or lack of it is the resultant of all the events of life and of the ability of the individual to deal with them, it is to a large extent the result of early childhood interpersonal relations. If these early relations occurred in an atmosphere which Erikson (1953), Buber (1952), and myself (1957) have in different contexts called trust or basic trust, a severe impairment in the ability to relate is not liable to occur. Basic trust is an "atmospheric feeling" which predisposes one to expect "good things" and is a prerequisite to a normal development of self-esteem.

In the therapeutic situation relatedness will be reestablished if the therapist is able to elicit an atmosphere of basic trust. The therapist must convey to the patient the feeling that he has faith in him and in his human potentiality, no matter how sick he is at present. In order to have such faith the therapist must like the patient and find something positive in him, or at least some problem with which he can identify his own. Since he cannot feel in this way toward every human being, he must limit the treatment to those for whom he can have these feelings.

This atmosphere of basic trust can be established in many ways, in accordance with the personality of the patient and of the therapist. However, some general techniques can be differentiated in a broad sense. It will be soon realised that all of them to a great extent rely on the countertransference. Whereas in the treatment of typical neurotics the transference plays a much more important role than the countertransference, almost the reverse is true for the treatment of psychotics. In the treatment of the neurotic the therapist may or may not play the role of "the mirror". We know, for instance, that with certain neurotics a transference is possible only if the analyst remains impersonal. This is absolutely untrue in the treatment of the schizophrenic. Paraphrasing Racamier (1959) we may say that the schizophrenic must feel the presence of the analyst, must feel that he is there as a tangible, reasonable, benevolent, and strong human being. The following general indications may help to establish this atmosphere of relatedness at the beginning of the treatment: The therapist (1) must assume an attitude of active and intense intervention; (2) must make attempts to remove the fear that is automatically aroused by the interpersonal therapeutic situation and offer general reassurance; (3) may offer short interpretative formulations, which the therapist has grasped at once in his first contact with the patient. They are "passing remarks" or "appropriate comments" (Semrad, 1952) and not detailed interpretations. The importance of these early explanations lies in conveying to the patient the feeling that somebody understands his troubles and feels with him. They should not be confused with deeper interpretations given later; (4) may find useful some nonverbal meaningful acts, like touching the patient, holding his hand, walking together. This procedure, however, must be implemented with great cautiousness, especially with catatonics and some apparently lucid paranoids.

Relatedness should not be considered just part of "supportive" therapy. It is in fact more nutritional than supportive, an attempt being made by it to offer to the patient what he did not have before in sufficient quantity.

The Acquisition of Insight

The value of acquisition of insight through interpretations in the treatment of schizophrenia is variously estimated. Many therapists, including the present writer, have changed their view on this subject several times, in accordance with what new experience indicates. Some therapists have remained impressed by the remarkable results obtained in some cases only with the establishment of relatedness. To many other authors, including the writer, however, a reevaluation of cases previously treated seems to indicate that the best results were obtained when the patient had acquired a deep understanding of his past and present life and of his ways of operating.

Insight is acquired predominantly, but not exclusively, through interpretations. Interpretations are beneficial in three ways: (1) an enlightenment; (2) as experiences, inasmuch as they are accompanied by changes in the emotional status of the patient; (3) as triggers to different patterns of behaviour.

Interpretations may be divided into two types: (1) referring mostly to the psychotic mechanisms or forms in accordance with which the patient functions; (2) referring to the psychodynamics of the patient.

Interpretations Concerning the Formal Mechanisms

Although dynamic interpretations are much better known, the present writer believes that interpretations concerning mechanisms and forms are also important, especially at an early phase of the treatment, and has devised special technical procedures with which to implement them. The patient is helped become aware of the ways with which he transforms his psychodynamic conflicts into psychotic symptoms (Arieti, 1961, 1962a, 1962b, 1963). Whereas the benefit from traditional interpretations is due or believed to be due to acquisition of insight into repressed experiences and to the accompanying abreaction, and therefore is supposed to be immediate, the effectiveness of the second type of interpretation consists of the acquisitions of methods with which the patient can work at his problems. They do not consist exclusively of insights passively received, but predominantly of tools with which the patient has to actively operate.

In what follows I shall take into consideration only auditory hallucinations, but the same procedures could be applied to other types of hallucinations after the proper modifications have been made.

With the exception of patients who are at a very advanced stage of the illness or with whom no relatedness whatsoever can be reached, it is possible to recognise that the hallucinatory voices occur only in particular situations, that is, *when the patient expects to hear them.*

For instance, a patient goes home after a day of work and expects the neighbours to talk about him. As soon as he expects to hear them, he hears them. In other words, he puts himself in what I have called *the listening attitude.*

If we have been able to establish not only contact but relatedness with the patient, he will be able under our direction to distinguish two stages: that of the listening attitude and that of the hallucinatory experience. At first he may protest vigorously and deny the existence of the two stages, but later he may make a little concession. He will say, "I happened to think that they would talk, and I proved to be right. They were really talking".

A few sessions later another step forward will be made. The patient will be able to recognise and to admit that there was a brief interval between the expectation of the voices and the voices. He will still insist that this sequence is purely coincidental, but eventually he will see a connection between his putting himself into the listening attitude and his actually hearing. Then he will recognise that he puts himself into this attitude when he is in a particular situation or in a particular mood, for instance, a mood on account of which he perceives hostility, almost in the air. He has the feeling that everybody has a disparaging attitude toward him; then he finds corroboration for this attitude of the others; he hears them making unpleasant remarks about him. At times he feels inadequate and worthless, but he does not sustain this feeling for more than a fraction of a second. The self-condemnation almost automatically induces him to put himself into the listening attitude, and then he hears other people condemning him.

When the patient is able to recognise the relation between the mood and putting himself in the listening attitude, a great step has been accomplished. He will not see himself any longer as a passive agent, as the victim of a strange phenomenon or of persecutors, but as somebody who still has a great deal to do with what he experiences. Moreover, if he catches himself in the listening attitude, he has not yet descended to or is not yet using abnormal or paleologic ways of thinking from which it will be difficult to escape. He is in the process of falling into the seductive trap of the world of psychosis but may still resist the seduction and remain in the world of reality. He will intercept the mechanism; he acquires the power to do so.

If an atmosphere of relatedness and understanding has been established, patients learn with not too much difficulty to catch themselves in the act of putting themselves into the listening attitude at the least disturbance, several times during the day. Although they recognise the phenomenon, they sometimes feel that it is almost an automatic mechanism which they cannot prevent. Eventually, however, they will be able to control it more and more. Even then, there will be a tendency to resort again to the listening attitude and to the hallucinatory experiences in situations of stress. The therapist should never be tired of explaining the mechanism to the patient again and again, even when such explanations seem redundant. It is seldom redundant, as the symptoms may reacquire an almost irresistible attraction.

But now that we have deprived the patient of his hallucinations, again you can ask, how will he be able to manage with his anxiety? How can we help him to bear his burden or a heavier but less unrealistic cross? An example will perhaps clarify this matter. A woman used to hear a hallucinatory voice calling her a prostitute. Now, with the method I have described, we have deprived her of this hallucination. Nevertheless, she experiences a feeling, almost an abstract feeling coming from the external environment, of being discriminated against, considered inferior, looked upon as a bad woman, etc. She has almost the wish to crystallise or concretise again this feeling into a hallucination. If we leave her alone, she will hallucinate again. If we tell her that she projects into the environment her own feelings about herself, she may become infuriated. She says, "The voices I used to hear were telling me I am a bad woman, a prostitute, but I never had such a feeling about myself, I am a good woman". The patient, of course, is right, because when she hears a disparaging voice, or when she is experiencing the vague feeling of being disparaged, no longer has she a disparaging opinion of herself. The projective mechanism saves her from self-disparagement. We must instead point out to the patient that there was one time when she had a bad opinion of herself. Even then she did not think she was a prostitute but had a low self-esteem, such as she probably thought a prostitute would have about herself.

In other words, we must try to reenlarge the patient's psychotemporal field. As long as he attributes everything to the present, he cannot escape from the symptoms. Whereas the world of psychosis has only one temporal dimension – present – the world of reality has three: past, present, and future. Although at this point of the illness the patient already tends to live exclusively in the present, he retains a conception of the past, and such conception must be exploited. We direct the patient to face longitudinally his deep feeling of inadequacy. At the same time the therapist with his general attitude and firm reassurance and sincere interest will be able to share the burden.

The realisation of the low self-esteem is not yet a complete psychodynamic explanation of the symptom, but at this stage of the treatment we stop at this explanation. The matter will be pursued later, when we shall examine factors in the early family environment which led to this negative self-appraisal. We have seen, however, that any formal mechanism which is pursued to its origin discloses not purely the nature of its form but its psychodynamic counterpart. This multifaceted nature of the symptom is seen even more clearly in other psychotic phenomena which can be called at the same time hallucinatory, illusional, delusional, or referential. For instance, a patient has the idea that people laugh at him. He actually hears them laughing, and he turns his head; he looks at them and sees them smiling. They may not smile at all, and he may misinterpret their facial expression. If they do smile, they may do so for reasons which have nothing to do with him. Again we must help the patient to recognise that he sees or hears people laughing at him when he expects to see or hear them. However, when the treatment is more advanced, the patient recognises that he feels people *should* laugh at him because he is a laughable individual. He hears them laughing because he believes that they should laugh at him. What he thinks of himself becomes the cause of his symptoms. For the patient it is a painful procedure to acknowledge that that is what he thinks of himself. In this case, too, the psychotic mechanism will dissolve itself when it is understood both formally and psychodynamically and the patient, with the help of the therapist, is able to bear the unpleasant psychodynamic meaning. In some delusions and ideas of reference there is an element of reality, which is valid at a realistic level as well as at a symbolic level (Arieti, 1962a). For instance, the boss of a patient used to hit an out-of-order water cooler, ostensibly to make the water flow. The patient interpreted the gesture as equivalent to hitting her. Later discussions seemed to indicate that the patient was not referring to herself an irrelevant happening. Her boss was given to acts of displaced hostility.

The patient is praised for this insight, but the insight is enlarged to include not only the realistic episode but its symbolic meaning. The coincidence between psychosis and reality is exploited to make contact with the patient and to develop consensual validation in some areas.

This insight of the patient I call punctiform because it concerns a small segment of reality. Although its presence is important and should be acknowledged, it should not be confused with the ideas of the antipsychiatry psychiatrists who see in the expressions of the schizophrenic patient a revelation of the supreme truth.

Concerning R. D. Laing's conceptions, I believe that we must agree with him that there are grains of truth in what the patient tells us; but, again, let us not see these grains of truth under a magnifying glass. If we do that, we may actually do a disservice to the patient. We may admire the patient for removing the masks, for saying what other people do not dare to say. But we must also recognise that the fragments of truth he uncovers assume grotesque forms, and that he will apply these grotesque forms to the whole world, so that whatever insight he has achieved will be less pronounced and less profound than his distortion. And his distortion not only has no adaptational value, but is inimical to any form of adaptation even in a liberal community of men. The psychotic outcome is thus only a pseudosolution. We must help the patient find real solutions. Sooner or later in the treatment, he must recognise that the environmental circumstances are responsible for his illness, not in a simple relation of direct causality, but because in different stages of his development, they facilitated intrapsychic mechanisms which later permitted the disorder to feed on itself. In my opinion it would be too simple and too naïve to join the patient in blaming solely the environment. When the psychosis is already active, it is no longer just an external drama; it is inner drama and inner metamorphosis. As a matter of fact, I have already mentioned that the main defensive aspect of the psychosis is the transformation of an intrapsychic danger into an external one. It is beyond the scope of this paper to illustrate the important role played by cognition in this psychotic transformation. This topic is referred to in the original writings (Arieti, 1948, 1955, 1957, 1969, 1971, 1974).

Psychodynamic Analysis

As soon as a degree of relatedness has been established and the major psychotic mechanisms have been abated, treatment must be oriented toward an acquisition on the part of the patient of awareness of his unconscious motivation and of insight into the psychological components of the disorder.

In order to help the patient during this difficult phase of treatment the therapist must be familiar with the characteristics of the psychodynamic development of schizophrenia. Elsewhere I have described in detail this development and divided it into four periods, which I shall summarise here (Arieti, 1968, 1974).

It is in the first period (early childhood) that, for a variety of reasons, the future patient cannot accept entirely the "Thou", the other person, generally the mother, who is necessary for the formation of the child's "I" or self. This is the beginning of the schizophrenic cleavage. The other comes to be perceived as a *malevolent Thou* and the I as a *bad me*. In most cases this cleavage is patched up and the psychological status is protected by defences. In the second period (late childhood), either because of the acquisition of a schizoid personality that blunts feelings or a stormy personality that is capable of a variety of responses, the Thou tends to be transformed and experienced as a *distressing other* and the bad me is transformed into the weak, inadequate me. The child will see himself as a weakling in a world of strong and distressing adults.

The third period, which generally starts at puberty, is characterised not only by sexual urges but most of all by conceptual life. What may prove most pathogenetic are not instinctual impulses or instinctual deprivations but ideas — the cognitive part of man, which has been neglected in psychoanalysis as well as in general psychiatry. From now on the self-image will consist predominantly of such concepts as personal significance, one's role in life, and self-esteem. The defences that the person had adopted in the previous two periods and that were adequate for the little world of the family become less reliable now that the patient is extending his relations with the big social world. He does not feel prepared for what he experiences as perennial challenge. The patient comes to believe that the future has no hope, the promise of life will not be fulfilled. He feels unaccepted and unacceptable, unfit, alone.

He may undergo a prepsychotic panic that is caused by a strange emotional resonance between something that is very clear (like the devastating self-image brought about by the expansion of conceptual life) and the unrepressed experiences of the first period of life, when he sensed with great intensity the threat of the world. The concordance and unification of the experiences of the first and third periods complete and magnify the horrendous vision of the self. In the totality of his human existence, and through the depth of all his feelings, the individual sees himself as totally defeated, without any worth or possibility of redemption.

In most cases only one solution, one defense, is still available to the psyche: to dissolve or alter his cognitive functions, the thought processes that have brought about conceptual disaster and that have acquired an ominous resonance with the original and preconceptual understanding of the self. It is at this stage that the fourth, or psychotic, period begins.

A detailed analysis of psychodynamic therapy would require repetition of a great part of the second edition of my book *Interpretation of Schizophrenia*. I shall focus here only on one fundamental point. In the beginning of treatment the parental role is generally shifted in a distorted way to the persecutors. In a minority of cases it is shifted not to persecutors, but to supernatural, royal, or divine benefactors who, in these grandiose delusions, represent figures antithetical to the parents. When the patient reestablishes relatedness and discovers the importance of childhood and of his relations with his parents, he goes through another stage. The original parental image comes to the surface and he attributes to the parents full responsibility for his illness and despair. Many analysts and psychiatrists (Lidz, 1952, 1965; Rosen, 1947, 1953, 1962) have accepted as real insights and as accurate accounts of historical events these explanations given by patients. It was easy to believe in the accuracy of the patients' accounts, first of all because some parents seem to fit this monstrous image; secondly, because the patients who had shifted their target from the persecutors to the parents had made considerable improvement, were no longer delusional or to a minimal degree, and seemed to a large extent reliable. The therapist must be careful. In a minority of cases the parents have really been as the patient has depicted them, but only in a minority. In by far the great majority of cases the patient who comes to recognise a role played by the parents, exaggerates and deforms that role. He is not able to see his own deformations until the therapist points them out to him. Fortunately, some circumstances may help. In this newly developed antiparental zeal the patient goes on a campaign to distort even what the parent does and says *now*. Incidentally, this tendency is present not only in schizophrenics, but also in some preschizophrenics who never become full-fledged psychotics. By being fixated in an antiparental frame of reference they may not need to become delusional and psychotic. To a much less unrealistic extent, this tendency occurs in some neurotics, too. At times the antiparental campaign is enlarged to include parents-in-law and other people who have a quasi-parental role.

The therapist has to help in many ways. First, he points out how the patient distorts or exaggerates. For instance, a white lie is transformed into the worst mendacity, tactlessness into falsity or perversion. These deformations are caused by the need to reproduce a pattern established in childhood, a pattern which was the result not only of what historically happened but also of the patient's immaturity, ignorance, and misperception. At times these deformations are easy to correct. For instance, once the mother of a patient told her, "Your mother-in-law is sick". The patient interpreted her mother's words as if they meant "With your perverse qualities you have made your mother-in-law sick as you made me sick once". On still another occasion the mother spoke about the beautiful apartment that the patient's newly married younger sister had just furnished. The patient, who, incidentally, was jealous of the mother's attention for her sister, interpreted this remark as meaning "Your sister has much better taste than you". Second, the patient must realise that the negative traits of parents or other important people are not necessarily arrows or weapons used purposely to hurt the patient. They are merely characteristics of these people and should not be considered total qualities.

For instance, in the remarks of the mother of the patient, which we have just reported, there might have been some elements of hostility. In every human relation and communication, in every social event, however, there are many dimensions and meanings, not only in the so-called double bind talk of the so-called schizophrenogenic mother. But the patient focuses on this negative trend or aspect and neglects all the other dimensions of the rich and multifaceted communication. The patient is unable to tolerate any ambivalence, any plurality of dimensions.

Thirdly, and most important, the original parental introject must lose importance. The patient is an adult now; it is up to the patient to provide for himself or to search for himself what once he expected to get from his parents.

Again lack of time prevents me from talking about other important aspects of the treatment, like the psychodynamic analysis of the transference and countertransference of the self-image, of dreams, and finally, of the general participation in the patient's life, at times with the help of a therapeutic assistant (Arieti, 1972; Lorraine, 1972).

In conclusion, psychotherapy aims at reestablishing the bond of human relatedness with the patient, attacking psychotic symptoms with specific techniques, understanding the psychodynamic history, especially in the misinterpreted relations with the family, and helping the patient to unfold toward new, nonpsychotic patterns of living. Thus, although the psychotherapy of schizophrenia retains the interpretative technique and the uncovering of the repressed, as in the original Freudian psychoanalytic therapy, it expands in many directions. It is just as nourishing as it is interpretative. Although it helps the patient to reacquire communication, concern, and love for the other, it promotes autonomy, individuality, and self-assertation.

References

ARIETI, S. Special Logic of Schizophrenia and Other Types of Autistic Thought. *Psychiatry*, **XI**, 325, 1948.
ARIETI, S. *Interpretation of Schizophrenia.* New York: Brunner, 1955.
ARIETI, S. The Two Aspects of Schizophrenia. *Psychiatric Quarterly*, **31**, 403, 1957.
ARIETI, S. Introductory Notes on the Psychoanalytic Therapy of Schizophrenia. In A. Burton (ed.), *Psychotherapy of Psychoses.* New York: Basic Books, 1961.
ARIETI, S. Hallucinations, Delusions and Ideas of Reference Treated with Psychotherapy. *American Journal of Psychotherapy*, **XVI**, 52, 1962a.
ARIETI, S. Psychotherapy of Schizophrenia. *Archives of General Psychiatry*, **6**, 112, 1962b.
ARIETI, S. *The Psychotherapy of Schizophrenia in Theory and Practice.* American Psychiatric Association Psychiatric Research Report, 17, 1963.
ARIETI, S. The Schizophrenic Patient in Office Treatment. In *Psychotherapy, Schizophrenia, 3rd International Symposium, Lausanne, 1964.* Basel: Kargel, 1965.
ARIETI, S. The Psychodynamics of Schizophrenia: A Reconsideration. *American Journal of Psychotherapy*, **22**, 366-381, 1968.
ARIETI, S. Current Ideas on the Problem of Psychosis. *Excerpta Medica International Congress*, Series No. 194, 3-21, 1969.
ARIETI, S. The Origins and Development of the Psychopathology of Schizophrenia. In M. Bleuler and J. Angst (eds.) *Die Entstehung der Schizophrenie.* Bern: Huber, 1971.
ARIETI, S. The Therapeutic Assistant in Treating the Psychotic. *International Journal of Psychiatry*, **10**, 7-11, 1972.
ARIETI, S. *Interpretation of Schizophrenia*, 2nd ed. New York: Basic Books, 1974.
BUBER, M. *I and Thou.* Translated by R.G. Smith. Edinburgh: Clark, 1953.
ERIKSON, E.H. Growth and Crises of the Healthy Personality. In C. Kluckhohn and H.A. Murray (eds.), *Personality in Nature, Society, and Culture,* 2nd ed. With the collaboration of D.M. Schneider. New York: Knopf, 1953.
FEDERN, P. *Ego Psychology and the Psychoses.* New York: Basic Books, 1952.
FREUD, S. On Psychotherapy. (1905) *Collected Papers,* 1, London: Hogarth Press, 1946.
FROMM-REICHMANN, F. Notes on the Development of Treatment of Schizophrenia by Psychoanalytic Psychotherapy. *Psychiatry,* **11**, 3, 1948.
FROMM-REICHMANN, F. *Principles of Intensive Psychotherapy.* Chicago: University of Chicago Press, 1950.
KLEIN, M. *Contributions to Psycho-analysis.* London: Hogarth Press, 1948.
KLEIN, M. *New Directions in Psychoanalysis.* New York: Basic Books, 1955.
LAING, R.D. *The Divided Self.* London: Tavistock, 1960.
LIDZ, R.W. and LIDZ, T. Therapeutic Considerations Arising from the Intense Symbiotic Needs of Schizophrenic Patients. In Brody and Redlich, *Psychotherapy with Schizophrenics.* New York: International University Press, 1952.
LIDZ, T. The Influence of the Family Structures in the Treatment of Schizophrenia. *Psychiatry*, **32**, 237-251, 1969.
LIDZ, T. *The Origin and Treatment of Schizophrenic Disorders.* New York: Basic Books, 1973.
LIDZ, T., FLECK, S. and CORNELISON, A.R. *Schizophrenia and the Family.* New York: International Universities Press, 1965.
RACAMIER, P.C. Psychoanalytic Therapy of the Psychoses. In S. Nacht (ed.), *Psychoanalysis of Today.* New York: Grune & Stratton, 1959.
ROSEN, J.N. The Treatment of Schizophrenic Psychosis by Direct Analytic Therapy. *Psychiatric Quarterly.* 2, 3, 1947.
ROSEN, J.N. *Direct Analysis: Selected Papers.* New York: Grune & Stratton, 1953.
ROSEN, J.N. *Direct Psychoanalytic Psychiatry.* New York: Grune & Stratton, 1962.
SEARLES, H.F. The Differentiation Between Concrete and Metaphorical Thinking in the Recovering Schizophrenic. *Journal of the American Psychoanalytic Association,* **10**, 22-49, 1962.

SEARLES, H.F. *Collected Papers on Schizophrenia and Related Subjects.* New York: International Universities Press, 1965.
SECHEHAYE, M.A. *Symbolic Realization.* New York: International Universities Press, 1951.
SECHEHAYE, M.A. *A New Psychotherapy in Schizophrenia.* New York: Grune & Stratton, 1956.
SEMRAD, E.J. Discussion of Dr. Frank's Paper. In E.B. Brody and F.C. Redlich (eds.), *Psychotherapy with Schizophrenics.* New York: International University Press, 1952.
SULLIVAN, H.S. *Conceptions of Modern Psychiatry.* New York: Norton, 1953.
SULLIVAN, H.S. *Schizophrenia as a Human Process.* New York: Norton, 1962.
WILL, O.A. The Psychotherapeutic Center and Schizophrenia. In B. Cancro (ed.), *The Schizophrenic Reactions.* New York: Brunner-Mazel, 1970.

The Treatment of Psychotic States, Particularly Schizophrenia, by Psychoanalysis

HERBERT ROSENFELD

In this paper I shall give first a brief historical outline of the psychoanalytic approach to the psychosis. Second, I shall give a short survey of my own research and contributions to psychoanalysis of the psychosis. Third, I shall make certain comparisons between Fromm-Reichmann's and Searle's theoretical and clinical work with psychotic patients, and my own. Fourth, I shall describe some of my recent work on the narcissistic delusional structures in schizophrenia. And fifth, I shall attempt to give some suggestions about the future of the psychoanalytic approach to schizophrenic patients.

In my paper on The Treatment of Psychotic States by Psychoanalysis: An Historical Approach (1969), I described in some detail how the psychoanalytic approach to the psychoses developed. Freud from 1896 onwards contributed to our psychopathological understanding of the psychosis particularly by his notes on the Schreber Case (1911), his paper on Narcissism (1914), his papers on Homosexuality and Paranoia, on Mourning and Melancholia (1917) and on Neurosis and Psychosis (1924). Freud was doubtful whether the psychoses could be approached by psychoanalysis because he believed that the psychotic patient was unable to form any transference. However, some of his close colleagues did not agree with him on this point. Abraham from 1907 made theoretical and clinical contributions to the Psychoanalytical Treatment of Severe Depressions and also Dementia Praecox. Federn (from 1905) and Waelder (1925) used their analytic knowledge for applying modified psychoanalytic therapy to psychotic states, but it took many years until the psychoanalytic treatment of the psychoses was well established. In the United States a number of non-analysts, such as Adolf Meyer and Harry Stack Sullivan, helped to break through the organic prejudice in the treatment of psychotic states. Meyer drew attention particularly to the reactive element in psychosis and many psychiatrists in the United States and England were deeply inspired by his work (Gillespie, Clifford Scott, etc.). Sullivan studied the interpersonal relations of his schizophrenic patients by creating psychotherapeutic treatment units in the Sheppard and Enoch Pratt Hospital. He found that even severely ill schizophrenic patients improved considerably in what may be called a "Therapeutic Community" where all the workers, doctors, nurses and helpers aimed at the reorientation of the schizophrenic patient towards interpersonal relations. Sullivan believed that from the very early post-natal state at which time the infant felt already the sense of approval and disapproval of the mother by empathy, some degree of interpersonal relatedness is maintained throughout life by everyone regardless of the state of mental health, and he believed that the disruption of this relatedness in the schizophrenic was only partial. In spite of his disagreement with many psychoanalytic theories Sullivan seemed to have inspired a number of psychoanalytic workers in schizophrenia such as Fromm-Reichmann, Arieti and

259

other members of the Washington Group of analysts. Fromm-Reichmann and Searles particularly worked for many years almost entirely with psychotic patients at the Chestnut Lodge Hospital and both of them have made very important contributions to the analytic therapy of schizophrenic patients. There are many other American analysts who have worked with schizophrenics such as Bychowski, Wexler, Pious, Reider, Knight, Arlow and more recently Kernberg, Bryce Boyer, Giovacchini and Hoedemaker discussed their intensive work with schizophrenic patients in their book in 1967.

The psychoanalytic treatment of psychotic patients in England has been stimulated by the work of Melanie Klein who investigated the earliest levels of infantile development through her analysis of seriously disturbed children and adults. She found that during infancy the child experienced anxiety reminiscent of the anxiety of the adult psychotic patient and for that reason she called the early phase from birth to about 4 to 6 months the paranoid-schizoid position and the phase following this the depressive position. In 1935 she wrote a paper on the psychogenesis of manic-depressive states and in 1946 "Notes on Schizoid Mechanisms". Winnicott, who was profoundly influenced by Melanie Klein's work on depression and mania worked with psychotic patients during World War II. Clifford Scott wrote a paper on The Treatment of Manic Depressive States in 1938 but he also treated some schizophrenics.

In my view Melanie Klein's paper on Schizoid Mechanisms has been the basic stimulus to the development of psychoanalytical treatment of schizophrenia in England. In 1947 I published a paper on "The Analysis of a Schizophrenic State with Depersonalisation" in which I had applied successfully Melanie Klein's work on schizoid mechanisms. In 1950 first Segal and then myself treated a deluded schizophrenic patient in a mental hospital. Later Bion, Sohn, Meltzer, Sidney Klein, Mason, Thorner and others carried out the analysis of schizophrenic and manic-depressive patients.

Notes on my Experiences with Psychotherapy and Psychoanalysis of Psychotic Patients

When I started in 1937 to treat schizophrenic patients in England by psychotherapy and from 1943 by psychoanalysis I found for many years not only little assistance but strong opposition from most of my psychiatric colleagues. John Rosen's visit to London in 1948 stimulated the interest in the psychological approach to schizophrenia. He had just published a paper reporting the successful treatment of 80 chronic schizophrenic patients who have been hospitalised for many years. Rosen demonstrated his approach at the Maudsley Hospital and managed to contact a catatonic patient who had been mute for many years. We know today that many of Rosen's patients relapsed and the so-called direct interpretive approach had many drawbacks, but some psychiatrists began more seriously to consider that the psychological treatment and research into the problems of schizophrenia had not been sufficiently explored. Since 1948 psychoanalytic research has clarified a great deal of the psychopathology of this disease, but still more research and opportunity for psychoanalytic treatment will be necessary to establish psychoanalytic treatment as the treatment of choice for many schizophrenic conditions. It is likely that there exist important hereditary or constitutional factors in children who later develop schizophrenia which manifests itself by abnormal psychological reactions very early on in infancy. This, however, often affects only a part of the mental apparatus, while certain aspects of the personality are able to develop more or less normally. Bion has contributed to our understanding of this problem in his paper Differentiation of the Psychotic from the Non-Psychotic Personality in 1957. The psychotic abnormal part of the personality remains cut off and latent and may be mobilised in a variety of ways through internal or external environmental pressures. Sometimes the internal problems are more significant, while at other times traumatic environmental factors play a more prominent role. Psychoanalytic treatment and research have investigated particularly the internal abnormal structures in schizophrenia and how they are inter-related with traumatic external experiences and influences.

In 1943 I started the analysis of Mildred who was suffering from a schizophrenic state with depersonalisation. When I began to observe that the psychotic manifestations had attached themselves to the transference I began to understand the meaning of the patient's behaviour and was able to communicate my understanding to her by means of verbal interpretations. It gradually led to a substantial improvement which continued after the patient had to interrupt analysis after 3 years to accompany her husband to another country. In 1950 I undertook the analysis of an acute catatonic hallucinated patient who was at the same time violent. He had difficulties in forming whole sentences and often communicated with me using only one or two words which he expected me to understand. In my paper on Transference Phenomena and Transference Analysis of an Acute Catatonic Patient I tried to illustrate that (a) an acute schizophrenic patient was capable of forming a positive and negative transference, (b) that it was possible to interpret this transference to the schizophrenic patient and (c) that the schizophrenic's response to interpretations can at times be clearly observed.

I also drew attention to my observations that schizophrenic patients showed one particular form of early object relations very clearly. Namely, as soon as they approached any object in love or hate they seem to become confused with this object and this seems to be due to impulses and phantasies of entering inside the object with a whole or part of the self. I related my observations to Melanie Klein's description of projective identification, a process originating in early infancy which has been investigated and described by many workers in England, France and the United States. In my paper on Projective Identification and Ego Splitting written for the Symposium on the Treatment of Psychosis in Montreal in 1969 I gave a detailed description of the various processes which have been discussed under the collective name "projective identification". I found it particularly important to distinguish between two types of projective identification, namely projective identification used for ridding the self of unwanted parts. Many psychotic patients use projective processes for communication with other people. These projective mechanisms of the psychotic seem to be a distortion or intensification of the normal infantile relationship which is based on non-verbal communication between infant and mother, in which impulses, parts of the self and anxieties too difficult for the infant to bear are projected into the mother and where the mother is able instinctively to respond by containing the infant's anxiety and alleviating it by her behaviour (Bion).

The psychotic patient who uses this process in the analytic transference may do so consciously but more often unconsciously. He then projects impulses and parts of himself into the analyst so that the analyst will understand and respond to his experiences. The analyst's capacity to contain the patient's projections is communicated mainly by the analyst's interpretive function, which helps the patient in making his distorted infantile responses and feelings accessible to the saner part of himself, which gradually diminishes the terror and apparent meaninglessness of the psychotic thought processes. The value of the analytic experience is also of fundamental importance for the development of introjective processes and so for the growth of the ego.

This is only one of the functions of projective identification and there are several other aspects of this process, which are essential for the understanding of psychotic states. We have to remember that projective identification is a primitive infantile mechanism, which is used by the schizophrenic for constantly projecting parts of himself into his objects and as this patient lives by projecting he believes that his objects do this too which results in fears of feeling invaded as soon as he comes close to any object.

When the projective identification is used for evacuation of libidinal parts of the self into external objects to deny psychic reality, emptiness or feelings of unreality become manifest. The evacuation is often combined with destructive devaluing attacks directed both against the libidinal self and the objects used for projection which produces intense feelings of uselessness and meaninglessness. When this situation attaches itself to the analytic situation verbal communication between patient and analyst becomes difficult as all interpretations are experienced as useless and meaningless. Fortunately projective identification used for communication and for evacuation may exist simultaneously or alternatively in our psychotic patients and it is essential to differentiate between these processes clearly in order to keep contact with the patient and make analysis possible.

When projective identification is used by the schizophrenic patient mainly to force destructive impulses and parts of the self into external objects, severe paranoid anxieties may result as the objects are experienced as retaliating and therefore intensely aggressive and intrusive, threatening to overwhelm and destroy the patient's self. Under these circumstances the patient often withdraws into a delusional psychotic structure for safety — a process which I shall discuss later.

In discussing the psychoanalytic technique in dealing with the schizophrenic patient I compared as early as 1952 the analysis of schizophrenic patients to the psychoanalytic treatment of children. Children and psychotic patients are not expected to lie on the couch and not only their talk but their behaviour and games are used as analytic material. In child analysis the cooperation between the children's parents and the analyst is necessary as the child has to be brought to the session and the parents supply the infantile history and sometimes keep the analyst informed about real events.

There is no question that in the treatment of severely ill, particularly acute schizophrenic patients the cooperation of parents and relatives is absolutely essential and the success or failure of the treatment of psychotic patients is to a large degree dependent on the cooperation of the parents. I have found it necessary to see my schizophrenic patients at least six times a week and I also found it advisable not to vary the length of time of any one session. I also felt it unwise to interrupt the treatment for more than a few days while the patient was still in an acute state as it often causes a long setback in the patient's clinical condition and in the analysis.

Comparisons Between Different Psychoanalytic Approaches

I shall now attempt to discuss the work of two experienced therapists of schizophrenic patients — Fromm-Reichmann and Harold Searles — and attempt to relate it to my own approach. After many years of work with schizophrenic patients Fromm-Reichmann changed her technique based on non-frustrating and appeasing the patient as she became aware that it had an infantalising effect on the patient. She began to differentiate the psychotic aspects of the patient's personality which she identified with the rejected infantile self or child in the patient from the non-psychotic part of the patient which she related to his adult personality. In the analysis she addressed most of her interventions and confrontations to the adult self. Nevertheless she indicated that she used only a minimum of interpretations of content while she was aware that the schizophrenic needed help in understanding the genetics and dynamics of his communications.

In her later work she stressed the devastating effect of the patient's hostility on his personality and showed that the universal conflict between dependency and hostility was overwhelmingly magnified in schizophrenia. Searles emphasised particularly the patient/analyst inter-relatedness in allowing the patient's transference psychosis to develop. He noticed that the patient projects into the therapist a variety of part object relations of a very disturbing kind and he uses his counter-transference feelings more than other therapists in reconstructing the patient's traumatic inter-relatedness with his early objects. He observed that the patient gradually improves and acquires ego strength through identification with the therapist who can endure the patient's primitive object relations. He also stresses the importance of the analyst being able to function as a part of the patient and he discusses the importance of projective identification in detail. He does, however, feel that the very deteriorated long hospitalised schizophrenic patient is too ill to be able to register verbal statements or interpretations by the analyst. He has worked with patients so deeply de-differentiated that only after several years of intense therapy do they become able to distinguish between an outside and an inside. He believes that verbal transference interpretations can be looked upon as one form of intervention which can at times be effective and which constitute an appeal for cooperation to the non-psychotic area of the patient's personality. I would agree both with Fromm-Reichmann and Searles that verbal interpretations are directed generally towards the non-psychotic aspects of the patient and therefore quite correct interpretations may be experienced by the patient as a rejection of his delusional relationship with the analyst, which is often related to desires for fusion or a symbiotic non-verbal relationship. But I think it is also essential for the analyst to understand that the schizophrenic patient is at times greatly in need of the analyst's capacity to understand and function, and his interpretations are needed by the patient to learn to think and to understand and to discriminate, in other words to recover mental functioning that has been lost or remained and undeveloped. Many of Fromm-Reichmann's and Searles' observations coincide with my own experiences, such as the importance of differentiating between psychotic and non-psychotic aspects of the patient. I also agree with Fromm-Reichmann about the inability of the schizophrenic patient to deal with his devastating aggression and his difficulty in acknowledging his dependency. Searles' experiences are very rich and have been gained through more than 15 years' intensive work with seriously ill schizophrenic patients. He has made use of many of Bion's and my own concepts. On the other hand he has drawn attention to the importance of the intense inter-relatedness which occurs between analyst and patient during the therapeutic involvement, particularly with severely ill schizophrenic patients who are often able to observe many details of the analyst's personality and difficulties. I agree with Searles that the capacity of the analyst to cope with the many primitive projections of part object relations and also parts of the patient's self in an accepting form is an essential therapeutic influence in the analysis of schizophrenic and other psychotic patients.

Some Recent Investigation of the Narcissistic Delusional Structures in Schizophrenia

I shall now concentrate on the discussion of a psychotic process, which I have studied for many years and which I believe to be of central importance in understanding and treating schizophrenic patients. In 1964 I described (with Dr. Meltzer) the delusional psychotic structure in some detail and more recently my investigation of destructive narcissism has revealed that in many schizophrenic patients the destructive narcissistic parts of the self are linked to a psychotic structure or organisation which is split off from the rest of the personality. This structure appears generally to be dominated by an omnipotent or omniscient part of the self which creates the notion that within the delusional structure there is complete painlessness and also freedom to indulge in any sadistic activity. The whole structure is committed to narcissistic self-sufficiency and is strictly directed against any object relatedness. The destructive impulses within this delusional world sometimes appear openly as overpoweringly cruel, threatening the rest of the self with death to assert their power but more frequently they appear disguised as omnipotently benevolent or life-saving, promising to provide the patient with quick ideal solutions to all his problems. These false promises are designed to make the normal self of the patient dependent on or addicted to his omnipotent self and to lure the normal sane parts into this delusional structure in order to imprison them. When schizophrenic patients of this type begin to make some progress severe negative therapeutic reactions occur as the narcissistic psychotic part of the self exerts its power and superiority over life and the analyst standing for reality by trying to lure the saner self of the patient into a psychotic omnipotent dream state which results in the patient's losing his sense of reality and his capacity for thinking. In fact there is a danger of an acute psychotic state if the dependent part of the patient which is the sanest part of the personality is persuaded to turn away from the external world and give itself up entirely to the domination of the psychotic delusional structure. This process has similarities to Freud's description of the giving up of object athexis and the withdrawal of the libido into the ego. The patient appears to be withdrawn from the world, is unable to think and often feels drugged. He may lose his interest in the outside world and want to stay in bed and forget what has been discussed in the previous session. If he manages to come to the analysis he may complain that something incomprehensible has happened to him because he feels trapped, claustrophobic, paralysed and unable to get out of this state. He is sometimes aware that he has lost something important but he is not sure what it is. Some patients develop an overwhelming anxiety which they often find difficult to explain since their fears have a nameless quality. Nevertheless, one has the impression that they feel threatened by death: For example, a patient may develop severe hypochondriacal fears of death or a delusion of being trapped by death which was expressed by a catatonic patient by his repeated question: "How can I get out of the tomb?" Detailed investigation of this process suggests that we are dealing here with pathological fusion because in this narcissistic withdrawal state the sane dependent part of the patient enters the delusional structure and a projective identification into a part of the self takes place in which the sane self loses its identify and becomes completely dominated by the omnipotent destructive process: it has no power to oppose or mitigate the latter while this pathological fusion lasts.

Harry Stack Sullivan and Arieti have drawn attention to the overwhelming panic which frequently occurs at the beginning of the schizophrenic illness. They attempt in the early part of the treatment to reduce this anxiety by reassurance and explanation. Arieti has stressed that successful psychotherapeutic treatment of acute schizophrenic conditions depends on the early treatment of the panic state. I myself have not only observed these severe anxieties during the early part of the psychotic illness but I have found that they are frequently repeated during the acute and later chronic stages of the disease. On escaping from the panic the patient often withdraws into catatonia, emptiness, paralysis, sleepiness and delusion.

During the last 6 years I have had the opportunity to observe both the panic and the withdrawn state in a patient who was struggling with a chronic psychotic state. Miss A had been in psychotherapy abroad for several years when she developed what appeared to be an acute psychotic state. From time to time she had a violent impulse to cut her wrists and when she succeeded in doing so she was hospitalised for more than 3 years. The hospital staff attempted sympathetically to understand her psychotic behaviour and thinking. She felt glad to be in hospital because for the first time in her life her sickness, as she called it, had been taken seriously. She had felt that her parents could not stand her being ill and would therefore not believe how ill she was and her manifest psychotic state was an attempt to be more open about her feelings. Previously she had felt so imprisoned by her psychotic rigidity that to make her blood flow out was felt by her not as a wish to die but as an attempt to become more alive. After very prolonged psychotherapeutic treatment in her own country where she made some progress her therapist felt that the treatment could go no further. The patient tried to cope on her own but after about a year she was again overwhelmed by severe paralysing anxieties. She felt forced to withdraw from life by just staying in bed or sitting in front of the fire eating, drinking alcohol, feeding herself on tranquilisers and reading detective stories. She felt helpless against the forces which prevented her from living and hopeless about any possibility of improving. She was also uncertain about her identity. After her acute breakdown she felt that she had an identity of being psychotic and she idealised this state and often longed to return to being the valued psychotic patient in the disturbed ward of the hospital where one could smash windows, cut one's wrists and fight against the forces who demanded that one should be part of life which was contemptuously referred to as conforming or being "goody-goody". When the patient approached me for analysis she was no longer able to idealise her withdrawal state as she was aware that it was cutting her off from any attempt to take part in life. Very soon after starting analysis with me she made quite clear that she felt it was dangerous to improve because as soon as she improved she became more and more terrified. So in order to appease the frightening forces within she would give up life and again withdraw into the paralysed state. These states repeated themselves frequently in the early stages of analysis with me and then she could again turn towards life but only in a very limited way. At this time I was able to observe that she had to obey the narcissistic principle of self-sufficiency which demanded that she should be able to do everything for herself and not accept any kindness, care, food or sexual satisfaction from anybody. To take something in from the outside world was felt to be bad, dirty or weak and subsequently she felt she had to be physically sick to rid herself of what she had taken in. In childhood and even much later she had not been able to bear her mother giving her food or presents and her mother's attention or interest in her was felt to be an intrusion into her privacy. But she also found it unbearable when her mother looked anxious, after the patient aggressively rejected her. The difficulties with her mother had obviously been in existence from early infancy. During the analysis it became clear that the patient was dominated by a psychotic narcissistic structure or self which threatened her whenever she attempted to come closer to life or any living person. This self posed as a friend and pretended to take care of her and give her whatever warmth and food she wanted so that she wouldn't have to be lonely. This situation was acted out during the withdrawal state. In fact, however, this so-called friend attempted to spoil any contact she was trying to make in relationship to work and people. During analysis she gradually became aware that this exceedingly tyrannical and possessive friend was the omnipotent destructive part of the self talking as a friend who seemed very threatening if she attempted to cooperate in the analysis and attempted to make any progress in her life situation. For a long time she felt too frightened to challenge the aggressive forces and whenever she came up against this barrier she identified herself with this aggressive narcissistic self and became aggressive and abusive towards me. Sometimes I seemed to represent her mother but at other times I was her normal infantile self which she rejected and belittled after projecting it into me. However, the main reason for her violent attacks related to my challenging the domination of her aggressive narcissistic state and my impudence in wanting to help her or even cure her and she demonstrated that she was determined to do everything to defeat me. But after these attacks had lasted some time I noticed that there was also a secret hope that I, and "I" included here also the self which was directed towards life, might win in the end. I also began to realise that the only alternative to her violent attacks on me was the admission that she really wanted to get well and this exposed her to the danger of being killed by the omnipotent destructive part of herself. After we had worked with this situation for many months she had a dream which seemed to confirm and illustrate the problem. In the dream the patient found herself in an underground hall or passage. She decided she wanted to leave and she found that she had to go through a turnstile to get to the staircase which led to the open air. The turnstile was obstructed by two people who were standing there. When the patient investigated she found they were both dead and in the dream she decided they had obviously been murdered recently. She realised that the murderer was still about and she had to act quickly to save herself. Nearby there was the office of a detective and she rushed in unannounced but had to wait in the waiting room for a moment. While she was waiting the murderer appeared and threatened to kill her because he did not want anybody to know his identity. She was terrified and burst into the detective's room and was saved. The murderer escaped and she felt that while she was temporarily safe the whole situation would be repeated. The dream story had then an idealistic ending because the detective was able to follow the trail of the murderer and catch him, to her almost unbelievable relief. The patient realised immediately that the detective represented me but the rest of the dream was a surprise to her. She had never allowed herself to think how frightened she was of being murdered if she allowed herself to trust me and come to me for help and give me all the information and cooperation she was capable of. The two dead people in the dream reminded her of the two previous unsuccessful attempts to get better from treatment. I understood the dream as a communication to me that a part of her had decided to get well and leave the psychotic narcissistic state which was equated by her with death but immediately the deadly power became actively murderous because of this decision. The dream explains the reason why the patient's anxieties had always been anonymous. She obviously knew that it was too dangerous to tell me about her dread of death because death was experienced as a person, a murderer, who would immediately punish her with death if she revealed its existence and her fear. After the dream it was slightly easier for the patient to talk about her problems and she occasionally was able to admit that she wanted to be alive but a negative therapeutic reaction threatened her frequently during the analysis. It is understandable that this patient always needed me to understand and interpret her anxieties and only very gradually was she able to express herself more openly and face her conflict between her own murderous feelings and her desire to live and love.

I have concentrated here only on one important aspect of the schizophrenic's psychopathology but I want to stress that I believe that our gradually increasing knowledge of the psychopathology of schizophrenia will make more schizophrenic patients accessible to analysis. The psychoanalytic treatment of the psychosis, particularly schizophrenia, does of course not only depend on the analyst's knowledge, but on his capacity to remain in contact with the patient so that he can perceive and understand the patient's communications.

Finally I want to raise the question which concerns us all — Will psychoanalytic psychotherapy or psychoanalysis of the psychosis ever succeed in playing the role in the treatment of schizophrenia which it deserves? I do not think that we can answer this question yet. I hope that it will be possible gradually to train more therapists in the psychoanalytic treatment of psychosis and create private or state-supported hospitals where most of the patients admitted will have the opportunity to have psychoanalytic treatment. There are so far only a few private hospitals where all psychotic patients admitted are being analysed. The therapeutic atmosphere in these hospitals not only creates an atmosphere which is helpful to the patient but it is also a creative working community for the therapist, who, particularly in the beginning, needs a great deal of help, supervision and support from colleagues working in the same direction.

References

ABRAHAM, K. (1907) On the significance of sexual trauma in childhood for the symptomatology of dementia praecox. In *Clinical Papers and Essays on Psychoanalysis.* London: Hogarth Press, 1955.

ABRAHAM, K. (1908) The psycho-sexual differences between hysteria and dementia praecox. In *Selected Papers.* London: Hogarth Press, 1950.

ABRAHAM, K. (1912) Notes on the psycho-analytical investigation and treatment of manic-depressive insanity and allied conditions. In *Selected Papers.* London: Hogarth Press, 1950.

ABRAHAM, K. (1913) Restrictions and transformations of scoptophilia in psycho-neurotics. In *Selected Papers.* London: Hogarth Press, 1950.

ABRAHAM, K. (1916) The first pregenital stage of the libido. In *Selected Papers.* London: Hogarth Press, 1950.

ABRAHAM, K. (1924) A short study of the development of the libido. In *Selected Papers.* London: Hogarth Press, 1950.

ARIETI, S. (1955) *Interpretation of Schizophrenia.* New York. Brunner.

ARLOW, J.A. and BREUER, C. (1969) The Psychopathology of the Psychoses. A Proposed Revision. *Int. J. Psychoanal.* **50.**

BION, W.R. (1954) Notes on the theory of schizophrenia. In *Second Thoughts.* London: Heinemann.

BION, W.R. (1956) Development of schizophrenic thought. In *Second Thoughts.* London: Heinemann.

BION, W.R. (1957) Differentiation of the psychotic from the non-psychotic personalities. In *Second Thoughts.* London: Heinemann.

BION, W.R. (1962) *Learning from Experience.* William Heinemann Medical Books Ltd., London.

BRODY, E.B. and REDLICH, F.C. (1952) (eds.) *Psychotherapy with Schizophrenics.* New York: University Press.

BRYCE BOYER, GIOVACCHINI, P. and HOEDEMAKER, E. (1967) *Psychoanalytic Treatment of Schizophrenia and Characterological Disorders.* Science House Inc. New York.

BULLARD, D.M. (1940) Experiences in the psychoanalytic treatment of psychotics. *Psychoanal. Q.* **9,** 493-504.

BULLARD, D.M. (1960) Psychotherapy of paranoid patients. *Archs gen. Psychiat.* **2,** 137-141.

BYCHOWSKI, G. (1952) *Psychotherapy of Psychoses.* New York: Grune and Stratton.

BYCHOWSKI, G. (1961) Introductory Notes on the Psychoanalytic Theory of Schizophrenics in *Psychotherapy of Psychoses.* New York: Basic Books.

CLARK, L.P. (1933a) The question of prognosis in narcissistic neuroses and psychoses. *Int. J. Psycho-Anal.* **14,** 71-86.

CLARK, L.P. (1933b) The treatment of narcissistic neuroses and psychoses. *Psychoanal. Q.* **20,** 304-326.

COHN, F.S. (1940) Practical approach to the problem of narcissistic neuroses. *Psychoanal. Q.* **9,** 64-79.

FEDERN, P. (1943) Psychoanalysis of psychoses. In *Ego Psychology and the Psychoses.* New York: Basic Books, 1952.

FREUD, S. (1905) On psychotherapy. *S.E.* **7.**

FREUD, S. (1916-17) Introductory lectures on psycho-analysis. *S.E.* **22,** 15-16.

FREUD, S. (1933) New introductory lectures on psycho-analysis. *S.E.* **22.**

FREUD, S. (1937) Analysis terminable and interminable. *S.E.* **23.**

FREUD, S. (1940) An outline of psycho-analysis. *S.E.* **23.**

FROMM-REICHMANN, F. (1939) Transference problems in schizophrenics. *Psychoanal. Q.* **8,** 412-426.

FROMM-REICHMANN, F. (1948) Notes on the development of treatment of schizophrenics by psycho-analytic therapy. In D.M. Bullard (ed.), *Psychoanalysis and Psychotherapy.* Chicago: Univ. of Chicago Press, 1959.

FROMM-REICHMANN, F. (1952) Some aspects of psychoanalytic psychotherapy with schizophrenics. In D.M. Bullard (ed.), *Psychoanalysis and Psychotherapy.* Chicago: Univ. of Chicago Press, 1959.

FROMM-REICHMANN, F. (1954) Psychotherapy of schizophrenia. In D.M. Bullard (ed.), *Psychoanalysis and Psychotherapy.* Chicago: Univ. of Chicago Press, 1959.

GREEN, Andre (1975) The Analyst, Symbolization and Absence in the Analytic Setting. *Int. J. Psycho-Anal.* **56.**

JACOBSON, E. (1954) Transference problems in the psychoanalytic treatment of severely depressive patients. *J. Am. psychoanal. Ass.* 2, 595-606.
JACOBSON, E. (1967) *Psychotic Conflict and Reality.* London: Hogarth Press.
KATAN, M. (1964) The importance of a non-psychotic part in schizophrenia. *Int. J. Psycho-Anal.* 35.
KERNBERG, O. (1972) Clinical Observations Regarding the Diagnosis, Prognosis and Intense Treatment of chronic Schizophrenic Patients. To be published.
KLEIN, M. (1935) A contribution to the psychogenesis of manic-depressive states. *Int. J. Psycho-Anal.* 16, 145-174.
KLEIN, M. (1940) Mourning and its relations to manic-depressive states. *Contributions to Psycho-Analysis (1921-45).* London: Hogarth, 1948.
KLEIN, M. (1946) Notes on some schizoid mechanisms. *Int. J. Psycho-Anal.* 27, 99-110.
KNIGHT, R.P. (1946) Psychotherapy of an Adolescent Catatonic Schizophrenic with Mutism. *Psychiat. Q.*
MAHLER, M.W. (1969) Perturbances of Symbiosis and Individualisation in the Development of the Psychotic Ego. *Problematique de la Psychose*, pp. 188-195. Excerpta Medica Foundation.
MELTZER, D. (1963) A Contribution to the Metapsychology of Cyclothymic States. *Int. J. Psyco-Anal.* 44, 83-96.
PIOUS, W. (1961) A hypothesis about the nature of Schizophrenic Behaviour. In A. Burton (ed.) *Psychotherapy of the Psychoses.* New York: Basic Books, 1961.
REICHARD, S. (1956) A re-examination of Studies in Hysteria. *Psychoanal. Quart.* 21.
ROSEN, John (1947) The treatment of Schizophrenic Psychoses by Direct Analytic Therapy. *Psychiat. Quart.* 21.
ROSENFELD, H.A. (1947) Analysis of a schizophrenic state with depersonalisation. *Int. J. Psycho-Anal.* 28, 130-139.
ROSENFELD, H.A. (1950) Note on the psychopathology of confusional states in chronic schizophrenias. *Int. J. Psycho-Anal.* 31, 132-137.
ROSENFELD, H.A. (1952a) Notes on the psychoanalysis of the superego conflict of an acute schizophrenic patient. *Int. J. Psyco-Anal.* 33, 111-131.
ROSENFELD, H.A. (1952b) Transference-phenomena and transference-analysis in an acute catatonic schizophrenic patient. *Int. J. Psycho-Anal.* 33, 457-464.
ROSENFELD, H.A. (1954) Considerations regarding the psycho-analytic approach to acute and chronic schizophrenia. In *Psychotic States.* London: Hogarth Press, 1965.
ROSENFELD, H.R. (1959) An Investigation into the Psycho-Analytic Theory of Depression. *Int. J. Psycho-Anal.* 60, Part II.
ROSENFELD, H.R. (1964) Object relations of an acute schizophrenic patient in the transference situation. In *Recent Research on Schizophrenia.* Psychiatric Research Reports of the American Psychiatric Association.
ROSENFELD, H.R. (1969) *The Negative Therapeutic Reaction.* To be published.
ROSENFELD, H.R. (1969) Contribution to the Psychopathology of Psychotic States. The importance of projective identification in the ego structure and the object relations of the psychotic patient. *Problematique de la Psychose*, pp. 115-128. Excerpta Medica Foundation.
ROSENFELD, H.R. (1971) A Clinical Approach to the Psychoanalytic theory of the life and death instincts: an investigation into the aggressive aspects of narcissism. *Int. J. Psycho-Anal.* 52, 169.
SCOTT, W.C.M. (1947) On the intense affects in treating a severe manic-depressive disorder. *Int. J. Psycho-Anal.* 28, 142. (The original paper was presented to the Paris Congress 1938).
SEARLES, H.F. (1955) Dependency processes in the psychotherapy of schizophrenia. In *Collected Papers on Schizophrenia and Related Subjects.* London: Hogarth Press, 1965.
SEARLES, H.F. (1963) Transference psychosis in the psychotherapy of schizophrenics. In *Collected Papers on Schizophrenia and Related Subjects.* London: Hogarth Press, 1965.
SEGAL, H. (1950) Some aspects of the analysis of a schizophrenic. *Int. J. Psycho-Anal.* 31, 268-278.
SEGAL, H. (1956) Depressions in the schizophrenic. *Int. J. Psycho-Anal.* 37, 339-343.
SEGAL, H. (1957) Notes on symbol formation. *Int. J. Psycho-Anal.* 38, 391-397.
STERN, A. (1938) Psychoanalytic investigation of therapy in the borderline group of neuroses. *Psychoanal. Q.* 7, 467-489.
STERN, A. (1948) Transference in borderline neuroses. *Psycho-Anal. Q.* 17, 527-528.
STONE, L. (1954) The widening scope of indications for psycho-analysis. *J. Am. psychoanal. Ass.* 2, 567-594.
SULLIVAN, H.S. (1947) Therapeutic investigations in schizophrenia. *Psychiatry* 10, 121-125.
TAUSCH, V. (1919) On the Origin of the Influencing Machine in Schizophrenia. *Psychoanal. Quart.* 1933.
THORNER, H. (1955) Three defences against inner persecution. In *New Directions in Psychoanalysis*, ed. Klein *et al.* London: Tavistock.
WAELDER, R. (1925) The psychoses: their mechanisms and accessibility to influence. *Int. J. Psycho-Anal.* 6, 259-281.
WEXLER, Milton (1951) The Structural Problem in Schizophrenia. *Int. J. Psycho-Anal.* 37.
WEXLER, Milton (1952) The Structural Problem in Schizophrenia: the Role of the Internal Object in Psychotherapy with Schizophrenics. *Int. Univ. Press,* New York.

WINNICOTT, D.W. (1945) Primitive emotional development. In *Collected Papers*. London: Tavistock Publications, 1958.

WINNICOTT, D.W. (1959-64) Classification: Is there a psycho-analytic contribution to psychiatric classification? In *The Maturational Processes and the Facilitating Environment*. London: Hogarth Press, 1965.

WINNICOTT, D.W. (1963) Communicating and not communicating leading to a study of certain opposites. In *The Maturational Processes and the Facilitating Environment*. London: Hogarth Press, 1965.

Synthesis and Concluding Remarks

Recent Contributions from the basic Biological Sciences toward an understanding of Schizophrenia

Schizophrenia, which has been an enigma since it was first described, affects a significant proportion of people in every country of the world. The magnitude of the problem in the face of ignorance regarding its components, their etiologies, pathogenesis and specific means of prophylaxis or treatment, has evoked a substantial number of doctrines, which, although unproven and contradictory, have attracted adherents to them and have been the basis for the establishment of numerous schools of thought.

As Dr. Richter points out, there have been many claims of a biochemical abnormality in schizophrenia, supported by flimsy and poorly controlled evidence. Equally inadequate is the evidence that any specific environmental factor such as parental personality or childrearing practices plays a crucial role in etiology. The widely promulgated treatment of schizophrenia with large doses of various vitamins is supported by enthusiastic and uncontrolled testimonials, while a number of carefully controlled laboratory and field studies have failed to adduce either a rational basis or acceptable empirical evidence for the treatment. Even more widespread in certain circles is the doctrine that schizophrenia is a myth or a "creative adaptation to an evil society" which is based upon emotional arguments and a series of illogical *non sequitors.*

In the course of the past two decades there has been an unprecedented increase in fundamental knowledge regarding the brain and behaviour. There has also been the discovery of several new classes of drugs which have significantly improved the treatment of schizophrenia as well as depression and mania. There has been a continuous dialogue between clinical observations and fundamental biological knowledge with the emergence, for the first time, of credible hypotheses, which do not attempt to answer the question of schizophrenia all at once, but rather to adduce information relevant to smaller questions. Much has been learned of the biological mechanisms on which these drugs appear to act, and in turn these have permitted the development of hypothesis relating their action to possible deficits in schizophrenia. A wealth of new biological techniques have been developed and are being used in studies of schizophrenia, while new and more compelling evidence, adduced in the past 10 years, for the importance of genetic factors lends renewed hope and substance to the search for biochemical mechanisms.

Dr. Shields has discussed the newer genetic studies. The observations on twins which he and Gottesman have carried out at the Maudsley Institute represent the most complete and best controlled study in this area. They have painstakingly minimized selective bias by resorting to a total twin register of patients and have ruled out subjective diagnostic bias by having a number of raters making independent diagnoses on the individual members of their sample without knowledge of their relationship. The appreciably higher concordance rate found by each rater in monozygotic twins as compared to the dizygotic pairs has laid to rest the claim that schizophrenia is a myth and that it cannot be recognised by psychiatrists. The collaborative international studies reported by Dr. Sartorius indicate the ability of psychiatrists in different cultures to recognise schizophrenia and make it difficult to maintain that it is the result of a particular type of sociocultural system.

Studies on populations of adopted individuals and their biological and adoptive relatives make it possible to disentangle genetic from the usually confounding environmental variables. In the most recent of these studies to be reported, a significant concentration of schizophrenia was found in the biological relatives of adopted individuals who eventually developed schizophrenia even though they had lived apart from them. A significant concentration of schizophrenia in the biological paternal half-siblings of such probands as compared with their controls rules out *in utero* and neonatal environmental influences. In the face of such evidence as this it is difficult to deny the importance of genetic factors in a substantial segment of schizophrenia. Population genetics, linkage and pedigree analyses are being applied to the problem although to date no particular mode of transmission has been established. Fibroblast and other cell culture techniques are available to examine any putative enzymatic defect such as the deficiency of monoamine oxidase in platelets which appear to be associated with schizophrenia, and such techniques have already been applied successfully in demonstrating a genetic reduction in N-5, 10-methylene tetrahydrofolate reductase in at least one case of schizophrenia.

Dr. Carlsson has reviewed the evidence, in which he pioneered, that a blockade of dopaminergic synapses constitutes the important pharmacologic action of the anti-psychotic agents. He pointed out questions that still require further research, such as the differential effects of these drugs on the mesolimbic and the striatal dopamine synapses, and the interaction of other neurotransmitters such as noradrenaline, GABA, and acetylcholine, in the search for the neurochemical deficit in schizophrenia. Dr. Richter brought up the possible involvement of endocrine and immunological factors which must also be considered. Dr. Pletscher, in a detailed review of the neuroleptic actions of five classes of antipsychotic drugs, points out a number of factors which must be taken into consideration in a more comprehensive account of the mechanism of action of these agents in schizophrenia. His approach, which also takes into consideration differential action on dopamine receptors in limbic system and striatal, on noradrenaline receptors, and on muscarinic receptors, yields a more precise correlation of pharmacologic action with clinical profiles.

Dr. Fuxe reviews evidence, accumulated over the past 15 years, that serotonin may be involved in schizophrenia as well as in the action of certain hallucinogenic indolamines. Two lines of reasoning suggest an effect of hallucinogens on pre- or post-junctional serotonin receptors. He suggests a novel pharmacological approach to accumulating further evidence, which in turn may lead to a new type of antipsychotic agent beneficial in schizophrenia but based upon serotonin receptor blockade.

The thing that I find most encouraging about biological research relevant to the problem of schizophrenia as exemplified by participants in this meeting is not so much that the answers to this old problem are at hand, but that specific and heuristic questions can now be raised on the basis of accumulated basic knowledge, that there are new tools which are capable of answering these questions and a substantial number of highly competent biologists throughout the world who are addressing these problems.

Clinical Sciences

MICHAEL SHEPHERD

In asking Dr. Kety and myself to attempt a synthesis of the material presented at this meeting the organisers have given me the more difficult task. This in no way reflects on the quality of the papers but rather indicates that the clinician's approach to schizophrenia is inevitably different from and in some ways more complex than that of the biological worker. The fundamental difference, I would submit, turns on the understandable reliance by biological scientists on the use of what are nowadays called reductionist tools. Regardless of whether their explanatory objectives are couched in molecular, mechanistic, genetic or behavioural terms these tools, as Professor W.H. Thorpe has recently put it,

> ". . . are those which, either by simplifying the system under study . . . or by limiting the aspects of the system chosen for examination make the experimental problem more approachable and subsumable with the general methods and theories of science developed for less complex systems. Living or non-living . . . There is no doubt that as a working hypothesis reductionism is the major basic tool to be in use among the great majority of experimental scientists."

But, as Thorpe goes on to point out, the adoption of *reductionist techniques* has to be distinguished from the *reductionist outlook* which assumes that all aspects of mental and physical activity can be brought under the same set of fundamental laws. The issue is a very real one for the subject of this meeting. It arises not merely in the questions one would like to put to Professor Carlsson about the intermediate steps leading from the post-synaptic receptor to his mad rats and his schizophrenic patients. The whole subject of mental disease in general, and schizophrenia in particular, seems to have entered the general debate which has been in progress among scientists since the publication of Kuhn's book on *The Structure of Scientific Revolutions*. For example, in a paper provocatively entitled, "Do not adjust your mind, there is a fault in reality", Professor Stephen Rose, himself a neurochemist, has recently grouped together the chemical, pharmacological and psychological explanatory models of schizophrenia as reductionist and to be contrasted with the non-reductionist sociological, psychological and psychoanalytical theories. "The dichotomy between the two approaches is such", he says, "that paradigms meet only at the level of mutual abuse".

This statement, in my view, goes much too far. Mutual incomprehension would have been a more accurate term than mutual abuse. The fact is that one need not be a reductionist to employ reductionist techniques. They are just as useful, within their limits, in the hands of a Cartesian or of an adherent of the so-called Double-Aspect Theory of the mind-body nexus or of a clinical psychiatrist who can also borrow them if he chooses, provided he makes his assumptions clear. Indeed, Dr. Davison did just this when he stated explicitly the view that schizophrenia is essentially an example of a "symptomatic psychosis . . . induced by cerebral biochemical disturbances . . . the end-product of a variety of pathogenetic syndromes, i.e. a syndrome". Dr. Richter implied something similar in his paper and it is implicit in the interesting communications of Dr. Itil and of Drs. Munkvard, Fog and Kristjansen. On this basis the schizophrenias might be regarded as analogous to, say, the pre-senile dementias or the cerebral palsies, a heterogeneous group of pathological conditions whose individual characteristics are to be specified individually until the term can be discarded as meaningless. On the other hand, if the comparison is with the mental deficiencies then, while the delineation of specific syndromes constitutes a similar procedure, the analogy would break down in the face of the large mass of non-specific polygenic mental handicap which is better regarded as deviation than disease. The notion of a "schizophrenic spectrum" of diseases arising from genetic studies is clearly relevant to such a view.

But it is apparent from the other papers presented to us that the outlook of the clinical scientist extends beyond the reductionist approach. In his review of the treatment of acute schizophrenia, Professor Cazzullo illustrates this broader approach and it is, I think, important to establish its general significance. Some years ago a distinguished English physician proposed the establishment of a Society for the Abolition of Clinical Psychiatrists. He did so on the grounds that psychiatry was no more than neurology without physical signs and needless to say, he is himself a neurologist. However, the potential range of the clinical sciences embraces at least four other types of activity, all of them well exemplified at this meeting. I should like to mention them in turn.

The first is phenomenological description, leading to a consequent abstraction of categories of illness and theories of disordered function. In my opening lecture I attempted to summarise the long history of this approach which is, after all, responsible for the outlines of our topic and which even now is a field which can be tilled with profit. A case in point is the intriguing group of patients whose initial illness is indisputably schizophrenic in form, but which then clears up to be followed by a relapse into a clearcut affective disorder with no trace of schizophrenic symptomatology. According to many authorities this sequence does not occur, though there are a few scattered reports on this outcome in the literature. Recently, however, we have been looking at the follow-up data of the WHO IPSS material with this in mind and have discovered that the pattern is not uncommon. Clearly such findings carry implications not only for nosological groupings but also for any theory of pathogenesis.

Secondly, there are the attempts to study the psychosocial correlates of people identified as schizophrenic. Dr. Brody gave us a broad survey of the many studies carried out in this field and, as he pointed out, much if not most of it is unsatisfactory in design and execution. This is particularly to be deplored at the present time since, as we have heard from several speakers, the accumulation of convincing evidence in favour of genetic factors playing a key role in the aetiology of schizophrenia also points to the significance of what are called "environmental" factors in their expression. The precise identification of these factors, however, remains to be ascertained, though Dr. Lambo would, I feel sure, have drawn our attention to the differences in the outcome of the groups of uniformly diagnosed schizophrenic illnesses in the WHO cross-cultural studies. There is now, I would suggest, clearly a strong case for carrying out properly planned epidemiological surveys of defined populations, not merely to count heads but to examine the possible associations of schizophrenic morbidity with the whole range of factors mentioned by Dr. Brody. This task could be rendered still more productive in the light of the distinction drawn by Professor Polani between defective enzymes (where it is appropriate to speak of gene linkage or synteny on the chromosome) and defective immune-responses where one cannot infer more than association or correlation.

And the whole sphere of correlation becomes all-important when we turn to the third area of clinical enquiry, namely the study of psychological disorder in the schizophrenias, the topic represented ably by Professors Tissot and Matte Blanco who draw on the concepts of Piaget and von Demarus respectively. In concentrating on the supposedly cognitive defects exhibited by schizophrenics, they were of course, able to do no more than touch on a vast number of investigations which have been conducted by experimental psychologists for many years. The general description of schizophrenic thought in such terms as concrete, overinclusive, a-holistic and idiosyncratic has been handed down by 3 generations of clinical observers, but it has needed only 1 generation of psychological inquiry to demonstrate such disturbing facts as that (1) so-called "thought disorder" is in part a form of perceptual aberration; (2) that it is non-specific; (3) that it is readily modifiable by operant techniques; (4) that the results of most controlled experiments are unreliable and non-replicable. Against this background it is surely wise to subject any broad theory of psychological function to the strictest experimental testing before its relevance to schizophrenia can be accepted.

The last of my four categories is what is often called intuitive or speculative interpretation, a form of activity which has long enriched clinical thinking in psychiatry. In allocating the carefully written papers by Drs. Rosenfeld and Arieti to this category I would readily acknowledge the value of their experience and the large investment of professional expertise required for its acquisition. To discuss the theoretical assumptions of their work would, I think, be misplaced here. The arguments for and against the psychoanalytical viewpoint have been repeated *ad nauseam* and seem to make surprisingly little difference to the views of either committed adherents of or opponents to the system.

I would, however, like to take up briefly the practical question raised by Dr. Rosenfeld at the end of his lecture. What, he asked, is the place of psychoanalysis in the treatment of the schizophrenias in the future? The answer to the question, I would suggest, will turn entirely on the readiness of psychoanalysts to have their results evaluated by the medical and scientific community at large. Here it may be relevant to mention that some years ago a committee was set up in Britain under the auspices of the Medical Research Council to examine the whole question of the efficacy of psychotherapeutic techniques. It failed to reach a conclusion for the simple reason that psychotherapists would not collaborate in the proposed clinical experiment. I gather that similar difficulties have been experienced elsewhere. This is, I think, now a matter of growing importance as systems of medical care all over the world move increasingly from private to public practice. In the discussion Dr. Brody asked for more attention to be paid to what he called the "epidemiology of psychotherapy". One factor with which he might well start is economic status, for most of the work on the psychotherapy of psychosis has been carried out on a private fee-paying basis. For this reason it constitutes, in the law of most countries, a private contract between persons and as such falls outside the public sector, provided certain conditions are met. The issue has, in fact, been publicly discussed in respect of scientology which, you will recall, claims to be the "only valid form of psychotherapy". But if Ministries of Health are to be expected to subsidise, at public expense, any long-continued and expensive form of therapy, they are entitled to and will certainly demand some evidence in favour of the effectiveness of that form of treatment. In view of the long history of psychotherapeutic activity with schizophrenics which Dr. Rosenfeld has summarised so clearly I hope very much that the evidence will not be delayed much longer.

So, in conclusion, it remains only for me to thank our lecturers for covering so adequately the spectrum of clinical enquiry in the schizophrenias and to say how keenly we await the appearance of their material in book form. The title of the volume, I gather, will be "Schizophrenia today", but it should serve to help us all anticipate and look forward to the developments we can confidently expect on "Schizophrenia tomorrow", if the multi-disciplinary outlook characterising this symposium is maintained.

Index

Gutted

TONY BLACK

Gutted

preface
publishing

Published by Preface 2009

10 9 8 7 6 5 4 3 2 1

First published in Great Britain in 2009 by Preface Publishing
1 Queen Anne's Gate
London SW1H 9BT

An imprint of The Random House Group

www.rbooks.co.uk
www.prefacepublishing.co.uk

Addresses for companies within The Random House Group Limited
can be found at www.randomhouse.co.uk

The Random House Group Limited Reg. No. 954009

A CIP catalogue record for this book is available from the British Library

Hardback ISBN 978 1 84809 052 1
Trade Paperback ISBN 978 1 84809 051 4

The Random House Group Limited supports The Forest Stewardship Council (FSC),
the leading international forest certification organisation. All our titles that are printed
on Greenpeace-approved FSC-certified paper carry the FSC logo. Our paper
procurement policy can be found at www.rbooks.co.uk/environment

Mixed Sources
Product group from well-managed
forests and other controlled sources
www.fsc.org Cert no. TT-COC-2139
FSC © 1996 Forest Stewardship Council

Typeset in Times by Palimpsest Book Production Limited,
Grangemouth, Stirlingshire

Printed and bound in Great Britain by Clays Ltd, St Ives PLC

For Madeline